The Rights Turn in Conservative Christian Politics

The Rights Turn in Conservative Christian Politics documents a recent
fundamental change in American politics with the waning of Christian
America. Rather than conservatives emphasizing morality and liberals
emphasizing rights, both sides now wield rights arguments as potent
weapons to win political and legal battles and build grassroots support.
Lewis documents this change on the right, focusing primarily on evangelical politics. Using extensive historical and survey data that compares
evangelical advocacy and evangelical public opinion, Lewis explains
how the prototypical culture war issue – abortion – motivated the
conservative rights turn over the past half-century, serving as a spring-
board for rights learning and increased conservative advocacy in other
arenas. Challenging the way we think about the culture wars, Lewis
documents how rights claims are used to thwart liberal rights claims as
well as to provide protection for evangelicals, whose cultural positions
are increasingly in the minority. Rights claims have also allowed evangelical elites to justify controversial advocacy positions to their base and
to engage more easily in broad rights talk in new or expanded political
arenas, from health care to capital punishment.

ANDREW R. LEWIS is Assistant Professor of Political Science at the
University of Cincinnati. He researches the intersection of religion, law,
and American politics. He contributes to FiveThirtyEight and other
media outlets and is currently Book Review Editor at the journal
Politics & Religion.

D0875130

Cambridge Studies in Social Theory, Religion, and Politics

Editors

David C. Leege, *University of Notre Dame*
Kenneth D. Wald, *University of Florida, Gainesville*
Richard L. Wood, *University of New Mexico*

The Rights Turn in Conservative Christian Politics

How Abortion Transformed the Culture Wars

ANDREW R. LEWIS
University of Cincinnati

CAMBRIDGE
UNIVERSITY PRESS

CAMBRIDGE
UNIVERSITY PRESS

University Printing House, Cambridge CB2 8BS, United Kingdom

One Liberty Plaza, 20th Floor, New York, NY 10006, USA

477 Williamstown Road, Port Melbourne, VIC 3207, Australia

314-321, 3rd Floor, Plot 3, Splendor Forum, Jasola District Centre, New Delhi-110025, India

79 Anson Road, #06-04/06, Singapore 079906

Cambridge University Press is part of the University of Cambridge.

It furthers the University's mission by disseminating knowledge in the pursuit of education, learning and research at the highest international levels of excellence.

www.cambridge.org
Information on this title: www.cambridge.org/9781108405607
DOI: 10.1017/9781108278171

First published 2017
First paperback edition 2018

A catalogue record for this publication is available from the British Library

Library of Congress Cataloging in Publication data
NAMES: Lewis, Andrew R., 1981- author.
TITLE: The Rights turn in conservative Christian politics : how abortion transformed the culture wars / Andrew R. Lewis, University of Cincinnati.
DESCRIPTION: Cambridge, United Kingdom ; New York, NY : Cambridge University Press, 2017. | Includes bibliographical references and index.
IDENTIFIERS: LCCN 2017017691| ISBN 9781108417709 (hardback : alk. paper) | ISBN 9781108405607 (pbk. : alk. paper)
SUBJECTS: LCSH: Christian conservatism–United States. | Religious right–United States. | Abortion–Religious aspects–Christianity. | Abortion–Political aspects–United States.
CLASSIFICATION: LCC BR526 .L489 2017 | DDC 261.7–dc23
LC record available at https://lccn.loc.gov/2017017691

ISBN 978-1-108-41770-9 Hardback
ISBN 978-1-108-40560-7 Paperback

To my wife, Kasey, for everything before, during, and after
And to my father, Tim, for inspiration

Contents

Figures

Tables

Acknowledgments

This book started with a question – a question posed *to* me, not *by* me. During the defense of my doctoral dissertation at American University, my advisor, Daniel Dreisbach, asked me what was the most surprising thing I uncovered in my research on the evolution of the Southern Baptist Convention's church-state advocacy. The answer was obvious and yet largely absent from the manuscript – abortion politics. Within this evangelical denomination, abortion had pervaded a seemingly separate political topic. From that question, the seed for this book was planted.

The seed needed an opportunity to germinate, and I am grateful for the James Madison Program at Princeton University and the University of Cincinnati for giving me the time and resources to develop this book. It also needed nutrition, space, and pruning, of which my colleagues and family gave abundantly. As I write these acknowledgments, I am overcome with gratitude.

In my professional life, there are many to acknowledge. Daniel Dreisbach, a rigorous scholar and thoughtful man, was my doctoral mentor and a scholarly role model. The James Madison Program at Princeton University, specifically Brad Wilson and Robby George, invested in me as a newly minted Ph.D., offering a postdoctoral fellowship. It was during that year at Princeton that this book sprouted, and I am appreciative of the encouragement and insight from all the fellows, specifically Dan Williams, Ben Kleinerman, and Ken Miller. My continued correspondence with Dan has been particularly beneficial.

For the past five years, I have served on the faculty in the political science department at the University of Cincinnati. I cannot thank the department enough for supporting me during this project. A few members deserve special mention. As Department Head, Rich Harknett helped me maximize research leaves to write the manuscript, while championing the project as a friend and colleague. Steve Mockabee partnered with me on various survey projects that I incorporate in the following chapters, and Brendan Green provided helpful comments as well as needed laughs. I must also thank my two graduate assistants, Tina Teater and Stuart Warren, who have been integral in various research and editing capacities. I also received research support from the university's Taft Research Center to help pay for some of the surveys and for assistance with the index.

As the book progressed, various colleagues have aided me immeasurably. Chief among them is Paul Djupe, who befriended me as a graduate student, endured my frequent questions, provided countless hours of feedback, and challenged me to make the project bigger. He remains a faithful mentor, colleague, and friend. Jim Guth helped introduce me to the study of religion and political behavior in 2008, and he kindly allowed me to use his two decades of surveys of Southern Baptist clergy, as well as his collection of Baptist newspapers and mailings.

For years, I presented drafts of various chapters at the annual meetings of the American Political Science Association and the Midwest Political Science Association, gaining helpful feedback. The discussants, panelists, and audience members who helped shape and improve this book are too many to name. I am also thankful for the occasion to present portions of the book at the University of Oxford, the University of Notre Dame, and the University of Denver, refining the project on each occasion. In particular, I want to thank Dave Campbell, Ted Jelen, Josh Wilson, Geoff Layman, Dan Williams, Paul Djupe, and two anonymous reviewers who have read various pieces of this manuscript and provided encouragement and support. Unquestionably, their comments improved the manuscript.

I am also beholden to the participants. For my dissertation, I spent several hours interviewing Baptist advocacy leaders, spending the most time with Richard Land and the late James Dunn, who passed away in 2015. I continue to appreciate their candor and time. I am also grateful for the clergy and citizens who took the time to complete surveys, for my work would not be possible without their participation.

The editorial team at Cambridge University Press has been wonderful. Sara Doskow and the series editors Ken Wald, Rich Wood, and David Leege have been thorough, timely, and enthusiastic. I am honored that they have found my book worthy of publication in the excellent Social Theory, Religion, and Politics series. I also appreciate the Cambridge journal *Politics & Religion* for allowing me to reproduce some of the material I previously published with the journal in Chapters 3 and 4.

Finally, I must recognize my family. They have been my support system for and distraction from this consuming project. My wife, Kasey, deserves immense credit and praise. When I started the project we did not have any children, and now we have three – Brooke, Ryan, and Claire – who are an endless source of joy and pride. Kasey's support, encouragement, and wisdom have endured, and our love has grown as our family has expanded. My parents, grandparents, siblings, and in-laws have sustained me by being both interested and benevolent. Their perspectives on the intersection of religion, law, and politics have been especially profitable during the project's development.

My family heritage is also my inspiration. As the son and grandson of pastors, I have witnessed the evolution of Christian politics firsthand. Yet, as also the son and grandson of public school teachers, I have been witness to a public faith, not a cloistered one – to living among. I have long observed the evangelical struggles of finding a home in a pluralistic society. I also draw on my pastoral lineage for more than the topic, as my formative years sitting in small-town church pews have ingrained in me the importance of narrative, storytelling, and grand themes. I seek to do them justice in the book.

I am grateful for the diverse and valuable contributions others have made to this book, both large and small, though any mistakes and errors in judgment, interpretation, and fact are solely mine. Like the politics that I study, institutions, people, history, opportunities, and perspectives have heavily influenced the book's development. I hope the readers can glean a portion of what I have received.

Abbreviations

ACA	Affordable Care Act
ACLJ	American Center for Law and Justice
ACLU	American Civil Liberties Union
AFL-CIO	American Federation of Labor and Congress of Industrial Organizations
AMA	American Medical Association
ANES	American National Election Study
BJC	Baptist Joint Committee for Religious Liberty / Baptist Joint Committee for Public Affairs
CIs	Confidence Intervals
CJRS	Criminal Justice and Religion Survey
CLC	Christian Life Commission
CRC	Christian Reformed Church
DOMA	Defense of Marriage Act
ERA	Equal Rights Amendment
ERLC	Ethics & Religious Liberty Commission
FACE	Freedom of Access to Clinic Entrances
FBI	Federal Bureau of Investigation
FRC	Family Research Council
GSS	General Social Survey
HHS	Health and Human Services
IRS	Internal Revenue Service
LCMS	Lutheran Church-Missouri Synod
LGBT	Lesbian, Gay, Bisexual, Transgender
MTurk	Amazon's Mechanical Turk
NAE	National Association of Evangelicals
NCC	National Council of Churches
n.d.	no date (on letter)

NFIB	*National Federation of Independent Businesses v. Sebelius*
NRLC	National Right to Life Committee
OR	Odds Ratio
RCIG	Religious Committee for Integrity in Government
RFRA	Religious Freedom Restoration Act
SBA List	Susan B. Anthony List
SBC	Southern Baptist Convention
SCHIP	State Children's Health Insurance Program
SEs	Standard Errors
SSI	Survey Sampling International
UN	United Nations
U.S.	United States

I

Introduction

Rights on the Right

In the spring of 2015, a diverse group of activists gathered to celebrate their victory in a hard-fought battle for the government protection of their rights. The achievement would fulfill essential constitutional guarantees and prevent this class of citizens from discrimination. Their victory was countered with prodigious backlash, resulting in a narrower protection than they desired, but the advocates prevailed. Those seeking the protection of their individual rights triumphed, which should come as no surprise. Rights are the currency of American politics, and rights-based arguments have been victorious for the better part of the past century.

What is surprising, however, is *who* was making this argument. This is not the story of gay marriage, with gay rights activists achieving the right for LGBT people to marry whom they wish via the Supreme Court's 5–4 decision in *Obergefell v. Hodges* (2015). Rather, this is the story of the 2015 Indiana Religious Freedom Restoration Act (RFRA), a measure passed by the Indiana legislature providing robust protections for religious freedom. This is the story of *conservatives*, not liberals.

More importantly, the battle over religious freedom in Indiana is emblematic of a seismic shift in American politics. Conservatives are now using typically liberal arguments, promoting *individual rights*. Conservatives are wielding these rights arguments with increasing frequency in judicial courts and courts of public opinion. And religious conservatives, such as evangelical Protestants and some Catholics, are at the helm, winning political victories and gaining legal protection. The result is a refashioning of the American "culture war." The political right has turned to rights. In the process, conservative Christians have shifted from protecting community morality to embracing certain liberties, particularly as free speech and religious liberty. Evangelicals, and their Christian Right allies, have been baptized into political liberalism. At least in *public* life, they have been converted; they now speak in the tongues of liberty, being filled with the rights spirit.

This change is monumental. Traditionally, as liberalism has been entrenched in rights,[1] conservatism, especially religious conservatism, has emphasized common morality, personal responsibility, and civic republicanism. In the process, religious conservatism has objected to liberalism's demand that religious and moral arguments be secularized.[2] These liberal and conservative viewpoints, while certainly not uniform, can be traced to variant perspectives on American democracy, with James Madison emphasizing pluralism and the respect for difference and Alexis de Tocqueville and John Adams emphasizing similarity. While liberals typically emphasized rights, conservatives typically promoted moral communities.

Building on this, Robert Bellah, the famed sociologist of culture, and his colleagues have identified different strands of American culture: biblical, republican, utilitarian individualist, and expressive individualist. The biblical and republican strands have been tied to political conservatism, while the individualist strands have been tied to liberalism.[3] The change for religious conservatives, then, is from a biblical conservatism to a utilitarian individualism, from communitarianism to pluralism, from morality to liberty.

Scholars are noticing this shift, with recent work identifying secular conservatives' transition toward libertarianism in free speech politics.[4] But scant attention has been given to religious conservatives in this process. Conservative Christians are now more supportive of political liberalism, though they continue to reject many items of expressive individualism, particularly individualist approaches to sexual morality. Rights then are more political, and less expressive in nature, for evangelicals and other religious conservatives.

The adoption of this form of liberalism is quite noteworthy. Only two decades ago some on the right argued that it was anathema to engage in liberal "rights talk." Harvard legal scholar Mary Ann Glendon, for example, in her 1991 book *Rights Talk*, delivered a sharp conservative critique of rights discourse. She argued:

Our rights talk, in its absoluteness, promotes unrealistic expectations, heightens social conflict, and inhibits dialogue that might lead toward consensus, accommodation, or at least discovery of common ground. In its silence concerning responsibilities, it seems to condone acceptance of the benefits of living in a democratic social welfare state, without accepting the corresponding personal and civic obligations. In its relentless individualism, it fosters a climate that is inhospitable to society's losers, and that systematically disadvantages caretakers and dependents, young and old.[5]

Despite this warning, religious conservatives, who were often seen as the last vestige of communitarianism as well as defenders civic republicanism in American politics, have come to embrace rights and rights talk. Notwithstanding setbacks in the 2016 presidential campaign, political liberalism seems to be triumphing, as evangelicals and their allies increasingly turn to rights, particularly the utilitarian, political version of individualism. Due to the changing demographics in America, with white Christians increasingly becoming less of a numerical and cultural majority, this is likely to persist. Diversity will foster pluralism and rights politics.

In this book, I identify the epic shift in evangelicals' approach to rights through some of the most pressing political issues – free speech, religious liberty, health care, capital punishment, and LGBT rights. I also trace the sources of this shift, identifying an under-appreciated cause – the politics of abortion.

THE RIGHTS SHIFT

On some level, we should not be surprised that conservatives have come to utilize rights arguments. Individual rights are central to both American culture and American politics, profoundly affecting politics and law.[6] Though there has been some debate about the nature of rights and individualism in the American Founding,[7] the language of rights permeates American politics. While not exclusive values, individualism and liberty have also been prominent in American religious culture, influencing approaches to church-life, personal morality, and public policy.[8]

The American rights culture, however, has long been the domain of liberals, especially as the role of rights has increased in law and politics over the past century in what has been called the "rights revolution."[9] Liberal legal organizations developed sophisticated strategies to gain short and long-term victories,[10] defeating conservatives with their rights-based arguments. These included victories in civil rights and civil liberties. In the area of civil rights, for example, African Americans gained access to the ballot box, black and white children were required to attend public school together, women and men were to generally receive equal legal treatment, and restaurants and hotels were required to serve all races. Extending civil liberties, women gained access to the birth control pill and abortions, the criminally accused received state-funded lawyers and the right-to-remain silent, gay sex was decriminalized and gay marriage was legalized, and Muslims were able to retain their beards in prison.

But even more, the secular and religious liberal successes in individual rights were largely responsible for activating the "culture wars" in American politics, pitting liberal individualists who were focused on rights against conservative traditionalists who were focused on morality.[11] Even after seeing their lost ground in the culture and before the Supreme Court in the latter half of the twentieth century, conservatives' initial push was not to pitch rights-based arguments, but to urge for limited government and law and order.[12] In fact, as discussed above, there was an aversion to doing so.[13]

I suggest that now the role of rights in American politics has been transformed; the paradox is that conservatives, particularly religious conservatives, have come to share the mantle of rights-based advocacy with liberals, though their focus on rights is centered more on political individualism than expressive individualism. These conservatives have shifted from defending cultural and biblical morality to cultivating a rights-based advocacy strategy, achieving considerable success in politics and especially law. In fact, some of this advocacy serves the dual purpose of expanding religious individualism while preserving elements of traditional morality.[14] Abortion politics are amenable to this opportunity.

Regarding morality, conservative rights talk has been used to counter other individual rights claims, seeking to reduce contraceptive coverage, fight non-discrimination provisions, and protect the role of religion in public life. In addition, conservative rights claims are proffered to counter common good policies favored by liberals, such as limitations on campaign contributions, the separation of church and state, and national health insurance. At the same time, conservative rights claims are supporting political rights of radicals and minorities. These rights claims use individualism to preserve traditional morality, if not for the entire country at least for the religious sect. In the process, conservative Christian activists are making legal and political justifications that would have been controversial, if not untenable, only a generation ago. Some of their issue positions are quite different too, though others are merely refashioned with the veneer of rights talk. In the process, the culture wars have been refashioned.

Free speech law is a notable example, and it is discussed in full in Chapter 3. For much of the twentieth century, minority and radical political groups, such as the Ku Klux Klan and the Socialist Party, libertine social critics and so-called "smut peddlers" like comedian Lenny Bruce and Hustler founder Larry Flynt, respectively, were the frequent participants in free speech cases. Liberal mainstays such as the American Civil Liberties Union (ACLU) often defended these organizations and individuals. Conservatives, and particularly conservative evangelicals, were the supporters of the rule of law, order, and common morality. In the past two decades, this has changed for conservatives, with evangelical elites and organizations promoting an expansion of the individual rights approach to free speech, particularly in the areas of public protesting, campaign finance, and student speech.[15] Now those suing for their free speech rights include a school-aged religious group, the Good News Club, an anti-abortion organization, the Susan B. Anthony's List, and a religious wedding photographer from New Mexico, Elaine Huguenin.

HOW HAVE WE GOTTEN HERE?

Some prior research has identified this shift in conservative politics, highlighting conservatives' coopting the language of liberalism,[16] engaging in deliberative discourse,[17] and embracing libertarian approaches to free speech and other rights advocacy.[18] But what underlies the rights-based advocacy change?

The previous studies suggest that political pragmatism, professionalization, and policy venue are causes, yet these works are largely silent on how religious conservatism cultivated rights arguments.[19] Scholars have underappreciated the breadth and underanalyzed the mechanisms that produced the religious conservative evolution in rights politics. In contrast, I tell the story of this rights evolution via its primary mechanism – abortion politics.

Following the Supreme Court's *Roe v. Wade* decision in 1973, anti-abortion activists became solidified as a political minority, and minority politics are often focused on rights and legal challenges. As I describe, among evangelicals abortion politics has prompted rights learning, rights claiming, and rights extension, what I call the LCE Process of rights politics. Moreover, because it is an "easy issue," elites have utilized abortion to expand the domain of evangelical advocacy. As evangelicals have grown more accepting of their minority status, prompted by abortion politics and rising cultural diversity, they have turned toward rights.

There are two primary areas where individual rights have found a home in conservative Christian politics – religious liberty and abortion. Some religious groups were long-engaged on topics of rights and liberties, though most are newcomers. For much of American history, the Baptists were fervent defenders of the individual right to religious liberty,[20] though they often did so via the communitarian approach of church-state separation.[21] In the post–New Deal period, Catholic Christians too developed a commitment for a universal, individual right – the *right to life* – though it was wielded in service of their desire to protect common morality and sexual mores.[22] As I describe in Chapter 2, Catholics increasingly framed their anti-abortion position in the language of human rights - the individual right to life - resulting in the creation of the National Right to Life Committee (NRLC) in 1968. Evangelicals were slow to adopt the Catholic position on abortion, and evangelicals and Catholics were often enemies in many public affairs battles.[23] Still, evangelicals increasingly opposed legalized abortion, though for a variety of reasons, including opposition to feminism and sexual freedom. Yet, in the mid-late 1970s evangelical thinker and apologist, Francis Schaeffer, helped bring the Catholic, rights-oriented opposition to abortion to evangelicalism, merging individual rights with cultural moral decline.[24] In short order, evangelicals joined Catholics to promote opposition to abortion, as the former enemies became allies.[25] By the second wave of the Christian Right activism in the 1990s, the right-to-life argument had come to the fore.[26] In due time, the Catholic human rights (or natural rights) approach to anti-abortion became the dominant public frame for evangelical activists. This prompted learning about the power of individual rights arguments and an application by activists to other policy areas.

I demonstrate that these two rights-based streams – right to life (abortion) and religious liberty – have formed the basis for conservatives to learn about individual rights and claim them. The pro-life movement in particular served to orient evangelical advocacy leaders toward a commitment to rights – *rights learning.* This has promoted an expansion of rights-based advocacy – *rights claiming* – as leaders found connections to these rights issues in abortion politics and other domains, and either expanded or altered their advocacy to support their pro-life and pro–religious freedom positions. The expanding rights sphere helped establish a minority politics perspective, often in service to protecting cultural morality. The activation of minority and rights politics among conservatives has also yielded secondary effects. The rights turn has yielded greater support for the rights to others, even disfavored groups – *rights extension* – fulfilling the LCE Process.

As the following chapters illuminate, this LCE Process is not often linear or perfectly consistent, as the illiberal components the Donald Trump presidential campaign and presidency illustrate. The broad arc of evangelical politics is bending toward rights, however, and this will continue to be bolstered by the growing religious and demographic diversity in America. In fact, much of evangelicals' support for Donald Trump was not that he would renew Christian majoritarian politics, but rather vouchsafe religious rights, both pro-life rights and religious freedom rights.

Rights and Representation

To understand the arc of rights politics within conservative Christianity, my approach is to pair elite activity and mass opinion. Doing so helps illustrate how political representation functions in rights politics.

In order for evangelical elites to take unorthodox, individual rights positions, the leadership must gain constituent credibility and/or mobilize the masses, lest they suffer representation problems from being generals without armies.[27] How can elites get the rank-and-file to support nontraditional, individual rights positions? Drawing on political behavior and interest group scholarship, I suggest that in order for elites to expand and alter their political advocacy, particularly in unorthodox ways, they need to appeal to their members (or respond to them) in ways that promote policy congruence and group stability. Advocacy on salient issues is important for this process,[28] and it has helped public affairs groups, particularly conservative religious political groups, thrive while membership associations have declined.[29] Further, elites can also frame issues in a salient way that appeals to their base.[30]

For evangelical groups, abortion may be central to this process of representation within interest groups, because most people have an opinion on abortion, and these opinions have remained quite stable in the face of growing liberalization of other attitudes, particularly same-sex marriage.[31] While aggregate abortion attitudes have long fallen somewhere in the middle regarding abortion,[32] mass attitudes have become more polarized of late.[33] Importantly, the politics of abortion are quite salient to evangelicals.[34] Abortion politics are also a "dominant dividing line" in American party politics.[35] Because of the salience and clear differences between the parties, abortion attitudes may even cause some to alter their party attachments.[36] In political behavior research, stable attitudes, like party identification, typically affect less stable attitudes, such as less salient issue positions. So, an attitude as stable and salient as abortion could be an effective tool to stimulate opinion change.

Moreover, prior studies have also demonstrated that rights-framing can alter public opinion,[37] tapping into Americans' common support for rights discourse.[38] Tying abortion to rights discourse could then be quite successful, especially in light of evangelicals' increasing minority status. Initial evidence suggests that the right-to-life framework is a potent counter to liberal rights claims.[39]

Rights become important as evangelicals lose prominence in American life, both in fact or in perception, and the nonreligious increase.[40] *Ordered* liberty is a majoritarian enterprise, while *individual* liberty is the domain of minorities. As such, the "moral majority" of a generation ago emphasized communitarianism, while today's religious minority emphasizes rights that seek protection, not domination. Despite the 2016 presidential election, this trend will continue.

THE HIDDEN IMPACT OF ABORTION POLITICS

There is an ongoing debate in social science and history about the importance of abortion politics in the mobilization of the Christian Right in American party politics. Abortion is given much popular and scholarly credit,[41] though some suggest the politics of race and gender played a greater role through the 1990s.[42] Thorough analyses suggest that the evangelical shift toward the Republican Party happened prior to *Roe v. Wade*, Jerry Falwell, and Ronald Reagan, developing throughout the middle of the twentieth century.[43] My research, however, investigates the role of abortion politics in areas beyond party politics and voter mobilization. I am interested in the impact of abortion on policy preferences, elite activism, and issue framing. Despite the history of partisan alignment, abortion matters here. For evangelical advocates, abortion is the focal point for cultural engagement and policy preferences. And in abortion politics, evangelicals came to understand the value of rights, particularly the value of rights arguments, both to protect elements of cultural morality and to protect evangelicals' individual rights. Much of this congruence has developed in the second wave of evangelical politics, coalescing in the mid-1990s. Moreover, this time period fits well with the findings of prior research on the impact of cultural politics on party mobilization and the rise of the individual rights approach to pro-life politics in evangelicalism.[44]

Abortion and Contemporary RFRA Battles

The link to abortion politics becomes quite clear as we consider the opening example from Indiana. In Indiana, one of the leading voices supporting the RFRA bill was the state's chapter of the National Right to Life Committee – a largely religious organization leading the anti-abortion movement.[45] Chapter 2 will provide more detail about the history of the NRLC and its relationship between Catholics and evangelicals. But for now, some background regarding RFRA is illustrative. While many now consider opposition to abortion and religious freedom to be congruent ideological positions of American religious conservatives, this was not always the case. In fact, when the national RFRA legislation was debated in the early 1990s, many pro-life groups were concerned that the legislation might *promote* abortion. Some conservative anti-abortion groups, including the Southern Baptist Convention (SBC) and the U.S. Conference of Catholic Bishops (USCCB), were afraid that individuals might bring suits claiming that their religious beliefs necessitated their access to abortion coverage.[46] Such claims could override limitations on federal funding for abortion, commonly known as the Hyde Amendment. In the 1990s, liberal religious freedom advocates convinced conservatives that this was unlikely, and the legislation eventually passed with little opposition.

Nonetheless, a much different situation currently exists. Shortly after the passage of the Indiana RFRA, Mike Fichter, President of Indiana Right to Life, praised the bill for protecting anti-abortion advocates. "RFRA is an important bill to protect the religious freedom of Hoosiers who believe that the right to life comes from God, not government," he said.[47] While the RFRA coalition in Indiana was diverse, pro-life, pro-family conservatives dominated it. They sought to use rights politics to promote traditional morality and religious pluralism.

The connection between abortion politics and other rights claims, such as religious liberty, is an important shift in conservative politics. It helps explain the fundamental tension in American democracy between rights and morality, and it is an exemplar of the shifting role of religion in society.

Pro-life groups became especially interested in religious liberty concerns following the 2010 Affordable Care Act (ACA), which expanded health care coverage, and the following contraceptive coverage mandate (both discussed in Chapter 5). Religious individuals and groups sought protection from being required to provide insurance that covered contraceptives, a handful of which were said to cause abortions by ending a pregnancy shortly after conception (e.g., the "morning after" pill). These anti-abortion groups used the federal RFRA statute to gain greater protections from the courts, resulting in the 2014 Supreme Court case *Burwell v. Hobby Lobby*, in which the pro-life groups prevailed. Abortion politics triggered an emphasis on religious liberty advocacy, which has since been transferred to the domain of gay rights (Chapter 7). As such, abortion politics has been instrumental to the expansion of conservative religious advocacy in the United States.

For most of the policy areas in the following chapters, abortion also contributed to evangelical Christians shifting their views over the past forty years. Abortion has been a prominent cause in evangelicals supporting a broader, more individual right to free speech, and it contributed to an increased focus on religious liberty as opposed to church-state separation. It has altered the considerations in debates regarding health care and the death penalty, and it is serving as an object lesson following the nationwide legalization of same-sex marriage. Consequently, the politics of abortion has transformed the landscape of conservative politics.

Certainly abortion is not the only thing affecting the conservative political views of the Christian Right, and the chapters will investigate other political, religious, social, and psychological arguments. Still, the politics of abortion remains central. Abortion politics, especially as combined with evangelical minority politics, has taught evangelicals about rights and the political process, and it is often the substantive frame motivating other issue positions.

SIGNIFICANCE FOR AMERICAN DEMOCRACY

The development of conservative, religious rights-based advocacy signals a profound political and cultural shift that has a broad ripple effect on American politics. American culture wars now largely involve competing rights claims, not simply rights versus morality. Does this reinforce our polarized politics and degrade our discourse?[48] Or does it enhance democratic norms, including deliberation and tolerance?[49] Does it signal the failure of American democracy or the vindication of Madisonian pluralism? Perhaps there are some lessons from the past for the present.

While Alexis de Tocqueville, the famed nineteenth-century French observer of American democracy, is often credited with describing the civic republican vision of America, he foreshadowed evangelicals' contemporary approach to politics. In a less-quoted section on religion in his seminal *Democracy in America*, Tocqueville discusses the republican nature of Catholics in nineteenth-century America. Intuitively, he declares:

Their social position, as well as their limited number, obliges them to adopt [democratic and republican] opinions. Most of the Catholics are poor, and they have no chance of taking a part in the government unless it is open to all citizens. They constitute a minority, and all rights must be respected in order to ensure to them the free exercise of their own privileges. These two causes induce them, even unconsciously, to adopt political doctrines which they would perhaps support with less zeal if they were rich and preponderant.[50]

Twenty-first-century American evangelicals have become like Tocqueville's nineteenth-century American Catholics, respecting the political process of secular rights claims in order "to ensure them the free exercise of their own privileges." They have been induced, whether unconsciously or consciously, to respect the hegemony of liberalism. The moral majority has shifted to become the pluralistic minority. Evangelicals embrace rights to protect their status in the increasingly diverse political community; they embrace rights to preserve cultural morality; and they embrace rights because it is an expected part of citizenship. In the process, religious conservatives may be exhibiting that our political theories have long promoted a false dichotomy of either rights or culture shaping citizenship. Instead, there may be room for a robust rights culture that is not inhospitable to society's losers and can promote common ground. Rather than *either*, the reality may be that *both* rights *and* culture shape our polity. This resembles Amy Gutmann and Dennis Thompson's "deliberative democracy," which provides procedural and institutional mechanisms to aggregate pluralist perspectives to promote common goals.[51] In fact, prior work has identified some of these qualities in the advocacy of the Christian Right.[52] The American culture war does not have to be a total war.[53]

TERMINOLOGY

My focus here is on evangelicalism, because evangelicals have become the most important religious group in American politics due to their size, their shifting political alignment in the past fifty years, and their role in conservative politics. Evangelicalism, though it is a diverse religious classification, has several identifiable traits: (1) a high view of the authority and trustworthiness of the Bible; (2) a belief in God's real, historical work of salvation; (3) a belief that salvation comes only through the atoning work of Christ; (4) a commitment to the importance of evangelism and missions; and (5) a commitment to living a spiritually transformed life.[54] In the modern era, many evangelicals participate in the National Association of Evangelicals (NAE), as opposed to mainline Protestants – an even more diverse group of more progressive, liberal, or neo-orthodox Protestants – who participate in the National Council of Churches (NCC). While many evangelicals are involved in the NAE, the largest evangelical denomination, the Southern Baptist Convention, has in the past resisted identification as evangelical. In recent decades, however, this resistance has subsided, with most Southern Baptist leadership embracing the term. The SBC, however, is not an official member denomination of the NAE.[55]

Evangelical Protestants are quite diverse, if one limits classification to the five articles of faith listed above. Yet for purposes of political analysis, scholars of religion and politics have typically limited their attention to white evangelical Protestants when discussing the politics of evangelicalism.[56] This is especially important when trying to understand the politics of the Christian Right, of which evangelicals are the primary players.[57] Following this approach, I too limit my analysis to white evangelical Protestants or traditionally Anglo-Saxon evangelical denominations, such as the SBC, the Presbyterian Church in America, the Evangelical Free Church of America, and others. When analyzing survey data, I follow the strategy of sociologist Brian Steensland and his colleagues in their categorization of evangelicals from survey questions about religious denominational affiliation.[58] Though there has been some recent consternation about the term "evangelical" in regard to its import for American politics, even from leading evangelicals,[59] focusing on this broad category of Protestants has historical, religious, and contemporary political merit.[60]

Even while limiting my discussion to white evangelicals, there remains political and ideological diversity within evangelicalism. Rank-and-file evangelicals are not in lockstep with the Republican Party or even with prominent evangelical advocates or organizations.[61] At the elite level, there are active evangelical advocacy groups on all sides of the major political issues. When writing about evangelicals or evangelicalism, however, I invoke trends or tendencies within this religious group, at both the elite and rank-and-file levels. When investigating elites, I focus my primary attention on the prominent, conservative political activists, as their size and influence warrant the most attention and depict the broadest swath of the movement.

In describing the politics of abortion, I have also chosen to often label opponents of abortion as "pro-life," following other recent works about the history of conservative abortion politics,[62] in addition to anti-abortion. Certain people may object to this usage of the pro-life label, particularly abortion rights supporters who take offense that supporting the right for women to choose abortion is somehow anti-life. Others critique pro-lifers for their inconsistency in supporting the death penalty, which I cover in Chapter 6, along with supporting war and gun rights.[63] In light of this, *The Associated Press Stylebook* recommends that journalists "use *anti-abortion* instead of *pro-life* and *abortion rights* instead of *pro-abortion* or *pro-choice*."[64]

Despite these objections, I have chosen to use the term pro-life primarily because that is what anti-abortion activists have called themselves for the past half-century. Chapter 2 will consider this further, but organized activism against abortion began in the late 1960s with the creation of the NRLC, and these activists chose the right-to-life language from the beginning. In addition, my focus here is on the language of rights and how conservative Christians transferred rights talk from the abortion domain to other policy domains. The movement began as a defense of inalienable human rights of the unborn; that message has persisted to the present, though frequently mixed with other messages. Using the pro-life descriptor reinforces the importance of rights in abortion politics.

METHODOLOGY AND DATA

The relationship between elite activism and mass opinion is central to my analysis of conservative Christian rights politics. To tell the story about how abortion politics has contributed to the shifting landscape of politics and religion, I analyze the historical development of evangelical advocacy positions and then pair them with attitudes of the clergy, the religious rank-and-file, and the mass public. I give particular attention to how political issues are framed, both to government officials and the religious base, uncovering the presence (or absence) of abortion politics. While investigating this, I focus on the shifting relationship between abortion politics, individual rights, and public morality.

To determine if abortion matters in regard to changes in elite and rank-and-file policy positions, as well as elite activism, I employ multiple analytic strategies. First, I investigate historical and qualitative evidence to establish both that abortion justifications developed prior to other individualism issues on the right and that other issues were framed in abortion terms. Second, I analyze longitudinal survey data of the mass public and evangelical clergy to investigate whether abortion attitudes had an independent effect on policy positions in different time periods, while also considering partisan, ideological, and demographic factors. I then compare the magnitude of the abortion effect to the magnitude of the other political effects. Third, I evaluate findings from multiple survey experiments to test whether the framing of political issues in rights-based, pro-life terms affects individuals' views toward conservative arguments and their political preferences on political issues other than abortion.

I make use of a variety of data, both qualitative and quantitative, to accomplish the analyses. The qualitative components are used to identify elite learning, framing, and position taking. The primary qualitative data are systematic analyses of historical records, including evangelical position statements, resolutions from prominent religious institutions, *amicus curiae* brief filings (also called "friend of the court" briefs) by critical players in court cases, and coverage in religious and secular news archives. Newspaper reports are a crucial component of this analysis, functioning as interviews with advocacy leaders in their historical place and time.

While the qualitative data are important to understanding advocacy, the quantitative data are used to link advocacy decisions with the opinions of the religious clergy, the rank-and-file, and the mass public. This connection is central to understanding the impact of abortion politics on the political representation of conservative evangelical politics.

The quantitative data come from a variety of surveys, both nationally representative surveys and online surveys employing experimental designs to help isolate the causal impact of issue-framing. I make frequent use of the General Social Survey (GSS) and occasionally the American National Election Study (ANES), as these surveys provide historical leverage, with the GSS dating to 1972 and the ANES to 1948. I also examine data from surveys of Southern Baptist pastors, dating to 1980 and collected primarily by James Guth of Furman University.[65] Finally, I incorporate data from several online surveys that incorporated experimental treatments, which randomized how elites framed arguments for or against political issues such as religious liberty, health care, free speech, and the death penalty. I detail the wording in each chapter, but in most cases survey takers were presented with an elite prompt about a pressing political issue. Respondents were randomly assigned to receive a treatment where the elite justified a conservative advocacy position because of its linkage to the pro-life movement (using rights language), because of general morality concerns, or without giving a specific reason (the control group). I then analyze if these frames affect individuals' political attitudes, support for the elite, or support for democratic norms, such as political tolerance. If abortion framing matters and other political issues can be tied to abortion politics, then religious advocates may have unappreciated abilities to leverage the culture of rights to preserve common morality, while simultaneously expanding support for political rights.

This variety of data allows for a thorough analysis of the evolution of evangelical political advocacy and the role that abortion politics has played in the shifts – both in the direction of the advocacy and its focus on rights. The historical evidence yields a rich understanding of advocacy changes, elite decisions, and context. The national survey data allow for opinion comparison over time, as well as statistical models that identify significant factors while employing extensive controls. The experimental analysis affords causal leverage regarding the effect of the way elites frame issues to the public. To enhance the narrative and readability, I utilize figures and graphs instead of tables in the text; complete statistical results appear in the corresponding tables in Appendix B. Details of the question wording and variable coding of the surveys can be found in Appendix A.

BOOK PLAN

As the book progresses, I first provide some background on evangelicals and abortion politics, before moving to the six substantive issue chapters. Chapter 2 analyzes the evolution of abortion politics, evangelicalism, Catholicism, and the Christian Right. It explores early evangelical ambivalence toward abortion, along with increasing opposition to the practice. The chapter also traces the relationship between evangelicals and rights. These two components, abortion and rights, are linked by the anti-abortion movement's turn toward rights – the right to life. As such, the chapter sets the stage for understanding how abortion politics have affected other advocacy decisions.

Chapter 3 begins with a substantive analysis of the First Amendment to the U.S. Constitution, specifically free speech. For much of the twentieth century, secular liberals and radical political groups dominated free speech politics. Yet of late, conservatives, including evangelical conservatives, have been the leading advocates of a broad, individual right to free speech. Evangelicals have come to support radical protest and unfettered political speech in ways that would have been unthinkable only a generation or two ago. The chapter shows that abortion lies behind this shift for conservative Christians.

Chapter 4 also focuses on the First Amendment, though here giving attention to the relationship between church and state. It addresses how abortion politics prompted evangelicals, particularly Baptists, to move away from supporting the separation of church and state. In the middle of the twentieth century, some evangelical groups were leaders in promoting church-state separation, but the issue is now the domain of secular liberals and mainline

Protestants. The chapter shows how the politics of abortion contributed to evangelicals splitting from traditional advocates for church-state separation for a more specific focus on religious liberty. This shift is the linchpin for the broader evolution in evangelical advocacy, as it is necessary to engage the base, move into the domain of individual liberty, and coalesce advocacy decisions around abortion and religious freedom.

Moving away from the First Amendment, Chapter 5 analyzes health care politics and law. At first blush, Christians would seem to support greater health care, especially for the poor, and in fact, many evangelicals supported national health insurance when it first gained political traction in the 1970s. In addition, the evangelical rank-and-file largely mirror the national population in public support for national health care. Yet, the Christian Right has been one of the primary opponents of national health care expansion since the 1990s. Using a variety of data, I show that abortion politics has tainted all efforts for health care expansion for evangelicals, and it has contributed to the recent fight against contraceptive coverage.

Chapter 6 addresses capital punishment and the conflicting ways that abortion has affected evangelicals' positions on the death penalty debate. In the 1970s, when the Supreme Court temporarily halted the death penalty, some evangelical groups opposed capital punishment. Catholics too have long opposed capital punishment, with Pope John Paul II arguing for a consistent pro-life ethic for the unborn and the convict. To the contrary, many Christian Right leaders have used their pro-life stances to support the death penalty, though there are diverse arguments within evangelicalism. I analyze the different conservative Christian perspectives on the death penalty and how they are linked to abortion politics, using survey experiments to anticipate how the issue might evolve in the near future.

The final substantive chapter, Chapter 7, addresses the politics of an issue that, on the surface, appears to be the outlier – gay rights. Abortion seems to be quite removed from gay rights; moreover, how can anti–gay rights advocacy be about rights? For the past several decades, most of the evangelical opposition to gay rights has been rooted in communitarian values, traditional morality, and concern for the family. As evangelicals have lost this cultural battle, however, they have tacked toward rights in their arguments. The post–*Roe v. Wade* pro-life movement has become the model for the Christian Right, the right to religious liberty has become the defense, and advocates have begun proffering rights-based arguments against gay marriage. Chapter 7 discusses this changing approach to gay rights.

Following the substantive chapters, Chapter 8 provides the conclusion. Here I transition from rights learning and rights claiming to rights extending, bringing the LCE Process to completion. I investigate how evangelicals' turn toward rights affects political tolerance. I then briefly examine the big picture, touching on the future of evangelical politics and rights politics, the culture wars, and the state of American democracy.

2

Cultivating the Value of Rights

Evangelicals and Abortion Politics

A self-confessed born-again president was in the White House, and he was comfortable talking about his faith and crafting homespun stories, often falling into a slower, southern drawl. At the end of his first year in office, he announced that he would convene a White House Conference on Families. In doing so, he called families "the foundation of American society and its most important institution."[1] If this happened today, we would expect American evangelicals to be ecstatic, but this president was not George W. Bush, but Jimmy Carter. Instead, the Conference on Families highlights Carter's degrading relationship with evangelicals, with some historians crediting his actions for the rise of the Christian Right and the success of Ronald Reagan.[2] Though this had already begun, evangelicals would increasingly abandon Carter's Democratic Party.

For Christian conservatives, there were a variety of problems with the White House Conference on Families. There was concern over the definition of families, the nontraditional roles of women, sex education, and gay rights.[3] Historically, one issue stands above the rest – abortion. Increasingly, "family values" meant opposition to abortion. In fact, by the 1990s, family values were synonymous with pro-life politics. The Conference on Families, however, avoided abortion divides, though taking a pro-choice position when prodded.[4] The same was true of Carter. In his 1976 presidential campaign, he declared himself personally opposed to abortion, but he opposed the Human Life Amendment, which would have altered the U.S. Constitution to ensure that fetuses had the status of persons, making abortion murder. Carter did support and sign the Hyde Amendment in 1977, preventing federal funds from paying for abortions, and he made overtures to pro-lifers in public statements. But, as historian Daniel Williams recounts, Carter shortly lost the confidence of pro-life Democrats, Catholics, and evangelicals.[5] This was especially perilous for Carter, as abortion was increasingly becoming a part of Christian Right politics with the parties diverging in their positions. This divergence was clarified in 1980, as Democrats established themselves as the pro-choice party with Republicans as the pro-life party.[6]

Political scientist Ryan Claassen shows that in 1976 Carter temporarily reversed growing evangelical support for the Republican Party that had been happening since the 1960s.[7] Evangelicals only narrowly favored Gerald Ford over Carter (50%–46%). In 1980, Carter's momentum with evangelicals was lost, as they chose Ronald Reagan over Carter by a wider margin (55%–37%). From 1984 to 2008, approximately 60–70% of evangelicals who turned out to vote supported Republican presidential candidates, with approximately 35% favoring Democratic candidates.[8] In the 2012 and 2016, evangelical support for Republicans has slightly increased.[9]

There are a variety of reasons for the Republican momentum. Some emphasize the growing moral and cultural conflict between the parties, especially party activists, which provided a ripe opportunity for evangelicals to settle in the Republican Party.[10] Others stress demographic shifts rather than party capture,[11] while still others underscore racial politics and the willingness of the Republican Party to mobilize (and demobilize) religious conservatives via political messaging.[12] The politics of abortion too were an important part of evangelical politics. Much has been written in political science and history regarding the role of abortion, the Christian Right, and Republican politics. Claassen finds support for racial politics over abortion politics. Recounting the evidence, he states that "a regional partisan realignment around issues concerning race and the concentration of evangelicals in the South explains voting trends among evangelicals, not the Christian Right thesis."[13] Still, some research gives abortion more credit for partisanship, especially after the 1980s.[14] A general consensus is that racial politics drove the first phase of party realignment through the 1980s,[15] while cultural politics contributed to partisan change in the second phase.[16]

Though there is some skepticism about the decisive role of abortion in party politics and the initial realignment of the political parties, it was certainly important to evangelical activism in the early 1980s. Moreover, as the Republican Party increasingly became the primary party opposed to abortion, racial, cultural, and moral politics coalesced, which may have contributed to polarization of abortion attitudes.[17] Most importantly, abortion has become a cultural and political touchstone of American politics, specifically evangelical politics. This, however, was not always the case.

EVANGELICALS, ABORTION, AND ADVOCACY SHIFT

Prior to the 1960s, there was little political agitation about abortion, and, as Williams's history describes, until the mid-1970s most Republicans and evangelicals were "reluctant" to restrict abortion.[18] What advocacy there was prior to the mid-1960s came from New Deal liberals, particularly Catholics. In the mid-1960s, however, Americans began to rethink the issue. With that rethinking came an emphasis on human rights, spawned out of New Deal liberalism. In 1967, Catholic bishops and some Lutheran pastors formed the Right to Life League, the country's first organization committed to ending abortion.[19] Evangelicals tried to walk a middle ground, with *Christianity Today*, the prominent, national evangelical magazine, holding a Protestant Symposium on the Control of Human Reproduction in 1968 that featured twenty-five leading evangelical scholars. The Symposium concluded that "abortion-on-demand" was sinful, but "therapeutic" abortion might at times be allowable. The conclusion was followed by a series of *Christianity Today* articles trying to navigate this differentiation.[20] Many evangelical leaders were early supporters that abortion should be safe, legal, and rare. There were, however, some dissenters, including Carl F. H. Henry, evangelical theologian and founder of *Christianity Today*. In an editorial in *Eternity* in 1971, he positioned himself as decidedly pro-life.[21]

Despite Henry's plea, many evangelicals supported a limited rights approach to abortion for much of the 1970s, affirming a limited right for a woman to choose to terminate her pregnancy. In 1971, the annual meeting of the Southern Baptist Convention passed its first resolution on this topic, epitomizing this balance. The resolution acknowledged different viewpoints on abortion and expressed society's responsibility to affirm a "high view of the sanctity of human life, including fetal life," but it also urged Southern Baptists to support pro-choice legislation. The resolution supported laws that "will allow for the possibility of abortion under such conditions as rape, incest, clear evidence of fetal deformity, and carefully ascertained evidence of the likelihood of damage to the emotional, mental, and physical health of the mother."[22]

While prominent evangelical bodies were supporting limited abortion rights, increasingly some evangelicals, particularly northern evangelicals, were becoming concerned with abortion. The National Association of Evangelicals, contrary to the SBC with its more supportive tone, passed a resolution in 1971 opposed to abortion on demand while allowing certain exceptions for rape, incest, and the mother's life.[23]

On January 22, 1973, the U.S. Supreme Court defined abortion politics for decades to come with its ruling in *Roe v. Wade*. In the 7–2 decision, more than two years in the making, the Court established a woman's fundamental right to terminate a pregnancy, with state restrictions only allowed as fetal viability grows in the final trimester.[24] Many evangelicals were supportive. The official Southern Baptist publication, *Baptist Press*, declared that the decision "advanced the cause of religious liberty, human equality and justice" in the lead of its article describing the case. It repeated this in the conclusion. *Baptist Press* went on to state that the decision was "strict constructionist." Further, it identified the "Roman Catholic hierarchy" as the primary opponents to the decision, with "most other religious bodies and leaders" approving of the decision.[25] A week after the Court's decision, *Baptist Press* also published a lengthy, positive interview with one of the *Roe* lawyers, who argued that state anti-abortion laws violated the woman's fundamental right to privacy. Linda Coffee, a thirty-year-old Southern Baptist lawyer who argued the seminal case with Sarah Weddington, differentiated between the legal freedoms afforded by the case and personal moral decisions.[26]

In the years following *Roe v. Wade*, several SBC leaders took clear positions favoring abortion rights. These included leaders of its advocacy groups, James Wood of the Baptist Joint Committee (BJC) and Foy Valentine of the Christian Life Commission (CLC). Wood argued that the anti-abortion position was inherently Catholic, and establishing such a view in law would violate the separation of church and state.[27] Valentine also thought that opposition to abortion was a Catholic position, though he sought to avoid getting entangled in the abortion controversy for much of the 1970s. In 1977, however, he signed an interdenominational statement that rejected the right to life arguments. He later described that abortion was not murder and was often the "lesser of the available evils."[28]

The denomination supported a moderate and nuanced pro-choice approach. Throughout the 1970s, the SBC's official position allowed for an abortion right, but it rejected a more absolute rights approach in favor of a limited rights approach that sought to balance common morality with individual rights.

The NAE, by contrast, remained opposed to abortion. Following *Roe*, the NAE reasserted its position, while vehemently opposing the ruling, stating that they "deplore in the strongest possible terms the decision of the U.S. Supreme Court which has made it legal to terminate a pregnancy for no better reason than personal convenience or sociological considerations."[29] Increasingly, Southern Baptists were joining their northern evangelical brethren in opposition to abortion, starting groups such as Baptists for Life in 1974 and Christians for Life in 1977.

Momentum metastasized in the late 1970s and early 1980s, resulting in a decisive shift in the SBC's view on abortion. The denomination became decidedly pro-life, bringing it more in line with the NAE. This is best seen in a 1980 resolution that unequivocally declared the SBC's opposition to "abortion on demand" and "the use of tax money or public, tax-supported medical facilities for selfish, non-therapeutic abortion," along with its support for "a constitutional amendment prohibiting abortion except to save the life of the mother."[30] In every resolution on abortion since 1980, the SBC has taken a firm pro-life stance, and it has become one of the religious leaders of the pro-life movement.

Abortion was also a primary factor in the SBC altering its official advocacy organizations. In the late 1970s and 1980s, there was a battle for control of the denomination between moderates and conservatives. For decades, the moderates had led the SBC, both its organizational structure and its political advocacy. In the late 1970s, an activist group of theological and political conservatives sought to gain control of the denomination, and they were quite successful at mobilizing the grassroots.[31] It took nearly a decade for the conservatives to alter their advocacy organizations, but in 1988 they replaced the leader of the Christian Life Commission, its advocacy group for moral and social affairs, with one of their own – the steadfastly pro-life and solidly conservative Richard Land. By 1988, being pro-life was a litmus test for denominational appointment. Further, in 1991 the denomination split with its church-state advocacy group, the Baptist Joint Committee, an umbrella group for several Baptist denominations of which the SBC was by far the largest contributor of members and money. The irreconcilable differences of the divorce primarily included abortion politics and the separation of church and state. Under Land, the SBC consolidated its moral and church-state advocacy, eventually changing the name to the Ethics & Religious Liberty Commission (ERLC).[32] Land led the SBC to be one of the most active pro-life denominations in America, with strong grassroots support.

Despite their once-tepid stance on abortion, evangelicals have become leaders in the cause to end legalized abortion, often in cooperation with Catholics. Evangelical elites now take unambiguous pro-life positions, lead national organizations, participate in public protests, champion legislative change, and fight legal battles. Evangelicals have transitioned both in their abortion views and their approach to rights, transitioning from supporting limited abortion rights to defending a broad right to life. As the next section shows, the evangelical mass public too has increasingly joined the pro-life cause advocated by elites.

Evangelical Opinion on Abortion

For the past four decades, scholars have been studying the mass public's opinion about abortion.[33] A few things stand out. First, people have an opinion about the issue, and these opinions are quite stable. In fact, they are nearly as stable as people's party identification.[34] Second, aggregate opinion is in the middle of the abortion debate, neither supporting abortion for any reason nor restricting abortion in all cases,[35] and this aggregate opinion is also quite stable. Third, because most have a moderate opinion that varies according to the specific rationale, question wording matters.[36]

Throughout the book, I examine abortion attitudes using the General Social Survey. Since 1977, the GSS has asked a nationally representative sample of individuals about their position on abortion. Instead of merely asking a general abortion question, the GSS asks people whether they support or oppose abortion in specific cases. These specific cases are: the woman's health is in danger; there is a strong chance of a serious birth defect in the baby; the pregnancy is caused by rape; the woman does not want any more children; the woman is single; the family cannot afford any more children; and the woman has any reason. I add these responses together into a Pro-Life Scale that ranges from 0 to 7, where higher values represent stronger opposition to abortion. These items scale quite well,[37] as is typical of abortion measures.[38]

The top panel of Figure 2.1 displays the results of the Index over time, for both evangelicals (solid line) and non-evangelicals (dashed line), with the gray horizontal bars representing standard errors. Even in 1978, evangelicals

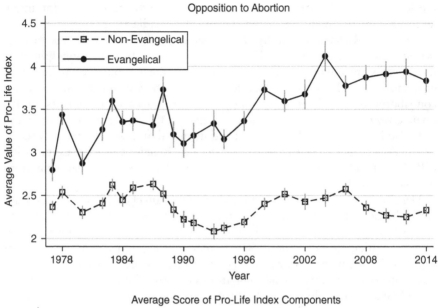

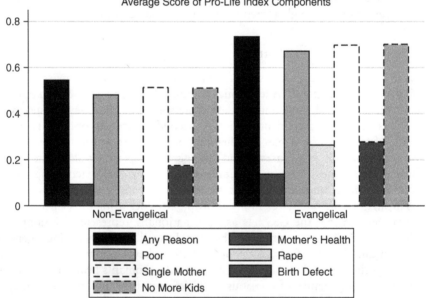

FIGURE 2.1. Average Evangelical and Non-Evangelical Scores on the Pro-Life Index and Its Components. GSS, 1977–2014.

were more opposed to abortion than non-evangelicals. This difference was statistically significant because the standard errors do not overlap, but it is substantively fairly minimal – an average difference of about a quarter point on the scale. The difference between evangelicals and non-evangelicals has continued to grow. Evangelicals were about three-quarters of a point more pro-life in the mid-1980s, one full point greater in the mid-1990s, and almost one and one-quarter point greater in 2010. Slight differences have become cavernous. In 1978, evangelicals only opposed abortion in less than three of the specific cases listed; in 2014, they opposed abortion in nearly four. The increasing religious polarization in the GSS is compatible, though even starker, than the increasing partisan polarization in regard to abortion.[39]

The bottom panel of Figure 2.1 displays how the average component scores for both groups across the entire time period. Evangelicals are more opposed to abortion in every component, but the largest differences between evangelicals and non-evangelicals are regarding the non-typical exceptions to anti-abortion laws. Evangelicals are much more likely to oppose abortion on demand (any reason), abortion because of financial circumstances (poor), and abortion due to preferred family size (no more kids).

While the evangelical masses became more pro-life over time, evangelical clergy have been consistently and strongly pro-life for more than three decades. Beginning in 1980, political scientist James Guth asked a representative sample of SBC clergy their views on a variety of theological, denominational, and political questions. From 1980 to 2008, these clergy were asked whether or not they agreed with an amendment to the U.S. Constitution outlawing abortion, similar to the Human Life Amendment. Clergy were presented with a Likert scale of options, ranging from "strongly disagree" to "strongly agree." While certainly some pastors who opposed abortion might not prefer to amend the Constitution to achieve their policy views, the question provides insight into the views of these pastors. The results are remarkably consistent. From 1980 to 1996, just under 80% of SBC pastors support an anti-abortion amendment, growing to just over 80% in the 2000s. Moreover, in 1980, when the denomination shifted to take a decidedly pro-life stance, this move was in line with SBC's pastors, as approximately 75% supported amending the Constitution to outlaw abortion.

All of these data suggest that by the early 1980s evangelicals were more opposed to abortion than non-evangelicals, though the elites were more pro-life than the rank-and-file. In the past thirty-five years, the elites have remained consistent in their opposition to abortion, while the rank-and-file have increased their opposition. In the collective, Americans hold a rather moderate position on abortion,[40] and the wording of the survey question matters.[41] But among this moderation there are groups solidly on each side of the pro-life and pro-choice debate. Evangelicals are the most prominent pro-lifers, and their shift to the Republican Party has contributed to partisan polarization on the issue.

MECHANISM FOR REPRESENTATION

While there is some academic debate about the role of abortion in the founding of the culture wars and the broader realignment of the Democratic and

Republican parties, abortion attitudes have been shown to be a potent force in politics. Political scientists Edward Carmines and James Stimson's classic work defines moral issues as "easy issues" because they are salient and simple to understand.[42] These easy issues have the ability to create an "issue evolution," where elites become polarized and public opinion follows. Conflict expansion is also prevalent in these easy issues. Importantly, political scientist Geoffrey Layman has shown that attention and importance of these easy, moral issues have increased considerably in the past four decades, as has the importance in the mass electorate.[43] Among these moral issues, the politics of abortion is a classic example of issue evolution and conflict expansion.[44]

A variety of data supports the evolving, expanding nature of abortion politics. Examining the 1992 election, one study of public opinion found that "abortion had a stronger influence on candidate choice than any other policy issue," and it even had a stronger influence than the state of the economy for those who considered abortion salient and who knew the parties' positions on the issue.[45] Similar evidence was found in state-level elections in the late 1990s.[46] Partisans who attach low value to abortion politics are likely to alter their views on abortion to match their political party,[47] but even more, abortion attitudes are so powerful that they can alter partisanship, especially when it is seen as an important issue.[48] In brief time periods, abortion shifts the strength of individuals' partisanship, from strong to weak and weak to leaning support of a party (and vice versa), if abortion is salient to them.[49] Across longer periods, the change is more substantial. Using panel data from 1982 to 1997, scholars found that abortion attitudes have contributed to party switching, with pro-life Democrats becoming Republican and pro-choice Republicans becoming Democrats.[50] One's view on abortion has been able to alter the most central and stable of all political positions – party identification.[51]

Because abortion has become a central part of evangelicals' political advocacy, it often serves as a mechanism for elites, particularly evangelical advocacy leaders, to represent their constituents. Many prominent evangelical organizations, especially those involved in conservative politics, are active participants in pro-life politics. This takes many forms, but it includes supporting pro-life candidates, bringing attention to pro-life issues, advocating for state or national pro-life legislation, and developing pro-life legal defenses, often through "friend of the court" briefs.[52] In fact, being pro-life is a de facto requirement of Christian Right politics. Pro-life politics are also prone to expansion into other arenas because abortion is more than a single issue position. Rather, it involves a "bundle of beliefs," a "worldview."[53]

Prior analyses have identified the centrality of anti-abortion politics to conservative religious organizations throughout the Christian Right movement,[54] but abortion's political leverage has been underappreciated. Because of its centrality, as conservative and religious organizations become more ingrained in politics and pursue new and different political issues, they can utilize abortion – the easy issue – to help their constituents understand the issue and to mobilize their constituents. Abortion, as the most stable issue attitude, can alter more fungible ones. Because abortion politics are stable and salient for evangelicals, it becomes a gateway to political representation. Stronger linkages between elites and their constituents have been a hallmark of conservative Christian politics,[55] and pro-life politics make that possible.

INFRASTRUCTURE OF RIGHTS

In addition to being the central issue evangelicalism used to represent its constituents, the politics of abortion also taught evangelicals about rights. While many accounts depict opposition to abortion as a conservative backlash against the equal rights of women,[56] there is little support for this in public opinion once controlling for other factors.[57] Even more, Williams's recent historical work capably documents how the early pro-life movement began as a liberal human rights campaign.[58] As early as the 1930s and 1940s, the largely Catholic anti-abortion activists drew upon the Catholic natural law tradition and the American liberal, individualist rights tradition. There was a clear emphasis in the 1950s among many Catholics that abortion violated the fetus's right to life, which was inalienable and deserved constitutional protection.[59] In turn, in 1968 the most prominent, ecumenical anti-abortion organization – the National Right to Life Committee – was intentionally named with an emphasis on universal rights, as was the Right to Life League that preceded it.

At its founding, the NRLC focused almost exclusively on the rights of the unborn, drawing connections from the Declaration of Independence, the United Nations' Universal Declaration of Human Rights, and the U.S. Constitution.[60] From the Declaration of Independence, emphasis was on the "inalienable rights" of "life, liberty, and the pursuit of happiness."[61] From the Universal Declaration of Human Rights it was that "everyone has the right to life, liberty and security of person" and that everyone is "entitled to all the rights and freedoms set forth in this Declaration, without distinctions of any kind," including "birth or other status."[62] From the U.S. Constitution, it was the Fifth and Fourteenth Amendments' guarantees of protection of "life, liberty, and property, without due process of law."[63] By the early 1970s, many Protestants had joined the NRLC, with some serving in leadership capacities. Early Protestant sympathizers were not conservative evangelicals, however, but liberal mainline Protestants with interests in a variety of human rights and social justice causes.[64]

Evangelicals began joining the movement during the 1970s, as discussed with the NAE's 1971 and 1973 resolutions, as well as the Southern Baptist shift on abortion culminating in 1980. Though evangelicals were brought into the pro-life fold in the mid-late 1970s, they often framed their opposition to abortion in terms of preserving proper sexual morality, not protecting the inalienable rights of the unborn. Majoritarianism was evangelicals' primary justification, not liberalism.

Two of the evangelicalism's most prominent figures, Francis Schaeffer and Jerry Falwell, inform this approach. Schaeffer, a Presbyterian theologian, was a cultural critic and a popular writer and speaker in the 1970s and 1980s.[65] Schaeffer's ministry influenced many evangelical leaders, including Jerry Falwell of the Moral Majority and Richard Land of the Southern Baptist Convention's advocacy organization,[66] and Williams credits Schaeffer for mobilizing evangelicals to stop abortion. Schaeffer brought much of the Catholic human rights approach to abortion into evangelicalism, yet simultaneously many of his appeals focused on lax morals, not human rights.[67]

Though Schaeffer had a hybrid approach to combatting abortion, the morality approach gained more traction with evangelicals, especially at first. Schaeffer's critiques came in the form of popular books and documentary film series, including *How Should We Then Live?* in 1976 and *Whatever Happened to the Human Race* in 1979.[68] Emphasizing rights, he compared abortion to slavery, when people stripped others of human dignity and human rights.[69] Yet, the central message of Schaeffer's primary works was that legalized abortion was the culmination of the legal and cultural shift away from biblical sexual morality.[70] The human rights component to anti-abortion advocacy, though evident, was secondary for many evangelicals.

Schaeffer's activism against abortion strongly influenced Jerry Falwell,[71] who epitomized the morality approach in opposing abortion. Falwell was a prominent pastor who had a large television and radio ministry, and he became the face of the Christian Right through his leadership of the Moral Majority, which he created in 1979. As its name signifies, the Moral Majority was focused on a communitarian vision – restoring society's moral order through majoritarian politics. Abortion became a primary issue for Falwell, though it was integrated with his opposition to secular humanism and sexual freedom.[72] Opposition to abortion was fused with opposition to the Equal Rights Amendment (ERA), gay rights, pornography, and church-state separation. In 1978, his short monograph *How You Can Help Clean Up America* linked abortion with sexual promiscuity and feminism. He declared that women who want an abortion were "pregnant because of sin" or had also been "caught up in the ERA movement and want to terminate their pregnancy because it limits their freedom and their job opportunities."[73] To Falwell, abortion was a morality project for the silent majority.

While early evangelical forays into the pro-life movement were often framed in terms of morality, not human rights, evangelicals too had a heritage of rights. For example, legal historian John Witte, Jr. describes the role of the Calvinist religious tradition in teaching Protestants about religious and political rights, including the rights of conscience, press, association, contract, and property.[74] Witte writes that "early modern Calvinism [is] one of the driving engines of Western constitutionalism."[75] Because of Calvinism's heritage in early America and evangelical Protestantism, these universal human rights were ingrained, though often dormant, in much of evangelical Christianity. Of particular note is the Baptist heritage of religious freedom in America, dating to the seventeentn century.[76] In the 1950s, the NAE appealed to this history when passing a resolution supporting human rights, though this was primarily focused on racial justice.[77] In 1978, the SBC harkened this tradition, passing a resolution affirming the UN's Universal Declaration of Rights.[78]

The religious and American tradition of rights provided the soil for the seeds the pro-life movement's rights culture to grow. Despite evangelicalism's early history with the pro-life movement mostly linking opposition to abortion with a failing culture and the need for improved sexual morality, there remained a stream of rights-talk within the pro-life movement. This was present in the Catholic wing of the pro-life movement, though they too occasionally framed abortion in morality terms. The pro-life rights culture grew in the evangelical wing, particularly as evangelicals and Catholics intermingled in groups such as the NRLC, which became less dominated by Catholics, and even parts of the Moral Majority, which was intentionally open to both Catholics and Protestants. Likewise, some leaders grasped Schaeffer's emphasis on human rights and dignity, especially as abortion politics became ingrained in minority politics following the cementing of the *Roe* precedent. As such, there was a dual foundation for the pro-life movement within evangelicalism – morality and rights.

Throughout, there was a continual appeal to universal rights. As Williams describes, "pro-lifers' central human rights claim – the claim that the fetus has an inalienable right to life – remained their guiding principle."[79] Following the Moral Majority, there was also a growth of the rights-based stream of the pro-life justification, as pro-lifers saw a need for their arguments to have more secular appeal, particularly in light of their political minority position.[80] Sociologist Matthew Moen describes that there was an increasing transition from moralistic language to liberal language, emphasizing rights, equality, and freedom.[81] In analyzing public opinion, political scientist Ted Jelen found that evangelicals were not motivated by rights justifications against abortion in the early 1980s,[82] but by the end of the decade they were.[83] The language of advocacy was changing with the cultural and political context.

There were also concerted efforts in the Christian Coalition, which replaced the Moral Majority as the forbearer of the Christian Right in the 1990s, to be more pragmatic in its politics and its public justifications.[84] Ralph Reed, who led the Christian Coalition from 1989 to 1997, was responsible for much of this effort.[85] In fact, in 1994, Moen wrote, "Virtually all of [the Christian Right's] issues have been recast" in the rhetoric of liberalism. "Using the rhetoric that Americans are accustomed to hearing both maximizes the appeal of issue positions and circumvents the problems connected to religious discourse in a pluralistic society."[86] Some analysts of the Christian Right suggest that it has been successful in employing "democratic virtues" even in their abortion positions.[87] The evolution of the SBC's anti-abortion resolutions highlights this approach. The SBC's 1980 resolution that shifted the denomination's abortion position focused on morality, condemning "selfish, non-therapeutic abortion."[88] By 1996, the SBC's resolution against partial-birth abortion was couched in liberal language, seeking to protect the "sanctity of the innocent, unborn babies" and working for "civil justice for these innocent victims."[89] In 2015, the denomination called on citizens to work "on behalf of justice, the protection of human life, and the cause of human flourishing."[90] Moralizing had given way to liberalizing. Rights and justice have taken precedence over right and wrong.

CRITICAL DEVELOPMENTS IN THE RIGHTS POLITICS OF ANTI-ABORTION ADVOCACY

Within the politics of abortion, this increasing dependence of rights was particularly noticeable in the legal and political battles over abortion protests in the 1990s. Abortion protests had been a hallmark of the pro-life movement from the beginning,[91] but Randall Terry's evangelical civil disobedience group Operation Rescue heightened the controversy. Operation Rescue members (often called Rescuers) engaged in street protests and sit-ins, blocked abortion clinics, and counseled (or pestered) clinic-goers. Not all anti-abortion protests were conducted by Operation Rescue, as many protesters simply picketed abortion clinics, but the Rescuers gained national attention for their tactics. Many protestors were aggressive in their tactics, however, and by the late 1980s cities such as Buffalo, New York saw frequent protest and blockade activity. Demonstrators were often arrested, and violence erupted in certain cities. David Gunn was the first abortion doctor shot and killed in 1993 in Pensacola, Florida. Another doctor and a clinic volunteer were killed the following year in Pensacola, and two Planned Parenthood receptionists were murdered in Boston that same year. In 1998, still another doctor was murdered at his home near Buffalo, and a bomb was detonated at a clinic in Birmingham, Alabama.[92]

The civil disobedience and clinic violence sparked a variety of lawsuits, as well as local and national legislation, to protect people seeking an abortion. These suits pitted abortion rights and public safety against free speech. Joshua Wilson's *The Street Politics of Abortion* describes the legal, political, and organizational maneuvering that pro-choice and pro-life activists engaged in regarding protests and civil disobedience.[93] As Wilson describes, at first the pro-choice advocates seemed to gain an advantage, with courts protecting clinic-goers and cities enacting regulations. But as the battle over abortion shifted from sidewalks to the courtrooms, pro-life advocates developed more sophisticated legal and political strategies, often reframing pro-life issues and appealing to bedrock First Amendment principles. Even more, conservatives became radicals, seeking protection of their rights against those on the left who sought to protect community safety and morality. The traditional roles of conservatism and liberalism had been flipped.

In the process, the religious advocates also became more professionalized and built institutions. Christian leaders and groups created legal advocacy organizations and cultivated legal practitioners to defend protesters. These included Pat Robertson's American Center for Law and Justice (ACLJ) and Jerry Falwell's Liberty University Law School and Liberty Counsel. These new groups are now prominent players in Christian Right politics, and their activities will be discussed in the chapters to come.[94] Wilson and others describe how the protest litigation altered the politics of abortion and broader evangelical advocacy, transforming from street politics to "advocacy conglomerates."[95] These religious legal advocacy groups joined with conservative legal organizations and conservative professional networks, such as the Federalist Society, which were also growing in prevalence and sophistication.[96] While initially focused on maintaining judicial fidelity to the text of the Constitution, conservative legal advocacy has recently shifted toward rights, seeking to protect broad personal freedoms, specifically in the areas of free speech and gun rights.[97] The rights stream of anti-abortion advocacy was in fertile ground.

ABORTION, RIGHTS, AND THE REIMAGINING OF CONSERVATIVE CHRISTIAN ADVOCACY

Within this milieu of conservative Christian activism, abortion has become a crucial focal point. First, the rights-based stream of the pro-life movement has been important for the stability, and even growth, of the mass support for the pro-life cause. The stability of aggregate abortion attitudes is impressive for the pro-life movement, especially when one considers the demographic and attitudinal changes in American society since *Roe* that should have encouraged increased support for abortion rights. Both political scientists, such as Jelen, and historians, such as Williams, have credited the movement's emphasis on rights for its staying power. Jelen describes the battle between a woman's "right to choose" and the fetus's "right to life": "Posed in this way, a fetal 'right to life' can plausibly be asserted to trump a woman's right to reproductive freedom." In his view, this approach helped alleviate the "tension between orthodox Christian values and the American culture of individual rights."[98] Similarly, Williams concludes:

As the other moral regulatory causes that the Christian Right championed – causes such as school prayer or opposition to pornography or gay rights – eventually lost public support and, in a few cases faded away entirely, the pro-life cause remained the one moral issue that was capable of attracting a younger generation to the Republican Party. It did so because unlike any of the other campaigns, it was a human rights cause that the millennial generation, which had grown up in an era of rights consciousness, could easily understand and claim as its own.[99]

Second, the politics of abortion have been used by activists to alter and expand the scope of evangelical advocacy, and much of this change is oriented around rights.[100] Wilson notes that the ACLJ's mission statement in 1999 was to be the "nation's pre-eminent public interest law firm and educational organization dedicated to defending and advancing religious liberty, the sanctity of human life, and the two-parent, marriage-bound family." By 2012, the ACLJ's mission had expanded to protecting "freedom and liberty in the United States and the world."[101] Liberty Counsel too is dedicated to "advancing religious freedom, the sanctity of human life, and the family," but its stated research and advocacy partnerships via its Liberty Center for Law and Policy institution have expanded of late to include "nominations and appointments, constitutional issues, and government oversight."[102] Conservative legal organizations have utilized and co-opted some pro-life and evangelical resources to achieve success,[103] as has the Republican Party in its attempt to mobilize evangelical voters.[104] Nevertheless, Wilson describes the expansion and professionalization of evangelical legal advocacy as a benefit to the movement: "This broadening of substantive political interests reflects one of the important ways that the New Christian Right is different from, and more politically potent than, earlier Christian conservative political iterations."[105] The right to life is both a powerful, easy issue and one ripe for conflict expansion.

CONCLUSION

While some of the previously referenced scholars have discussed the role that abortion politics have played in the evolution and expansion of evangelical politics, prior work has paid little attention to the specific ways in which abortion politics have spawned evangelical advocacy in other issue domains. Scholarship on public opinion, abortion, and cultural change has been heavily focused on partisan politics,[106] while the studies of the Christian Right legal and political movements have focused almost exclusively on elite and organizational changes.[107] Both types of work omit the interplay between mass opinion and elite advocacy. The forthcoming chapters seek to weave together this holistic picture.

   Moreover, the expansion of issues within evangelical activism often comes with a repackaging of political discourse, focusing on rights. Again, studies of rights politics have tended to focus on elites or public opinion, with scant analysis of how changing elite advocacy interacts with changing mass opinion. Studies of evangelical rights politics have also overlooked the centrality of abortion. Because abortion is critical to evangelical politics, elites are able to expand the sphere of their advocacy by tying issues to abortion. In addition, because the pro-life movement has had an active rights-based justification that has grown more important in evangelical circles, the politics of abortion have taught evangelicals about the public value of rights-talk. The politics of abortion have contributed directly to both *rights learning* and *rights claiming*, and they are a signpost for *rights extending*. In the coming chapters, I explore how abortion has coalesced both advocacy expansion and rights politics within conservative evangelicalism.

3

But Words Can Never Hurt Me

Learning the Value of Free Speech

On a chilly January day in 2015, religious fundamentalists resorted to violence to avenge the defamation of their religious beliefs. A satirical tabloid, known for its disrespectful cartoons lampooning religious leaders, had repeatedly depicted the leader of the fundamentalists' faith in cheeky and insensitive ways. At about midday in a major international city, two gunmen approached the tabloid offices and murdered eleven people, injuring another eleven. Following the attacks, the world responded – decrying the attacks, showing sorrow for the dead and injured, and defending a broad right to free speech, even radical anti-religious speech.

In this case the fundamentalist assailants were Islamic radicals who targeted the French tabloid paper *Charlie Hebdo* for its caricatures of the Muslim prophet Muhammad. In the United States and around the world, the response to the devastating attack was overwhelming in its support for *Charlie Hebdo*. The phrase *Je suis Charlie* (I am Charlie) became ubiquitous, filling social media profiles, newspaper headlines, and television news reports. Along with the support came strong commitments to free speech, decrying radicals who would resort to violence in the face of public expression.

American Christians were no exception in defending free speech. Even though the tabloid was religiously offensive and had sharply criticized Christianity at times, evangelicals and Catholics overwhelmingly offered public support for a broad right to free speech (and directly or indirectly supported the magazine) through social media accounts, interviews by leaders, and organizational statements. Following the attacks, conservative *New York Times* columnist Ross Douthat, who is a Catholic ally to conservative evangelical elites, argued, "The right to blaspheme (and otherwise give offense) is essential to the liberal order."[1] Tony Perkins, leader of the Christian Right organization the Family Research Council (FRC), declared, "While many believe the satirical work of *Charlie Hebdo* was in bad taste and of poor form, we recognize the freedom that they had to speak without fear of reprisal or the threat of violence. Make no mistake about it, last week's violent assault was designed to intimidate and silence others who would dare exercise that fundamental human right of the freedom of speech."[2]

There were some exceptions, recommending more nuanced support for free speech. John Stonestreet of the Chuck Colson Center for Christian Worldview offered, "I am not going to post [*Je suis Charlie*] on Facebook. I'm not going to claim that. I want to march against Islamic terror, but not for the sort of thing that we see out of *Charlie Hebdo*."[3] Prominent evangelical pastor Franklin Graham, son of the famed evangelist Billy Graham, presented a similar response,[4] while Southern Baptist commentator Joe Carter reluctantly supported free speech in this case, arguing for liberty though not license. "Yes, offensive speech must be defended," said Carter while writing at the outlet for the Southern Baptist Convention's advocacy group, "but 'good men' ought to carry out the task with a sigh of opprobrium."[5] Notably, Pope Francis suggested that there should be limits to religious mockery. Francis declared, "One cannot provoke, one cannot insult other people's faith, one cannot make fun of faith. ... In freedom of expression there are limits."[6]

Despite cautions, broad support for free speech, even radical speech, was the recurrent message from American conservatism and evangelicalism, appearing on conservative websites such as The Federalist, the Heritage Foundation, the Family Research Council, and others.[7] Conservatives and evangelicals staked broad, liberal support for free speech rights.

Advocacy for expansive free speech rights, even religiously insensitive speech, is quite new for American evangelicals. For most of the twentieth century, it was liberals and radicals who supported extensive free speech rights. Evangelicals considered these groups antithetical to American moral values, as they often supported pornography and sexualized art, while defying American patriotism. In fact, in the 1980s, one of evangelicalism's most prominent leaders, Jerry Falwell, had a bitter legal battle over a satirical advertisement in the pornographic magazine *Hustler*, founded by Larry Flynt.[8] Falwell's case bears some resemblance to *Charlie Hebdo*.

In its November 1983 issue, *Hustler* printed a parody of a liquor advertisement suggesting that the pastor and prominent political activist's first sexual encounter had been a drunken rendezvous with his mother. Falwell sued the magazine for libel, invasion of privacy, and the infliction of emotional distress, seeking damages from the magazine. Falwell raised money for his legal fees in two direct mailings: one to his Moral Majority organization and one to the fans of his *Old Time Gospel Hour* television show, asking for his supporters to help defend him "against the smears and slander of this major pornographic magazine." In response, Falwell raked in more than $700,000 in financial support.[9]

While the legal battle was certainly personal, Falwell was also seeking to narrow the free speech protections offered by the First Amendment. His legal team argued that the parody cartoon in *Hustler* was "outrageous,"[10] differentiating it from traditional parody cartoons. The implication would be that outrageous speech or parodies were exempt from settled First Amendment protections, such as the normal standards for public figures to prove libel. The litigation progressed all the way to the U.S. Supreme Court in the case *Hustler Magazine v. Falwell*. In 1988, the Court unanimously sided with *Hustler*, protecting the right of individuals and media to publish even outrageous political cartoons against public figures. Conservative Chief Justice William Rehnquist defended "robust political debate ... which will not always be reasoned or moderate."[11] Falwell was not convinced by this interpretation of the First Amendment, commenting after the decision, "No sleaze merchant like Larry Flynt should be able to use the First Amendment as an excuse for maliciously and dishonestly attacking public figures as he has so often done."[12] Ordered liberty and common morality were Falwell's theme.

What happened in the thirty years between *Hustler Magazine v. Falwell* and *Je suis Charlie* that would alter evangelical support for outrageous political cartoons? Was it merely that evangelicals opposed extensive free speech in Falwell's case because the outrageous parody affected one of their leaders, while they supported broad speech rights in *Charlie Hebdo* because it was targeted at Muslims – a prominent enemy? Or do the examples signify a broader ideological shift of increasing support for free speech, as has been documented in other areas of conservative politics?[13] The rest of the chapter suggests that it is the latter, and, coincidentally, the shift was facilitated by evangelical commitment to anti-abortion politics, with which Falwell and his Moral Majority were heavily involved.[14]

EARLY EVANGELICAL FREE SPEECH ADVOCACY: OBSCENITY, CAMPAIGN FINANCE, AND RADICAL PROTEST

In the middle of the twentieth century, evangelical organizations were infrequently involved in major free speech debates. For example, prior to the 1988 conservative change in leadership of the Southern Baptist Convention's advocacy organization (discussed in Chapter 2), the denomination had little activity in free speech legal advocacy beyond the "equal access" cases that developed in the 1980s and argued that religious groups should have equitable access to public facilities and public funding based on free speech grounds.[15] When the denomination engaged on free speech issues, it focused largely on nonjudicial advocacy, such as making public statements, supporting local activity, and encouraging legislation. On the whole, evangelicals emphasized a "common morality" or "ordered liberty" legal framework in the area of free speech, reflective of their cultural and demographic dominance in American society. Drawing on Robert Bellah's categories,[16] they supported biblical and republican moral values in regard to speech, not individualist ones. In what follows, I trace these developments in three areas: obscenity, campaign finance, and radical protest.

Obscenity

Anti-obscenity advocacy was the primary free speech issue that evangelicals were engaged in for much of the twentieth century, as most evangelicals have long been opposed to public distribution of pornography and have supported laws outlawing various forms of obscenity and profanity. At its 1953 annual convention, the SBC first went on record opposing obscenity in literature, which "serv[es] no good purpose at all," and supporting legal restrictions on obscene materials. The denomination also commended a congressional investigation into obscene literature.[17] The SBC's initial foray into free speech advocacy was to protect common morality.

Though evangelicals stood firm against obscenity and pornography, they were fighting a losing battle. Beginning in the late 1950s, the Supreme Court facilitated the easing of anti-obscenity laws in a string of decisions beginning with *Roth v. United States* (1957). *Roth* established that obscenity was not protected by the First Amendment's free speech clause, but to qualify as obscenity a work would have to be wholly obscene and violate the contemporary community standards for obscenity. The decision liberalized obscenity law.

Evangelical organizations were slow to recognize these important legal shifts, at first praising the decision in *Roth* for declaring that obscenity was outside the bounds of the First Amendment. Two months after the Supreme Court released the *Roth* decision, the Southern Baptist Christian Life Commission (the denomination's primary advocacy organization for moral and ethical issues) held a conference on obscene literature, urging churches to take action opposing its spread. Of particular concern to the speakers was the effect of pornography on American's youth. The conference urged Southern Baptists to push for stricter laws and stronger enforcement of existing laws, while "join[ing] hands with other Protestant groups and other forces for morality in their communities." Yet, evangelical leaders seemed to underestimate the potential impact the recent *Roth* decision would have on obscenity law. Instead of being outraged that the standards for obscenity had been decreased, Glenn D. Everett of the *Christian News Service* emphasized that the decision continued to hold that obscenity is outside the accepted boundary of the First Amendment, serving as a "powerful weapon" to enact anti-obscenity legislation.[18] The lack of appreciation for the impact of the Court's decision signals evangelicals' (and particularly Baptists') general deferential posture toward the Court, which was also evident in other areas of law.

In the years following *Roth*, the status of obscenity laws was unsettled. Evangelicals continued to advocate for strict laws and tough enforcement – moral majoritarianism. Importantly, the National Association of Evangelicals joined this effort in 1958, opposing all forms of alcohol advertisements and supporting the end of "indecent and obscene publications."[19] The next year, the SBC passed a resolution specifically supporting efforts of Postmaster General Arthur E. Summerfield to eliminate the use of the mail to distribute pornographic materials.[20] Summerfield garnered attention for a federal case that resulted from the confiscating of uncensored copies of D. H. Lawrence's novel *Lady Chatterley's Lover* from the U.S. mail. Lawrence's graphic sexual descriptions had for many decades been subject to obscenity restrictions in the United States and Europe, and its distribution through the mail violated the Comstock Act's restrictions on mailing obscene materials. However, the Post Office's decision to seize shipments of *Lady Chatterley's Lover* was a narrow reading, and potentially a rejection, of *Roth's* standards. In supporting General Summerfield, the SBC was advocating for tighter obscenity laws and tighter reigns on free speech. The Post Office lost the case after the District Court sided with the bookseller, declaring that the novel was not "utterly without social importance," affording it free speech protections.[21] While evangelicals were arguing for limited rights, expansive individual rights were prevailing.

At the 1959 annual Southern Baptist convention, CLC leaders admitted that in *Roth* and successive cases the Court had unleashed sweeping changes in obscenity law, stating that because of the Court's decisions, "obscene publications were let loose on the country in greater volume than ever."[22] In the annual report given by A. C. Miller, the CLC declared that "the most effective instruments in this struggle [defeating obscenity] should be the home, the school and the church; and that one of the objectives of this united effort should be to arouse informed and active public opinion that will not tolerate the distribution of this offensive material in any form or by any method."[23] In the address, the CLC appeared to have ceded the legal definitions of free speech protections and obscenity to the Supreme Court, while seeking to motivate a morality ground war at home.

Despite the judicial defeats for their positions on obscenity, the SBC and the NAE continued to express their opposition to obscenity and pornography. The SBC's advocacy occurred primarily through the Christian Life Commission, and both large evangelical organizations periodically passed resolutions. The NAE passed five resolutions that sought to narrow the First Amendment between 1960 and 1970. In 1965, the SBC urged booksellers and newsstand proprietors "to refuse to sell such literature as appeals to the prurient interests" (a nod to the language of the majority opinion in *Roth*) and expressed its support for state laws, which would allow proprietors to restrict the sale of "objectionable materials."[24]

Notwithstanding their efforts, evangelicals continued losing ground before the Supreme Court, as it was further liberalizing obscenity law, defining contemporary community standards as the nation as a whole in *Jacobellis v. Ohio* (1964) and declaring that a work of art could not be considered obscene if it had a "modicum of redeeming social value" in *Memoirs v. Massachusetts* (1966). In 1965, the NAE publicly opposed the Court's liberalizing of obscenity laws in a firm critique from the religious tradition that was often deferential to the Court and political institutions. The resolution declared that the NAE "deplores any of the court's decisions which undercut the responsibilities of the states to deal effectively with obscenity cases, thus significantly encouraging the traffic in obscenity."[25] On the ground, evangelicals continued to push for localities to establish community morality rules to limit broad free speech rights.

The Supreme Court provided good news in 1968, ruling that minors can be restricted from purchasing non-obscene materials that contain nudity, though it may be suitable for adults (*Ginsberg v. New York*). The SBC praised this decision in a 1968 resolution, calling for additional legislation to protect minors from pornography.[26] The NAE, however, further admonished courts for liberalizing obscenity law in 1969, asking Congress to limit appeals for pornography cases and "permit local communities to establish and enforce their own standards of decency."[27] In a nod to contemporary evangelical advocacy, the NAE was quick to lay blame on the courts.

Despite their anti-obscenity positions, evangelicals were slow to develop a robust legal justification for their positions. In the more than a dozen SBC resolutions on the topic, the First Amendment is rarely referenced, and the NAE largely avoided crafting a legal defense against liberal rights claims. When evangelicals did develop constitutional arguments, they emphasized ordered liberty and the boundaries of rights rather than competing rights. For example, in a 1970 Congressional testimony, SBC advocacy leader Harry Hollis argued that, despite the fact that Baptists embrace liberty, he would support laws that would prevent adults from reading and viewing what they would like. Citing Justice Brennan, who wrote the majority opinion in *Roth*, Hollis declared obscenity to be outside "the area of constitutionally protected free speech and press." Hollis explained, "Constitutional controls are needed not to abridge freedom but to provide a stable moral climate in which freedom can be enjoyed."[28] To help promote this stable moral climate, Hollis advocated for a government initiative that would become the target of much SBC protest in the coming decades – sex education in public schools.

Hollis's proposal was part of the CLC's local, multilevel approach to opposing obscenity through churches, schools, and local businesses. "If funds can be provided to help parents and teachers understand the new math, why should there not be an expenditure of money to help adults communicate the old and wonderful phenomenon of sexuality?!" Hollis exclaimed. His proposal called for the teaching of biblically based sexual ethics in schools, though he made no caveat about how this might fit with the First Amendment's Establishment Clause, of which the SBC was a prominent defender at the time (see Chapter 4).[29] The key theme of both is community morality, where individual action cannot trump community standards.

Beyond the church-state dilemmas, there is a naïveté in Hollis's testimony. In advocating for ordered liberty that protects the right of the community to narrow free speech and free press rights, Hollis approvingly cited Justice Brennan, the author of the majority opinions in *Roth*, *Jacobellis*, and *Memoirs*. Hollis seems to have failed to realize that Brennan's individual rights approach directly contradicted his focus on the community's morals. The ground had shifted from underneath evangelicals. Hollis was defending moral majoritarianism, while the prevailing doctrines had been recast in individualism.

Evangelicals failed to see the turning constitutional tide and counter liberal rights claims with competing rights. Instead, their default constitutional position was to assume that pornography and obscenity were outside the bounds of the First Amendment's protections, and leading organizations did not attempt to define these boundaries. Though evangelicals were not directly involved in obscenity cases, they continued to publicly support anti-obscenity laws despite losing legal ground. The SBC, for example, passed resolutions condemning pornography, obscenity, and child pornography at its annual convention nine out of the eleven years between 1977 and 1987. Taking a limited rights, communitarian approach, the Southern Baptist resolutions condemned the use of pornography and called for tougher legislation and enforcement to restrict its production and sale. Resolutions typically called the nation toward the standards of biblical morality in the area of sexual relations and referenced the danger pornography caused to American youth and families. This is classic biblical conservatism.[30] The First Amendment was rarely referenced, though the SBC carved out a more robust legal defense than the NAE did.

While the SBC's default constitutional approach was to assume that pornography and obscenity were outside the bounds of the First Amendment's protections, it did not attempt to define these boundaries. A 1986 SBC resolution epitomizes this approach, declaring that "the Supreme Court of the United States has set forth clear and precise standards which allow for a determination of obscenity applying the local community standards."[31] This is in reference to the Court's perspective following *Miller v. California* (1973), though the SBC's confidence in the Court's "clear and precise standards" was and is not shared by most legal scholars who point to Justice Potter Stewart's vague "I know it when I see it" obscenity standard from *Jacobellis v. Ohio* (1964). Imprecise standards on the right opened the door for the left's liberalism to triumph.

Even more, major religious organizations, the SBC in particular, were largely deferential to the Supreme Court, perhaps related to their moral conservatism. (The NAE, by contrast, was vocal in opposing the Court's view of obscenity and free speech, as mentioned earlier.[32]) The SBC showed little outrage when the Court narrowed its definition of obscenity, allowing more sexually explicit content to become legal. In fact, the SBC clung to the Court's statements that obscenity was outside the bounds of free speech, while failing to understand that the definition of obscenity had changed in a way unfavorable to most Southern Baptists. This deference to the Supreme Court characterized the SBC's approach in other areas, including the Court's controversial decisions on school prayer and abortion that many evangelicals strongly opposed. As evangelicals would become more focused on rights, they would no longer accede to the

Court, an outlook learned following *Roe v. Wade*. Growing rights consciousness coincided with reduced deference, signaling an acknowledgment of a
growing cultural minority status. In rights politics, the stakes of Supreme Court
decisions are higher.

Campaign Finance

While obscenity and pornography were the most prominent components of
mid-century evangelical free speech advocacy, evangelicals also engaged other
prominent free speech issues, including issues of campaign finance reform
and radical protest. While they only engaged in a smattering of advocacy,
evangelicals consistently supported ordered liberty over individualism.

In the 1970s, President Richard Nixon's Watergate scandal set the stage for
campaign reform. In the spring of 1974, the Senate took steps to have presidential elections publicly financed and reduce campaign spending by limiting
individual contributions, requiring financial disclosures, and imposing broadcast restrictions. At the same time, nineteen religious organizations, including the
Baptist Joint Committee, an umbrella group for various Baptist denominations
including the SBC,[33] formed the Religious Committee for Integrity in Government (RCIG) to respond to Watergate and support campaign reform efforts.

The RCIG was an interfaith coalition comprised of the BJC, the National
Council of Churches, the Unitarian Universalist Association, the United Methodist Church, and the United Church of Christ. It had the hallmarks of
social justice, mainline Protestantism, not evangelicalism. Because the SBC
was represented, however, a major player in evangelical politics participated.
Moreover, evangelicals seemed to be warming to campaign finance reform.
When United Press International covered the launch of RCIG, it noted "some
indications" that the coalition might be joined by "some heretofore unlikely
allies – evangelicals."[34]

With its formation, the RCIG announced that Watergate was a moral crisis.
It had five "initial objectives" related to morality of government, campaign
reform, and the seeking of a moral resolution to the Nixon crisis.[35] The
coalition explicitly supported public financing of elections and encouraged
Congress to move on the issue. After the Senate approved of public campaign
financing, James E. Wood, executive director of the BJC and member of the
RCIG, praised the Senate for taking "an historic . . . significant step toward the
goal of assuring integrity in government" and limiting the detrimental influence
of corporations and the wealthy on elections. Wood went on to state that
campaign reform would improve the country's confidence in politics. "Any
restoration of public confidence in the nation's political process must include
high priority campaign reform, including some form of public financing of all
federal elections."[36] Wood made no mention of free speech concerns, and it is
likely that at this time much of the SBC supported reform, as Gallup reported
that 67% of Americans supported public financing of elections in 1974.[37]

Following the resignation of President Nixon, several SBC leaders discussed the crisis of confidence in American politics and again pointed to the need for campaign finance reform. Wood declared that Americans need to dedicate themselves to probity in government and that this should include "campaign reform." Similarly, SBC Vice President Stewart B. Simms urged Congress to pass campaign finance reform, along with measures to insulate the FBI and IRS "from executive or any other manipulation."[38] Again, these leaders did not cite any First Amendment concerns. Common morality was the primary concern.

In 1974, when Congress eventually passed the campaign finance reforms by amending the Federal Election Campaign Act of 1971, some conservatives were troubled. For example, Congress passed the legislation over President Gerald Ford's veto, and Senator James Buckley of the Conservative Party initiated a legal challenge to the regulations (*Buckley v. Valeo*), citing a violation of free speech. Despite the lawsuit, there was scant conservative momentum behind the free speech opposition to campaign finance reform, as Amanda Hollis-Brusky's work on the evolution of conservative legal advocacy shows.[39] Even more, there was no activity among conservative religious activists. *Baptist Press*, for example, did not run a story on the legislation, and it also refrained from covering the ensuing legal challenge, even after the Supreme Court limited some of the campaign restrictions. The Court declared that certain restrictions violated free speech in *Buckley v. Valeo* (1976). Despite this historic conservative free speech win, the right's advocacy against campaign finance would not begin in earnest for two decades.[40]

Notwithstanding the lack of public evangelical reaction to *Buckley*, James Wood of the BJC and other leaders who were active in the RCIG surely did not agree with the Court's perspective. Like anti-obscenity laws, campaign finance restrictions nevertheless emphasized the need for ordered liberty and deference to the political process, though they arose from the politically liberal, not the conservative, perspective.

Radical Protest

Evangelicals also supported a similar limited rights approach to radical protest, which often involved protests against the government. In the second half of the twentieth century, antiwar protests exemplified radical protests, and one of the biggest free speech battles was over the legality of burning the American flag in protest. Evangelicals, like the broader public, were fervent supporters of limited rights and community morality in this area of law, promoting patriotism over individual rights.

During the Vietnam War, numerous prominent antiwar protests included some type of destruction or defilement of the American flag, such as burning the flag or hanging it upside down. Congress sought to combat this type of expression, and in 1967 several bills proposed to make it a criminal offense to desecrate the flag. Neither the NAE nor the SBC took official positions on flag burning or the legislation, though *Baptist Press* reported on the issue during the 1960s and 1970s. Some insights about the evangelical position can be gleaned from this reporting.

When the U.S. House of Representatives voted to ban flag mutilation in 1967, *Baptist Press's* article, though presenting both sides, included quotes from two Baptist Members of Congress who strongly supported the legislation. Representative John Buchanan (R-AL), a Southern Baptist pastor and Southern Baptist Seminary graduate, presented a community rights approach, stating, "This body [the House of Representatives] has the right and the duty to protect our flag." Representative Roy A. Taylor (D-NC), a Baptist deacon, declared that it was "a disappointing state of national affairs" that the legislation was needed, but it was necessary "to curb a minority of misguided Americans who do not yet know the meaning of citizenship or patriotism." Taylor reemphasized the communitarian, majority rights perspective, saying, "It is time for patriotic people to speak out ... the voice of America must not be that of the pacifist, unpatriotic minority."[41] The Senate followed suit in 1968, passing the Federal Flag Desecration Law, which was signed into law by President Lyndon Johnson. Johnson's signature did not end the controversy, however, as protests increased.

Throughout, prominent evangelicals spoke out in favor of limiting radical, flag-based protests. Even evangelist Billy Graham gave an impassioned speech defending the flag against protestors at a July Fourth religious service on the National Mall. Graham chastised the "relatively small extremist element, both to the left and the right in our society, [which has] knocked our courts, desecrated the flag, disrupted our educational system, laughed at our religious heritage."[42] Though *Baptist Press* did not take a specific position, in tracking various flag cases and events it appeared to be catering to those who would oppose the protests. During the 1970s, *Baptist Press* continued to track several flag burning laws and cases, including the Supreme Court case *Spence v. Washington* (1974), which overturned a Washington law and upheld an individual's right to hang a flag upside down in protest.[43] While the evidence here is scarce, evangelicals certainly were opponents of the radical protests in the 1960s and 1970s, preferring community rights to individual rights. There was little direct advocacy in the era, but the evidence supports limits on, not expansion of, free speech.

SHIFT IN FREE SPEECH ADVOCACY

Chapter 2 discussed the evangelical shift in abortion advocacy, but it is useful to briefly recall this development in order to draw the connection to free speech. As with free speech, many evangelicals supported a limited rights approach to abortion for much of the 1970s – affirming a limited right for a woman to choose to terminate her pregnancy. Opposition to abortion grew in the 1970s, gaining critical mass by 1980. Within evangelicalism, opposition to abortion initially brought together several streams of Christian Right advocacy, support for morality and family values, opposition to feminism and sexual liberation, and frustration with the supposed activism of the Supreme Court. Yet, by the end of the 1970s, some evangelicals began to appropriate the Catholic human rights approach, supporting the "right to life." Evangelical apologist and cultural activists Francis Schaeffer has been credited with bringing this Catholic, rights-based argument to evangelicalism, though merging it with morality-based anti-abortion positions.[44] Within Christian Right politics, an emphasis on individual rights began to emerge, especially as conservative Christians took an embattled minority approach to abortion politics. Opposition to abortion increasingly came to be framed in individualist, right-to-life terms. Similarly, the individual-based free exercise of religion sought to trump the ordered liberty protection against religious establishments. These individualist approaches were gaining momentum by the 1990s.

The focus on rights took root in free speech too. Evangelicals became more accustomed to the need for expanded speech rights, following proposed restrictions on religious broadcasting in 1974 and the success of conservative Christian groups using an individual rights-based free speech argument to support religious liberty claims of equal access to public accommodations.[45] At the same time, conservative religious advocates, in line with Reagan politics, expressed ire toward the Supreme Court, backing away from the deference shown by the SBC leaders in previous periods.

A speech in June 1984 at the annual Southern Baptist convention underscores the synergies. Franky Schaeffer, son of Francis Schaeffer, spoke to the Pastor's Conference prior to the convention, an annual event that was the scene for the conservative pastors within the denomination. In his speech, Schaeffer brought together abortion, free speech, and religious liberty in a message that could have been delivered in 2016. He encouraged courthouse picketing and demonstrations at abortion clinics, opposing "secular zealots who seek to use the law to curb our religious liberties." "We must refuse to bow to the secular zealots who would curb the freedom to preach the gospel, whether it be in public school or elsewhere," said Schaeffer. "We must stand against those who would seek to strip the right of freedom of assembly and speech from those such as pro-life demonstrators who picket outside abortion clinics to save babies' lives. In short, we must stop being an apathetic, silent, wishy-washy and compromising evangelical church."[46]

Though Franky Schaeffer has since had a tenuous relationship with evangelicalism, renouncing the faith and its political activism, his message lives on.[47] For the past two decades, evangelicals have been expanding their free speech advocacy. The SBC altered its approach largely under the leadership of Richard Land who took over the denomination's advocacy in the late 1980s, leading the Christian Life Commission, now called the Ethics & Religious Liberty Commission. In addition, several religious legal advocacy groups have been founded, giving increased attention to explicit free speech advocacy.

While not all exclusively evangelical, they are prominent in the domain of evangelical advocacy. These organizations include: Alliance Defending Freedom (ADF), the Becket Fund for Religious Liberty, the Christian Legal Society, the American Center for Law and Justice, and Liberty Counsel. These legal organizations joined a growing list of conservative religious advocacy organizations, such as the Christian Coalition, the Family Research Council, and Concerned Women for America. Together, these coalitions have become free speech advocates,[48] advancing their own causes as well as the causes of others.

Abortion politics have played an important role in this process, as the pro-life issue has provided both the need for supporting expanded speech rights and the mechanism to promote rank-and-file support of such controversial advocacy. The increasing prevalence of the individualized right-to-life arguments within evangelical life has transferred to a broader, more-individualized right to free speech. Yet, the relationship between abortion politics and liberal free speech arguments is more nuanced in surveys of the evangelical rank-and-file than it is among advocacy elites. This incongruence might impel activists' choice of tactics, encouraging them to concentrate on legal cases when rank-and-file support is low.

Radical Protest

Longitudinal survey data on free speech are limited, but the General Social Survey provides the best opportunity to evaluate the views of rank-and-file evangelicals over time. The GSS has consistently asked a battery of questions regarding whether or not controversial people should be able to speak in one's own community. I combined the responses to these items into a free speech scale ranging from 0 to 5, with higher scores representing more tolerance of speech.[49] These items scale quite well and are often used as a measure of political tolerance.[50] Here I focus specifically on support for an individual right to free speech.

Figure 3.1 presents a comparison of evangelicals and non-evangelicals over time. The plotted lines represent the means, while the vertical bars are one standard error above and below the mean. Though evangelicals have become prominent advocates for strengthening free speech protections, the rank-and-file continue to trail the general public, as non-evangelicals are consistently more tolerant of radical free speech than evangelicals are. Both groups have become more accepting over time, however, with non-evangelicals being more linear. While evangelicals lag the general public, they are more supportive of expanded speech rights than forty years ago, and their tolerance has increased at a greater rate.

The rank-and-file data present some puzzles. How can evangelical elites be on the forefront of free speech advocacy, and how have rank-and-file evangelicals learned to support the expansion of free speech rights for non-allies – *rights extending*? Investigating elite advocacy should provide some insight.

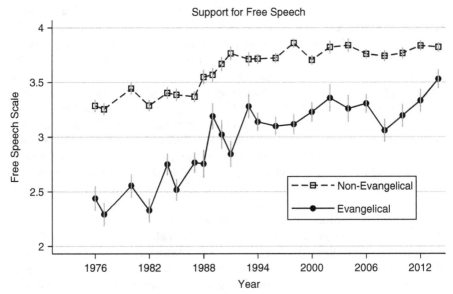

FIGURE 3.1. Evangelical and Non-Evangelical Support for Free Speech over Time, Using Free Speech Scale. GSS, 1975–2014.

If abortion is a primary mechanism for evangelical elites to expand their advocacy, as outlined in Chapter 2, the relationship between abortion and free speech deserves considerable attention. In what follows, I consider the prominent areas of free speech advocacy, which were discussed earlier in the pre–Christian Right era.

Elites and Support for Radical Speech

In some cases, the elite relationship between abortion and free speech is direct. The clearest example of this develops from the abortion protest cases that emerged in the 1990s following the rise of Operation Rescue and the increase in street protests. These cases have been credited for transitioning Christian Right advocacy, making it more professional and secular.[51] The dynamics between abortion politics and increasing support for free speech, however, have been under-analyzed.

Highlighting the direct relationship between abortion and free speech, the third *amicus curiae* brief the SBC filed under Richard Land was a defense of Operation Rescue abortion protestors in *Bray v. Alexandria Women's Clinic* (1992) who had blocked access to an abortion clinic.[52] The brief, in partnership with the National Right to Life Committee, marshaled free speech rights and a narrow view of Fourteenth Amendment civil rights to support the protestors.[53] Related, in 1994, many evangelical groups opposed the Congressional Freedom of Access to Clinic Entrances (FACE) legislation, which was signed into law in

1994 by President Bill Clinton. During the legislative process, the SBC's Christian Life Commission sharply criticized FACE for its diminution of free speech, arguing that the Act was an attempt "to squash politically incorrect pro-life dissent."[54] Other evangelical organizations and pro-life allies, including the Christian Coalition and the National Right to Life Committee, joined the SBC in opposing the legislation on free speech grounds. The legislative director of the NRLC warned that FACE would "crush peaceful protestors' free speech with Federal lawsuits."[55] In a resolution detailing its pro-life position and opposition to pro-choice policies, the SBC declared its opposition "to any legislation which would have the effect of denying First Amendment freedom of speech rights, especially as a means of responsible, non-violent protest at abortion clinics."[56] Evangelicals firmly defended broad, individual free speech rights to protect anti-abortion activism.

The pattern continued in *Madsen v. Women's Health Center* (1994), when a broad array of evangelical and Catholic groups, including the Southern Baptist CLC, the Christian Legal Society, the National Association of Evangelicals, and the Catholic League for Religious and Civil Rights, filed an *amicus* brief objecting to abortion protest restrictions. These groups continued to oppose abortion-related free speech zones in *Schenck v. Pro-Choice Network* (1997) and *Hill v. Colorado* (2000). After the Court upheld the free speech zone in *Hill*, the SBC's Land, declared, "The majority of this court is so committed to the preservation of its supreme value, abortion, that it denies other explicitly guaranteed constitutional rights when they may conflict with the recently discovered right to abortion.... [I]n order to protect an undisturbed right to abortion they explicitly deny the guaranteed First Amendment right of freedom of speech."[57]

Most recently, in 2014 the Supreme Court heard *McCullen v. Coakley*, another anti-abortion protest case, with the Supreme Court ruling unanimously that the buffer zone in Massachusetts was too restrictive on free speech. The Christian Legal Society wrote an *amicus* brief signed by many evangelical groups, including the SBC's advocacy arm (the ERLC), supporting the protestors and declaring *Hill* to be in "deep tension with longstanding First Amendment values." The brief begins by quoting favorably the language from the liberal *New York Times v. Sullivan* (1964) case that protected the press from libel suits. It then opposes neutral time, place, and manner restrictions because they "deny access to places of symbolic significance [and] undermine the expression that depends upon connection to place." It further argues that these restrictions can strip speech of its "emotive" content, echoing *Cohen v. California* (1972), where the Court ruled that "one man's obscenity is another's lyric" – possibly the individual rights apex of free speech jurisprudence. The brief closes with an argument for a broad protection of the individual right to free speech, citing *Snyder v. Phelps*'s (2011) approval of "even hurtful speech, expression, and protest."[58] In 1972, *Cohen* was the epitome of liberal, individualist protections for vulgar, obscene, anti-American acts. In 2014, it became a precedent to protect activists' promotion of traditional moral beliefs.

This is quite the contrast to *Falwell* only twenty-five years prior. Rather than trying to limit free speech law, evangelicals were building on the most liberal free speech precedents and taking quotations from cases they would have certainly opposed in decades past.[59] In fact, they were using obscenity precedents to defend their rights, changing course with decades of free speech advocacy. Biblical conservatism had given way to individualism, even supporting expressive individualism. Under the banner of promoting the pro-life cause, evangelical leaders have embraced liberal free speech clause jurisprudence.

Evangelicals and Non-Abortion Protest Speech

While anti-abortion protests provide the direct link between abortion and expanded free speech advocacy, evangelicals have also come to promote the expansion of non-abortion protest speech, citing potential pro-life concerns. A prominent example is *Morse v. Frederick*, a 2007 case where a high school student was suspended for holding a "bong hits for Jesus" banner at a school event to watch the passage of the Olympic torch. Though evangelical legal scholar, Kenneth Starr, represented the school district in the case, many evangelical organizations, including the Christian Legal Society, Alliance Defense Fund (now called Alliance Defending Freedom), Rutherford Institute, and American Center for Law and Justice, backed the student, even though he was vaguely supporting drug use and promoting religious mockery. The Christian Legal Society argued that, while it "has no sympathy for Frederick's tasteless banner and his juvenile stunt," this case could bestow "broad power on public school officials" and "they would almost certainly employ that power to suppress controversial religious expression, including the right to associate around shared convictions and moral standards."[60] Such "controversial religious expression" is clearly a reference to abortion and same-sex marriage. Driving home this point, the ACLJ declared, "While we strongly disagree with the student's message in this case, the fact is that unless student speech is protected, a message considered appropriate today could be deemed offensive tomorrow. We want to ensure that students who hold pro-life and pro-family positions will continue to be able to present those messages without censorship."[61] For evangelical elites, the expression of their abortion convictions was at the forefront of their concern, causing them to defend pro-drug, religious mockery.

Evangelicals similarly supported broad free speech protections in the Westboro Baptist Church protest case – *Snyder v. Phelps* (2011). The Westboro Baptist Church is a fringe religious group that was led by Fred Phelps and his family. Since the 1990s, the church has been actively protesting against homosexuality. These protests expanded to include the American military and other institutions, as Westboro considered America's defense of homosexuality a scourge. The church gained national attention by picketing funerals of gay murder victims and American military members. In *Snyder v. Phelps*, the family of Matthew Snyder, a Marine killed in battle in Iraq, sued the Phelps family, seeking damages after the Westboro Baptist Church had protested their son's military funeral using offensive language.

Due to the toxic nature of the case, some of the typical conservative religious advocates refrained from filing briefs, though Liberty Counsel and the Rutherford Institute participated in support of Westboro. As has become a frequent occurrence in free speech cases, evangelical advocacy groups joined the ACLU in promoting individual free speech rights. This partnership is quite a change from the ordered liberty approach of the mid-twentieth century.

Though Liberty Counsel, a legal advocacy organization connected to the Jerry Falwell–founded Liberty University Law School, strongly opposed Westboro's actions, Staver said that the "bad facts of this case could have negatively affected the legitimate free speech rights of law-abiding Americans. ... Free speech needs breathing room. I would rather tolerate a person's offensive speech than be silenced by the force of law."[62] In a press release, Liberty Counsel went on to warn that not extending Westboro free speech protections could produce future trouble for the pro-life cause. "This case could give a veto right to anyone who claims that speech of another is 'offensive.' Today the offensive speech of the Phelpses was on trial, but tomorrow it could be religious, pro-life or pro-family speech or any other speech for that matter."[63] Departing from the legacy of Falwell in his case against *Hustler*, Liberty Counsel tied an individual rights approach to abortion advocacy.

The Southern Baptists, like many other religious groups, refrained from participating. When the case initially developed, Richard Land promoted an ordered liberty approach arguing that the Constitution does not permit "verbal terrorism," classifying the church's signs as a type of "verbal pornography and obscenity" that is outside the protections of the First Amendment.[64] Nevertheless, as the case developed, Land reluctantly supported the church on free speech grounds:

> My heart tells me they should be outlawed from doing this; however, my head tells me that anytime we allow the government to restrict religious speech and activity for any reason, we are setting a very dangerous precedent and we are embarking on a steep and slippery slope to dark and dangerous places. What government is allowed to do to Westboro Baptist Church today, they could be allowed to do to other religious groups tomorrow or the day after.[65]

Land's internal processing about the commitment to liberalism is insightful. His instincts were to order and patriotism, but he became convinced that such a position could lead to the government restricting evangelicals from speaking out against abortion or same-sex marriage. Evangelical advocates were moving toward liberalism via the vehicle of abortion. A desire to promote the pro-life movement shifted them toward the ACLU's free speech position.

Flag Burning, the Difficult Radical Protest Case
For the right, radical protest has largely been reframed to focus on how broad free speech protections may be helpful to conservative advocacy causes,

particularly the right to protest against abortion and speak in favor of traditional morality. The issue of flag burning, however, brings more nuance and hesitation, though evangelical elites seem to be increasing in their support.

In the 1960s and 1970s, evangelicals were firm supporters of laws limiting the desecration of the American flag. Following the Supreme Court's seminal decision to strike anti–flag burning laws in *Texas v. Johnson* (1989), major evangelical groups were largely silent.[66] *Baptist Press* did not report on the outcome of the case, though they did report on a telephone pornography case decided the same day, suggesting that they were not ignoring the Court, but instead chose to ignore the flag burning case.[67] There was a strong public backlash to the Court's decision, however, including broad swaths of rank-and-file evangelicalism. President George H. W. Bush pushed for a constitutional amendment to protect the flag, and he received considerable support. *Baptist Press* again refrained from covering the proposal for a constitutional amendment to protect the flag, which failed in October 1989. This lack of coverage suggests a shift from the 1970s, when flag cases were regularly covered in the Baptist newspaper. That said, many Christian Right groups advocated for a constitutional amendment in 1989, 1990, and 1995, though the measure repeatedly failed in the Senate.

By the 2000s, many evangelical elites seemed to accept the constitutionality of flag burning. In 2002, evangelicals rallied to support Michael McConnell, a contested federal appeals court nominee of President George W. Bush, despite McConnell's opposition to an amendment to ban flag burning. McConnell was endorsed by Jay Sekulow of the ACLJ, and approvingly covered by *Baptist Press*, which directly mentioned his stance on flag burning.[68] Yet, in 2006 the Senate fell only one vote shy of approving a constitutional amendment banning flag burning, and several evangelical organizations pushed for its passage, including Jerry Falwell's *National Liberty Journal*, the Family Research Council, and the Christian Coalition.[69]

Evangelicals seem to be of two minds on the issue of flag burning, and it represents the tension on the right between supporting free speech and patriotism. Elites have also refrained from discussing the issue in the terms of abortion, which was common for other radical protests. Perhaps the lack of a direct link to abortion politics has kept evangelicals as opponents to flag burning. Elites are also better able to engage in divisive advocacy in court than in the legislature. But still, there remains a growing acceptance of the practice within evangelicalism. For example, in 2010, a *Baptist Press* columnist defended flag burning and the *Texas v. Johnson* precedent, stating: "While I personally find burning a U.S. flag or a Bible in protest offensive, I accept both as part of comprehensive freedom of speech. The price we each must pay to enjoy our own freedom of speech is to endure being offended by someone else's."[70] This approach epitomizes a liberal, individual rights approach to free speech, and it is quite a change for an SBC elite. Though flag burning is the more nuanced case, evangelical organizations have come to embrace radical speech, even for political opponents, much more than they did several decades ago.

Results of the Rank-and-File's Views on Free Speech

Evangelical organizations have grown to support free speech and employed free speech arguments to gain political and legal victories, especially since the 1990s. They often did so with the rationale of protecting anti-abortion advocacy, which was learned during the 1980s and 1990s era of prominent abortion protests. How does this activity compare to the evangelicals in the pews, the constituents of these organizations?

Recall from Figure 3.1 that evangelicals have lagged behind their non-evangelical counterparts in support of radical free speech since the questions debuted in the GSS more than forty years ago, but evangelicals have been gradually gaining ground on non-evangelicals. Has abortion contributed to this increasingly positive response?

In comparing support for anti-abortion measures and support for free speech, there is a consistent negative correlation for both evangelicals and non-evangelicals. Anti-abortion attitudes are related to decreased support for free speech. As Figure 3.2 shows, this negative correlation is steady across decades for non-evangelicals, but it consistently declines for evangelicals. This signals that the negative relationship is weakening among rank-and-file evangelicals, though perhaps a far cry from the elite activity.

Multivariate statistical analyses provide more insight into the relationship between evangelicals, abortion, and free speech attitudes over time. I created models predicting free speech support, with religious affiliation (evangelical Protestant, Catholic, black Protestant, mainline Protestant, Jewish, and other

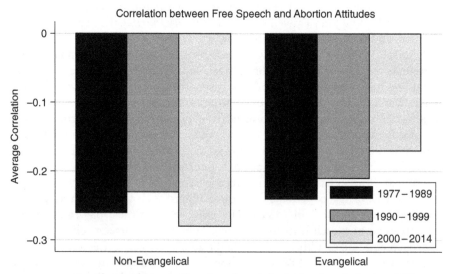

FIGURE 3.2. Correlations between Free Speech and Anti-Abortion Attitudes. GSS, 1977–2014.

faiths),[71] a composite score of abortion attitudes, political party identification, and political ideology as key independent variables, while also controlling for government confidence, church attendance, demographic characteristics, and time. In addition, I added an interactive effect, which combines the effect of abortion attitudes and being an evangelical. This captures the contingent effect signaled by the elite activity. This interaction explores whether evangelicals who are more pro-life are more likely to favor free speech. The full variable coding is in Appendix A, but each variable except free speech is coded in the conservative direction.

The standard statistical model for the entire time period confirms Figures 3.1 and 3.2, as well as conventional wisdom. Evangelicals as well as all other faith traditions are more opposed to expansive free speech than the unaffiliated, with evangelicals being the most strongly opposed. Similarly, individuals who are more strongly opposed to abortion are less supportive of free speech. Interestingly, Republicans are positively disposed to radical speech, though conservatives are less likely to support broad speech rights. The interaction between evangelical and abortion attitudes is not significant.

While the full period model is useful for understanding the lay of the land, it is likely to obscure the change over time, especially since evangelical elites only really started advocating for expanded free speech in the 1990s. To investigate this, I split the GSS into three periods corresponding to the growth of free speech advocacy by evangelical organizations: 1977–1989, 1990–1997, and 1998–2014. Table 3.1 in Appendix B shows the full results of these models, along with the cumulative model, but Figure 3.3 displays the results graphically. The hollow squares signify the point estimates, with the gray bars representing the confidence intervals. If the bars do not cross the dashed vertical line, the relationship between the independent variable and the dependent variable are considered statistically significant. The independent variables have been standardized on a 0–1 scale to ease the comparison.

Most of the independent variables are consistent over time, as can been seen when comparing the three panels stacked vertically in Figure 3.3. The variable of interest is the evangelical and abortion interaction, labeled "I: Evang. & Abortion" in the graph. Over time this variable changes directions. In the pre-1990 period, more pro-life evangelicals are likely to be more opposed to free speech. Abortion attitudes multiply the negative effect evangelical affiliation has on free speech. In the middle period, the interactive effect becomes positive, though it is not statistically significant. We see the beginnings of the change in this relationship, which is realized in the last period. From 1998 to the present, more pro-life evangelicals are likely to be more supportive free speech. Being more pro-life counteracts the ordered liberty tendencies of being an evangelical. This rank-and-file pattern follows the trajectory of the elites, with anti-abortion attitudes having a positive effect on free speech, especially since the 1990s. Abortion politics seem to be teaching evangelicals, both the mass public and the elites, about the value of free speech, though the elites have been more convinced.

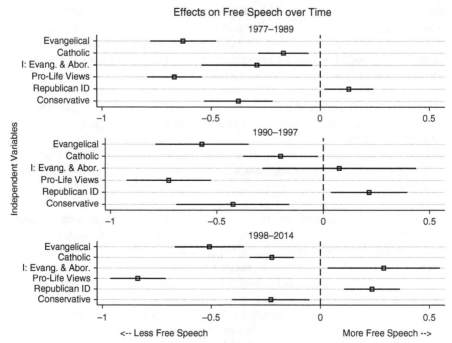

FIGURE 3.3. Effects on Support for Free Speech in Three Time Periods. Linear Regression Models with Standardized Coefficients and 90% Confidence Intervals. GSS, 1977–2014.

The effect of party ID is also quite important, as Republicans are more likely to favor free speech in each time period. It is static, however, not evolutionary. As evangelicals become more pro-life and more Republican, they are increasingly likely to support free speech. Evangelical support for free speech seems to have pro-life and Republican origins, which would comport with the even stronger elite positions. A 1996 survey of Southern Baptist clergy supports this conclusion, as the clergy found Republicans more likely to be supportive of free speech than Democrats are (50%–13%). Evangelicals have followed their party in support of free speech, but abortion seems to be an important trigger.

Though evangelicals continue to trail their non-evangelical counterparts, their tolerance has grown at greater rates, suggesting a growing free speech liberalism. Contrary to a simple individual rights thesis, those with more pro-life views are likely to have decreased tolerance for free speech. Rather, the positive effect of the abortion position seems to be contingent, finding a home in evangelicalism and Republicanism. This has led to evangelicals closing the rights gap on their non-evangelical citizens, following the pattern of the elites.

Campaign Finance

In addition to supporting broad protest rights, for both abortion protests and disfavored groups, evangelical elites have recently engaged in broader pro-speech advocacy, often informed by recognition of their support for pro-life and pro-family advocacy. For example, while some evangelical elites championed campaign finance reform in the 1970s, evangelicals have been leading opponents of such legislation since the dawn of the twenty-first century, arguing that it infringes on free speech. Campaign finance is an instance of expansive Republican free speech advocacy.

Data in national surveys on campaign finance reform and religion are scarce, but in 2000 the American National Election Study asked respondents if they preferred that we "protect the government from excessive influence by campaign contributors" or that we protect "the "freedom of individuals." More than 75% of all respondents with an opinion stated they preferred to protect against excessive campaign contributions. This dropped to 70% for evangelicals. The issue also lacks public awareness, as more than 36% of both evangelicals and non-evangelicals reported having no opinion. In total, 81% of evangelicals either supported or had no opinion on campaign finance reform. If 70% of the rank-and-file with an opinion supported campaign finance reform, how were activists able to oppose it? A look at the history of evangelical advocacy provides insight.

Elite Campaign Finance Advocacy

In 2001, when Senators John McCain and Russell Feingold collaborated to pass the Bipartisan Campaign Reform Act, conservatives, evangelicals, and other pro-life groups were critical of how the reforms would infringe on free speech. Prior work has detailed the growth of conservative legal advocacy against campaign finance reform in the 1990s and early 2000s, utilizing free speech arguments. This work focuses on the conservative Federalist Society and its legal networks and lawyers,[72] as well as the libertarian stream of conservatism,[73] but it overlooks how religious conservatives were brought into this conservative coalition. Abortion was central to this process. In fact, anti-abortion groups' opposition to campaign reforms dated back to the mid-1990s when McCain and others first championed the reforms. The pro-life National Right to Life Committee was a leader, linking evangelicals to the burgeoning conservative legal culture against campaign finance.[74]

When the McCain-Feingold bill became law, NRLC argued that the bill would prevent the organization from sponsoring advertisements opposing partial-birth abortion, and the Christian Coalition, Family Research Council, and others organizations joined them.[75] The SBC passed a resolution at its annual convention in June 2001 "object[ing] vigorously to any attempts to abridge the free speech rights of any American citizen or group" and "reject [ing] any campaign finance legislation that hinders or abridges free speech."

In the resolution, the SBC also approvingly cited the Court's limitations on campaign finance reforms in *Buckley v. Valeo* (1976).[76] Evangelical anti–campaign finance advocacy had become mainstream.

Richard Land, as head of the ERLC, argued in 2002 that because of the legislation's limits on free speech, the "price is too high" for this reform. In fact, he reasoned that it would increase the power of the media while decreasing the role for religious advocacy,[77] engaging the talking points of both the conservative Federalist Society and the Christian Right.[78] As such, Land supported constitutional challenges led by evangelical lawyer Jay Sekulow of the American Center for Law and Justice and former Solicitor General Ken Starr,[79] though the ERLC did not participate in *amicus* activity. When the Supreme Court upheld the McCain-Feingold bill in *McConnell v. FEC* (2003), evangelical and pro-life leaders were outraged. Land called the decision "a disaster for Americans' First Amendment guarantee of freedom of speech." He went on to define his free speech–based opposition to the outcome, arguing:

If we want true campaign finance reform, we should pass laws that require full and timely disclosure of all contributions from all sources that sponsor political speech. That way people are free to spend their money promoting their political views, which until now was guaranteed under the Constitution. Voters would know who is paying for what and supporting whom, and make their electoral decisions accordingly.[80]

Evangelical organizations continued to oppose campaign finance reform that would inhibit advocacy, citing individualist free speech grounds. Such strong stands seem unlikely without an abortion connection, especially considering the lack of public awareness of these issues and the absence of evangelical advocacy in earlier cases that were not linked to abortion politics, including *Buckley v. Valeo* (1976) and *Austin v. Michigan Chamber of Commerce* (1990).

In 2004, Wisconsin Right to Life, the state chapter of the NRLC, sued the Federal Election Commission, challenging the constitutionality of the provisions of the 2002 McCain-Feingold law that prohibited the organization from airing "issue advertisements" in the sixty-day blackout period prior to the election. Wisconsin Right to Life argued that the ban prevented them from running advertisements against Democratic Senators for filibustering President Bush's judicial nominees. Coincidentally, one of these Democratic opponents was Russ Feingold, namesake of the legislation. The pro-life group argued that this was a violation of their free speech.

After bouncing around federal courts, in 2007 the U.S. Supreme Court heard the case *Federal Election Commission v. Wisconsin Right to Life* (2007), where conservative legal scholars, as well as an array of evangelical organizations such as the ACLJ and the Family Research Council, supported Wisconsin Right to Life. Liberal advocates, the ACLU and the AFL-CIO, also joined the pro-life group.[81] In June 2007, the Supreme Court ruled in favor of Wisconsin Right to Life in a 5–4 decision, with Chief Justice John Roberts writing in the majority opinion that the Court "gives the benefit of the doubt to speech, not censorship." Following the victory, Richard Land of the ERLC called the ruling "a tremendous victory for freedom of speech [which] helps to restore the most basic of constitutional guarantees."[82] Christian conservatives had become invested in broad free speech rights.

Evangelical and pro-life groups did not stop with the victory in the Wisconsin Right to Life case. In 2009, the Supreme Court heard a larger challenge to McCain-Feingold, *Citizens United v. Federal Election Commission*, which sought to remove limitations on independent, corporate campaign expenditures. There are many pro-life links to the case. James Bopp, the Federalist Society member who litigated the Wisconsin case and served as general counsel for National Right to Life Committee for thirty-five years, also argued the case for Citizens United. In addition, the religious legal group ADF formally supported the case at the *certiorari* stage (asking the Court to hear the case) and at the merits stage (encouraging an outcome). Other prominent religious groups refrained from participating, likely because there was not an explicit connection to abortion politics, as there had been in Wisconsin Right to Life. Nevertheless, after the Court struck down part of the McCain-Feingold legislation in their 2010 decision, evangelical organizations praised the outcome. In fact, when Elena Kagan was nominated to be a Supreme Court justice, one of Richard Land's objections to her nomination was her free speech perspective presented in her oral argument in support of campaign finance regulations in *Citizens United*.[83] And in 2013 the National Right to Life honored James Bopp, lead lawyer in *Citizens United* and *Wisconsin Right to Life*, with a glowing resolution.[84]

Most recently, in 2014 several Christian Right groups supported the pro-life Susan B. Anthony List (SBA List), as it challenged an Ohio campaign law that prohibited advertisements that make false statements in *Susan B. Anthony List v. Driehaus* (2014). In the case, SBA List posted a billboard in the district of Ohio Representative Steve Driehaus, stating that his vote to support the 2010 Affordable Care Act (often called Obamacare) was also a vote for taxpayer-funded abortion. Driehaus filed a complaint with the Ohio Elections Commission, arguing that the advertisement violated Ohio law that forbids false campaign ads. SBA List countered that Ohio's limitation is a violation of their federal right to free speech.

The Christian Legal Society, NAE, and others filed a joint brief supporting SBA List, while ADF filed independently. The liberal ACLU joined these religious groups in their support of SBA List. While the ERLC did not participate in this campaign advertisement case that again pits pro-life advocacy against campaign finance regulations, the organization did offer public support for the SBA List, a common partner in pro-life causes.[85] When the anti-abortion group was victorious, senior counsel for ADF declared, "The First Amendment forbids government from acting as a 'truth commission' on matters of public debate." He then went on to say that Representative Steve Driehaus lost his job because Susan B. Anthony list made public warnings about "abortion funding in Obamacare [that] were objectively true," and "his constituents, like most Americans, reject taxpayer-funded abortion."[86]

In a mere thirty years, evangelical activists have sharply changed their positions in support for political speech and in opposition to campaign finance reform. No longer is common morality central; instead, an individual rights perspective prevails. Evangelicals' role in abortion politics, at least at the elite level, had much to do with this, as campaign reform has largely been opposed by pro-life organizations such as the National Right to Life Committee, the SBA List, and ADF. Abortion brought pro-lifers and evangelicals into the broader conservative legal fold to fight against campaign finance regulations and for expanded political speech.

The Rank-and-File and Campaign Finance
Returning to the survey data, are the evangelical rank-and-file in line with the elites? Do statistical models support this relationship between abortion and opposition to campaign finance? The results, presented in Table 3.2 in Appendix B, are suggestive, but not conclusive. The model signals that individuals who oppose abortion rights are more likely to oppose campaign finance reform, though this does not reach statistical significance ($p = 0.18$). If anti-abortion attitudes promote opposition to campaign finance reform, these are not localized within evangelicalism, as the interactive effect (not shown) is also insignificant.

In the survey, party identification is the biggest factor in opposition to campaign finance reform, with strong Republicans being nearly twice as likely to oppose campaign finance reform as strong Democrats, holding the other variables at their means. Those with negative views of the government are also more likely to support reform, as are those who are more educated.

If the results for abortion are only suggestive, how have evangelical and pro-life organizations become leading opponents of campaign finance reform? Part of the answer lies in the fact that few understand the issue,[87] which allows partisanship to dominate. Recall that 36% of people did not have an opinion on the issue. In addition, in statistical models predicting whether one responds with "don't know" to the survey question, abortion stands out. Those who state that abortion is an important issue are more likely to have an opinion on campaign finance reform. Holding the other variables constant, those who state that abortion is "not at all important" are 7% more likely to not have an opinion than those who state it is "extremely important." An interactive effect (not shown) also suggests that this effect may be more important for evangelicals ($p = 0.13$). Therefore, while partisan politics are central, survey data indicate that pro-life arguments against campaign finance restrictions might break through the morass of campaign finance reform. Evangelical elites have made these connections to support the free speech position.

Obscenity – The Exception

While evangelical elites have become broad supporters of expanded free speech rights, they continue to oppose obscenity and pornography, arguing that these categories of expression are outside the bounds of First Amendment protection. The rank-and-file are also strongly opposed. Since 1973, the GSS has asked for people's views on the legality of pornography, with the options of it being always illegal, illegal for those under the age of eighteen, and always legal. Figure 3.3 shows a comparison of these responses over time for evangelicals and all other respondents. Non-evangelicals have become more accepting of pornography, with an increase (and now majority) in those holding that it should be legal for those over age eighteen, as shown in the line with gray, hollow squares. Evangelicals, on the other hand, have remained stable in their positions. Since 1973, there has been nearly an even split between those who say it should always be illegal (solid, black circles) and those who say that it should be illegal to those under age eighteen (solid, gray circles).

Elites Advocacy Regarding Pornography and Obscenity
The trend in evangelical opinion about pornography laws is matched by evangelical organizations and elites. Unlike radical protest and campaign finance,

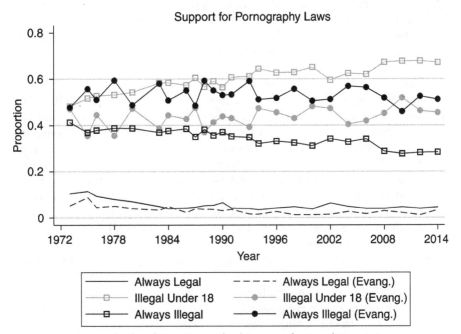

FIGURE 3.4. Evangelical and Non-Evangelical Support for Legal Restrictions on Pornography over Time. GSS, 1973–2014.

their positions on obscenity and pornography have not liberalized. In fact, early in Land's tenure, the SBC group filed a legal brief in support of tough obscenity standards. The case was *Alexander v. United States of America* (1993), and the NAE and the Southern Baptists filed a brief with several religious groups, including the United Methodist Church, Episcopal Church, and National Council of Churches, supporting the government's obscenity penalties. The SBC's advocacy arm also filed briefs with other evangelicals urging the court to uphold the constitutionality of child pornography statutes in *United States of America v. X-Citement Video* (1994) and *Ashcroft v. American Civil Liberties Union* (2002). Further, evangelical groups attacked the National Endowment for the Arts (NEA) in the 1990s for funding what they determined to be obscene and profane art. Evangelical groups helped oust NEA chairman John Frohmayer in 1992,[88] and in *NEA v. Finley* (1998) conservative Christian groups, including Liberty Counsel, the ACLJ, the National Family Legal Foundation, and Morality in Media, supported obscenity and profanity speech restrictions implemented by the NEA.[89]

In recent years, these groups' attention to issues of obscenity has decreased, but their positions have remained strongly opposed. How does this fit with their rights-oriented shift in the areas of radical protest and campaign finance?

In liberal obscenity law, there is no logical or practical connection to pro-life politics. The higher-order policy position – abortion – is not affected by protecting the common morality of obscenity standards. In fact, some evangelical leaders argue that anti-obscenity laws reduce abortions. Elites' decreased emphasis on obscenity cases, however, may suggest that they understand the tension in the scope of their free speech advocacy.

Rank-and-File Views on Pornography

The elite findings are buttressed by the survey data from the GSS. Multivariate statistical models, shown in Table 3.1 in Appendix B, indicate that evangelicals are less supportive of pornography legalization than the unaffiliated, having the most conservative views. Pro-life attitudes also run counter to the free speech argument of legalization of pornography in all periods (not shown in Table 3.1). In the early period between 1977 and 1997, anti-abortion attitudes actually enhanced evangelicals' opposition to pornography, as the interactive effect is robust. This contingent effect fails to achieve statistical significance in the later period, though the general effect of abortion attitudes predicting support for strong pornography laws remains.

For evangelical elites and rank-and-file, pornography and obscenity are the exception to their growing support for free speech. Their liberalization has limits. Since support for the legalization of pornography cannot be applied to the pro-life movement, there is no incentive to shift opinions. In fact, evangelical leaders may have a stronger case with their constituents if they argue it is outside the bounds of First Amendment protection. This dichotomy may be more tenuous with First Amendment advocates, however, which could yield less activity in legal cases and congressional legislation.

The comparison of radical speech, campaign finance, and obscenity provide insight into how abortion politics and party politics work together to structure free speech advocacy. Evangelical advocates continue to support free speech regulations when it is salient to the rank-and-file and there is no abortion link (i.e., obscenity). When it is salient to the rank-and-file to oppose the free speech topic but there is an abortion link (i.e., radical protest), then evangelical activists are increasingly likely to support broad speech protections, especially in legal cases, despite rank-and-file objections. The pro-life cause gives them cover. Finally, when the free speech topic is not salient, but there is an abortion link (i.e., campaign finance), evangelical activists have ample opportunity to support broad speech positions, in court and in legislation, particularly when bolstered by partisanship.

EXPERIMENTING WITH ABORTION AND FREE SPEECH SUPPORT

The historical and survey data presented provide strong evidence of the role abortion has played in increasing evangelical support for free speech. For more than two decades, leading evangelical organizations have effectively framed free speech issues in the terms of abortion in order to liberalize the religious tradition's approach to free speech. The rank-and-file appear to have moved in concert on most issues.

To more explicitly test the relationship between the framing of free speech in anti-abortion language and support for free speech, I developed a survey experiment. In June 2015, my colleagues and I conducted a framing experiment with an online panel of 1,500 evangelicals obtained through the company Survey Sampling International (SSI). Evangelicals were obtained in two ways. Half of them were secured by screening for people affiliated with an evangelical denomination, and the other half were secured by screening for people who identified as born-again Christians. We administered a survey experiment about free speech to half of the sample, directing an experiment about health care to the other half, as discussed in Chapter 5.

Half of the sample was randomly assigned to receive the free speech experiment, and out of those, individuals were then randomly assigned to receive one of three prompts from a "local minister" supporting free speech "even to those with whom [the pastor] may disagree."[90] The first minister supported speech in anti-abortion terms, saying, "Decisions about free speech should be guided by the politics of abortion. I oppose abortion, and I do not want others to deny my ability to express these views." I refer to this as the Anti-Abortion Frame.

The second pastor also supported free speech citing abortion, but he instead uses the right-to-life construction. The minister states, "Decisions about free speech should be guided by our understanding of rights. I am pro-life, and

I want to ensure that my free speech to protest abortion is protected. We must protect the rights of disfavored groups, because we may become disfavored." I refer to this as the Right to Life Frame.

The final minister simply supported free speech without stating a reason. He merely said, "Yes, I support expansive free speech." I refer to this as the Control Frame.

Following the prompt, the evangelical respondents were then asked two questions related to the topic. First, they rated how persuasive the minister's comments were on a 0–10 scale. Second, they were asked to rate on a 0–10 scale whether "there are circumstances in which the First Amendment's protections of free speech should be limited." Because the experiment employs random assignment, I use linear regression statistical models to investigate the effect of the frames on the outcomes, with independent variables for each frame (with the Control as the comparison group) and two demographic controls (education and race), as these variables did not randomize across treatments.[91]

The results of the persuasiveness model are displayed graphically in the top panel of Figure 3.5. The black circles represent the standardized coefficients, with the black bars identifying the confidence intervals. If the bars do not overlap with the vertical, dashed line, then the effect is statistically significant.

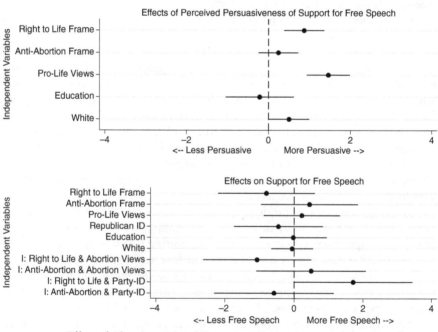

FIGURE 3.5. Effect of Abortion-Related Frames on Persuasiveness of Free Speech Arguments and Support for Free Speech. Linear Regression Models with Standardized Coefficients and 95% Confidence Intervals. SSI Evangelical, 2015.

The figure shows that the Right to Life Frame is the most persuasive, being statistically more effective than the control. This suggests that evangelicals are responding to rights-oriented arguments.

Moving to support for free speech, the results of the model are displayed in the bottom panel of Figure 3.5. There were no independent effects of the individual frames, but I investigated if there were contingent effects through interactive variables. At the bottom of the lower panel, there are four interactive effects, combining party-ID and abortion attitudes for both the Right to Life and Anti-Abortion Frames. Of these, it is the Right to Life and party-ID interaction that yields a significant effect ("I: Right to Life & Party-ID"). Republicans who received the Right to Life justification for supporting expanded free speech, even for those with whom they disagree, were more supportive of speech without restrictions. The combination of abortion and partisanship had a potent effect, mirroring the historical evidence from the evangelical movement.

CONCLUSION

Evangelical elites' long-term framing of free speech rights in pro-life terms has been effective. Though still trailing the general population, evangelicals have increased their support for speech, outpacing their non-evangelical peers, and this is linked to abortion politics. In what began as legal and political support for anti-abortion protestors, evangelicals now leverage free speech arguments to support non-allies and to defeat campaign finance restrictions. They champion individualist free speech principles and lean on liberal legal precedents, taking positions that would have been unthinkable to evangelical forbearers, including Jerry Falwell. Common morality has largely been replaced by liberal pluralism, reflecting the status of evangelicals in politics.

While the shift in evangelical free speech advocacy is clear, it is not without its exceptions, pornography and flag burning being chief among them. Both issues lack the connection to abortion politics, and flag burning, in particular, has been counterbalanced by a potent appeal to patriotism. These issues confirm evangelical hesitance with expressive individualism, though evangelicals support political individualism. The competing components of free speech politics (expressive versus utilitarian or political individualism) are also why the evangelical rank-and-file may be generally less supportive of speech than others are. Nevertheless, these issue areas seem to be a reduced priority among evangelical organizations of late.

The exceptions to free speech advocacy also shed some insight into instances of late where evangelicals have seemingly been less supportive of free speech. Donald Trump's 2016 Republican presidential primary campaign, for example, was marked by lack of support for free speech, as protestors were badgered and assaulted, the press was belittled, dissidents were threatened, and flag burning was opposed. How does the fact that a large percentage of evangelicals supported Trump fit with the evangelical commitment to free speech? The Trump example certainly suggests a split within evangelicalism, particularly between the elites and the masses. The majority of evangelical organizations who have championed free speech did not support Trump throughout most of the primary.[92] In fact, his early support was greater from evangelicals who did not attend church often.[93] Non-churchgoing evangelicals are less likely to hear elite framing of free speech and respond to elite appeals. In addition, the Trump campaign's silencing of speech in the Republican primary was disconnected from the elite pro-life movement. In the past, Trump had been quite supportive of legal abortion, and his consistency on the issue was not a priority for his early supporters based on exit polls.[94]

The lack of evangelical and pro-life connections to the Trump campaign may account for the perceived lack of commitment among Trump primary supporters, but evangelical voters as a whole supported Trump at near-record levels in the 2016 general election.[95] This suggests a few implications for free speech politics. First, the growth in evangelical support for free speech is episodic rather than linear and tenuous rather than salient among the rank-and-file. In particular, other issues can crowd out free speech advocacy for the grassroots, as was the case in 2016. Second, Trump's evangelical support belies the importance of elites to build the case for free speech. Third, evangelicals' support for Trump indicates the utility of connecting free speech rights to abortion politics. Without the connection, the rank-and-file may be prone to illiberal views and actions. And so the Trump campaign's seeming diminution of free speech is consistent with the history and the statistical models – evangelical commitment to liberal free speech views is contingent upon abortion and elite leadership. Yet on the whole, the trajectory is toward promoting broad free speech rights, especially as evangelicals have become ensconced in minority politics.

4

Separation Tranquility

Abortion and the Decline of the Strict Separation of Church and State

In late September 2015, Pope Francis made his first visit to the United States, holding court along the eastern corridor in Washington, DC, New York City, and Philadelphia, Pennsylvania. His visit captivated the nation, in large part because of the Jesuit's celebrated status as a Latin American and a reformer. While some American Catholics are wary of Francis, he had become renowned since his installation in 2013, especially by those pushing for the Catholic Church to modernize in either doctrine or approach (or both).

American Catholics and the American media anticipated the pope's visit for nearly a year, and religious leaders largely welcomed the five-day event, as it would bring renewed attention to faith in America. Some evangelicals, though, lamented Francis's "decidedly mixed signals" on several cultural issues, specifically homosexuality.[1]

The three cities prepared for throngs of parishioners, media, and onlookers who would gather to hear and see the pontiff. Philadelphia, in particular, employed enormous provision. The City of Brotherly Love, not as used to visiting foreign dignitaries as New York and DC, is the home of a large Catholic contingent and was also hosting the World Meeting of Families, where Francis was the keynote speaker. The city closed bridges, roads, and schools and commissioned a massive security enterprise.[2]

At final tally, the event cost Philadelphia $18 million, of which the city would pay $8 million from taxpayer funds, receiving $9 million from the World Meeting of Families.[3] To some, this might raise questions. Does an American city providing $8 million in tax money to pay for a religious leader's visit implicate constitutional questions, specifically the separation of church and state? Is it proper to mix government services and expenditures with religion, especially to this degree?

Such constitutional questions are not merely rhetorical. In fact, in 1979, the also-beloved Pope John Paul II visited Philadelphia as well, and his visit ignited a protracted controversy over the expenditure of public funds for the event. The American Civil Liberties Union sued the city over its construction of a 28-foot-wide outdoor altar and its provision of chairs for guests, arguing that such expenditures violated the First Amendment's Establishment Clause. The Board of National Ministries of the American Baptist Church joined the lawsuit, with a communications specialist from the denomination bringing the case jointly with the ACLU. The Baptist Joint Committee, which represented the Southern Baptist Convention at the time along with several other Baptist bodies, supported the lawsuit with a resolution, and the affair was covered widely in *Baptist Press*.[4] The federal Third Circuit court ruled that the city's actions were unconstitutional, as the construction of the papal platform equated to "public sponsorship of a religious service."[5]

In 2015, no such controversy over the pope's visit developed. Americans United for Separation of Church and State, an advocacy group focused on Establishment Clause questions, issued a public statement prior to the pope's visit, urging the cities to "take pains to protect church-state separation," citing the 1979 incident, among others.[6] Certainly, Philadelphia took better measures to ensure constitutional fidelity. In his public statements, Mayor Michael Nutter took care to assure reporters that no public funds were used for religious purposes.[7] Some in Philadelphia were frustrated with the cost the city paid for the event, but there was scant discussion of potential constitutional impropriety.

This inaction is particularly noteworthy for Baptists, who for most of the twentieth century were the leading Christian voices cautioning about the constitutional concerns of government intermingling with Catholicism, seeking to maintain robust Establishment Clause protections.[8] Baptist legal activists sought to protect the religious liberty of minorities while preventing large religious groups from gaining favored status with the government. The ACLU, Americans United, and the Baptist Joint Committee, along with a few Jewish organizations, were prominent in the fight to protect the separation of church and state. Baptists were specifically on guard against Catholic encroachments to the wall of separation, opposing ambassadors to the Vatican, resisting public funding of parochial schools, and, as discussed earlier, cautioning against public support for papal visits.

In contemporary politics, this dynamic has changed. Most Baptists and their evangelical brethren are now allies with Catholics. For these evangelicals, the perceived threat is not state-preferred majoritarian religion, but the denial of rights of orthodox believers who have become disfavored minorities. When Pope Francis came to the United States, some Southern Baptist leaders did call his address to Congress "problematic," harkening back to the prior era. R. Albert Mohler, Jr., president of Southern Baptist Theological Seminary and frequent public commentator, noted, "No Roman Catholic pope has ever been invited to address a joint session of Congress. And Baptists historically have been very opposed to the United States government recognizing any religion or religious leader in such a way."[9] Yet Mohler refrained from calling the address unconstitutional. Instead, the typical evangelical plea sounded like the statement from Russell Moore, the current president of the Southern Baptist Convention's Ethics & Religious Liberty Commission, who called for a unified Christian witness on ethical and moral concerns. "I hope the pope speaks with clarity about the dignity of all human life, including that of the unborn; the stability of the family, including the necessity of mothers and fathers for children; and religious liberty for all."[10] Primary concern was over what the pope would say, not where he would say it.

After the pope spoke to Congress, Southern Baptists were critical, though mostly of his tepid support for the core of American conservative religious advocacy: abortion, gay marriage, and religious liberty. While some Southern Baptist leaders took the opportunity to encourage that the government return to refraining from extending diplomatic privileges to the Vatican,[11] the loudest and most prominent cajoles came from those wishing that the pontiff were stronger on life, traditional marriage, and religious liberty. Again, Russell Moore opened by expressing gratitude for Francis's statements "about the dignity of all human life, whether the unborn, the elderly or the immigrant." But he went on to lament, "I do think that the Pope's address was an opportunity to address urgent moral issues like abortion culture and religious liberty with more clarity and directness than what was delivered."[12] Mohler called Francis's message regarding abortion and marriage "very fuzzy and evasive."[13]

The primary anxieties, however, concerned the positions of the new pope, not the prudence of his visit. The concerns were over content, not constitutionality. Baptists were most disquieted about Francis's re-crafting of the evangelical-Catholic cultural and political partnership, not the American church-state relationship.

The comparison of these papal visits more than three decades apart is instructive about a broader political and legal shifts in the American religion landscape. No longer are most Baptists (and some other evangelicals) guarding the wall of separation between church and state; now they have joined their Catholic brethren to guard against the encroachment of secularism and the infringements to religious liberty, especially the religious liberty of evangelicals and Catholics. The First Amendment to the U.S. Constitution has two religion clauses – one forbidding religious establishments and the other protecting against the infringement of religious exercise. Evangelicals, Baptists in particular, have shifted their emphasis from the Establishment Clause to the Free Exercise Clause. How has this happened? I suggest that much of the answer lies at the beginning of both of Russell Moore's statements regarding Pope Francis – in the politics of abortion.

THEORETICAL CONTEXT

The change in emphasis among prominent Baptists is representative of a broader shift in the politics of the First Amendment. In the past thirty years, the landscape of church-state relations has undergone a consequential jurisprudential shift away from the strict separation of church and state (focused on the Establishment Clause) and toward the government accommodation of religion (focused on the Free Exercise Clause). In 1991, legal scholar Ira Lupu declared that "the constitutional era where separation is the dominant theme appears to be over."[14] Evidence of this shift can be seen in Supreme Court's decisions favoring religious organizations on "equal access," free speech, and free exercise grounds in the face of no-establishment challenges.[15]

Evangelical Protestants have played an important role in this shift, as they have been some of the strongest supporters for the public accommodation of religion, in both their public opinion and their legal advocacy work.[16] Arguably, no evangelical group better exemplifies this change in church-state relations than the Southern Baptist Convention, the largest Protestant denomination in America, which, despite its historical ties to the separation of church and state, officially began lobbying for accommodation in 1991.

While this shift away from the separation of church and state is evident in the literature, little attention has been given to its causes. Many scholars have debated the historical merits of both the separation and the accommodation positions,[17] whereas others have analyzed public opinion on church-state matters,[18] as well as the activity of religious groups involved in church-state litigation.[19] Those focusing on Southern Baptists have given some attention to the denomination's declining support for church-state separation, within a broader discussion of the SBC's recent denominational divide.[20] In doing so, these scholars identified the rise of conservative evangelicalism as promoting the theological, political, demographic, and organizational factors that contributed to the Southern Baptist shift in church-state politics. Yet what is missing is an appreciation of how the central issue of conservative evangelical politics – abortion – affected church-state advocacy change. Understanding this link provides greater insight into the political and religious divisions that have shaped Christian Right politics. It also illuminates conservative Christianity's increased emphasis on rights-based political arguments by tying together abortion and religious liberty.

Abortion's role in shaping legal advocacy may be especially true in the crafting of the prudential relationship between church and state, as the need for abortion advocacy demands an open public square for religious viewpoints. These issues – abortion and church-state relations – are two of the central issues of the cultural divide in American politics,[21] so one would expect a connection. Yet while abortion has been shown to influence voting behavior, political activity, and even partisanship,[22] as shown in Chapter 2, there is little analysis of how it might have shaped church-state politics. Legal scholar Thomas Berg references abortion's role in contemporary church-state politics when discussing the decline of anti-Catholic separationism among evangelicals,[23] and historian Barry Hankins suggests that abortion may have been the "most important factor" in the SBC's move toward accommodation.[24] Yet neither work engages in a full treatment of how abortion altered

church-state relations. Here, I analyze the relationship between abortion politics and evangelical church-state advocacy, with a specific focus on the Southern
Baptist Convention.

SOUTHERN BAPTISTS AND CHURCH-STATE RELATIONS

As a religious group, Baptists have a heritage of dissenting from the religious
establishment favored by the government and supporting the separation of
church and state. The Baptists, while not solely responsible, made an important
contribution to securing religious liberty, the institutional separation of church
and state, and religious equality in America.[25] The dominant Baptist position
on the separation of church and state is that separation is vital to protecting the
church from the state. For most of the twentieth century, the SBC was a leading
proponent of church-state separation and religious liberty. Its Washington,
DC–based advocacy organization, the Baptist Joint Committee, was active in
promoting these issues before the Supreme Court and in other political arenas.
The BJC is an umbrella group of several Baptist denominations in America of
which the SBC was the largest and most important until its split with the BJC in
1991, following conservatives gaining control of the denomination.[26]

The BJC was an active proponent of the Court's Establishment Clause
jurisprudence, beginning with the early Court decisions on the topic – *Everson
v. Board of Education* (1947) and *McCollum v. Board of Education* (1948).
Everson applied the Establishment Clause to state and local governments,
though it ruled in favor of a New Jersey town reimbursing parents from public
funds for transportation costs to local parochial schools, while *McCollum*
outlawed a Champaign, Illinois, school district's practice of releasing public
school students from school to take religious education classes on a voluntary
basis. These two cases laid the groundwork for the Supreme Court promoting
the strict separation of church and state in the mid-twentieth century, with
Everson providing the rationale and rhetoric and *McCollum* providing the
legal outcome.

Though *Everson* is noteworthy for its strict separation language, including
the "high and impregnable" "wall of separation between Church and State," the
BJC was quite concerned with the Supreme Court's refusal to strike down
the New Jersey bussing program. The BJC had encouraged the Court to strike
the practice on Establishment Clause grounds, filing an *amicus* brief with the
General Conference of Seventh Day Adventists that asked the Court to preserve
the "time-honored doctrine of the separation of Church and State safeguarded
by the Constitution."[27] Further, the BJC's chairman, E. Hilton Jackson, joined
the counsel for Arch Everson in the oral argument before the Court.[28]
Following the ruling, the BJC adopted a resolution deploring the *Everson*
decision for "turning back the hands of the clock as far as religious liberty
and the separation of church and state are concerned."[29] In fact, the BJC's
first executive director, James Dawson, stated, "We consider this another

encroaching step toward changing the Constitution in a manner to give the Catholic church a privileged position."[30]

In *McCollum*, the BJC again submitted an *amicus* brief supporting the separationist position. While the Joint Committee was more satisfied with the Court's outcome in the case, some of its Southern Baptist constituents were not, with the executive secretary of the SBC, Duke K. McCall, calling the BJC's position in the case "ill advised" and not supported by Southern Baptists.[31] The BJC, however, was vindicated when the SBC supported the outcome of *McCollum* in resolutions at its 1949 and 1953 annual convention. In 1953, the resolution referenced *McCollum* before asserting its "unwavering devotion to the separation of church and state" and its "strong opposition to the use of tax funds and tax-supported schools in favor of any or all religious organizations."[32]

Southern Baptists also helped found Protestants and Other Americans United for Separation of Church and State, currently called Americans United for Separation of Church and State, to express a broader Protestant voice on church and state issues and to promote church-state separation. In the early days, both the BJC and Americans United opposed public funding for religious schools and hospitals, religious practices in public schools, and diplomatic relations with the Vatican, while promoting religious liberty domestically and internationally.[33] Both also had an anti-Catholic animus.[34]

Despite some criticism, from the 1940s to the 1970s the denomination approved of the BJC's and the Supreme Court's separationist positions. The Southern Baptist Convention gave its formal support for Americans United in resolutions in 1948, 1960, and 1965. In ten of the twenty-five annual conventions from 1947 to 1972, Southern Baptists passed resolutions opposing the use of public funds to support religious schools, hospitals, and other institutions. On three occasions, the SBC passed resolutions opposing diplomatic relations with the Vatican. The SBC also officially affirmed the *McCollum* decision and the Court's Establishment Clause doctrine in resolutions at the annual conventions in 1949 and 1952.

Regarding prayer in schools, neither the SBC nor the BJC was directly involved in the Supreme Court's controversial 1962 and 1963 rulings that decided that prayers and Bible readings directed by public school employees were a violation of the Establishment Clause.[35] Despite this, the BJC was active in defending the Court's decisions to its members and before Congress. The school prayer rulings were publicly unpopular, though, and many members of Congress (along with many religious leaders and activists) supported a constitutional amendment to overrule the Supreme Court. The BJC opposed these efforts in congressional hearings, and it was able to persuade the SBC to pass a resolution in 1964 that expressed concern about "public officials ... us[ing] public or official powers for the advancement of religious commitments or ideas" and opposed "the adoption of any further amendment to that Constitution respecting establishment of religion or free exercise thereof."[36] The SBC

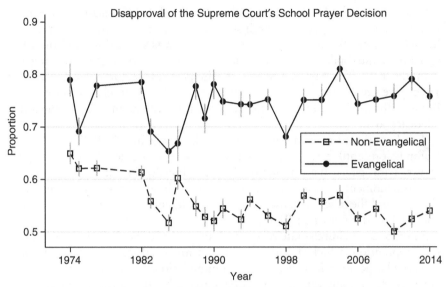

FIGURE 4.1. Evangelical and Non-Evangelical Disapproval of the Supreme Court's Rulings Declaring Prayer and Bible Readings in School Unconstitutional. GSS, 1974–2014.

also implied its support for the Supreme Court's school prayer decisions in a 1971 resolution, which explained that it supported only truly voluntary prayer, not prayer coerced by government involvement.[37]

The SBC resolution supporting the Supreme Court, as well as the BJC's arguments opposed to prayer in schools, was unpopular, especially among evangelicals. Figure 4.1 plots evangelical and non-evangelical opposition to the Supreme Court ruling from 1974 to 2014, using data from the General Social Survey. While the majority of Americans have disagreed with the Court since 1974, evangelicals have been statistically stronger in their disagreement, generally hovering between 70% and 80 % opposed to the ruling. Even when the general public's objection moderated in the late 1980s to 50–55% disapproval, evangelical disapproval remained high.

Changing of the Guard in the SBC

In the late 1970s, the SBC began to change. In a well-documented denominational battle over theology, politics, and control that spanned from the late 1970s to the early 1990s, Southern Baptist "conservatives" gained control of denominational leadership positions from the "moderates," who had long controlled the Convention.[38] During this turmoil, the embattled BJC promoted equal access legislation, which was later expanded upon by evangelical legal groups using free speech arguments. Despite broad support for its equal access advocacy, at the end of this struggle the SBC defunded the BJC and authorized a conservative-led, SBC-only group, the Christian Life Commission, to serve as its advocacy arm regarding church-state and other moral and political issues. In 1988, active SBC conservative Richard Land was selected to head the CLC. Quickly, Land built an independent SBC advocacy presence, breaking ties with the BJC. The SBC secured a Washington office for the CLC and by 1990 gave Land's organization the authority to lobby on church-state issues. In 1991, the SBC voted to sever ties with the BJC, leaving the CLC as the SBC's advocacy arm.

Land continued to lead what is now called the Ethics & Religious Liberty Commission until 2013, when Russell Moore succeeded him. During his tenure, Land paved the way for the SBC to officially alter its approach to the First Amendment in regard to both the free speech (as discussed in the previous chapter) and the religion clauses. He was an influential entrepreneur in the SBC and the broader Christian Right.

In the area of church-state relations, Land rejected the BJC's type of church-state separation, which it had championed for a half-century. Instead, Land promoted a position he called the "accommodation" of religion, which "seeks government 'accommodation' of individuals' rights to express religious beliefs in government locales."[39] This is generally similar to the position of conservative legal scholar Michael McConnell, among others.[40] To Land, Southern Baptists never agreed with the style of separation of church and state that the BJC promoted. In fact, he argued that some Southern Baptists' preferences might even lean toward the unconstitutional establishment of religion. In an interview with the author, Land said, "The majority of Southern Baptists, you give them a choice between the Joint Committee's separation and establishment and they're going to choose establishment."[41] To him, accommodation protects against the negative implications of both establishment and separation.[42] Land described his perspective, saying, "What I want to do is restore maximum accommodation. Government maximally accommodates your right and my right to speak our religious beliefs to others in the public square and in the classroom when appropriate. But the majority doesn't silence the minority; the minority doesn't silence the majority."[43]

Under Land, the ERLC accepted non-preferential aid to religious organizations on the basis of equality, allowed the government to recognize America's Christian heritage, and rejected the idea that the government "entanglement" of religion violates the Establishment Clause. Land's emphasis on accommodation and rejection of much of the Supreme Court's prior separationist doctrine was matched by the Southern Baptist membership. For example, the left panel in Figure 4.2 shows that the majority of SBC pastors approved of a school prayer amendment (as did the evangelical rank-and-file), especially from 1980 to 1996, when a voluntary prayer amendment was on the political agenda. The BJC consistently opposed such an amendment, but in the mid-1990s Land supported a narrowly tailored one that protected voluntary prayer.[44]

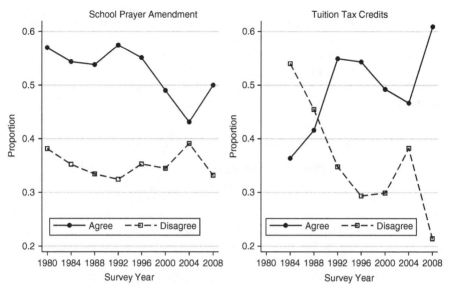

FIGURE 4.2. Clergy's Views on a School Prayer Amendment and Tuition Tax Credits. SBC Clergy, 1980–2008.

The same is true with tuition tax credits, which the BJC also consistently opposed as being a violation of the Establishment Clause. Land personally supported vouchers and other types of indirect funding to religious and non-religious groups and individuals. He helped move the SBC in this direction, though he admitted that during his leadership the SBC lacked consensus on the issue.[45] As the right panel of Figure 4.2 shows, SBC pastors were increasingly inclined to accept tuition tax credits and other voucher programs as a favorable policy, effectively switching their positions.

ABORTION AND CHURCH-STATE POLITICS IN THE SBC

During the process of the SBC's transition from moderate leadership to conservative leadership and from *support for separation* to *support for accommodation*, the denomination also experienced an important shift in its position on abortion, as detailed in Chapter 2. In the 1970s, the denomination's official stance was a qualified defense of pro-choice abortion rights, though rejecting abortion on demand. In 1980, the denomination decisively altered its position with the passage of a strong pro-life resolution. When Land was appointed director of the SBC's Christian Life Commission in 1988, he moved the denomination's abortion advocacy unambiguously in the pro-life camp and positioned it as one of the religious leaders of the anti-abortion movement.

The shifts in abortion and church-state separation occurred almost synchronously, but the concurrence of these shifts is not coincidental. The relationship between abortion and church-state relations is also more explicit than a broad culture war occurring within American society and the denomination.[46] In the SBC, abortion politics played an instrumental role in promoting its shift away from the separation of church and state. The BJC's version of the separation of church and state did not commingle well with pro-life advocacy and the political and theological conservatism of Southern Baptists.

PRO-LIFE POLICIES AND THE ESTABLISHMENT CLAUSE

Pro-life Southern Baptists' frustration with the denomination's Establishment Clause interpretation stemmed from events beginning in the era of *Roe v. Wade* (1973), though not necessarily with the case itself. Rather, the problem was that the strict separationists, including the BJC, often supported abortion rights through First Amendment arguments. Pro-life Southern Baptists also became frustrated with the BJC as an organization, because they viewed it as being pro-choice and liberal.

Much of the pro-life Southern Baptists' disdain for the BJC begins with James E. Wood, Jr., the executive director of the BJC from 1972 to 1980. Early in his tenure, Wood supported abortion rights. In order to avoid a territorial conflict with the CLC, which was charged with advocating on social issues, he couched pro-choice advocacy in terms of promoting religious liberty for those who favored abortion and the promotion of the separation of church and state in the face of the potential establishment of religious beliefs.[47]

Proffering Free Exercise and Establishment Clause arguments to oppose pro-life policies was not unique to Wood and the BJC of the 1970s. These arguments were frequent among strict separationist lobbies and mainline Protestant groups. Before the Supreme Court, evidence of this first appears in an *amicus curiae* brief submitted by the American Ethical Union, American Jewish Congress, Episcopal Diocese of New York, United Methodist Church, and others in *Roe v. Wade* and *Doe v. Bolton* (1973). At the end of the brief, the groups pithily argue that religious beliefs underlie the moral concern for the fetus. As such, "The police power cannot be employed in the service of sectarian moral views without violating the Establishment Clause of the First Amendment."[48] The BJC did not participate in *Roe* or *Bolton*, but these filers were its allies. In addition, the year of the *Roe* decision, Wood first went on record supporting abortion rights at the Joint Committee's board meetings.[49]

Separationist groups and defenders of abortion rights continued to advance First Amendment arguments against pro-life policies that were challenged at the Supreme Court in the 1970s and 1980s. In 1976, the American Jewish Congress, the United Methodist Church, and others filed an *amicus* brief in *Poelker v. Doe* (1977), a case concerning the city of St. Louis' policy of not allowing therapeutic abortions in its state-run hospitals. In the brief, these religious groups placed even more emphasis on the religious nature of pro-life policies, believing this should engender the policies to run afoul of the Establishment Clause. They declared, "The mayor's action violates the First Amendment's dual guaranty of church-state separation and the free exercise of religion by imposing upon the entire community the religious doctrine of those to whom abortions are sinful."[50]

While neither the BJC nor the moderate Southern Baptist leadership joined the early briefs supporting abortion rights, evidence suggests that their sentiments were in favor of defending abortion on First Amendment grounds. The religious strict separationist groups and mainline Protestant groups were frequent allies of the BJC. In addition, in the late 1970s, the BJC opposed a constitutional amendment to ban abortion except to protect the life of the mother, arguing that the pro-choice position was a matter of religious liberty. In October 1979, Wood endorsed a pro-choice statement released by the Religious Coalition for Abortion Rights that also expressed this position. The statement declared:

The position that a fetus is a human being with full human rights from the moment of conception is a particular theological position. Other theologies take other positions. If, therefore, those opposing abortion are successful in incorporating their particular religious doctrine into the supreme law of the land, our religious liberties will have been seriously eroded.[51]

This strain of legal argument reached its apex with the federal courts following the 1976 passage of the Hyde Amendment, which prohibited federal funds from being used to supply abortions. Wood testified before a U.S. District Court that the Hyde Amendment was a violation of the First Amendment. He stated that "while the Hyde Amendment is manifestly discriminatory in public policy against the poor, even more alarming is that one's free exercise of conscience and religion in this matter is abrogated." During his testimony, Wood also declared that the Hyde Amendment violated the Establishment Clause by being a "gross entanglement of institutional Government into the moral and religious values of the people of this Country."[52] He linked the policy to aid to parochial schools and seemed to be implying that, in agreement with some other religious groups involved in advocacy against the Hyde Amendment, the end result is the establishment of the Catholic religion in America.

When the district court invalidated the anti-abortion legislation, Wood called the decision "supportive of the guarantees of the First Amendment for all citizens and for the inviolability of one's individual conscience in facing what is intrinsically a complex moral issue" and "a profoundly significant one for maintaining the integrity of the First Amendment."[53] The Supreme Court agreed to hear the challenge to the Hyde Amendment in *Harris v. McRae* (1980), but the BJC chose not to join an *amicus* brief. Yet several other like-minded religious groups did file. The brief of the American Ethical Union, United Methodist Church, and others opposed the Hyde Amendment, focusing entirely on First Amendment considerations. In fact, Foy Valentine, the director of the SBC's Christian Life Commission, and four Southern Baptist seminary professors signed on to the brief. The *amici* deemed the anti-abortion statutes "religious rather than secular" and a violation of both the Free Exercise and Establishment Clauses. Regarding the Establishment Clause, the brief argued that the Hyde Amendment "constitutes a law which prefers those religions that forbid abortion over those which do not and injures women who do not profess a religious belief forbidding abortion by withholding from them a government benefit available to others."[54] Using the standards culled from the Court's previous Establishment Clause decisions, in particular the three-part "Lemon Test" from *Lemon v. Kurtzman* (1971), the brief argued that the Hyde Amendment lacked a secular purpose, had a primary effect of advancing religion, and entangled the government with religion. For these religious advocates, strict separation was a tool to vouchsafe abortion rights.

Two other mainline Protestant groups, the National Council of Churches and the Presbyterian Church in the U.S.A., also filed briefs opposing the Hyde Amendment, but they grounded their objections in the Free Exercise Clause, arguing that the amendment violated the liberty of conscience of women.[55] Only the United States Catholic Conference filed a brief objecting to these First Amendment claims against the Hyde Amendment, outlining that it is acceptable and even normal for laws to articulate public morality.[56] Evangelicals had yet to join Catholics in opposing strict separationist arguments to invalidate anti-abortion measures.

In its 5–4 decision allowing the Hyde Amendment to stand, the Court rejected the Establishment Clause argument. The majority opinion stated, "We are convinced that the fact that the funding restrictions in the Hyde Amendment may coincide with the religious tenets of the Roman Catholic Church does not, without more, contravene the Establishment Clause."[57] The majority avoided the Free Exercise issue, though, declaring that the appellees lacked standing.

While the decision in *Harris v. McRae* directly rejected church-state arguments for invalidating pro-life policies, separationists and abortion rights groups continued to utilize them. For example, in two abortion-related cases in the 1980s, *Bowen v. Kendrick* (1988) and *Webster v. Reproductive Health Services* (1989), groups filed *amicus* briefs objecting to pro-life policies because they violated the separation of church and state. Pro-life, Southern Baptist conservatives rejected this brand of separationist jurisprudence, moving them away from supporting church-state separation and toward supporting the government accommodation of religion. These pro-lifers promoted a broad version of religious rights, which were more vital than church-state limitations that protect the political community. The linking of abortion and church-state politics imperiled the separationist movement to many pro-lifers.

Of particular concern to Southern Baptists was the Joint Committee, both its brand of church-state separation and its tacit defense of abortion rights.

The BJC's pro-choice advocacy during this period remains one of its most controversial positions, and it played a significant role in the growing division between the BJC and Southern Baptists. When James Dunn was appointed leader of the BJC in 1980, he vowed to avoid the abortion issue, in large part because Southern Baptist conservatives were upset with Wood and the BJC's involvement with the issue. Yet for SBC conservatives, this was not enough. The inaction on abortion troubled them, causing many to suspect Dunn and the BJC were pro-choice. For example, conservative leader Paige Patterson said that Dunn's lack of a clear stance on abortion was "probably the signal" that he did not agree with them more broadly.[58]

While the BJC did not take any public positions on abortion under Dunn, there were a few incidents, beyond the organization's inaction, that distressed pro-life conservatives. First, in a 1983 criticism of President Ronald Reagan, Dunn made a statement that alluded to his probable pro-choice views. He declared, "The complex issue of abortion is reduced to the simple cry of 'infanticide' by Mr. Reagan, who would redress 'a great national wrong' in the name of civil religion, making it virtually impossible for mothers to make their own decision in this very private, very *religious* matter."[59] To many, this statement was similar to the arguments made by Dunn's BJC predecessor.

Conservatives were also disgruntled about the BJC inviting Sarah Weddington, the lawyer who argued the pro-choice position in *Roe*, to speak at its religious liberty conference in 1981. Weddington spoke against Senator Jesse Helms's proposal to strip the federal courts of the jurisdiction to hear school prayer cases. Though in its press release the BJC did not mention her ties to *Roe*,[60] her appearance angered pro-life Southern Baptists who were aware of it.[61]

The Joint Committee additionally filed a brief with the American Jewish Committee and Americans United in *Bowen v. Kendrick* (1988), regarding the constitutionality of the Adolescent Family Life Act, which provided federal funding for a partnership of religious and government agencies to provide counseling to teenagers on issues of sexual activity. The BJC argued that this act violated the Establishment Clause by advancing religious views and entangling government and religion. Part of its argument directly addressed abortion on church-state grounds, declaring that religious organizations are promoting religion when they counsel teens on sexual morality, as it is "fundamentally a religious doctrine." The brief follows with a statement that discouraging abortion is fundamentally a religious component of sexual morality.[62] For many pro-life leaders in the denomination, this indicated that pro-life values were unwelcome in the advocacy strict separationists.

The abortion issue continued to hamper the BJC's relationship with the SBC until the very end. When Richard Land was appointed the new director of the CLC, putting it firmly in control of the SBC conservatives and pro-lifers, he sought to counteract prior Baptist arguments that abortion rights should be defended on First Amendment grounds. In *Webster v. Reproductive Health Services* (1989), the CLC filed its first-ever *amicus* brief.[63] Filing with the

Lutheran Church-Missouri Synod and the National Association of Evangelicals, the Southern Baptist agency argued that while being pro-life is a religious belief, it is also a belief of fundamental morality, directly opposing the separationist arguments. The brief proclaimed, "We do not advocate the imposition of our religious views by law in order to impose upon others our religious beliefs. Rather, those religious beliefs are also deeply seated in the moral and ethical system that forms that basis of much of the civil and criminal law of this nation and therefore, if the state legislatures so decide may coincidentally be expressed in legislation."[64] As such, these organizations argued that "state laws prohibiting abortions are not unconstitutional establishments of religion."[65] In this brief, Land, the CLC, and the new conservative SBC leadership were clearly opposing the past positions of the BJC and developing a view of the relationship between church and state that would be friendly to pro-life policies and advocacy.

The division between these two Southern Baptist lobbies over abortion is evident in a conflict between the BJC and the CLC in the waning days of the BJC's partnership with the denomination. In 1991, the BJC was a leading proponent of the Religious Freedom Restoration Act that combated the Supreme Court's ruling in *Employment Division v. Smith* (1990), which limited the scope of free exercise of religion claims, giving greater deference to the government.[66] RFRA was a legislative remedy to restore free exercise rights to the standard used before the *Smith* decision. The CLC, under Land's leadership, also opposed *Smith*, but they were hesitant to support RFRA, being concerned that it might be used to advance pro-choice positions in the name of religious freedom. Dunn was somewhat critical of the CLC's slow response, and Land used this opportunity to attack Dunn on the pro-life issue. He wrote a pointed letter asking Dunn to "state for the record whether abortion is a practice which should prevail as a free exercise of religion claim." Land also wanted Dunn to commit to Southern Baptists that the BJC "will never advocate, especially in the courts or in Congress, the view that abortion claims would prevail as religious liberty claims."[67] Dunn responded, "As everyone knows, or should know quite well, the BJCPA [BJC] since I have been here has never addressed abortion as a free exercise right, nor have we addressed the issue of abortion in any fashion."[68] Dunn further declared, "Our position on the free exercise/abortion issue is clear: We oppose any effort to amend the Religious Freedom Restoration Act that would keep any free exercise claim from being made; we take no position, however, on whether such claims should be successful." Land and the new, pro-life CLC were not satisfied with Dunn's response because it equivocated on abortion.[69]

Eventually, Land and the CLC agreed to support RFRA, as their abortion concerns were satisfied.[70] At its 1991 annual convention, the SBC passed a resolution supporting a legislative remedy to *Smith*. In that same convention, however, the SBC would also vote to end its financial ties with the BJC.

The SBC's split with the BJC is the event that allowed Southern Baptists to officially embrace accommodationism. It gave Land the ability to craft the denomination's new approach to church-state issues, and it gave SBC

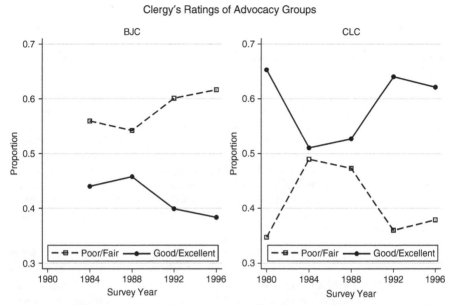

FIGURE 4.3. Clergy's Views of the Performance of the Baptist Joint Committee (BJC) and Christian Life Commission (CLC). SBC Clergy, 1980–1996.

conservatives almost complete control over the decision-making. Yet it should be noted that it was not a small band of conservative SBC elites that had a disregard for the BJC. Southern Baptist clergy also disapproved of the BJC. Figure 4.3 shows that from 1984 to 1996, more SBC pastors thought the BJC was doing a poor or fair job than those who thought it was doing an excellent or good job. There is also a statistically significant correlation between pastors rating the BJC negatively and being pro-life.[71] Similarly, the ordered logistic regression models (see Table 4.1 in Appendix B) show that abortion attitudes were a strong, constant predictor of one's view toward the BJC, even when controlling for political and religious views. Pro-life clergy were more likely to disapprove of the BJC.

Pro-life attitudes are also highly predictive of support for school prayer among SBC clergy and the general public, when controlling for political and demographic measures. Being pro-life consistently increases opposition to the Supreme Court's school prayer decision, though the effect is not greater for the pro-life evangelical rank-and-file than non-evangelical pro-lifers, as the interaction effect is insignificant. The same goes for the clergy and support for the school prayer amendment. The complete results for the clergy are in Table 4.1 and for the rank-and-file are in Table 4.2 (see Appendix B).

Considering the foregoing evidence, abortion appears to have affected the SBC's church-state positions and views in large part because those promoting the separation of church and state attacked pro-life policies, and defended pro-choice decisions, on First Amendment grounds. The SBC's relationship with the

BJC was a casualty of this strategy by the separationists. In an interview, Dunn, former BJC head, understood this, calling it an "excuse" used to attack him and the BJC.[72] Land, in describing the view of conservative elites, recognized that abortion was one of several factors that led to the defunding of the BJC and the changes in the CLC.

It was a significant factor, but it wasn't the only factor. Almost all the moderates were pro-choice, the theological moderates. They have never understood, they still don't understand, and I suspect they never will understand the depth of the outrage that pro-life Southern Baptists felt that Southern Baptists were being portrayed in Washington as pro-choice, when they were so strongly and convictionly pro-life. I think that's why this agency [the Christian Life Commission] changed first, because it was the point agency on the life issue. I've talked to a lot of pro-choice people, and they just don't get it. They just don't get how huge this was, and how angry and upset Southern Baptists were over having themselves be described as a pro-choice denomination when they weren't.[73]

To Land and most of the SBC conservatives, abortion was a legitimate concern with both the BJC and its strict separationist fellow-travelers, not merely an excuse. The usage of the separation of church and state as a reason to reject pro-life policies tainted separationism for Southern Baptist conservatives and helped the denomination embrace accommodation.

CATHOLICISM AND CHURCH-STATE SEPARATION

Intertwined with the linkage between abortion and church-state politics is Baptists' evolving relationship with Catholics. For much of the twentieth century, Baptists battled Catholics, especially in the church-state arena. Baptists opposed an ambassador to the Vatican, championed a legal battle against transportation reimbursements to parochial schools in *Everson*, passed numerous resolutions opposing funding for church schools (e.g., Catholic schools) at the annual convention, and helped start Protestants and Other Americans United for Separation of Church and State, to impede the Catholic Church. Legal historian Philip Hamburger argues that Southern Baptists saw church-state separation as "attractively antihierarchical," being congruent with their opposition to Catholicism.[74] This is evident in Southern Baptist pastor George W. Truett's famous 1920 sermon on the steps of the U.S. Capitol, where he developed a lengthy contrast between the Baptist and Catholic views of church-state relations and church polity, calling the two religious messages "the very antipodes of each other."[75]

Following *Roe*, Catholics were the primary religious group opposing abortion rights. As such, separationists were able to paint pro-life policies as establishing a particular religion – Catholicism – in *amicus* briefs, hearings, and public statements. For example, the *amicus* brief of the American Jewish Congress, United Methodist Church, and others in *Poelker v. Doe* (1977) identifies the Catholic theology that a soul is given at conception as being the driving force behind anti-abortion laws.[76] This view had also taken hold among some of the Southern Baptist leadership.[77] A 1981 pamphlet on abortion by Christian Life Commission even stated, "Christians may properly work to change [using abortion for birth control] without moving to the other extreme and insisting that the whole nation be required to accept the Roman Catholic dogma related to abortion as the law of the land."[78]

For much of the 1970s, Baptists, the BJC, and Americans United took the position that they had taken before on parochial school issues, opposing the Catholic Church on separation of church and state grounds. But, by the late 1970s and early 1980s, pro-life issues became one of the two central issues for Southern Baptist conservatives. In the process, Southern Baptists and Catholics became comrades in the battle against abortion. In *Bowen v. Kendrick* (1988), Concerned Women for America, ally to Southern Baptist conservatives and founded by Beverly LaHaye, the wife of SBC pastor Tim LaHaye, partnered with the Catholic League for Religious and Civil Rights supporting the Adolescent Family Life Act against its Establishment Clause challenge. The newly conservative-controlled CLC filed a brief alongside, though not in partnership with, the United States Catholic Conference in *Webster v. Reproductive Health Services* (1989), supporting the pro-life position. In *Planned Parenthood v. Casey* (1992), the CLC partnered directly with the United States Catholic Conference and the National Association of Evangelicals arguing that *Roe* should be "reconsidered and ... abandoned."[79] Catholics and Baptists were now allies and co-belligerents.

Land also originally signed the joint declaration "Evangelicals & Catholics Together" in 1994, recognizing both the religious and moral common ground between evangelicalism and Catholicism. Abortion played a prominent role in this statement. In fact, the statement recognized that the cooperation between these two groups was in large part due to their agreement against abortion. "The pattern of convergence and cooperation between Evangelicals and Catholics is, in large part, a result of a common effort to protect human life, especially the lives of the most vulnerable among us," the statement said. "Abortion on demand ... must be recognized as a massive attack on the dignity, rights, and needs of women."[80] In April 1995, however, Land and another prominent Southern Baptist signer removed their names from the document after a year of criticism. Their disassociation with the document was for theological and missiological reasons. Despite his departure, Land affirmed joint "efforts which consolidate the influence of evangelicals and Catholics in addressing moral issues," abortion being prominent.[81]

While elites were coming together, it should be noted, however, that data from the General Social Survey do not show that evangelicals' feelings toward Catholics have improved between 1986 and 2004.[82] Evangelicals' views of Catholics have remained flat (or slightly declined) over time, even for more pro-life evangelicals.[83] The improved relationship is primarily among the evangelical advocacy groups, like the ERLC. Despite the lack of improvement in feelings toward Catholics, evangelical activists and the evangelical base have warmed to Catholic issue positions.

Public Funding for Religious Schools

One of the areas that display how Southern Baptists' church-state views have been altered by the improvement in their relations with Catholics is the government funding for private schools. From the founding of the BJC in the 1940s, the SBC frequently went on record opposing government aid to religious schools and institutions. Throughout the 1960s and 1970s, the SBC explicitly and consistently opposed even indirect government aid to religious institutions, with the SBC declaring its opposition in 1966, 1967, 1968, 1971, and 1972. In 1972, the SBC extensively opposed vouchers and proposals from the Nixon Administration to provide public support for parochial schools, while at the same time affirming the Court's separation doctrine.[84]

During the 1980s, and continuing to the present, the BJC opposed direct and indirect aid to religious schools. Southern Baptist conservative elites, however, were increasingly becoming more favorable to neutral, indirect funding to religious schools.

For many SBC moderate elites committed to church-state separation, any type of funding for religious schools was unconstitutional. For example, Dunn criticized tuition tax credits for being unconstitutional, as well as "regressive," "expensive," "inflationary," "unfair," "divisive," "destructive," "undemocratic," "dishonest," and "intrusive."[85] In staking their opposition to tuition tax credits for religious schools, these leaders frequently cited the SBC's commitment to the separation of church and state through numerous resolutions and official positions at least dating back to the 1940s.[86] The separationists were emphasizing what they considered common sense limits on religious rights – the communitarian necessity of separation.

Conservatives countered the separationist Baptist perspective, arguing that vouchers for students to attend religious schools are not direct funding for religious institutions. In fact, they maintained, vouchers promote neutrality and religious liberty. Land, for example, stated that the government does not have to provide vouchers to religious schools, but, if it wants to provide tax money to support private schools, it must, as a matter of neutrality, allow that money to go to religious schools. Forbidding vouchers to religious schools in this scenario, would be a denial of the rights of religious citizens. Conservative rights arguments were being cultivated.[87]

The conservative elites' positions on tuition tax credits also began to be reflected in the opinion of the Southern Baptist clergy. According to Figure 4.2, in 1984 only 36% of pastors agreed or strongly agreed with the policy of tuition tax credits, while 54% disagreed or strongly disagreed with the policy. Support for tuition tax credits increased, reaching 54% in 1992 and 61% in 2008. SBC pastors' support for tuition tax credits effectively switched between 1984 and 1992 in favor of the accommodationist view, and in 2008 the approval gap

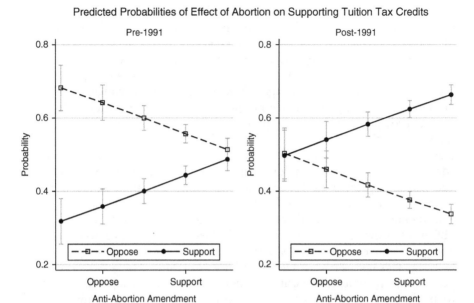

FIGURE 4.4. Predicted Probabilities of the Effect of Abortion Views on Supporting Tuition Tax Credits with 95% Confidence Intervals. SBC Clergy, 1984–2008.

widened. The switch happened after they had moved to the Republican Party, though it coincided with the party's increased emphasis on school choice.

The survey data also suggest that there is a strong relationship between abortion and views on tuition assistance to religious schools. The correlation between abortion and tax credits is statistically significant from 1984 to 1996, and the correlation increases as the pastors change their views.[88] The results of ordered logistic regression models are shown in Table 4.1 in Appendix B. Even with the inclusion of extensive controls, views on abortion remain statistically important. Figure 4.4 takes these models and collapses the outcome variable (tuition tax credits) to a simple agree/disagree response. It shows that pastors who were in favor of an anti-abortion amendment to the Constitution were in general more likely to be supportive of tuition tax credits in all of the surveys, even in 1984 while the majority of SBC pastors disagreed with such tax credits. Moreover, the two graphs in Figure 4.4 show the increasing support for tuition tax credits across the denomination, as the supporting and opposing lines switch places between the left and right panels.

The confidence intervals, shown by the vertical gray bars, provide further insight. If the vertical bars in the two horizontal lines do not overlap, the probabilities are statistically significant at the 95% confidence level. In the pre-1991 period (left panel), the only predicted probability that is not statistically different is between those who strongly support an anti-abortion amendment. These strongly pro-life pastors are almost completely split in their views on tuition tax credits. This changes drastically after 1991 (right panel), where there is a clear significant difference among pro-life pastors, with the least pro-life pastors having an insignificant difference in their views on tax credits. Abortion attitudes yield increasingly accommodationist views.

As the conservatives gained more control of the SBC, its official positions on tuition tax credits began to change. These official position changes were surely bolstered, in part, by the change in opinion of the denomination's clergy, as well as growing Republican support for tax credits and vouchers. In 1991, the year that the SBC voted to defund the BJC, the annual convention passed a resolution supporting tax credits and voucher-type programs for religious education, breaking from a long-standing position that the SBC and BJC had taken. The resolution "encourage[d] choice in education initiatives which include proper tax incentives for families." It clarified that as long as the educational choice proposals did not "constitute direct aid to churches" the SBC would view them as "keeping with the First Amendment protections."[89] In 1996, the Convention expressed a similar sentiment in a resolution, though its language was not nearly as qualified as it was in 1991. Instead, the resolution "encourage[d] our legislators, at all levels of government throughout our nation, to develop the means and methods of returning educational and funding choices to parents."[90] Parental religious freedom rights were the overriding rationale.

The CLC followed the positions in the 1991 and 1996 resolutions by filing *amicus* briefs supporting a school choice program in Wisconsin in 1995 and 1997 (*Warner Jackson v. John T. Benson*) and programs in Cleveland, Ohio (*Zelman v. Simmons-Harris*) and Arizona (*Arizona Christian School Tuition Organization v. Winn*) in 2002 and 2010. Though in 2010 Land said that he "probably wouldn't file" in vouchers cases because the SBC lacks consensus on the issue,[91] the ERLC has filed briefs supporting these tuition assistance programs on the basis of religious freedom. In the Arizona case, the brief the ERLC joined argued that by striking down this law the lower court "chills private religious conduct and expression."[92]

While the SBC is not an ecumenical denomination, its partnership with Roman Catholics to combat abortion and other social issues has improved its regard for the Catholic Church. In the process, Southern Baptists have become friends with their former foe in the church-state arena. No longer do they view religious schools with contempt. Instead, Baptists and Catholics are fighting the same culture war for the role of faith in politics and social issues such as abortion. The denomination's improving relationship with Catholics is partly responsible for its shift away from church-state separation, and it can be see in Baptist support for the funding of religious schools.

EMPHASIS ON FREE EXERCISE

As alluded to in the prior sections, another impetus in the SBC's shift away from the separation of church and state was its evaluation that the separationist

Establishment Clause doctrine limited the ability of religious individuals to live their faith in public. Land described the differences between the conservative ERLC and the BJC, saying:

There is a genuine philosophical difference between the Joint Committee and us [the ERLC] over where the threat is. They [the BJC] remain convinced that there is a threat to the Establishment Clause, which I think is loony. I think that there would have to be a spiritual revival of incredible proportions in the United States before there would be any possibility for there to be any significant violations of the Establishment Clause. But I think there is diminution of the free exercise clause every day.[93]

Much of this belief regarding the "diminution" of the Free Exercise Clause has ties to abortion. Two factors contributed to the connection between anti-abortion advocacy and anti-church-state separation advocacy, and both of these shifted Southern Baptists' focus to the Free Exercise Clause. First, the critics of pro-life evangelicals frequently attacked their political involvement by declaring that church and state should be separate. Because their pro-life attitudes were religiously informed, they did not belong within the public arena. Second, and related, pro-life advocates saw a decline of religious values within American culture, which they viewed as one of the primary reasons why abortion had come to be legal and accepted. Because of these influences, pro-life Americans were more likely to take positions protecting their ability to express their religious views within political conversations and promoting America's religious heritage. Both positions contributed to them opposing the strict separation of church and state.

Historian Barry Hankins credits two evangelical intellectuals, Carl F. H. Henry and Francis Schaeffer, for being especially important in activating SBC conservative elites against abortion and the separation of church and state.[94] Their leadership on cultural issues had an important connection to the way conservative evangelicals came to understand the culture wars and the relationship between church and state. Underlying the scholarship and apologetics of both was a resistance to a view of American church-state politics, which would require American Christians to separate their faith from politics and allow America's religious heritage to be expunged by secular humanists. Land credited Schaeffer for convincing him that there was "a real attempt to suppress the religious free speech and the religious free exercise rights of the people in the public square in general and in public schools in particular."[95] To Land and other conservatives, pro-life and pro-democracy advocacy should not be inhibited by the strict church-state separation which had the effect (either direct or indirect) of inhibiting the exercise of religious faith in politics.

To guard against strict Establishment Clause jurisprudence restricting religious advocacy, particularly on abortion issues, Land and other evangelicals argued that the Court should move away from the Lemon Test – the three-part test used by the Court in *Lemon v. Kurtzman* (1971) to determine if a policy amounted to an unconstitutional establishment of religion. To Land, the Lemon Test was "broodingly hostile to religion" and it violated the Supreme Court's purpose in striking down government sponsored prayer in the 1962 and 1963 cases.[96]

The SBC's distaste for the Lemon Test was not merely about church-state separation. The SBC's displeasure for it was also precipitated by the strategy employed by mainline Protestant groups, Americans United, and even the BJC, to rebut pro-life policies and programs with the Establishment Clause. Briefs filed by religious groups and separationist groups in abortion cases often analyzed pro-life policies through the lens of *Lemon*, determining if the policy had a secular legislative purpose, advanced religion, or resulted in an excessive government entanglement with religion. Three cases serve as examples. First, in *Harris v. McRae* (1980), the *amicus* brief joined by organizations including the United Methodist Church, the Unitarian Universalists, a division of the Disciples of Christ, and signed by moderate SBC leader Foy Valentine among others, argued that the Hyde Amendment should be struck down because it violated the "Purpose-Effect-Entanglement Test," what is now typically called the Lemon Test.[97] Second, in *Bowen v. Kendrick* (1988), the BJC and Americans United argued that the Adolescent Family Life Act violated the second prong of the Lemon Test because the program which encouraged religious institutions to provide services regarding teenage sexuality had the primary effect of advancing religion.[98] Finally, in *Webster* (1989), Americans United argued that the state of Missouri violated the second prong of the Lemon Test, because by the preamble declaring that life begins at conception, the legislation improperly advanced a religious belief.[99]

When Land took over the CLC, he guided it in filing a brief in *Lee v. Weisman* (1992), a public school graduation prayer case, arguing that the Court should reject *Lemon*. Aided by constitutional law scholar, Michael McConnell, the CLC argued that a no-coercion test would be more prudent than the Lemon Test. In the same case, the BJC argued that the Court continue to use the Lemon Test. Directly attacking the CLC's position, the BJC's brief declared that those who seek to change the test require "the court to abandon the fundamental requirement that government be neutral toward religion, and substitute instead that requirement that government refrain from 'coercion.'"[100] In *Lee v. Weisman*, the Court did not strike down the Lemon Test, but the CLC continued to express this opinion before the Court, making a similar argument in *Kiryas Joel School District v. Grumet* (1994).[101]

Land grounded his agency's shift away from focusing on the Establishment Clause in the desires of Southern Baptist congregants.[102] According to the survey data from pastors on their church-state views and their disapproval of the BJC, Land's perspective is accurate, as the clergy's positions were far from the BJC's model of separation. Land viewed his accommodation approach as a middle way that adhered both to Baptist tradition and the denomination's preferences. In fact, the ERLC's shift away from focusing on the separation of church and state to promoting the government accommodation of religion appears to have been positively received. Figure 4.3 above shows that after

Land was appointed to lead the SBC's religious liberty and moral agency (the Christian Life Commission) in 1988, Southern Baptist pastors increasingly gave the agency positive ratings.

This focus on accommodation and religious liberty has remained under Russell Moore. As an example, in 2014 the Supreme Court heard *Town of Greece v. Galloway*, regarding the constitutionality of sectarian prayers preceding a town meeting, a practice frequent before many local government activities. The Second Circuit Court of Appeals had previously decided that for the opening prayers to be constitutional, they should be religiously neutral. The ERLC solely filed an *amicus* brief supporting the constitutionality of these prayers, arguing that they did not violate the Establishment Clause and stating that the neutrality provisions proposed by the lower court "threatens the religious liberty of participants in civic councils." It based its argument in free speech and religious liberty, contending that "forcing prayer to conform to a state orthodoxy of 'neutrality' discriminates against those religious beliefs that require prayer in a form prohibited by that 'neutrality'" (i.e., praying in Jesus' name.).[103] Additionally, several prominent Southern Baptist seminary presidents, as well as Baptist and other evangelical theologians, submitted a brief arguing that the religion clauses of the Constitution "do not require legislative invocations to be religiously 'neutral' prayers," arguing that such restrictions on content would violate religious liberty and freedom of conscience.[104]

By contrast, the BJC filed a brief opposing the town's practice of opening their municipal meetings with prayer. It argued that the practice violated the Establishment Clause because it "infringes the liberty of conscience of not just religious minorities, but also of Christians who believe worship should be voluntary." Instead, the focus should be on separation of church and state – "prayer is an expression of voluntary religious devotion, not the business of the government." "By opening a local government meeting with an exercise of religious devotion, a political assembly is transformed into a religious congregation,"[105] which, if true, would amount to an establishment of religion. In this case, the Court narrowly sided in favor of the town (and the ERLC), supporting the practice of opening meetings with prayers given by different area religious leaders. Religious freedom continued to prevail over separation.

The Big Picture of Religious Freedom

In church-state relations, Southern Baptists have shifted most of their concern from the Establishment Clause to the Free Exercise Clause, matching the emphasis of most evangelical activists and expanding the discourse of rights politics.[106] Yet heretofore scholars have largely overlooked abortion's important role in this change. To the Southern Baptist leadership, the high wall of separation that characterized the Court's church-state jurisprudence from the 1940s to the 1980s and still infects the advocacy of many separationists groups has served to hamper political advocacy against abortion. For them, this has caused free exercise to be a greater concern. If religious groups are able to actively participate in public life and religious institutions are able to receive the same benefits as secular groups, then America's culture war, of which abortion is a central battle, has a better chance of being won by the traditionalists. Moreover, evangelicals are increasingly coming to terms with the decline of "Christian America." The focus has shifted from an emphasis on majoritarian Christian values to the protection of minority rights, such as religious liberty. Russell Moore has called this "post-Christian America,"[107] and Southern Baptists appear to be realizing this. In fact, by 2008, 90% of SBC clergy agreed that religious freedom was threatened in America, growing 20% from 1988. As a response, evangelicals like the SBC have rejected contemporary Establishment Clause arguments for their "hostility toward religious people." In a recent *amicus* brief filed to support a religious daycare, the ERLC developed this hostility argument, saying it "cuts against the values undergirding the Free Exercise, Establishment, and Equal Protection Clauses." Moore elaborated, "Separation of church and state means, among other things, that the state should not discriminate against religious people simply because they are religious."[108] The emphasis of the SBC's First Amendment advocacy has clearly changed. Despite success in the 2016 presidential election, the focus on free exercise will remain the way forward, either through minority (legal) or majority (legislative) politics.

CONCLUSION

Though the connection between abortion and church-state advocacy has been under-analyzed by previous scholars it is clear that, while not the sole cause, abortion played an important role in the Southern Baptist shift away from the separation of church and state in the past thirty years. Abortion politics was central to the SBC's separation from the BJC, the separationist stalwart, because the BJC had been tainted for its usage of the religion clauses to support pro-choice advocacy and for refusing to take a pro-life position. The SBC's commitment to pro-life advocacy has also established an advocacy partnership with the Catholic Church, its former enemy in church-state relations. As such, Southern Baptists are less cautious of indirect government support for religious schools and institutions. This alliance is further support for James Davison Hunter's premise that the new cultural landscape pits the orthodox, like Southern Baptists and Catholics, against progressives and seculars.[109] Finally, Southern Baptist engagement in abortion politics seems to have motivated a greater emphasis on the free exercise of religion, while eschewing Establishment Clause retorts. This attention to pro-life politics and emphasis on free exercise characterizes much contemporary conservative Christian legal advocacy, as seen in opposition to the 2010 Patient Protection and Affordable Care Act and its contraceptive mandate, as well as gay rights. These topics are explored further in Chapters 5 and 7. One particular episode, however, is instructive for the changing emphasis on church-state relations for Baptists (and the broader evangelical community).

Following the passage of the health care law in 2010, the Obama Administration's Department of Health and Human Services (HHS) implemented instructions about what medication and procedures insurance providers would be required to cover. The bill was highly controversial, and the divides were partisan. After the enactment, the requirement for contraceptive care became the most controversial for religious organizations, as employers were required to provide contraceptive coverage at no charge to the insured. These included traditional hormonal contraceptives, barrier methods, intrauterine devices, and emergency contraception – often known as "morning after" pills.

Religious organizations and religiously owned businesses objected to this "contraceptive mandate." Catholic doctrine rejects to any form of artificial birth control, and evangelicals were primarily opposed to emergency contraception, which they regarded as causing abortions because they end pregnancy after conception. While the original mandate exempted houses of worship from the coverage, it required religious nonprofits (e.g., schools, hospitals) and religiously run businesses with more than fifty employees to offer contraceptive coverage or face stiff financial penalties. Many religious groups insisted that the contraceptive mandate violated their religious conscience and their First Amendment right to religious freedom. After much resistance, HHS revised their rules in June 2013 to try and accommodate religious nonprofit institutions (though not for-profit companies) that object to contraceptive coverage. Under the updated rule, religious employers need to fill out a government form (or write a letter) to alert the government that they consciously object to providing contraceptive coverage. The government would then provide free access to the contraceptives via the employer's insurance plans.

Many religious nonprofits were unsatisfied, arguing that by assisting the government in using their insurance plans they were violating their religious conscience by aiding the procurement of contraceptives and abortifacients. Simultaneously, the for-profit companies filed legal challenges, which would end in their favor in the 2014 *Burwell v. Hobby Lobby* Supreme Court decision discussed in the next chapter. Dozens of religious charities, universities, and denominational entities – most of these Catholic and evangelical – too filed suit in federal court. Evangelicals and Catholics were partnered to litigate for religious liberty, spurred by their opposition to abortion. In fact, two of the primary plaintiffs in these cases were the Catholic nonprofit Little Sisters of the Poor and the Southern Baptist nonprofit insurance company GuideStone Financial Resources. As these cases progressed through federal courts, the U.S. Conference of Catholic Bishops and the Southern Baptist Convention were leading advocates opposed to the rules for religious nonprofits. Their decades-long growing political relationship had been realized. The religious legal advocacy group The Becket Fund for Religious Liberty aided the Baptists and Catholics. The federal government countered that broad access to free contraceptives was a compelling government interest, not to be overridden by religious objections.

In March 2016, the U.S. Supreme Court heard appeals from these cases, consolidating seven lower court cases into *Zubik v. Burwell*, though popularly the legal challenge took the name Little Sisters of the Poor from the amenably named plaintiff. A broad array of evangelical and Catholic advocates supported the religious nonprofits in these cases, arguing for a broad right to religious freedom as protected by the First Amendment and the federal Religious Freedom Restoration Act. These included the Southern Baptist Convention, its seminaries, and mission agencies, the National Association of Evangelicals, the Assemblies of God, the Christian Missionary Alliance, and the Seventh-Day Adventists. The SBC's brief argued was the epitome of the linkage between abortion and religious liberty. It argued that "compel[ing] individuals to participate in what they believe to be an unjustified taking of life imposes a grievous burden on the exercise of their beliefs."[110]

While Southern Baptists were joining their Catholic and evangelical allies in defense of a broad religious liberty rights, the Baptist Joint Committee rejected this argument, again opposing the SBC at the Supreme Court. In fact, not only did the BJC refrain from joining religious groups arguing for religious liberty, for the first time in the history of the organization it asked the Supreme Court to reject the religious liberty arguments for the plaintiff when there was no Establishment Clause issue at stake. In a brief filed with constitutional scholar and University of Virginia Professor Douglas Laycock, the BJC argued that there was no "substantial burden" to these religious nonprofits' free exercise rights. Further, their brief argued, "But religious liberty can be endangered by exaggerated claims and overreaching as well as by government intransigence and judicial under enforcement. Petitioners endanger religious liberty, both legally and politically."[111]

The arguments by the competing Baptist groups are instructive for the evolution of church-state politics. The SBC and their partners sought to advance an *expansive right* to religious liberty, motivated by pro-life views being implicated by the government's regulation. These evangelical and Catholic groups viewed themselves as threatened minorities, facing stiff government penalties. The BJC, less concerned about pro-life issues, sought a narrower, *limited right* to religious liberty. It was unconvinced of the minority status of these prominent players in American politics, as they have been for nearly all of the Christian Right's religious freedom claims. Instead, the BJC was oriented toward political compromise, the rights of the community, and preserving the delicate constitutional balance that protects traditional minorities. This fits well with a primary advocacy position of protecting the separation of church and state, which can be seen as establishing community norms for religion and politics.

In all, this fight between estranged organizations is indicative of the shift in Baptists' approach to church-state politics. For the Southern Baptists, the largest, most powerful Baptist contingent, the politics of abortion have enabled a change from primarily protecting church-state separation to primarily defending a broad right to religious liberty, and this has been exacerbated by a change in the status of evangelicals, from cultural majority to threatened minority.

In May 2016, the Supreme Court released a complicated *per curiam* ("by the Court") opinion, which did not resolve any of the legal questions but granted a victory for the religious nonprofits by exempting them from penalties. The opaque opinion set no precedent for future cases, ensuring a continued debate over the extent of religious liberty and reproductive rights. What is clear, however, is that evangelicals have become entrenched in the pursuit of broad religious freedom protections, eschewing Establishment Clause concerns. Republican allies have pursued religious freedom rights on their behalf, as well. Religion in public life has become about individual freedom, not separation of church and state boundaries, and abortion politics underlie this evolution.

5

First, Do No Harm

Abortion and Health Care Opposition

In the Gospel of Luke, Jesus is recorded teaching his followers and the religious elites how they could inherit eternal life. Jesus' short answer cited two central tenants of the Pentateuch – the Jewish Law: "Love the Lord your God with all your heart and with all your soul and with all your strength and with all your mind" (Deuteronomy 6:5),[1] and "Love your neighbor as yourself" (Leviticus 19:18). An expert in the Jewish law sought to test Jesus, asking him, "And who is my neighbor?" Jesus responded with a story that has now become familiar: the parable of the Good Samaritan.

In this parable, a man was attacked, beaten, robbed, and left "half dead" on the side of one of the most dangerous roads of the day. Both a priest and a scholar of the Jewish law, a Levite, passed by the wounded, helpless man without giving aid. But a Samaritan, a man of an ethnic origin despised by the Jews, stopped to care for the victim. The Samaritan bandaged the victim's wounds, provided him with lodging, and paid for his health care expenses.

Jesus then asked his critic, "Which of these three do you think was a neighbor to the man who fell into the hands of the robbers?" The Jewish expert replied, "The one who had mercy on him." Jesus then commanded, "Go and do likewise."

The Good Samaritan is a central parable in the Gospels. For evangelical Christians who are committed to both the authenticity of the Bible and the achievement of eternal life, the teaching of the Good Samaritan story is vital. The parable is Jesus' description of how to both fulfill the Law's commands and inherit the Kingdom of God. This passage is also reinforced by Jesus' other teachings about caring for the poor and needy. In the Gospel of Matthew, for example, Jesus declares that at the end of time God will welcome those who cared for others: "For I was hungry and you gave me something to eat, I was thirsty and you gave me something to drink, I was a stranger and you invited me in, I needed clothes and you clothed me, I was sick and you looked after me,

I was in prison and you came to visit me" (Matthew 25: 35–36). He proclaims that providing mercy to the needy is providing mercy directly to Jesus (Matthew 25:40), but failing to provide mercy is rejecting Jesus (Matthew 25:45). These decisions have eternal implications, as those who failed to act "will go away to eternal punishment, but the righteous to eternal life" (Matthew 25:46).

Jesus' commands to care for the needy and provide health care for the hurting present an interesting puzzle. How have evangelicals, who are marked by their commitment to following the Bible and the commands of Jesus as well as their focus on eternal life, been leading much of the recent opposition to national health care proposals? Even more, why are those who would benefit from increased health coverage, such as low- to middle-income evangelicals, so often opponents of these policies?

Certainly, part of the answer lies in who is mandated to distribute care to the sick and needy, with conservatives emphasizing the individual and liberals asserting the state. But if this were merely a question of ideology, we would expect more of a debate within evangelicalism, not primarily hearty opposition. So what has spawned evangelical opposition to national health care proposals?[2] In the historical accounts of the Christian Right, there has been scant attention paid to health care politics,[3] while analyses of public opinion on health care have focused on demographic, political, and organizational factors, largely ignoring religion.[4] Recent attempts to frame the issue of health care, particularly by opponents of reform, have been credited with altering public opinion,[5] despite failing to mention religious mobilization or fully investigating issue frames.

I posit that the politics of abortion have been central to evangelical health care politics. Framing health care politics in abortion terms has brought conservatives into the broader conservative fold opposing national health care initiatives. The addition of religious conservatives has also given rise to a conservative rights-based opposition to liberal human rights calls for national health care, with abortion politics combining with party politics to produce strong opposition to prominent national health care initiatives.

THE ABSENCE OF CONSENSUS

In postwar America, Christians lacked consensus regarding the expansion of national health coverage. President Harry Truman proffered the first realistic proposal in November 1945, advocating for national health insurance, among several other reforms to health care. The American Medical Association (AMA) responded with sharp criticism, mobilizing opposition that eventually led to the proposals' defeat.

In the process, Christians could be found on both sides of the debate. Many progressive, Social Gospel Christians favored some version of national health care, with leading theologians within the movement, including Reinhold Niebuhr, supporting the Truman plan and attacking the AMA's obstruction.

Some fundamentalist evangelicals, on the other hand, opposed the Truman proposal. Criticism came from prominent fundamentalist leader Bob Jones, who in a conference in South Carolina[6] called the proposal "Santa Claus, MD," while other fundamentalists opposed the legislative efforts in large part because of their disdain for European socialism and Russian communism, which had penetrated leftist American politics.[7] The American Protestant Hospital Association also unanimously rejected the proposal, siding with the AMA.[8] Yet, among the bulk of evangelicals, there was little consensus and scant discussion about the national health insurance proposal.

Despite the defeat of Truman's proposal, support for national health care persisted in both domestic and international politics. In 1948, the United Nations helped reframe the debate, touting health care as an individual right with the passage of the Universal Declaration of Human Rights, in which Article 25 addressed health care directly, stating:

Everyone has the right to a standard of living adequate for the health and well-being of himself and of his family, including food, clothing, housing and medical care and necessary social services, and the right to security in the event of unemployment, sickness, disability, widowhood, old age or other lack of livelihood in circumstances beyond his control.[9]

Eleanor Roosevelt shepherded the passage of the Declaration, serving as the chair of the drafting committee.

The UN Declaration signaled universal health care coverage as a central pillar in New Deal politics, which for many Christians, especially working-class Democrats, was a welcome change. But for fundamentalist evangelicals, the connection to the United Nations fueled apocalyptic opposition, with anti-God communism (and socialism) joining forces with the Beast – the one-world government that signaled the "end times" prophesied in the Old Testament book of Daniel and the New Testament book of Revelation.[10] They believed the UN's rights should not have been honored, and opposed New Deal programs with vigor. Nevertheless, the Universal Declaration made prominent the argument that health care was an individual right, and bolstered its supporters' contention that the way to achieve universal health care was through the language of liberalism.

In the decades that followed, social welfare policies were further removed from anticommunist politics (and UN politics), though activists continued to focus on human rights. In turn, evangelicals became increasingly ambivalent about the proposals, with certain pockets showing support and others opposition. On the whole, by the mid-1970s, evangelical attitudes toward government-supplied social services mirrored the general population. In the 1975 General Social Survey, the averages for evangelical and non-evangelical respondents were nearly identical in terms of their support for the government improving the standard of living, the government being too involved in economic policy, and whether the government should pay for health care.

Both evangelicals and the general population took moderate positions, slightly favoring more government involvement.

Within this environment in the 1970s, Senator Edward Kennedy (D-MA) was the leading political advocate for increased national health care coverage, touting it as an individual right to the American public. Building on the UN's Universal Declaration of Human Rights, Kennedy proposed his Health Security Act in 1971, which called for a single-payer system of universal health care. Kennedy's plan was strongly supported by organized labor, while economic conservatives and medical interest groups mounted opposition. President Nixon sought to co-opt the issue by developing a market-based health care policy; however, the ensuing Watergate scandal halted the progress.

Evangelicals remained conspicuously quiet – by today's standards – in regard to these health care proposals, in part because of a lack of agreement on particular health policies among religious advocacy organizations, whose number was significantly fewer in the mid-1970s. But of the organizations that did exist, they did not agree to a particular perspective on health policy. The National Association of Evangelicals, for example, did not issue a resolution on the matter. In fact, they would not deliver an official statement on health care policy until the 1990s.

The Southern Baptist Convention provides insight into evangelical politics of the day. In 1975, the advocacy arm for the SBC and other Baptist bodies, the Baptist Joint Committee, considered a resolution to support Senator Kennedy's national health care plan. The BJC's discussion of the issue was covered positively in *Baptist Press*, but the organization failed to reach an agreement on language in support of the plan.[11] That same year, SBC Christian Life Commission director C. Welton Gaddy declared that health care was an individual right[12] and urged Congress to pass "a significant program of national health security" guided by moral principles. Gaddy had supported a national health care plan throughout the mid-1970s, but was unable to convince the denomination to take an official position at the time,[13] as a clear, unified view did not exist.

In 1978, however, the SBC did ultimately signal its support for the right to health care, following leadership from the CLC. At its annual convention, the denomination passed a resolution supporting the Universal Declaration of Human Rights, affirming the Declaration and identifying health care as a human right. It stated:

And we believe with the framers of the United Nations' Universal Declaration of Human Rights that human rights include freedom from involuntary servitude, arbitrary arrest and imprisonment, torture, unfair trial, cruel and unusual punishment, invasion of privacy; rights to family life, property, work, and equal pay for equal work as well as food, shelter, health care, and education; and freedom of thought, speech, assembly, religion, movement, and participation in government.[14]

At the prompting of the CLC, the SBC supported health care as an individual right on the basis of the dignity of humanity, and that "all persons are 'made in the likeness of God.'" The convention declared in the resolution that these rights "coincide with the Bible's teachings in support of justice, mercy, peace, and righteousness," and that these "basic human rights ... may not be relinquished, abridged, or denied." The individual's right to health care had found a home within evangelicalism, at least for the time being.

Despite its overall support, the denomination did not pass a stand-alone resolution in favor of the right to health care, and it avoided backing any specific policy proposal. Nevertheless, the largest and most prominent evangelical denomination had signaled support for individuals' right to health care, at the dawn of the Christian Right. Thirty years later, such a position seems far-fetched.

CHANGE IN EVANGELICAL APPROACH

In the decades that followed, evangelicals became primary opponents of national health care legislation, despite growing rights-based rhetoric in favor of health care among the American public. Opposition culminated three decades after the SBC resolution supporting the UN's Universal Declaration, when Republicans, the Tea Party, and their Christian Right allies fought President Obama's 2010 Affordable Care Act at every conceivable stage – in Congress, within bureaucratic rulemaking procedures, on the campaign trail, and inside the U.S. Supreme Court. While evangelicals were generally noncombatants or, at most, tepid supporters of universal health care in the 1970s, many evangelical organizations have of late been on the front lines, even willingly engaging in battles doomed to fail such as shutting down the government and goading President Obama into vetoing legislation defunding health care.

Survey data further supports grassroots evangelical opposition to government-provided health care as being a recent phenomenon. When the Southern Baptists supported universal health care in the late 1970s, the denomination was not on an island within evangelicalism, but rather within the mainstream of evangelicalism on health care policy, as data from the General Social Survey in Figure 5.1 shows. Additionally, evangelicals nearly mirrored the national population in support for universal health care. This was especially true in 1975 and 1984, when the GSS first asked their now-standard question about support for the federal government paying for health care. With responses ranging from 1 (government should help) to 5 (people should help themselves), the average evangelical response of 2.54 in 1975 was somewhat supportive of the federal government providing health care. Evangelicals (shown by the solid line) were slightly more likely to oppose government health care than all others (shown by the dashed line). It was not until the 1990s, and especially after 2008, however, that evangelicals started meaningfully diverging from the general public in their opposition to national health care.

The trend of early evangelical support and growing opposition to universal health care is also evident in survey data of evangelical clergy. In every

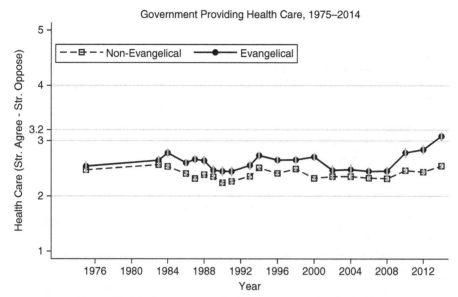

FIGURE 5.1. Evangelical and Non-Evangelical Views on National Health Care.
GSS, 1975–2014.

presidential election year between 1980 and 2008, political scientist James Guth of Furman University and his colleagues surveyed Southern Baptist clergy about their political views. From 1988 to 2008, the survey asked about the pastors' support for "government-sponsored national health insurance," soliciting responses ranging from strong agreement to strong disagreement. Figure 5.2 shows that even as late as 1988, at the height of the Christian Right, nearly 20% more Southern Baptist pastors supported national health insurance than opposed it. Despite support in the mid-1980s, compared to the rank-and-file, the clergy shifted earlier and more decisively against national health insurance policy.

Figure 5.2 demonstrates that between 1988 and 1996 evangelical pastors flip-flopped in their support for universal health insurance. While support for national health insurance garnered nearly a 20 point advantage in 1988, opposition surged to a 35 point lead in 1996, extending to more than 75% of Southern Baptist pastors opposing national health insurance in 2008. What accounts for such a considerable change?

By 1988, when more of them supported national health insurance, clergy were already identifying as Republican in party politics. But the change in the pastors' health care views was not solely about partisan politics, as Republican identity preceded the switch in health care views. For example, in 1980, Southern Baptist clergy were more likely to be Democrats (45%) than Republicans (28%). By the 1988 survey, however, approximately 65% of

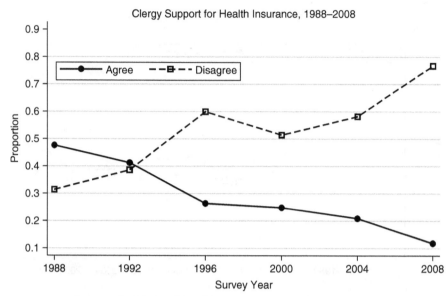

FIGURE 5.2. Support for National Health Insurance. SBC Clergy, 1988–2008.

pastors claimed Republican identity. This continued to grow, with 85% identifying as Republican in 2008.

By contrast, the evangelical rank-and-file did not diverge sharply from the general public in their support for government provided health care until 2010, long after they had become a key Republican constituency. From 2010 to 2014, evangelicals were significantly more likely than other individuals to oppose national health care. In the three surveys conducted between 2010 and 2014, evangelicals averaged nearly a half-category more opposition to the federal government paying for health care than did non-evangelicals.

These data intimate that party identity alone did not account for the change in evangelical opposition to heath care. Rather, there were two mechanisms. First, the evolution in evangelical health care politics was tied to the salience of health care politics within partisan politics, as opposition to universal health care became a key Republican issue in the 1990s. The second, less-appreciated mechanism was the coupling of the predominant evangelical policy position – abortion – with health care politics and Republican Party politics, which activated evangelical opposition from the 1990s to the present.

HEALTH CARE AND THE POLITICS OF ABORTION

Chapter 2 develops the history of abortion and evangelical politics, documenting the pre-1980 moderate evangelical position of not supporting abortion on demand but allowing for limited abortion rights. This changed sharply for evangelicals by the early 1980s, as they transitioned to being strongly anti-abortion and supplanted Catholics as the leading pro-life voice in American politics, particularly at the mass level. This change is particularly evident in data from Southern Baptist clergy. By 1980, 73% of SBC pastors favored a constitutional amendment banning abortion, and that number rose to more than 80% from the mid-1990s to 2008.

The Coupling of Abortion and Health Care

While evangelicals' abortion attitudes are now settled, they were in a state of flux in the 1970s, particularly following *Roe v. Wade* (1973). After the Court's decision, pro-life activists failed to achieve a constitutional amendment outlawing abortion, and the pro-choice position became more settled. The establishment of a woman's right to an abortion forced the issue into most health care policy debates. If women had a right to abortion, did the government have to pay for these procedures? What are the implications for poor women, as well as the taxpayers who object to abortion? While pro-life activists failed to defeat a broad, general right to abortion, they did succeed in restricting public funding.

The Hyde Amendment

In 1976, Congressman Henry Hyde (R-IL), a Catholic, pro-life Republican from Illinois, authored an amendment to the appropriations bill for the Departments of Labor, Health, Education, and Welfare. The amendment, now known as the Hyde Amendment, barred federal dollars from being spent to reimburse states for abortion procedures under the Medicaid program. It only permitted federal funding "where the life of the mother would be endangered if the fetus were carried to term." The provision passed the U.S. House of Representatives by a vote of 207–167 in September 1976, and President Jimmy Carter signed it into law, along with the broader appropriations bill, after coming into office in 1977. Although Carter supported abortion rights and opposed the anti-abortion constitutional amendment, he also supported the controversial Hyde Amendment. At a news conference on July 12, 1977, Carter outlined his position, stating, "I do not think that the Federal Government should finance abortions except when the woman's life is threatened or when the pregnancy was a result of rape or incest."[15] For Carter and other pro-choice moderates, the right to an abortion did not guarantee that the government would pay for the abortion; the right did not mean an obligation. With its passage, health care politics were promptly embroiled in the politics of abortion.

The Hyde Amendment was immediately challenged by pro-choice supporters, and federal judge for the Eastern District of New York, John F. Dooling, Jr., issued an injunction on the funding prohibition forty minutes after it went into effect. When the U.S. Supreme Court vacated the injunction, Dooling followed with a temporary restraining order, allowing the Medicaid payments to continue.[16] Meanwhile, the U.S. Congress continued to pass versions of the Hyde Amendment with each year's appropriations bills, adding or removing exceptions for rape, incest, or threats to the life and health of the mother.[17] The anti-abortion National Right to Life Committee strongly supported the strictest prohibitions, condoning only exceptions to save the life of the mother. After the House approved a strict measure without exceptions for rape and incest in 1977, the National Right to Life Committee proclaimed a "clear-cut human rights victory."[18]

Between 1977 and 1980, the Hyde Amendment was attached to appropriations bills each year, while at the same time being continually litigated, before finally being settled affirmatively by the U.S. Supreme Court. Many evangelicals, even those like President Carter who supported *Roe v. Wade*, applauded the measure prohibiting federal funding for abortion. *Christianity Today*, for example, editorialized in favor.[19] Yet, other, mostly pro-choice, mainline Protestant denominations, such as the United Methodist Church, United Church of Christ, Lutherans in America, and Presbyterian Church U.S.A., opposed the Hyde Amendment.[20]

Southern Baptist leaders were the most prominent evangelicals to oppose the measure. During the legal challenges to the Hyde Amendment, Baptist Joint Committee leader James Wood was actively involved in opposing the constitutionality of the legislation, as described in the prior chapter. Wood testified before a U.S. District Court that the Hyde Amendment was a violation of the First Amendment, stating that "while the Hyde Amendment is manifestly discriminatory in public policy against the poor, even more alarming is that one's free exercise of conscience and religion in this matter is abrogated." During his testimony, Wood also declared that the Hyde Amendment violated the First Amendment's Establishment Clause by being a "gross entanglement of institutional Government into the moral and religious values of the people of this Country."[21] He linked the legislation to aid for parochial schools and seemed to imply that, in agreement with some other religious groups involved in advocacy against the Hyde Amendment, the end result would be the establishment of the Catholic religion in America, and would violate both the Constitution and the collective responsibility of ordered liberty. For Wood and the mid-twentieth-century SBC, religious liberty was the most absolute of all individual rights, bounded by Establishment Clause concerns for communal responsibility. When the District Court invalidated the legislation, Wood called the decision "supportive of the guarantees of the First Amendment for all citizens and for the inviolability of one's individual conscience in facing what is intrinsically a complex moral issue" and "a profoundly significant one for maintaining the integrity of the First Amendment."[22]

After the Supreme Court agreed to hear the challenge to the Hyde Amendment in *Harris v. McRae* (1980), the BJC chose not to join an *amicus* brief, likely signaling the competing views in the SBC. Yet, several other like-minded religious groups did file. The brief of the American Ethical Union,

United Methodist Church, and others opposed the Hyde Amendment, focusing entirely on First Amendment considerations. In fact, Foy Valentine, the director of the SBC's Christian Life Commission, and four Southern Baptist seminary professors signed on to the brief. As discussed in Chapter 4, the *amici* deemed the anti-abortion statutes "religious rather than secular" and a violation of both the Free Exercise and Establishment Clauses. Regarding the Establishment Clause, the brief argued that the Hyde Amendment "constitutes a law which prefers those religions that forbid abortion over those which do not and injures women who do not profess a religious belief forbidding abortion by withholding from them a government benefit available to others."[23] Using the standards culled from the Court's previous Establishment Clause decisions, in particular the three-part "Lemon Test" from *Lemon v. Kurtzman* (1971), the brief argued that the Hyde Amendment lacked a secular purpose, had a primary effect of advancing religion, and entangled the government with religion.

Two other mainline Protestant groups, the National Council of Churches and the Presbyterian Church in the U.S.A, also filed briefs opposing the Hyde Amendment, but they grounded their objections in the Free Exercise Clause, arguing that the amendment violated the liberty of conscience of women.[24] Only the United States Catholic Conference filed a brief objecting to these First Amendment claims against the Hyde Amendment, outlining that it is acceptable and even normal for laws to articulate public morality.[25]

In its 5–4 decision allowing the Hyde Amendment to stand, the Court sidestepped the Free Exercise argument and plainly rejected the Establishment Clause argument. Regarding the Establishment Clause, the majority stated, "We are convinced that the fact that the funding restrictions in the Hyde Amendment may coincide with the religious tenets of the Roman Catholic Church does not, without more, contravene the Establishment Clause."[26]

For many evangelicals, the constitutional fight over the Hyde Amendment was the final act in their transition to the pro-life cause. Three weeks prior to the release of the Supreme Court's decision in *Harris v. McRae*, the Southern Baptist Convention passed a decidedly pro-life resolution at their annual convention in St. Louis, calling for a constitutional amendment prohibiting abortion. Chapter 2 discusses this resolution at length, which ended the SBC's equivocation on abortion and signaled a broader shift within evangelical life. In addition, the resolution took a strong stand in favor of the Hyde Amendment, declaring that the Convention "abhor[ed] the use of tax money or public, tax supported medical facilities for selfish, non-therapeutic abortion."[27] In staking out these positions, the SBC rejected attempts to moderate the resolutions at the convention.[28]

With this change, the SBC's health care advocacy positions were badly damaged. The Convention explicitly rejected the BJC and CLC's opposition to the Hyde Amendment and support for abortion rights, and distrust of these advocacy groups grew. Moderate, pro-choice advocacy would not be sustained within evangelical politics. The Convention was at war with its advocacy leadership.

In addition, it was becoming increasingly evident that on the national level, health care politics and abortion politics were interrelated. Because of *Roe*, the right to an abortion would now be intertwined with policy decisions about the funding of health care. The Hyde Amendment, though narrowly constitutional, was a legislative provision, not a right to protect the unborn. Therefore, restricting funding for abortions would have to be fought legislatively during every health care battle. As a result, common ground between health care advocates and anti-abortion advocates was disappearing. Defending a right to health care overlapped with supporting a right to abortion, which evangelicals could not support. For evangelicals, abortion politics became primary after 1980, and remained stable. The salience and stability of the abortion position allowed it be used to alter a less stable position – health care.

Reagan-Era Politics

With the election of Ronald Reagan in 1980 and the increase in pro-life Republicans in Congress, the environment for pro-life policies changed. While an anti-abortion amendment did not pass, evangelical and Catholic pro-life activists were pleased with other actions. Presbyterian and staunch anti-abortion advocate C. Everett Koop, who had joined with theologian Francis Schaeffer in bringing the pro-life cause to evangelicalism, was appointed Surgeon General. Koop's Senate approval was aided by Southern Baptist Jesse Helms (R-NC).[29] A strong Hyde Amendment also remained, with Reagan signing the Supplemental Appropriations and Rescission Act of 1981 that declared: "None of the funds appropriated under this Act shall be used to perform abortions except where the life of the mother would be endangered if the fetus were carried to term." Federal funding for abortions was not without conflict, as fights arose between Baptists Mark Hatfield (R-OR) and Jesse Helms in the Senate, with Hatfield seeking to take a more moderate stance.[30] To the chagrin of pro-life advocates, Hatfield prioritized passing appropriations bills as chair of the Senate Appropriations Committee over incorporating measures that would narrowly limit abortion funding.[31] Nevertheless, the Hyde Amendment stayed in effect, with the strict language from the 1981 Supplemental Appropriations and Rescission Act remaining constant from 1981 to 1993.

Though not all Republicans were of a like mind, in heath care politics evangelicals rallied around the primacy of abortion. In December 1982, *Christianity Today* published an editorial praising the pro-life activities in a variety of health care arenas. Evangelicals were lauded for consistently supporting the Hyde Amendment, barring federal money for research on living fetuses, eliminating abortion coverage under federal health insurance, and appointing Koop as Surgeon General. In the process of evolving on health care, evangelicals had come to defending rights. They had moved away from the right to health care, swiftly framing their activity as defending the right of the unborn. The *CT* editorial praised evangelicals for "battling for the right to life and other freedoms."[32] Rights talk was taking hold on the right, and it was being used to combat human rights on the left.

Due to the linkage between abortion and health care, evangelical groups began moving away from the right to health care. The SBC, for example, implied an official change in its position on health care policy in a 1987 convention resolution. Instead of health care being an individual right that governments owe their citizens, health care was described as a need to be met by the local church. The resolution acknowledged that compassion and mercy demand physical care, but the provider should be the church, not the government.[33]

In ten years, the SBC shifted from being social justice advocates on the issue of health care to embracing a conservative, localized approach that refrained from calling health care a right.[34] Limited government had replaced social justice. This sentiment began to be reflected in the views of the clergy, as shown in Figure 5.2.

A Gathering Storm of Opposition

In the 1980s and early 1990s, there was little need for evangelicals to advocate against health care policy, as this was not on the Republican agenda. Health care was a growing part of the Democratic agenda, however, as Jesse Jackson was able to add it to the party platform in 1988 following the success of his Democratic presidential primary campaign. After being nominated by the Democrats to face Republican George H. W. Bush, Michael Dukakis's presidential campaign pulled back from seeking broad health care reform. Health care largely remained out of the national spotlight.[35] One exception was in 1989, when congressional Democrats sought to weaken the language of the Hyde Amendment, but President George H. W. Bush responded with a veto.

The election of President Bill Clinton in 1992 brought newfound urgency to anti–health care advocacy on pro-life terms. Clinton made health care reform a priority in his campaign, and he was also committed to loosening restrictions on federal funding for abortion.

On the twentieth anniversary of *Roe v. Wade*, Clinton's third day in office, he signed executive orders rescinding four anti-abortion policies, including bans on federal funding of abortion counseling, fetal tissue research from elective abortions, and international organizations that provide abortion as a family-planning service. Clinton also ordered the Food and Drug Administration to review its ban on importing RU-486, the so-called "morning after" pill deemed "emergency contraception" or an "abortion pill" by pro-choice and pro-life advocates, respectively.

At the signing ceremony, Clinton stated, "We must free science and medicine from the grasp of politics and give all Americans access to the very latest and best medical treatments." Speaking to the abortion issue directly, he declared, "As a nation, our goal should be to protect individual freedom while fostering responsible decision-making, an approach that seeks to protect the right to choose while reducing the number of abortions. Our vision should be of an America where abortion is safe and legal, but rare."[36] The tension between health policy and abortion politics was reignited.

Evangelicals were not pleased with these developments by the Southern Baptist president from Arkansas. Richard Land, director of the SBC Christian Life Commission, avowed, "Today is a sad day for America and a horrifying day for unborn children.... As if to add insult to injury, President Clinton takes these actions on the 20th anniversary of the Supreme Court's *Roe v. Wade* decision. These are truly cruel and spiteful acts meant to break the will of the pro-life movement.... It will not work."[37] The National Right to Life Committee also sharply criticized Clinton's actions, and *Christianity Today* gave the decisions prominent coverage, captioning a photo: "In their face: As prolifers march, Clinton rescinds abortion regulations."[38]

Clinton was not finished antagonizing pro-life evangelicals. In announcing his plans for the federal budget in April 1993, he proposed to follow through on a campaign promise and rescind the Hyde Amendment, lifting the ban on federal financing of abortions. In covering the Hyde Amendment, the *New York Times* perceptively foresaw the looming battle regarding abortion and health care reform. "Perhaps most important," the *Times* declared, "both sides of the abortion issue are preparing for a fight over the health-care program being drafted by the White House task force headed by Hillary Rodham Clinton."[39]

Throughout his campaign, Clinton had committed to reforming the nation's health care system. Following his inauguration, he established the Task Force on National Health Care Reform, led by his wife, Hillary Rodham Clinton. The goal was to develop a proposal for a universal health care plan, succeeding in the policy area advanced by Harry Truman and Ted Kennedy. Throughout the process, the National Abortion Rights League demanded that abortion and contraceptive services be included in basic health benefits packages.[40] The January executive orders and the proposal to revoke the Hyde Amendment sent strong signals to evangelicals that abortion would be covered in the eventual Clinton proposal.

Following the announcement about seeking to retract the Hyde Amendment, evangelicals pushed back on the newly inaugurated Clinton. Doing so, they set the groundwork for a broader fight over the Clinton health care reform. In June 1993, at the annual Southern Baptist convention in Houston, Texas, the denomination targeted Clinton specifically, along with his health care proposals. First, the denomination meeting passed, with what *Baptist Press* called only "scattered opposition," a strongly worded resolution condemning the pro-abortion activities of the administration.[41] This resolution focused particularly on the January executive orders and the Hyde Amendment. The SBC "call[ed] upon Congress to maintain the Hyde Amendment and other pro-life policies that prohibit the use of federal funds to encourage, promote, or perform abortions except to save the life of the mother, thereby protecting the unborn and the consciences of millions of pro-life taxpayers." The denomination then established its position on health care, declaring that it "oppose[d] the inclusion of abortion in any health care plan which may be proposed by the President and adopted by Congress."[42]

If that was not enough, the denomination wrote a resolution that explicitly targeted Clinton – "On President William Jefferson Clinton." It is a tradition for Baptists for encourage the membership to pray for the president, particularly newly elected presidents, following the Bible's direction in 1 Timothy. But these encouragements had not been enshrined in specific denominational resolutions. It is also common for resolutions to take positions on potential policy proposals, though avoiding personalizing criticism. The Clinton resolution broke both conventions. While the resolution on Clinton called for prayer, the substance of the resolution took specific, critical aim at the president, his public morality, his positions on abortion, and his health care proposals.

Regarding health care, the resolution declared that the president and his advisors were "seriously contemplating the inclusion of abortion coverage in the national health care insurance program which would coerce private employers as well as taxpayers to pay for elective abortions." For Southern Baptists, this was a nonstarter. To further accentuate the point and the denomination's opposition to Clinton, a Southern Baptist, the resolution detailed several other pro-life objections, including the administration's actions to repeal pro-life executive orders, its push to authorize morning after "abortion pills," and its nomination of pro-choice advocate, Joycelyn Elders, to be the Surgeon General of the United States.[43]

The SBC's criticism of Clinton reverberated throughout evangelicalism, garnering coverage at *Christianity Today* and major national newspapers. The resolution "On President William Jefferson Clinton" was particularly controversial, as it was the first time that the SBC had "singled out a politician for criticism by name."[44] Chair of the SBC resolutions committee, James Merritt, reported that Clinton and his policies were the most frequent submissions for potential resolutions.[45] In pursuing the specific resolution on Clinton, Merritt said that the denomination wanted to focus a resolution on Clinton's policies because he is "a fellow Southern Baptist" and "represents the most severe shift in moral perspective and policy formulation of any president in history."[46] He also noted that if the public saw "what we didn't say, we'd be getting pats on the back."[47] Evangelicals were ready to fight against the inclusion of abortion in health policy.

Opposition to the Clinton Health Plan

The stage was set for an intense fight over the Clinton heath care proposal, and in the fall of 1993, the administration delivered the Health Security Act to Congress. The legislation sought to promote universal health care via a national managed care system, with the federal government subsidizing premiums for small companies and low-income individuals. On arrival, the proposal was strongly opposed by Republicans and the health care industry, who preferred market-based reforms. Initial public response was favorable, with a September Gallup poll suggesting clear majority support at 59%. Even C. Everett Koop, the former Reagan Surgeon General and anti-abortion activist, signaled his early support.[48]

Despite the early backing, three words and one hyphen in the Health Security Act stymied support for many evangelicals and Catholics – "pregnancy-related services." This phrase signaled that the Health Security Act would require coverage for abortions and, potentially, "morning after" pills. In fact, Hillary Clinton testified before a House committee, saying, "We don't want to add or subtract from the rights for services that are currently available. And in most instances where there is insurance coverage, pregnancy-related services has been deemed to include abortion where that is appropriate between a physician and a patient." Health and Human Services Secretary Donna Shalala also made clear that the administration sought to keep abortion services as part of the legislation.[49]

Conservatives, including some religious groups, were slow to rally around abortion as the mechanism for opposition. When the Heritage Foundation released its extensive critique of the plan, abortion coverage played a small role, buried within a thick report. Republican activist William Kristol, who led the organization Project for the Republican Future in 1993 and 1994, did not mention abortion when he delivered his proposed critiques to Republican leaders in December 1993.[50] *Christianity Today* featured an editorial that began with praise for the "ambitious" Clinton health care plan, seeking needed reform. While *Christianity Today* did not fully endorse the Health Security Act, calling for "something less ambitious and costly than the Clinton plan," it certainly did not doom the proposal for evangelicals.[51]

By contrast, the United States Catholic Conference, which first supported universal health care coverage in 1919, was quick to oppose the measure, and a number of evangelical and pro-life groups followed, though incrementally. The National Right to Life Committee quickly declared, "We are not against having pregnancy-related services in the basic benefits package. But Congress time and time again has recognized that abortion is different."[52]

In January, Southern Baptist and Catholic leaders testified before a House subcommittee, both arguing that while health reform is needed, the government should not subsidize abortion as part of a health care plan. Southern Baptist leader C. Ben Mitchell testified, "By making abortion a requirement of the comprehensive benefits package, health-care reform of the President's variety would compel every denomination and local congregation to either fund abortion or else break the law and suffer its penalties. Every congregation, as an employer, would be required to take money from the offering plate and offer it to abortionists."[53]

The Catholic Church printed 19 million postcards, encouraging parishioners to contact their legislations in opposition to abortion funding. In February, the

Christian Coalition, led by Ralph Reed, announced a $1.4 million campaign to oppose the Clinton heath proposal. As part of the campaign, the organization distributed 30,000 postcards for church attendees to send to Congress and initiated radio and print advertisements opposing the legislation. The Christian Coalition emphasized abortion, though focused heavily on reduced care and inflated bureaucracy and American opposition to socialism.[54] In April, an editorial in *Christianity Today* chastised evangelicals for being "remarkably quiet" about the Clinton health care reform plan. The editorial emphasized that the legislation would force the healthy to subsidize the sick, only tangentially mentioning that the plan would "also force Christians to pay for benefits such as mental health care, counseling for drug and alcohol abuse, and abortion services."[55]

Increasingly, evangelical organizations tied their opposition specifically to abortion, escalating their voice. The National Association of Evangelicals issued their first-ever statement on health care in 1994, passing a resolution on "Health Care Reform." The NAE opened by "welcom[ing] health care reform," suggesting principles to guide the debate. Its first principle was clear: "Abortion is not health care." The resolution went on, "Any health plan which includes coverage for elective abortion should be rejected. This includes abortion referral, payment for abortion, or the training of medical personnel for abortion practices." The second principle also emphasized the pro-life position: "Euthanasia should never be endorsed by government or surrogates."

Though the Clinton Health Security Act was on life support in the summer of 1994, the Southern Baptist Convention directly attacked the legislation on pro-life grounds at its annual meeting. Like the NAE, the SBC resolution conceded that there was a need for "revision in the health care delivery system in order to provide affordable care for all those in need," but it declared that President Clinton's plan was "morally objectionable." The resolution cited the absence of language that would forbid funding of abortion, the distribution of contraceptives to minors, potential for rationing of care, and "inadequate conscience clauses" to protect religious people from being required to deliver morally objectionable services (i.e., abortion).[56] While prominent Republicans emphasized cost, quality of care, and the growth of government,[57] religious organizations and leaders honed their opposition in pro-life terms, helping mobilize the Christian conservatives.

Evangelicals had coalesced around abortion in opposition to universal health care, shifting the early emphasis of oppositional efforts from Republicans and the Christian Coalition. As other legislative proposals were presented, anti-abortion concerns remained at the forefront for evangelicals. For example, in 1994, Representative Jim Cooper (D-TN) proposed a Managed Competition Act, which gained bipartisan support. Regarding abortion, however, the Cooper plan sought to remain "abortion neutral." Pro-life groups, including the SBC, NRLC, Family Research Council, Concerned Women for America, American Family Association, Christian Coalition, and Eagle Forum, stated they would oppose the plan unless it prohibited funding for abortion.[58] For evangelicals, the politics of abortion trumped health care policy.

After languishing in Congress, the Clinton Health Security Act officially perished in September 1994, when Senate Majority Leader George Mitchell (D-MA) declared it dead. Republicans presided over the burial, with their overwhelming success in the 1994 midterm elections. In a eulogy to the press, Hillary Clinton acknowledged that the administration was not prepared for the extent of the opposition, especially the direct mail and media advertisements that evangelical and conservative groups had used to combat the plan.[59] Many of these directly referenced the abortion issue.

Even after the demise of the Clinton health care proposal, pro-life objections were continually raised when evangelical leaders discussed national health care reform. For example, in 1998, when a journal for the liberal Center for Ethics (partially funded by the moderate Cooperative Baptist Fellowship) published an essay supporting national health care and expanded abortion rights, the SBC published a strong critique in *Baptist Press* of these policy proposals on religious and political grounds.[60] Even more directly, Richard Land, head of the Southern Baptist advocacy arm, the Ethics & Religious Liberty Commission, argued that *Roe v. Wade* had led to a "new ethic" where euthanasia and health care rationing could be acceptable. "The acceptance of *Roe v. Wade* by this society made Jack Kevorkian inevitable.... It made physician-assisted suicide inevitable. It made the rationing of health are to seriously ill and elderly and infirm people inevitable."[61] The pro-life concerns of abortion and end-of-life issues such as health care rationing were the primary issues with national health care reform.[62] The right to life had come to overshadow the right to health care.

Evangelicals and Contemporary Health Care Advocacy

While evangelicals have downplayed pro-health care advocacy since the 1980s, they did support reforms, at least in theory. Notably, in 2003, many faith leaders, including Richard Land of the SBC, joined together to encourage the federal government to tackle the "national dilemma" of health care. Land argued that Americans and Christians have a duty to care for the less fortunate. Stopping just short of calling health care an individual right, Land said "The Ethics & Religious Liberty Commission believes that a nation so blessed by God and so dedicated to the proposition that all men are created equal would decide that some among us should not have access to the basic building blocks of a better life."[63]

Evangelicals increasingly warmed to health care reform in the 2000s. In the George W. Bush administration, evangelical groups, including the ERLC, strongly supported the State Children's Health Insurance Program (SCHIP) legislation that expanded health care benefits to unborn children.[64] The SCHIP legislation was a means not only to promote health reform but also to expand the pro-life cause. Rather than being at odds, the pro-life mission and the health care mission supported each other with this endeavor. It also certainly helped that a Republican was in the White House.

In addition, *Christianity Today* positively covered the passage of Governor Mitt Romney's program requiring health insurance in Massachusetts in 2006. The pro-life Massachusetts Family Institute declared, "We are very pleased that Massachusetts is taking the lead on this issue. It is [about] reaching out to those who are impoverished, those who are in need, visiting those in the hospital, tending to the sick. It's all part of the great social mandate that we [Christians] have." SBC leader Richard Land was described as "laud[ing] the bill as an innovative attempt, at least, to address an important moral and human rights issue."[65] Perhaps health care as a right was returning to evangelicalism.

Further, in 2008, the editorial board of *Christianity Today* advocated for national health care reform, endorsing a prudent plan giving access to the marginalized but, importantly, protecting the freedom of conscience, especially avoiding an "insurance plan [that] makes all members subsidize abortions."[66] During the national debate over expanded health care in 2009 under the Democratic President Obama, evangelicals again came out in favor of reform. Evangelical leader Chuck Colson wrote an editorial in *Christianity Today* titled "We Need Health-Care Reform," calling Christians to advocate for reform under the principles of "human dignity, care for the poor, and prudence." Colson was especially troubled by the number of uninsured Americans, though he did not provide a direct policy recommendation. Instead, he and his coauthor offered guiding principles. While Colson did not mention abortion directly, he was particularly concerned about pro-life issues of rationing and euthanasia.[67]

Related, the ERLC produced a 2009 white paper: "Fifteen Principles for Successful Health Care Reform." The document opened with a strong statement that faithful Christians are "compel[led]" through biblical principles to "help our nation find a way to provide for the health care needs of all of our fellow citizens."[68] Yet, the organization opened by grounding its advocacy in a pro-life framework, stating that "our commitment to the sanctity of human life and love for our neighbor" necessitates health care reform. In fact, the "sanctity of life" is principle number one for the ERLC. The white paper also called for conservative, limited-government principles, including a rejection of a single-payer system (point three), the maintenance of provider competition (point six), and support for small, community-level innovations (point eight).[69] For most evangelicals, health reform was a good, but only after vouchsafing their anti-abortion commitments.

The Affordable Care Act and the Aftermath of Its Passage

Despite theoretical evangelical support of expanded health care, evangelicals strongly opposed President Obama's Affordable Care Act of 2010. As with the Clinton Health Security Act in 1993–1994, the persistent theme of evangelical opposition was abortion.

After Obama was elected president in 2008, health care reform was again on the agenda. Though evangelical leaders had recently been on record supporting health care reform, many prominent evangelical groups objected the health care actions of the Obama administration. SBC leader Richard Land opposed Kathleen Sebelius being appointed to head the Health and Human Services department because of her pro-choice record, and Americans United for Life called her "unfit" to lead HHS.[70] Though many of these organizations had supported the expansion of SCHIP to cover unborn children during the Bush administration, Southern Baptist leadership, for example, called an unrealized proposal to expand SCHIP under the Obama administration "universal health care by stealth" and a "Trojan horse."[71]

Despite resistance, President Obama continued to push for major health care reform. Prior to Obama's major health care speech in September 2009, Land encouraged him to include language in the legislation specifically excluding abortion.[72] After not getting the compromise from the president that they wanted, thirty conservative Christian leaders agreed to form the Freedom Federation, declaring that "abortion is not healthcare,"[73] harkening back to the *Christianity Today* editorial of 1993.

Abortion remained central to evangelical opposition to health care reform during the final stages of the legislative process. An op-ed in *Baptist Press* in November 2009 praised the bipartisan efforts of Democratic Representative Bart Stupak (D-MI) and Republican Representative Joe Pitts (R-PA) for securing an amendment that incorporated that Hyde Amendment language into the health care bill.[74] Tony Perkins of the Family Research Council supported Stupak's efforts as well,[75] and *Christianity Today* reported being positively "Stunned By Stupak" as the pro-life Democrats secured the anti-abortion language.[76]

Had the Stupak compromise remained, evangelicals may have yielded their strong opposition. At the last minute, however, Stupak and his Democratic allies withdrew their demand for the Hyde Amendment language, agreeing to an Obama Executive Order as a compromise to allow the passage of the Affordable Care Act. Pro-life leaders, from the National Right to Life Committee and Susan B. Anthony List to the FRC and the SBC, castigated the decision.[77] The SBC's Land declared, "Pro-lifers across the country are rightly both chagrined and disillusioned with Rep. Bart Stupak's cave-in on protecting unborn lives in the ObamaCare legislation that just passed." Land called Stupak's defense of the Executive Order "pathetic," comparing it to saying that "a bikini can cover the fat lady in the circus," because an executive order is an insufficient protection for the pro-life concerns.[78] Perkins of the FRC was also displeased. After Stupak announced his retirement shortly following the passage of the legislation, Perkins commented, "For two decades Rep. Bart Stupak stood firm for the pro-life cause. It is a shame that he will leave Congress remembered for his vote on the Obama health care bill, the largest abortion promoting piece of legislation in the last 30 years."[79] Following suite, the Susan

B. Anthony List retracted a "Defender of Life" award they had planned to give Stupak for his stance in the health care legislation.[80] The politics of abortion ignited fierce evangelical opposition to the ACA.

The Contraceptive Mandate and Hobby Lobby

Even after evangelicals and other pro-lifers lost the battle over the health care law, they continued to trot out pro-life objections to their rank-and-file. For example, the SBC scrutinized Donald Berwick, Obama appointee as an administrator for the Centers for Medicaid and Medicare Services, for suggesting that health care rationing could save the government money. Land stated that his appointment made life more dangerous for the elderly.[81]

The strongest pro-life critique following the passage of the Affordable Care Act, however, came following the HHS rule mandating that employers provide free contraceptives in their health plans. This contraceptive mandate was first attacked by pro-life Catholic organizations, which objected to the required provision of any contraceptives, as they violate Catholic doctrine. Catholic groups quickly framed the regulation as a violation of religious freedom. To start, evangelicals were less concerned because there is no doctrine of opposing contraceptives in their faith tradition. Yet, the inclusion of "morning after" pills in the HHS requirement mobilized pro-life evangelicals, as they believed that these contraceptives cause abortion by ending life after conception. Evangelicals had protested emergency contraception since these drugs emerged in the 1990s.[82]

Quickly, the pro-life perspective gained traction. The day the contraceptive mandate was formally announced, Land linked the two rights – religious liberty and right to life. "[HHS] Secretary Sebelius is stating that people who have religious convictions against contraceptives or particular type of contraceptives that are abortifacients will have a one-year reprieve before they will be forced to pay for health insurance for that which they find unconscionable."[83]

Evangelicals were slower to mobilize on the contraceptive mandate, but the pro-life issue helped frame the importance for them. Evangelical objections to the mandate almost always referenced the "morning after" pills and the abortion issue. During the comment stage on the proposed HHS contraceptive mandate, the Southern Baptist ERLC filed a comment objecting to the HHS plan. The ERLC cited the "SBC's long history of opposing abortion and supporting religious freedom." In the comment, the ERLC distinguished its position on contraception from Catholics, though it declared that "the overwhelming majority of Southern Baptists do, however, object to the use of 'emergency contraception,' which can result in the abortion of a human embryo." It concluded its comment by declaring that the contraceptive mandate "is the first time the government has forced pro-life citizens to fund, directly or indirectly, insurance coverage for abortion-causing activities. This is an egregious abuse of federal power."[84] The ERLC was appealing to the heritage of the Hyde Amendment.

The National Association of Evangelicals urged the Obama administration to drop the HHS rule on "contraceptive and abortifacient coverage" in an official policy statement. The NAE framed their objection in terms of religious liberty, but the importance of abortion was unmistakable.[85] In addition, nearly sixty evangelical leaders sent a joint letter to President Obama in December 2012 opposing the HHS mandate for its impact on the conscience of religious organizations. They wanted to be clear that the contraceptive mandate, because of its coverage of the "morning after" pills, was not only a concern for Catholics.[86] Many Republicans joined the effort too, with Representative Steve Scalise (R-LA) gathering 154 cosigners to urge the Obama administration to reverse its policy,[87] though early Republican efforts were more muted than those of the evangelical and Catholic activists.[88]

HHS and the Obama administration, while providing some compromises, persisted in requiring non-church employers to provide all FDA-approved contraceptives. Many affected religious organizations prepared to challenge this in federal court. The Becket Fund for Religious Liberty, a religious legal advocacy group, began equipping to defend religious institutions. In doing so, it declared, "Religious colleges, universities, and hospitals will never pay for abortion drugs in violation of their religious beliefs – this year or any other year."[89]

Dozens of Catholic organizations, including the University of Notre Dame and Catholic University, were quick to challenge the HHS requirements.[90] In July 2012, they were joined by Wheaton College, arguably the most prominent evangelical college in America. Wheaton argued that the HHS rule "runs roughshod over Wheaton's religious beliefs ... by forcing them to provide insurance coverage for abortifacient drugs."[91] The SBC's insurance and pension provider, GuideStone Financial Resources, also objected to the contraceptive mandate, directly citing abortion. In a message at the annual SBC convention, GuideStone's president declared that it will "never allow this administration to tell us that we have to provide abortive drugs like morning-after-pills or provide for same-sex marriages."[92] After first stating that it would seek a legislative remedy, GuideStone too filed suit in 2013, winning an injunction against the mandate.

In total, 140 evangelical and Catholic plaintiffs filed 56 cases opposing the contraceptive mandate, yet the most high-profile case came from the evangelical owners of the Hobby Lobby retail chain.[93] The Green family operated Hobby Lobby "in a manner consistent with Biblical principles," and because of this they objected to providing four of the twenty forms of contraception the HHS mandate required, all of which, they felt, violated their religious faith of opposing abortion. Facing stiff penalties for refusing to comply, the Green family brought their case to federal court, eventually resulting in a monumental case before the U.S. Supreme Court, *Burwell v. Hobby Lobby* (2014).

The end of the chapter returns to this case, along with the other legal challenges to the 2010 Affordable Care Act, but the trajectory of evangelical health care advocacy is clear. While Republicans have opposed national health care plans, arguing that such policies are expensive, inefficient, and socialist, these arguments alone did not motivate evangelical opposition to health care. Rather, abortion brought evangelicals (and some Catholics) into the anti–health care fold. The politics of abortion, and its rights-based elements, were effective antidotes to the pro–health care emphases of Christianity. The right to life trumped the right to health care, and this has remained the central concern of evangelical health care advocacy, as seen in the 2010 Affordable Care Act and the proceeding HHS Contraceptive Mandate.

ABORTION, HEALTH CARE, AND SURVEY DATA

The history of evangelical health care advocacy shows that abortion politics played an important role as evangelicals shifted from being ambivalent to greater levels of national health care – even at times affirming a right to health care – to being an opponent of the major national health care initiatives. In the past twenty years, the most prominent evangelical organizations have formally opposed major national health care reform, even though some of these same evangelicals had supported national health care plans in the 1970s. From an advocacy standpoint, evangelicals' general commitment to the right to life trumped any, often tepid, support for caring for the needy through expanded health care. Evangelical leaders utilized pro-life positions to gain support for their opposition, targeting government leaders, other evangelical advocacy organizations, and rank-and-file members. This still leaves an important question. Did rank-and-file evangelicals connect pro-life politics with health care opposition, or is this merely an elite phenomenon? In what follows, I marshal two data sets, Southern Baptist Clergy from 1980 to 2008 and the General Social Survey from 1975 to 2014, to help answer these questions.

The opinions of the clergy largely mirror the advocacy efforts of evangelical organizations. Recall that Figure 5.2 shows that in 1988 more SBC clergy favored national health care than opposed it. This position switched between 1992 and 1996. Following the Clinton health care plan, more SBC clergy opposed national health insurance, and the gap widened every year through 2008.

The responses of rank-and-file evangelicals are similar, though not nearly as stark. Largely evangelicals in the pews mirrored the national population's views on health care until 2008, though slightly more opposed to more government provision. Figure 5.3 zooms in on the divergence between evangelicals and non-evangelicals in the GSS, with the vertical, gray tick marks identifying the standard errors for each survey year. Though there is little substantive difference in views between 1980 and 1988, evangelicals are more conservative on health care. After a downturn in opposition, evangelicals are significantly more opposed to the national government providing health care following the Clinton election in 1992. This opposition again narrows during the George W. Bush years (2000–2008), before a wide gap between evangelicals and others

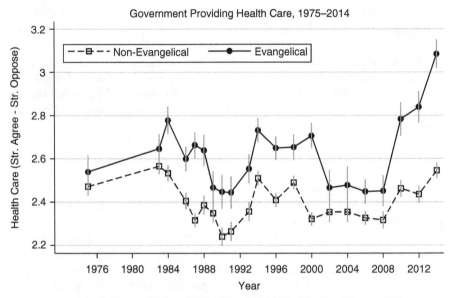

FIGURE 5.3. Gap in Evangelical and Non-Evangelical Health Care Views. GSS, 1975–2014.

develops from 2008 to 2014 corresponding with the Affordable Care Act and the aftermath of its implementation.

What explains the widening gap in the GSS data and the switch in preferences in the clergy data? The qualitative research on health care political and legal advocacy indicates that abortion politics has been a driving factor of evangelical opposition to national health care proposals, though party politics matter too. Analyses of the survey data provide insight for the rank-and-file and the clergy.

The descriptive statistics show that the clergy, and also the rank-and-file (especially since 2008), agree with much of the evangelical advocacy efforts to oppose health care reform. And the trend toward opposing reform seems to follow evangelicals' views on abortion, as evangelicals have become increasingly opposed to abortion. In fact, as shown in Figure 5.4, health care attitudes and abortion attitudes are increasingly correlated for evangelicals over time. Before the dawn of the Clinton health plan in 1993, rank-and-file evangelicals' health care attitudes are essentially uncorrelated with their abortion attitudes, but this connection develops with a dramatic rise in average correlations after 1992. After 2008, with the introduction of the Affordable Care Act and the controversy over contraceptive coverage, the average correlation is even higher, with a peak (0.29) in 2010. All the while, the correlation between non-evangelicals' health care and abortion attitudes are fairly stable, rising only slightly in the post-1992 years. Even after 2008, the average correlation of non-evangelicals'

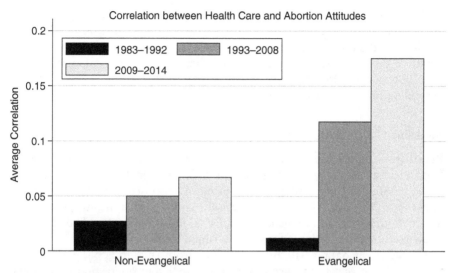

FIGURE 5.4. Correlation between Abortion and Health Care Attitudes among Evangelicals and Non-Evangelicals. GSS, 1983–2014.

abortion and health care attitudes is only slightly higher, and it remains less than half of the evangelical correlation.

The clergy data follows the trend from the GSS, as the correlations grow from 1988 to 2008, though less starkly. The correlation between abortion and health care spikes from 0.16 to 0.31 between 1988 and 1996, signaling that the Clinton health care plan helped bring these issues together for the clergy. Unfortunately, the clergy data end prior to the controversial Affordable Care Act.

While the correlations provide evidence of an increasing relationship between abortion and health care over time for evangelicals, more is needed to analyze these effects. To thoroughly gauge whether a relationship exists between abortion and health care, I created statistical models that test the relationships in the clergy data and the GSS, while controlling for partisan, ideological, religious, and demographic factors. Appendix A provides the methodological details for the models. For the clergy, support for an anti-abortion amendment and party identification are the key independent variables. The models also include a measure of ideology that is less correlated with abortion – support of government social services,[94] the party of the president at the time of the survey, a scale of orthodox religious beliefs, secular and seminary education measures, church size, age, and survey year. For the rank-and-file, separate variables for a respondent's religious affiliation are included, with unaffiliated as the comparison category. For my purposes, evangelical affiliation, party ID, and an anti-abortion scale are the key independent variables. The rank-and-file models also include a measure of ideology similar to the clergy models – support for government spending on social services, as well as church attendance, education, age, gender, race, having children, and survey year. In all the models, variables are coded in the conservative direction (low to high). Controlling for the political party of the sitting president helps account for the possibility that attitudes might change depending on who proposes the reform.

Modeling Clergy Opposition to Health Care

Recall from Figure 5.2 earlier in this chapter that the majority of Southern Baptist clergy supported government-provided national health insurance in 1988, before switching and becoming primarily opposed to such a plan in the mid-1990s. This switch happened precisely as the Clinton health plan gained national attention and evangelical (and Republican) criticism spiked. The data allow consideration of what factors contribute to this switch.

For the clergy data for all the survey years from 1988 to 2008, party ID and ideology stand out as the primary factors predicting opposition to national health care. Table 5.1 in Appendix B presents the results in full. The ideological opinions have the largest effect on opposing national health insurance, with the pastors opposing the government fixing social problems being the most likely to also oppose national health care. This makes intuitive sense, as it is quite similar to national health care, where the government is providing health care as a social service. Clergy who identify more strongly with the Republican Party are also more likely to oppose health care, as are those with more education and from bigger churches. The partisan nature of the issue is clear. As for abortion, the key theme in the qualitative findings, the data support that, while controlling for the other political and demographic factors, favoring an anti-abortion amendment produces greater opposition to national health insurance. The full model also suggests, in line with the general trends, that clergy are less supportive of national health care over time. Perhaps, as the correlations suggest, the relationship to abortion is more significant over time.

To investigate the role of time in the models, I split the data into two separate time periods, before and after the Clinton health care proposal (1988–1992 and 1996–2008). Again, these results are presented in Table 5.1 in Appendix B. For most of the independent variables, the relationship to clergy's attitudes about national heath insurance is consistent between the time periods. Clergy who identify as more Republican and who oppose the government solving social problems are stable in their opposition to health care. The demographic factors remain insignificant. There is a change, however, in the relationship between abortion and health care in the time periods. Prior to 1993, there is no significant relationship between abortion and health care, but this emerges in the 1996–2008 period,[95] with those more opposed to abortion also being more opposed to national health insurance. There is a similar movement among religious beliefs, with the more orthodox becoming more opposed to government-provided health insurance.

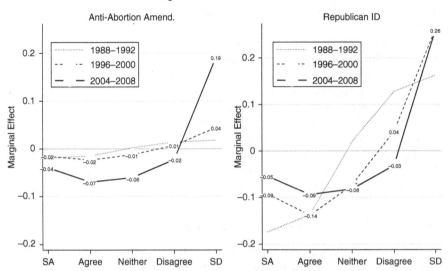

FIGURE 5.5. Marginal Effects of Support for Anti-Abortion Amendment and More Republican Party ID on Clergy's Health Care Attitudes. Ordered Logistic Regression Models. SBC Clergy, 1988–2008.

The models from the later period also suggest that opposition to national health insurance grows over time, as the survey year variable is statistically significant. To investigate this increasing relationship further, I broke down the data into three two-survey periods: 1988–1992, 1996–2000, and 2004–2008. The most recent period even more strongly supports the growing relationship between abortion and health care attitudes among Southern Baptist pastors.[96] While the effects of party and ideology on health care opinions remain constant across the data, the effect of abortion grows in the later period with opposition to abortion more strongly predicting opposition to national health insurance.

The change in the effect of abortion attitudes on opposition to national health insurance over time can be seen is Figure 5.5. The figure compares the marginal effect of support for an anti-abortion amendment and individual party identification. The lines in each graph track the marginal effect of the independent variable for each category of opposition to national health insurance, when opinion moves from the lowest to highest levels in the abortion and party ID items (strongly oppose to strongly support an anti-abortion amendment and strong Democrat to strong Republican). For party identification, on the right, the slope of the lines for all three time periods is essentially the same. While the effects of partisanship and ideology are strong and constant, the effects of abortion grow in strength. The dashed line (1996–2000) in the left panel is stronger than the dotted gray line (1988–1992), but the difference is especially clear with the solid, black line in the 2004–2008 period. This fits with evangelical organizations and elites increasingly opposing health care proposals because of abortion. In fact by 2004–2008, abortion views have a similar, though smaller, effect as partisanship does on health care attitudes for the clergy.

To summarize the clergy data, as the SBC became more conservative and more Republican in the 1980s and 1990s, its clergy were less likely to support government provided health insurance. But this change occurs later compared to partisanship regarding other political issues, as the majority of pastors did not switch their views until the 1992–1996 period. Abortion seems to be a trigger, as it plays an important and growing role in clergy's views, tracking with the public statements of evangelical elites and organizations. Unfortunately, I do not have data for the clergy following the 2010 Affordable Care Act or the high-profile Hobby Lobby Supreme Court case, but I expect that this would have made the pro-life issue more salient to the pastors.

Modeling Rank-and-File Opposition to Health Care

While the clergy flipped their views on national health insurance from 1988 to 1996, evangelical respondents in the GSS did not have nearly as drastic a change. Since 1983, evangelicals have been slightly more conservative on health care than non-evangelicals, but, as Figure 5.4 shows, that gap has grown since the mid-1990s. Statistical models suggest that abortion politics plays an important role in this shift.

To assess opinion on government providing health care over time, I created a full model for all GSS survey years from 1983 to 2014 and two models that split the time period before and after the introduction of the Clinton health care proposal (1983–1992 and 1993–2014).[97] The results of all the models are in Table 5.2 in Appendix B.

In each time period, evangelicals are more opposed to government-provided health care than seculars are, as are mainline Protestants. As expected, Republicans and those ideologically opposed to government spending are also more likely to oppose health care. Public opinion is also less favorable when Democrats are in office, likely because this is when the issue is most salient. Healthier and older individuals are more likely to oppose health care, as are whites.

As for abortion, once more the time period matters. Like the clergy data, there is a growing relationship between opposing abortion and opposing the government providing health care, while the partisan and ideological relationships are constant. In the full model containing all years from 1983 to 2014, being pro-life has a statistically significant relationship predicting opposition to health care, but this model obscures the over-time change in effect. In the pre-Clinton years, there is no significant relationship between abortion and health care, but this develops in the post-1992 models. In fact, this relationship only grows during the Obama administration.

Figure 5.6 shows the changes in the effects of some of the key independent variables in the pre- and post-1993 periods. In the top panel, it is clear that

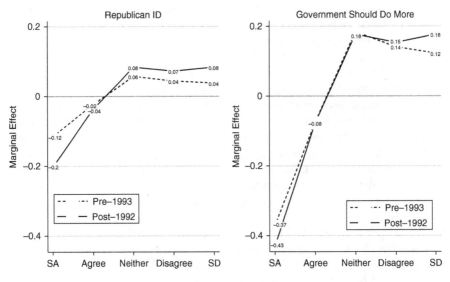

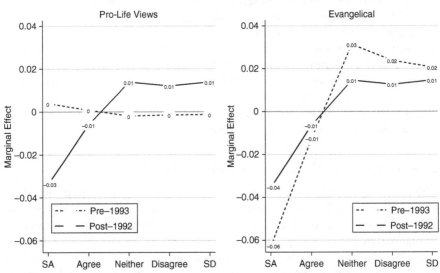

FIGURE 5.6. Marginal Effects of Key Independent Variables on Health Care Attitudes. Ordered Logistic Regression Models. GSS, 1983–2014.

one's ideological position about how active the government should be in social service spending (upper right) has the greatest effect on health care attitudes, with those most opposed to government spending being disfavored to the government paying for health care. Partisan identification too has a strong effect. Yet, like the clergy data, it is clear that these marginal effects remain fairly consistent before and after the Clinton health plan, with the slopes of the lines and the marginal effects being nearly identical.

In the bottom right panel, being evangelical has a smaller though statistically significant effect in both periods. This marginal effect is also fairly consistent in its slope, though stronger in the pre-1993 period. Abortion, however, is the outlier (bottom left). The marginal effects are flat and insignificant prior to 1993, growing to become statistically significant in the latter, post-1992 period. While the rank-and-file's view of abortion is less important than partisanship and ideology, it becomes a more important factor as religious organizations and elites are justifying their opposition to national health care initiatives in anti-abortion terms. Elite messages, whether from television, newspapers, religious outlets, or pulpits, resonated with the rank-and-file. Party politics certainly mattered, but abortion appears to be an effective trigger to activate opposition.

While being more pro-life has an increased correlation with opposing national health care since 1993 and being an evangelical yields more opposition to health care in both periods, these two variables do not work in concert for the rank-and-file. There is no interactive effect pertaining just to evangelicals. Evangelicals more strongly opposed to abortion are not more strongly opposed to health care reform than other pro-lifers are. Likewise, pro-life evangelicals are not more strongly opposed to health reform than pro-choice evangelicals are. Rather, these variables have independent effects. The pro-life effect on opposition to government-provided health care is not localized in evangelicalism, but the public seems to be responding to the linking of abortion and health care, which was often led by evangelical elites and activists. The right to life appears to combat the right to health care in the public, as it did in the examination of evangelical elites and organizations.

Experimenting with Abortion and Opposition to Health Care

The longitudinal data from the clergy and the rank-and-file suggest that abortion has increasingly become a wedge issue, driving evangelicals away from national health care reform. This comports with the qualitative findings, as evangelical advocacy groups enhanced their opposition to health care as abortion coverage became integral to national health policy. While evangelical leaders were wary of engaging on the prudence of health care policy before the 1990s, they increasingly attacked these policies for their support for abortion beginning with the Clinton plan in 1993 and continuing to the Obama plan in 2010. The combination of the qualitative elite findings and the quantitative survey findings suggest that elites were able to reframe the issue of health care in the terms of abortion to mobilize evangelical opposition.

To further verify the impact of reframing opposition to national health reform because of opposition to abortion, my colleagues and I conducted a survey experiment in June 2015. We conducted this experiment with an online panel of 1,500 evangelicals obtained through the survey company Survey Sampling International. Evangelicals were obtained in two ways. Half of them were secured by screening for people affiliated with an evangelical denomination, and the other half were secured by screening for people who identified as born-again Christians. We administered a survey experiment about health care to half of the sample, administering an experiment about free speech to the other half, as discussed in Chapter 3.

For those who received the health care experiment, individuals were randomly assigned to receive one of three prompts from a "local minister" opposing a "national health insurance program." The first opposed health care in anti-abortion terms, with the minister saying, "I oppose abortion, and every national health care proposal for the past 25 years has expanded and funded the abortion industry." I refer to this as the Anti-Abortion Frame. The second also opposed health care citing abortion, but instead engages in the right-to-life formulation of arguing for the rights of the unborn. In the second, the minister states, "Decisions about health care should be guided by our understanding of rights. I am pro-life, and every national health proposal for the past 25 years opposes the right to life of the unborn by expanding and funding the abortion industry." I refer to this as the Right to Life Fame. In the final prompt, the minister merely says, "I oppose creating a national health insurance program." I refer to this as the Control Frame.

After receiving one of the three prompts, the survey takers were then asked two questions. First, they rated how persuasive the minister's comments were on a 0–10 scale. On the whole, evangelicals rated the persuasiveness at 5.01 out of 10. This suggests more evangelical support for national health care coverage than popular media accounts might reflect. The Right to Life frame was viewed as the most persuasive (5.60), while the Control Fame was the least persuasive (4.20).

Second, respondents were asked about their opinion regarding health care policy. They were presented with four options: (1) federal government directly provides health insurance; (2) federal government requires individuals to obtain health insurance, while offering subsidies; (3) federal government provides funding to states to assist people in gaining coverage; (4) federal government should not be involved in providing health coverage. They were also able to select that they did not know or had no opinion.

Surprisingly, evangelicals had quite a bit of variation in their health care views. At 29%, a plurality selected that the government should not be involved in health care, though 25% selected the single-payer option and 24% selected that states should manage health insurance with federal subsidies. Only 12% selected the individual mandate approach that the 2010 Affordable Care Act prescribes, while 9% offered no opinion. There is little variation across treatment groups, except that fewer people selected the most liberal, single-payer option after receiving the Anti-Abortion Frame.

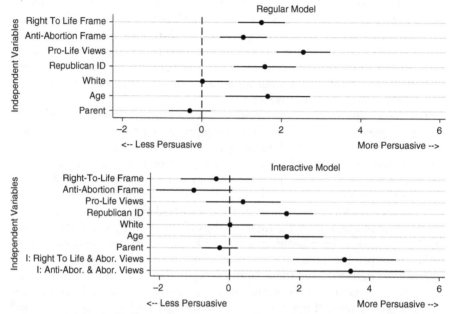

FIGURE 5.7. Marginal Effects of Persuasiveness of Frames in Opposition to Health Care. Linear Regression Models with Standardized Coefficients and 95% Confidence Intervals. SSI Evangelical, 2015.

These initial results suggest that the while the frames may enhance persuasiveness, they have less effect on policy positions, at least in this isolated test. Analyzing more thorough models with multiple variables provides more robust results. As such, I investigate regression models that compare the effects of the frames on persuasiveness and health care attitude. I also include two political controls (party ID and abortion attitudes) and three demographic control variables (race, age, and being a parent), as these were not randomly distributed across the frames. In addition, I investigate interactive effects to see if the frames had different effects on different people with different attitudes. The full models are in Table 5.3 in Appendix B, and the results of randomization on the demographic variables are in Table 3.4.

The results of the persuasiveness models are displayed graphically in Figure 5.7. The black circles represent the marginal effects, with the black bars identifying the confidence intervals. If the bars do not overlap with the vertical, dashed line, then the effect is statistically significant.

As the top panel shows, both the Right to Life and the Anti-Abortion Frames are more persuasive than the Control Frame, with the rights-based, pro-life justification being stronger. Those who are more Republican, more pro-life, and older are also more likely to view the anti–health care statements

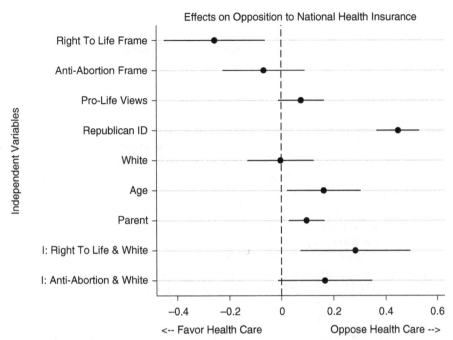

FIGURE 5.8. Marginal Effects of Frames on Opposition to Health Care. Logistic Regression Model with Standardized Effects and 90% Confidence Intervals. SSI Evangelical, 2015.

as more persuasive. The bottom panel adds interactive effects between the frames and people's views of abortion (the only interactions that were statistically significant). Since the frames do not function independently in this panel, the bottom two marginal effects points are of primary interest. The strong, positive effect for both interactions identify that those who are more opposed to abortion are more likely to view the frames as persuasive. This makes intuitive sense, since the justifications are in abortion terms, but it is important to understand that religious elites can prime positive responses by tapping into people's views on abortion.

To more simplistically model health care policy, I collapsed the four response options into two options, either favoring (0) or opposing (1) a version of national health insurance. The models are in Table 5.3 in Appendix B. Regarding health care policy, the frames have no direct, independent impact. But there is an important contingent effect. The abortion arguments for opposing national health insurance are especially effective on white evangelicals, as compared to nonwhite evangelicals. The bottom two effects in Figure 5.8 show that the minister's Right to Life justification for opposing abortion has a strong, significant effect in white evangelicals opposing national health insurance, only trailing party identification. The Anti-Abortion justification is also suggestive,

though it fails to achieve typical standards of statistical significance ($p = 0.13$).
Clergy framing of the health care opposition as a pro-life position is likely to be
effective, particularly for white evangelicals. This solidifies the longitudinal
public opinion and historical evidence presented earlier in the chapter.

ABORTION AND HEALTH CARE LEGAL CHALLENGES

The survey data suggest that the abortion issue has become a growing reason
why evangelicals oppose national health care reform efforts. Along with partisanship and ideology, abortion has come to define the debate for the right. This
corresponds well with the way elite evangelical advocates frame health care
topics. Their opposition is almost always couched in pro-life terms. This
presents a final question. How would evangelical leaders respond if abortion
was removed from the health care debate? Would they engage or stay on the
sidelines? The three Supreme Court challenges to the Affordable Care Act
between 2012 and 2015 provide insight into these questions.

The greatest challenge to the constitutionality of the Affordable Care Act
came in the 2012 Supreme Court case *National Federation of Independent
Businesses (NFIB) v. Sebelius*. In the case, NFIB argued that the Affordable
Care Act's central mechanism, the "individual mandate" that required individuals to purchase health insurance or face a penalty, was an unconstitutional
violation of the U.S. Congress's powers. The plaintiffs argued that while
Congress has the power under Article 1 of the U.S. Constitution to "regulate
commerce," it may not require individuals to engage in commerce.

NFIB was organized and championed by several conservative and libertarian organizations and scholars, but conservative Christian groups were largely
absent. Certainly these organizations were opposed to the Affordable Care Act;
they had lobbied against it in Congress, but most of them did not engage in the
legal challenges.

Only two religious right groups filed *amicus* briefs in the case: the American
Center for Law and Justice and the Family Research Council. The ACLJ, in
particular, is one of the religious legal organizations most ingrained in broader
conservative legal advocacy, having networks with the Federalist Society.[98]
When these organizations justified their activity to their constituents, they
clearly implicated the abortion issue. The ACLJ proclaimed, "Federal funds
should never be spent for elective abortions."[99] Following the Supreme Court's
June 2012 decision to uphold the law as valid under Congress's taxing powers,
a chagrined FRC declared that the individual mandate is "only one section
among hundreds of provisions that will force taxpayers to fund abortions."[100]

The Supreme Court heard another legal challenge in 2015 regarding the
constitutionality of the Affordable Care Act, *King v. Burwell*. In *King*, challen-
gers argued that the health insurance tax credits offered by the Affordable
Care Act are only valid when they are set up by states, not when offered by
the federal government, as was the case in thirty-four states. *King* was a

more technical case than *NFIB*, with longer odds. But like *NFIB*, there was little religious engagement. The ACLJ was the only prominent conservative Christian group to file an *amicus* brief.[101] Following the Court's ruling in the summer of 2015 to uphold the Affordable Care Act, the FRC delivered a critical press release, again linking the health care law to abortion. "Obamacare subsidizes abortion," said the FRC. "Americans should not be forced to pay for other people's abortions."[102]

Notably, in the two direct legal challenges to the Affordable Care Act, nearly all of evangelicalism stayed on the sidelines, with the exception of two of the most conservative advocacy organizations that also had ties to the broader conservative legal movement.[103] And when mainstream evangelical groups chose to engage in the Supreme Court cases, they justified their involvement to their constituents by citing abortion.

The lack of activity in *NFIB* and *King* pales in comparison to the flurry of evangelical advocacy in *Burwell v. Hobby Lobby*, the case brought seeking to limit the HHS contraception mandate. *Hobby Lobby* was explicitly about the two hallmarks of modern, rights-based evangelical advocacy: abortion and religious freedom. Fifty-nine *amicus* briefs were submitted in favor of the Christian retailer, with approximately 60% explicitly involving religious organizations or individuals. A broad swath of evangelical organizations submitted or joined *amicus* briefs supporting the craft chain, including the National Association of Evangelicals, the Southern Baptist Convention, the Christian Legal Society, the Liberty Institute, the Ethics & Public Policy Center, Prison Fellowship, Eagle Forum, the ACLJ, and the FRC. They also were joined by major Mormon and Catholic organizations. In highlighting their involvement to both the Court and their constituents, these groups consistently emphasized their objection to abortion and their support for religious freedom. For example, the NAE declared in its press release that Hobby Lobby does not "object to contraception generally" only to "so-called 'morning after' drugs that may act as abortifacients." The NAE's president asserted, "Business owners in America should be able to run their businesses according to their religious faith and values."[104]

While the leadership of most evangelical advocacy organizations surely opposed the Affordable Care Act, as did many of their constituents, they appear to be constrained in their advocacy approach on health care. The politics of abortion is the switch that initiates their effort, allowing these advocates to engage an issue generally thought to be outside of their domain. The linkage between abortion and health care has grown among both the elites and the rank-and-file over the past four decades, but the absence of abortion politics makes less likely.

CONCLUSION

In the practice of health care, the Hippocratic Oath, "First, do no harm," looms large as a foundational principle. In fact, this quote comes not from the Hippocratic Oath, but from *The History of Epidemics*, a part of the fifth-century BC Hippocratic corpus. The actual Hippocratic Oath is less pithy in its covenant between physician, God, and patient. Yet part of the original Oath references abortion, stating: "I will neither give a deadly drug to anybody who asked for it, or will I make a suggestion to this effect. *Similarly I will not give to a woman an abortive remedy*. In purity and holiness I will guard my life and my art" (emphasis mine).[105]

This is a reminder that considerations of abortion have long been a part of health care principles. Following *Roe v. Wade,* this has become all the more evident. It is nearly impossible to disentangle government provided health care coverage from abortion. Because of this, the politics of abortion have come to override health care reform for evangelicals. Drawing on the Hippocratic Oath, evangelicals' foundational principle may be thought of as: First, do no harm to the unborn. In health care politics, evangelicals have engaged in rights claiming. The rights of the unborn and the rights of conscience have trumped the right to health care, bringing evangelicals into the conservative coalition against expanded government health care.

6

Whose Rights

Abortion Politics, Victims, and Offenders in the Death Penalty Debate

On Patriot's Day, April 15, 2013, two brothers detonated homemade bombs at the finish line of the Boston Marathon, terminating the New England holiday. Across the nation, spring tranquility transitioned to terror as the public watched in distress the citywide hunt for the attackers, Dzhokhar and Tamerlan Tsarnaev. Television and social media gripped the nation while the events unfolded. Surveillance images of the brothers were released to the public; the Tsarnaev brothers shot a Massachusetts Institute of Technology security officer and carjacked a resident. A gunfight between the police and the brothers broke out, where Tamerlan was killed and Dzhokar escaped. The next evening, Dzhokar was captured aboard a family's winterized boat.

The events and the terror remained in the public consciousness for the next year, as the story was relived as the Boston Red Sox advanced to win baseball's 2013 World Series and runners and supporters redeemed the 2014 Boston Marathon. The second anniversary, however, brought a different debate. In January 2015, the federal trial of Dzhokar Tsarnaev began with jury selection, followed by opening statements in March. On April 8, 2015, Tsarnaev was found guilty on thirty counts. The federal prosecutors urged the court to sentence Tsarnaev with the death penalty, and on May 15 the jury agreed.

During the process, the "Boston Bomber" trial re-exposed a national debate about capital punishment. In fact, the death penalty seemed to be on trial in 2015, and there was a hung jury in the court of public opinion. Despite the Tsarnaev verdict, several signs pointed toward waning support for the death penalty. The Connecticut Supreme Court declared the death penalty unconstitutional under the state's constitution, and Pennsylvania Governor Tom Wolfe issued a moratorium on capital punishment in the Keystone State. More surprising, a diverse coalition of fiscal conservatives, religious conservatives, and humanitarian liberals joined forces to ban the death penalty in Nebraska, even overriding Governor Pete Ricketts's veto.[1] Further, 2015 saw the fewest instances of capital punishment since the U.S. Supreme Court halted the practice for four years between 1972 and 1976, in part due to the low availability of execution drugs.

Broadly, the public was experiencing reservations. Public support for the death penalty seemed to have peaked in the mid-1990s, falling to the lowest levels in more than forty years in 2015.[2] In their extensive study of public opinion and the death penalty, Frank Baumgartner and his colleagues show that the public discovery of innocent people on death row, brought to light through media accounts, advocacy work, and politicians' responses, has altered the landscape, causing more to oppose capital punishment.[3] Advocates for abolition of the death penalty have been successful in framing the issue in light of innocence.

The Boston Bomber trial and sentencing worked against this trend, however, especially at first. Dzhokhar Tsarnaev was clearly guilty, so the concerns about sentencing a guilty person to death (the innocence frame) failed to apply. Perhaps related, shortly after the bombing, a Washington Post-ABC News poll found that 70% supported the death penalty for Tsarnaev.[4] This strong support eroded, however, with only a small majority of Americans preferring the death penalty instead of life in prison for Tsarnaev at the time of the sentencing.[5] The *Boston Globe* too reported deteriorating support for the death penalty in the Northeast,[6] though a CNN poll reported a 10% jump in support for the death penalty among residents of the Northeast when polled specifically about Tsarnaev, as compared to general support for the death penalty the year prior.[7] This suggests that public opinion about the death penalty is particularly prone to external effects, such as the Boston bombing. The eroding of effects also suggests that something more than innocence is driving opposition to the death penalty.

RELIGION AND THE DEATH PENALTY

At its heart, the political debate over capital punishment is about justice, morality, and rights. In regard to the death penalty, American society has often looked to religion, particularly Christianity, to help ground the justice requirements and the moral dimensions. Because of this, for decades religious elites have been at the center of the debate, staking claims both for and against capital punishment. Even in the case of Tsarnaev, many major news outlets, such as the *LA Times*, the *Washington Post*, and CNN, featured articles about the religious perspective about sentencing him to death, and there were vocal supporters on both sides.

For most of modern Western history, Christianity has supported capital punishment. Yet, some religious traditions have been strongly connected to the abolition movement, even prior to the rise of the innocence frame. For the past half-century, mainline Protestant denominations and the Catholic Church have been leading opponents of capital punishment, though the rank-and-file do not always mirror the church leadership. Evangelical Protestantism too has had some abolitionists, especially from its more pacifist traditions, though this has typically been a small minority.[8] The overwhelming majority of evangelicals have supported the death penalty, however, at least in theory if not always in practice.

Still, within American religion, there too has been declining support for the death penalty, though there remains a religious divide. Can this only be explained by the emergence of the innocence concept, or, as the Tsarnaev case suggests, is there more going on with capital punishment? More specifically, how does the growing religious rights culture affect positions on the death penalty?

Many empirical scholars have examined the effect of religion on public support for capital punishment. Some have found a relationship between fundamentalism,[9] church attendance,[10] and biblical literalism and support for the death penalty.[11] Others suggest that the primary differences in death penalty support are not among the religious, but between the religious and the nonreligious.[12] Some find that orthodox Protestants are more likely to attribute wrongdoing to individual choices, not societal circumstances, leading to support for capital punishment.[13] Despite this attention to the relationship between religion and capital punishment, there has been little consideration given to elite-level framing and the connection between the religious rank-and-file and religious advocacy leaders.[14]

Competing Christian Arguments Regarding Capital Punishment

Both supporters and abolitionists are focused on justice, and in particular the value of human life, but their focus is oriented on different actors in the criminal justice system. Supporters of capital punishment focus on victims, seeking retribution for the loss of their life, while opponents focus on offenders, seeking to protect their human dignity. This is demonstrated in the way they approach the Bible.

Those who support the death penalty turn to Genesis 9, God's covenant with Noah. Genesis records God saying, "Whoever sheds human blood, by humans shall their blood be shed; for in the image of God has God made mankind" (Genesis 9:6). This is supplemented by Romans 13, which outlines the relationship between Christians and governing authorities. Romans 13:4 seems to justify the state's use of capital punishment, declaring: "But if you do wrong, be afraid, for rulers do not bear the sword for no reason. They are God's servants, agents of wrath to bring punishment to the wrongdoer" (Romans 13:4).

Christian leaders who oppose the death penalty also point to the Bible, though focusing on how it treats offenders. In Jesus' famed "Sermon on the Mount," he calls his followers to "not resist an evil person" and, if slapped on the right check, to "turn to them the other cheek also" (Matthew 5:39).

Additionally, Jesus refrained from applying a capital punishment to a woman caught in adultery, instead asking, "Let any one of you who is without sin be the first to throw a stone at her" (John 1:7) and then saying, after her accusers had departed, "Then neither do I condemn you" (John 1:11). Abolitionists also point to God's punishment for Cain after he murdered his brother Abel in Genesis 4. Rather than enacting the death penalty, as Genesis 9 would suggest, God cursed Cain to a life of restless wandering (Genesis 4:12).

While evangelicals have traditionally been the staunchest religious proponents of capital punishment, of late there has even been some formal opposition to the death penalty from evangelical circles. In March 2015, the National Latino Evangelical Coalition urged its member congregations to oppose the death penalty.[15] Younger evangelicals have also been shown to be less supportive,[16] and some younger evangelical elites have taken prominent positions supporting abolition. Evangelical author and leader of the new monastic movement, Shane Claiborne, is one of the most prominent young advocates for abolition,[17] leading its advance. Other more established organizations, such as the evangelical group Prison Fellowship, have long opposed the current death penalty procedures in the United States,[18] with many of their leaders seeking abolition.[19] Perhaps most importantly, in October 2015, the National Association of Evangelicals updated its stance on the death penalty. In the past, the NAE had declared that the pro-death penalty approach was the only biblical standard regarding capital punishment. In 2015, however, its new resolution "affirmed the conscientious commitment of both streams [pro-death penalty and pro-abolition] of Christian ethical thought."[20]

Despite some recent calls for abolition and acceptance of different opinions, evangelicals continue to be some of the leading supporters for the legality of the death penalty, with Catholics and mainline Protestants in opposition. In fact, the Public Religion Research Institute recently pegged their support for capital punishment at 59%, 15% higher than the general public.[21] Many prominent evangelical organizations also continue to support the capital punishment, though they rarely engage on the issue.

How has mainstream evangelicalism maintained resilience on the issue of capital punishment, as the much of the political ground is shifting beneath them? In particular, as evangelicals have become more aligned with Catholics in the culture war battles, particularly in viewing issues through the anti-abortion, pro-life lens, how have evangelicals resisted the Catholic Church's opposition to the death penalty? Like the prior chapters, I suggest that for an answer we look to an issue where these two religions agree – abortion.

Evangelical and Catholic Divergence

Largely, evangelicals have been united with Catholics, particularly in elite politics, in regard to their anti-abortion commitment. As Chapter 2 shows, Catholics were first to use the rights-based, right-to-life framework, with evangelicals joining this effort by the late 1970s and early 1980s. In turn, these religious traditions have become partners on a variety of topics, including religious liberty, church-state relations, and health care, as discussed in prior chapters. Despite this, these groups have diverged on the death penalty.

In 1980, a majority of the National Conference on Catholic Bishops approved a negative statement on the death penalty, and during his time as pope, John Paul II routinely expressed his opposition to the death penalty during his reign that began in 1978.[22] In the 1980s, the Catholic leadership began emphasizing the "seamless garment" approach to the sanctity of human life. This seamless garment is a reference to Jesus from the Gospel of John, which describes his tunic as a "seamless garment" in chapter 19. The garment was of such great value that the soldiers did not want to tear it after his fructification, but instead cast lots to determine who would keep it.

Cardinal Joseph Bernardin of the Chicago archdiocese coined the seamless garment teaching in 1983, and he sought to represent a holistic, treasured teaching of Jesus. The seamless garment approach considered the interrelatedness between abortion, the death penalty, euthanasia, human trafficking, just war, and other issues,[23] seeking to consistently value human life from "womb to tomb," as the saying goes. Pope John Paul II became the most visible proponent of this approach to opposing the death penalty. Often opposition was explicitly couched in pro-life terms, as it was on January 27, 1999 in St. Louis, Missouri, when John Paul II stated:

The new evangelization calls for followers of Christ who are unconditionally pro-life: who will proclaim, celebrate and serve the Gospel of life in every situation. A sign of hope is the increasing recognition that the dignity of human life must never be taken away, even in the case of someone who has done great evil ... I renew the appeal I made ... for a consensus to end the death penalty, which is both cruel and unnecessary.[24]

But just seventeen months later, the Southern Baptist Convention, the largest evangelical denomination in the United States, would formally adopt a resolution affirming "fair and equitable" capital punishment applied via "humane means."[25]

Further, in February 2016, Pope Francis called for a worldwide abolition of capital punishment. Speaking to a crowd in St. Peter's Square at the Vatican, the pope called on political authorities to take action. "I appeal to the consciences of those who govern to reach an international consensus to abolish the death penalty." He went on, saying, "The commandment 'You shall not kill' has absolute value and applies to both the innocent and the guilty."[26] From John Paul II to Francis, the emphasis was on the rights of the accused.

Shortly following Pope Francis's speech, Russell Moore, leader of the SBC's advocacy arm, publicly penned his disagreement with the pope. While admitting there are "serious problems with the application of capital punishment," including "racial and economic disparities," Moore stated bluntly, "I cannot agree with Pope Francis that the death penalty is, in all circumstances, a violation of the command not to murder." Moore, who has been called evangelicalism's Pope Francis by *Washington Post* religion reporters,[27] went on to declare, "We must not lose the distinction the Bible makes between the innocent and the guilty."[28]

It is surprising that these culture war partners diverge on such an important moral issue. Some prior research suggests that evangelicals, even pro-life evangelicals, are more persuaded by their punitiveness than Catholics are.[29] I refine this, submitting, in the case of the death penalty, that evangelicals and Catholics have used the framework of abortion and rights differently to support opposing outcomes. While Moore praised Pope Francis for his unwavering support for the "value of human life,"[30] Catholics, like Pope Francis, focus on the application of the pro-life ethic to the *convicted*, while evangelicals, like Moore, focus on its application to the *victims*. Both views were pro-life at heart and had an emphasis on rights, but their attention was on different parts of the capital punishment equation. These competing pro-life approaches to death penalty politics have contributed to continuing evangelical dual-mindedness on the death penalty.

The competing approaches to capital punishment are also indicative of the nature of the representation dynamics within evangelicalism. In the past few decades, evangelical organizations, more so than Catholic ones, have crafted their advocacy positions to be amenable to the political positions of their base. Tying capital punishment to abortion helps elites craft justifications for supporting or opposing capital punishment that are conducive to mass tolerance, if not support, of these positions.

The Evolution of Evangelical Support for Capital Punishment
While evangelicals have long been considered stalwarts in their support for capital punishment, in the mid-twentieth century there was a push by prominent Protestant organizations to oppose the death penalty. Though many of these efforts were championed by mainline Protestant organizations, except the SBC, much of this activity occurred before the wave of evangelical/mainline denominational splits in the later part of the twentieth century. As such, there was certainly some evangelical involvement in mid-century efforts to oppose capital punishment. Notably, much of this advocacy was prior to the U.S. Supreme Court halting capital punishment in 1972 in the *Furman v. Georgia* decision.

In 1956, the Methodist Church (U.S.A)'s (now United Methodist Church) General Board of Church and Society became the most prominent Protestant organization to officially oppose the death penalty.[31] The United Presbyterian Church in the U.S.A. (now the Presbyterian Church (U.S.A.)) followed suit in 1959.[32] In the 1950s, there were still a considerable number of evangelical churches, clergy, and people in these denominations, by today's classifications. The official mainline Protestant stance opposing the death penalty came in 1968 when the National Council of Churches advocated for the abolition of capital punishment.[33] The NCC's opposition was grounded in the "worth of human life and the dignity of the human personality as gifts of God," though, like Pope Francis, it focused attention on the offender, not the victim. According to the resolution, the death penalty results in "institutionalized disregard for the sanctity of human life," which sounds like it could be written by twenty-first-century pro-life activists.[34]

Notable early evangelical efforts began in the Southern Baptist Convention in 1962 and 1963, when leaders of the Christian Life Committee in the North Carolina state Baptist convention put forth a proposal for the North Carolina Baptists to go on record supporting the abolition of the death penalty. The delegates defeated this in 1962, though the North Carolina Baptists approved the statement supporting abolition on the final day of the meeting in 1963.[35] *Baptist Press* commented that the measure passed after many of the delegates had departed. Virginia Baptists, in 1965, also approved a resolution condemning capital punishment and all but calling for the abolition.[36]

These were not isolated incidents. At the 1964 annual meeting of the Southern Baptist Convention, the Christian Life Commission, the SBC's arm for handling moral and social issues, proposed a resolution to the general convention opposing the death penalty. The recommendation declared that "while recognizing that capital punishment is taught in the Old Testament, we affirm that it is contrary to the spirit and teaching of Christ." The recommendation also based its opposition in sanctity-of-life terms, focusing on the life of the criminal, not the victim. The logic was that because "we reaffirm our historic position concerning the sacredness of human life in general and the worth and dignity of the individual in particular ... we therefore call for the abolition of capital punishment in the states and federal jurisdictions where it is now legally prescribed."[37] Nevertheless, on the floor the resolution was altered, deleting the call for the abolition of the death penalty.[38]

In the early 1970s, the SBC continued to have an internal debate about capital punishment. *Baptist Press* reported that a representative poll taken in January 1971 found that 66% of SBC pastors and 56% of SBC Sunday School teachers approved of capital punishment, low numbers by today's standards. In 1968, Arkansas Governor, Winthrop Rockefeller, a Baptist and Republican, declared a moratorium on executions until the U.S. Supreme Court decided on their constitutionality. As he was leaving office in 1970, Winthrop commuted the capital sentences of fifteen death row inmates in Arkansas, encouraging other states to do the same. In describing his decision, Rockefeller acknowledged the role of his Christian faith: "I cannot and will not turn my back on life-long Christian teachings and beliefs, merely to let history run out its course on a fallible and failing theory of punitive justice."[39] An editorial in an Arkansas Baptist paper praised the Arkansas governor's decision to commute the death sentences of those on death row, saying that the action was reminiscent of Jesus who set an example of "commuting the eternal death sentence for the penitent thief being crucified with him, giving this man the gift of eternal life."

Baptist Press distributed this message to a broader Baptist audience by covering the editorial.[40]

At the same time, the status of capital punishment was in limbo in the nation. No executions had been conducted since 1967, and several states had recently abolished or halted capital punishment, including Alaska (1957), Hawaii (1957), Oregon (1964), Iowa (1965), West Virginia (1965), Vermont (1965), Arkansas (1967), and Pennsylvania (1972).[41] Moreover, in 1965 Lyndon Johnson's Department of Justice declared its opposition to capital punishment, and in 1968 it asked Congress to end the practice. Attorney General Ramsey Clark, a Presbyterian, testified, "Executions cheapen life. We must cherish life."[42]

In 1971, the U.S. Supreme Court agreed to hear a case addressing the constitutionality of the issue – *Furman v. Georgia* (1972). *Furman* was a case that consolidated three death penalty convictions in Georgia and Texas for rape and murder, where the petitioners argued that the death penalty was unconstitutional under the U.S. Constitution's Eighth Amendment protection against cruel and unusual punishment. Eight *amicus* briefs were filed in the *Furman* case, with only the brief from the state of Indiana writing to support the practice.

When the Supreme Court heard the oral arguments in *Furman* in January 1972, *Baptist Press* reported on the diverse religious coalition, including Catholics, the National Council of Churches, and several mainline Protestants, asking the Court to abolish the death penalty. The religious coalition emphasized the innocence frame, arguing that the death penalty was cruel and unusual because of the "inherent fallibility of every judicial proceeding ... the possibility of executing an innocent man ... and because the evils of the death penalty are not remedial."[43] Further, the West Virginia Council of Churches declared that the death penalty violated the religious freedom of the prisoner by prohibiting him or her from seeking salvation.[44] Southern Baptists, however, did not participate in the case.

The Court delivered a one-page *per curiam* opinion, holding that the death penalty in these cases did amount to cruel and unusual punishment. But the justices were highly divided on their view of the death penalty, penning nine separate opinions. Two justices argued that it was always unconstitutional; three argued that death sentences were unconstitutional as currently imposed, specifically because they were applied arbitrarily and in racially biased manners; and four argued for upholding the practice. Despite the broad diversity of opinion, many Court observers considered capital punishment to be history. Notably, in private, Chief Justice Warren Burger bemoaned, "There will never be another execution in this country."[45]

Baptist Press did not cover the historic decision, but in 1973, the Christian Life Commission held a conference on criminal justice, where leading Southern Baptists remained divided on the issue of capital punishment.[46] Religious opponents of capital punishment, however, praised the *Furman* ruling.

Despite Justice Burger's claim that the death penalty would be forever halted in America, its impact seems to have had the opposite effect. Public support for the death penalty spiked after the ruling, and many states sought to ameliorate their practice of capital punishment, resolving the Supreme Court's objections. In total, thirty-five states revised their death penalty procedures to decrease the arbitrariness of the practice and its outsized application to African Americans. A common revision was the bifurcated trial, separating the conviction phase from the sentencing phase and adding specific requirements that must be met for the death penalty to be applied. President Richard Nixon too followed suit, asking Congress to authorize a bill calling for capital punishment for certain federal crimes.[47]

The Supreme Court ruled on these revised death penalty procedures in *Gregg v. Georgia* (1976), upholding the practice in a shocking 7–2 ruling. Justice Stewart wrote the opinion of the court, writing that "the punishment of death does not invariably violate the Constitution." Further, the Court praised the new bifurcated trial, stating, "No longer can a jury wantonly and freakishly impose the death sentence."[48] When the Supreme Court reversed course, upholding the constitutionality of capital punishment in *Gregg*, *Baptist Press* reported on the outcome, though Southern Baptists did not take a position.[49] The annual convention refrained from discussing capital punishment the following summer.[50]

Evangelicals, however, continued to be of two minds on capital punishment. In 1979, Watergate figure-turned-evangelical, Charles Colson, gave an address to the SBC's annual convention opposing capital punishment.[51] He would soon come to be the leading evangelical advocate for prison and death penalty reform, heading the organization Prison Fellowship. At the same time, other evangelical denominations were rethinking their stance on the death penalty, including the Christian Reformed Church (CRC). In a 1979 report on the death penalty, the CRC concluded, "The Scriptures lay no mandate on modern states to exercise capital punishment," though they "do permit modern states to inflict capital punishment." The document went on, "According to the spirit of Scripture, capital punishment is prudently exercised only under extreme conditions and not as a general rule."[52]

While some evangelical denominations, like the SBC and CRC, were conflicted on capital punishment in the 1970s, with many focusing their attention on the rights of the convicted and the accused, other conservative Christian institutions were focusing the debate on victims. The Lutheran Church-Missouri Synod (LCMS), for example, came down in favor of the death penalty. In 1967, it first declared, "capital punishment is in accord with the Holy Scriptures and the Lutheran Confessions."[53] Following the public and religious debate over the death penalty, the denomination released a "Report on Capital Punishment" in 1976. The Report reaffirmed the LCMS's 1967 position, basing the need for capital punishment in the "sacredness of human life" and acknowledging the authority of the government to apply the death penalty, while recognizing the need for an improvement in the fairness of the application.[54] The conservative Lutheran denomination was an early advocate of linking support for capital punishment to support for human life.

More importantly for evangelicalism, in 1972 and 1973, the National Association of Evangelicals went on record through two resolutions supporting the death penalty in limited cases – for premeditated capital crimes, murdering a police officer, or murder in connection with another crime.[55] In the resolutions, the NAE also framed its focus not on criminals, but on victims and community justice. The 1973 resolution opposed courts that have declared capital punishment unconstitutional, and the 1972 resolution developed the theoretical framework for death penalty support. The resolution declared, "If no crime is considered serious enough to warrant capital punishment, then the gravity of the most atrocious crime is diminished accordingly." The resolution then continued to emphasize that capital punishment, by seeking justice for victims, promotes a respect for human life. "From the biblical perspective, if capital punishment is eliminated, the value of human life is reduced and the respect for life is correspondingly eroded."[56]

As Chapter 2 describes, it was just in 1971 and 1973 that the NAE began taking nuanced pro-life positions on the issue of abortion, becoming the first prominent evangelical organization to do so. As it did in the area of capital punishment, the NAE's abortion resolutions sought to reframe this debate in the language of life and the consideration of victims, thus opposing abortion on demand but supporting abortion to save the life of the mother. "We believe that all life is a gift of God, so that neither the life of the unborn child nor the mother may be taken lightly," stated the 1973 resolution that also "deplor[ed] in strongest possible terms" the Supreme Court's decision in *Roe v. Wade*.[57] At the time, when the constitutionality of both capital punishment and the death penalty were on the minds of political, moral, and legal elites, this connection between abortion opposition and support for capital punishment was surely not lost on many evangelicals.

Recall, however, that the Southern Baptists had yet to reach a consensus on abortion. In the 1970s, they passed several nuanced pro-choice resolutions that sought to limit the frequency of abortion while protecting the rights of choice. Yet in 1980, the denomination passed an unequivocally pro-life resolution, and it has remained committed to this position ever since.

As the Christian Right grew, however, evangelical activists remained on both sides. Charles Colson became a prominent evangelical advocate for the elimination of the death penalty, staking his position in prominent evangelical outlets such as *Christianity Today*. He was joined by more liberal evangelicals, including Ron Sider of the American Baptist institutions Eastern University and Palmer Theological Seminary, Glen Stassen of the evangelical Fuller Theological Seminary, and David Gushee of the Southern Baptist college Union University.[58]

Christianity Today, which typically follows the mainstream, elite views of evangelicalism, seemed to lean toward abolition. In 1984, the evangelical magazine published a cover story titled "The Death Penalty: Two Sides of a Growing Issue," detailing Christian cases for and against capital punishment, mostly focusing on those supporting abolition. The story identified evangelical abolitionists, including Colson and others involved in prison ministries, as well as the executive director of the Christian Legal Society. The article describes evangelicals opposed to the death penalty as particularly concerned about mistakes and arbitrary enforcement, not yet linking the issue to abortion. Markedly, the feature did bring to evangelical audiences the "seamless garment" approach of Joseph Cardinal Bernardin and the Catholic bishops, seeking "a comprehensive and consistent life ethic."[59] The author concludes with his perspective, clearly linking opposition to abortion and capital punishment with a focus on the convicted: "While many see a difference between the unborn and convicted criminals, at least one argument against abortion probably applies to capital punishment as well: Doubt should always be resolved on the side of life."[60] *Christianity Today* foreshadowed what was to come, though it only captured one side of the anti-abortion argument.

REPRESENTATION AND DEATH PENALTY ADVOCACY

While evangelical elites debated the morality of the death penalty, the rank-and-file strongly supported capital punishment. Public opinion muted the efforts of evangelical elites in the 1960 and 1970s, and it surely prompted the NAE to advocate for the capital punishment. From 1972 to 2014, the General Social Survey has asked respondents about the death penalty. The item asks respondents whether they support capital punishment for murder, providing a binary, yes/no option. Using this question, Figure 6.1 plots the percentage of death penalty supporters for evangelicals with a solid black line and all others with a dashed gray line. The vertical gray lines depict standard errors for both evangelicals and non-evangelicals. If the standard error lines for the two groups (evangelicals and non-evangelicals) do not overlap, there is a significant difference.

Over the forty-year period, evangelicals have consistently supported capital punishment, with this support peaking in the 1990s at about 85%. Of late, this support has declined to less than 75%, though this remains quite high and largely matches the level of support in the late 1970s. Until 1990, evangelicals, though more supportive, largely mirrored the national population, with a solid majority supporting capital punishment as a punishment for murder. In the 1990s, however, evangelicals diverged from the others, whose support fell. Evangelicals peaked at higher levels of support for the death penalty in the mid-1990s (~85% vs. 78%). Yet from 1990 to 2012, both the non-evangelicals and Catholics (not shown) have had greater rates of decline than evangelicals have. Though their rates are declining too, from 2000 to 2014, evangelical support is approximately 10% higher, settling at 74% approval in 2014.

For SBC pastors, the results are even more consistent. From 1988 to 2008, a collection of surveys asked these clergy how strongly they agree or disagree

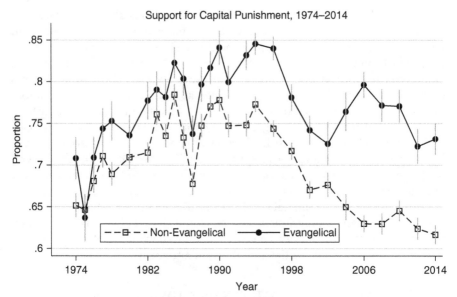

FIGURE 6.1. Evangelical and Non-Evangelical Views on Capital Punishment, GSS, 1974–2014.

with capital punishment, scaled from strongly disagree (1) to strongly agree (5) with a neutral option (3), the latter selected by only 5%. SBC pastors consistently supported the death penalty at high levels (with the average being just over the "agree" level). The standard deviations are consistent and small. For the twenty-year period, 80–85% of SBC ministers supported the death penalty. And while the general public's and the evangelical rank-and-file's support was declining between 1998 and 2008, there was a slight uptick in support among the clergy, from 80% to nearly 90%.

While there is some movement in favor of abolition, the strong level of grassroots support for the death penalty in the 1970s and 1980s caused tensions for evangelical abolition advocates. A prominent example is the Southern Baptist Christian Life Commission, which was the primary advocate for abolition in the SBC since the 1960s. As late as 1981, the CLC strongly urged an end to capital punishment. It issued a brochure in 1981, prominently distributed to SBC churches, which stated that Christians "should support the abolition of capital punishment."[61] Yet this position, along with its support for limited abortion rights, doomed the CLC. In the 1980s, conservative Southern Baptists gained control of key positions in the denomination, and part of their mission was to realign the SBC's political advocacy with that of the membership, particularly in the areas of abortion, church-state relations, and capital punishment.[62] Conservatives sought to oust CLC director N. Larry Baker in 1987 for his moderate views on abortion and capital punishment. In regard to capital punishment, Baker had declared that it "runs counter to the Christian ethic and the Christian gospel."[63]

Eventually Baker would resign his post, and the conservative-controlled Convention would select Richard Land to head the CLC, as described in Chapter 2. Land strongly opposed abortion, except when the mother's life was in danger, and he would lead the SBC to be the most prominent non-Catholic pro-life denomination. On capital punishment, Land submitted in his interview for the position, "I firmly believe in capital punishment as part of the biblically mandated authority of the civil magistrates."[64] He went on to champion the pro-life rationale for death penalty support, similar to the NAE's position in the early 1970s. He declared that capital punishment is "society's way of upholding the sanctity of human life. If human life is sacred and God has given it, then we must uphold its sanctity. When another person callously ... wantonly takes life, then capital punishment is one of the options of the magistrate."[65] Following the selection of Land to head the CLC, the organization stopped distributing its pamphlet calling for the abolition of the death penalty,[66] and it moved forward with a pro-life justification for capital punishment, focusing on the rights of the victims.

Change was also afoot in one of evangelicalism's most prominent supporters of abolition – Charles Colson. Colson was an evangelical social justice advocate, with conservative bona fides. His opposition to the death penalty fit well with his advocacy for prison reform and the leadership of his prominent prison ministry, Prison Fellowship. Colson had been active in trying to persuade evangelicals to oppose the death penalty, speaking to denominations like the SBC and writing in *Christianity Today*. But in 1994, Colson altered his position, favoring capital punishment "at least in principle, but only in extreme cases when no other punishment can satisfy the demands of justice."[67] Colson claimed that his visit with the serial killer John Wayne Gacy ultimately led to his "conversion."[68] He remained a reluctant supporter, however, actively championing reforms to improve the fairness of the application of capital punishment.

Rights and Death Penalty Support

Throughout the 1980s, 1990s, and 2000s, perhaps spurred by the rank-and-file, many evangelical elites and organizations promoted the justification of capital punishment, focusing on the value of the victim's life and linking the issue to abortion. The NAE's position from the early 1970s seemed to have triumphed. This perspective was codified in the SBC's most recent convention resolution on the topic in 2000. The resolution begins by declaring that "every human life has sacred value." It further highlights the connection between the right to life and death penalty support by acknowledging the denomination's "deep reverence for human life," "profound respect for the rights of individuals," and "respect for the law."[69] This had become the dominant position of evangelical elites.

Evangelical supporters of capital punishment were also susceptible to attenu-
ation, like Colson, based on context, however. Prominent evangelical conservatives, including Jerry Falwell and Pat Robertson, spoke out against the capital
sentence of death row convert, Karla Faye Tucker. *Christianity Today* prominently covered Tucker's case, as she gained national attention for her prison life
change from axe murderer to committed Christian. Robertson led a "crusade
for mercy" on his 700 Club television show, and he argued, "She is not the
same person who committed those heinous axe murders. She is totally transformed, and I think to execute her is more of an act of vengeance than it is
appropriate justice."[70] Nevertheless, Robertson's wish was not granted, as the
born-again Texas governor, George W. Bush, denied the stay of her execution
in February 1998, concluding that the "judgment[s] about the heart and soul of
an individual on death row are best left to a higher authority."[71]

Following Tucker's execution, *Christianity Today* officially supported an
end to the death penalty, in an editorial titled "The Lesson of Karla Faye
Tucker." The magazine stated that the death penalty was unfair and discriminatory, fraught with mistakes, lacks deterrent value, and fails to consol. *Christianity Today* criticized an approach oriented toward justice for the victims as
being focused on vengeance. Instead, argued the editors, punishments should
promote reconciliation of the offenders, which flows from the ministry of Jesus.
Certainly, the evangelical magazine was rejecting the pro-life orientation
toward victims' rights for the pro-life orientation toward offenders' rights.
The editorial concluded, "It seems clear that the death penalty has outlived its
usefulness. It has not made the United States a safer country or a more equitable
one. The potential of life imprisonment without parole and other protective
measures, however, offer better options for the state, which must continue to
deal with 20,000 murders each year."[72]

Though the SBC remained supportive of capital punishment, its news arm,
Baptist Press, published an interview with an anti–death penalty SBC pastor in
1998. David Crosby, pastor of New Orleans First Baptist Church, befriended
Tucker while she was on death row, and their relationship changed his view on
the death penalty. "We want to do this (capital punishment) at arm's length,
but we cannot. I hope we will take the death penalty personally and Karla's
death will help us all to experience execution as a personal responsibility," he
said. "Pope John Paul II and others have challenged us to a consistent pro-life
stand and that means doing away with the death sentence. I'm hearing that with
new ears today."[73] Though the denomination would pass a resolution in
support of capital punishment at its annual convention in 2000, the fact that
its news agency would highlight the pro-life case against capital punishment
acknowledged the validity of debate with evangelicalism.

Following Tucker's execution and the *Christianity Today* editorial, there has
been some momentum toward abolition among evangelical elites. Social justice
activist Shane Claiborne has received some attention, especially from the evangelical left for his opposition to the death penalty as part of his general

emphasis on nonviolence. Other, more mainstream evangelical elites have joined in their disapproval of the death penalty, including Marvin Olasky, editor of the evangelical *World Magazine*, and John Whitehead, founder and president of the Rutherford Institute, a conservative, Christian civil liberties legal organization. Some, like Whitehead and Claiborne, have argued that capital punishment goes against the Christian message. In 2008, Whitehead told *Christianity Today*, "It is anti-evangelical to kill people. Christianity is redemptive. But you can't redeem people by extinguishing them."[74] Others, including Olasky, argue more pragmatically that the way the capital punishment is practiced in the United States is unjust and unbiblical. Instead, they support life imprisonment without parole as the proper punishment for heinous crimes. As Olasky describes, capital punishment in the Bible is "a maximum rather than an obligation."[75] This resistance culminated in 2015. Many evangelical leaders opposed the execution of Kelly Renee Gissendander, who had become a theology student at Emory while on death row in Georgia,[76] before being the first woman in the state executed in seventy years.[77] Further, the National Latino Evangelical Coalition urged abolition, while the NAE declared that evangelicals could rightly either favor or oppose capital punishment.

Despite some vocal support for ending the death penalty, strong favorability for the practice of capital punishment remains, as the Tsarnaev trial exposed. Importantly, justification is increasingly grounded in the sanctity of life and dignity of humanity, language harkening evangelicals to the pro-life movement. The Southern Baptist Convention has taken over from the NAE as the leader in this approach. In a debate among evangelical leaders in *Christianity Today*, Richard Land then head of the SBC's advocacy arm, argued that it is "excruciatingly biblical to be both pro-life and pro-death penalty." Land went on, "It is also imperative that I support capital punishment because human life is sacred . . . . Life is sacred, and when men wantonly take other men's lives, they have transgressed a divine prerogative and forfeit their own right to life."[78] Moreover, SBC seminary president and prominent writer, R. Albert Mohler, wrote in a 2014 column on CNN.com, "The death penalty was explicitly grounded in the fact that God made every individual human being in his own image, and thus an act of intentional murder is an assault upon human dignity and the very image of God."[79] While opposing the economic and racial injustices related to the unfair application of the capital punishment, Mohler argued that the death penalty should be legal, but rare. For him, and much of the evangelical hierarchy, the death penalty promotes the right to life – what has become central to evangelical political advocacy. This rationale has transcended theology, as conservative leaders, including the Catholic convert and one-time presidential hopeful Bobby Jindal, have used pro-life rationale to support the death penalty. In a 2011 interview, Jindal declared, "We're made in God's image, and it's tragic that the modern world doesn't take the value of life more seriously. . . . We should do everything we can to go after these monsters."[80] Anti-abortion language has become an important conduit for pro-death penalty positions on the right, especially the religious right.

Abortion and Death Penalty Attitudes

Does this elite framework connecting the language of abortion politics to death penalty, either in support or opposition, gain credence with the evangelical masses? Correlations suggest that abortion might work differently for clergy and the rank-and-file. For Southern Baptists pastors, there is a strong, positive correlation between opposition to abortion and support for the death penalty, and this remains constant over time. For the rank-and-file, the correlations are weak and negative over time, with those more opposed to abortion also being opposed to capital punishment. Yet that relationship diminishes over time. In addition, correlations between abortion attitudes and views on capital punishment are nearly identical for evangelicals and non-evangelicals over time. Perhaps there is a disconnect between the clergy and the masses, or perhaps the connection between pro-life politics runs in different directions, since the religious elites use competing abortion-related frames to discuss support for or opposition to capital punishment.

Multivariate statistical models are necessary for more insight into the relationship between abortion politics and support for capital punishment among evangelicals. For the Southern Baptist clergy, data are available from 1988 to 2008, covering the decade before and after the peak of support for the death penalty. The dependent variable is a Likert scale, as the response options range from strongly opposing capital punishment (1) and strongly supporting it (5), with a middle, neutral option (3). The strength of opinion is important, as the model results vary when the data is collapsed to simple agreement or disagreement. Because of this, I use ordered logistic regression models to capture the change between all five categories. As in the previous chapters, the independent variables are party identification, political ideology, and religious beliefs, as well as controls for demographic factors and the survey year. The variable coding is in Appendix A.

Like the capital punishment preferences discussed earlier, the statistical models show consistency for the SBC clergy over time. Table 6.1 in Appendix B presents the results of a model for the whole time period, as well as separate models before and after 2000, the peak of death penalty opposition. Ideology and religious beliefs are the strongest and most stable predictors, with the more conservative political and religious beliefs being related to support for capital punishment. Republican party identification is only significant in the full and pre-2000 models, though this may be due to the lack of party variance in the later period. The connection with abortion is the opposite, as those who are more pro-life are more supportive of capital punishment, but only in the period from 2000 to 2008.

Figure 6.2 shows the impact that changing from low to high (liberal to conservative) on the abortion and ideology variables has on support for the death penalty. The solid, black lines represent the 2000 to 2008 period, while the dashed lines represent the earlier period. Two things are easy to determine. First, the magnitude of the effect is greater for ideology, though both are statistically

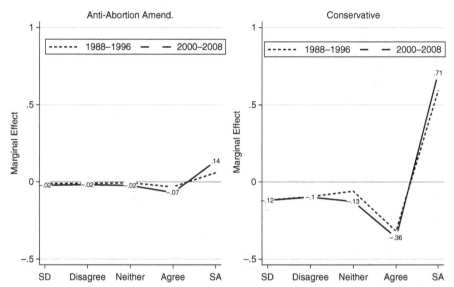

FIGURE 6.2. Marginal Effects of Support for Anti-Abortion Amendment and Conservative Ideology on Support for the Death Penalty. SBC Clergy, 1988–2008.

different than zero. Second, the action is really at the extremes, the shift from agreeing with the death penalty to strongly agreeing with it. Both strong conservatives and those who support an anti-abortion amendment are more likely to strongly support the death penalty. For the clergy, the conservative law and order impulses, as well as the victim-focused right-to-life approaches to death penalty politics, seem to have triumphed, especially since 2000.

For the rank-and-file, the GSS measure of death penalty support is dichotomous, as individuals either select whether they support or oppose capital punishment. Because of this, I employ logistic regression models. As in previous chapters, the abortion scale and the religious tradition variables are the primary independent variables of interest. Other independent measures used are: party identification, political ideology, societal distrust, survey year, and demographic controls. The political variables are coded from liberal (low) to conservative (high) to ease in interpretation again. Again, the variable coding can again be found Appendix A.

The top panel in Figure 6.3 presents graphically the results of the central independent variables in the basic model of all the survey years from 1977 to 2014. For ease of interpretation, the independent variables have been standardized, scaled on a 0–1 level, and some variables have been omitted from the figure. The top of Figure 6.3 is similar to those in the prior chapters. The black dots represent the point estimates for each independent variable, and the horizontal gray bars represent the 95% confidence intervals. If the bars do

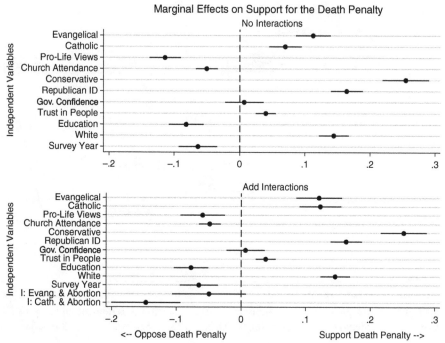

FIGURE 6.3. Marginal Effects on Support for the Death Penalty without and with Interactions. Logistic Regression Models with 95% Confidence Intervals. GSS, 1977–2014.

not overlap with the vertical, dashed line, then the measure is statistically significant. If the dots are to the right of the vertical line, then the relationship is positive; if it is to the left, it is negative. The full results can be found in Table 6.2 in Appendix B.

Evangelicals and Catholics are more supportive of the death penalty than are the unaffiliated, as are people from all religious traditions except black Protestants. Evangelicals are the most supportive. The political variables also operate as expected, with conservative ideology and Republican affiliation both predicting support for the death penalty. As with the clergy, ideology has the strongest relationship with the death penalty in the model. Abortion, however, functions differently in the GSS than it does for the clergy models. Those with stronger pro-life views are more likely to oppose the death penalty, considering all the other factors. In addition, religious commitment (i.e., church attendance) decreases support for the death penalty, which has been demonstrated in some prior work.[81] The demographic variables operate as expected. It is noteworthy that government confidence does not correlate with support for the death penalty. A high level of confidence in the government is not required to support the invoking of capital punishment.

Returning to the religious and abortion variables, are Catholics responsible for the negative relationship between anti-abortion attitudes support for the death penalty, or do evangelical rank-and-file have structure their thoughts about abortion and capital punishment differently than the clergy? To answer this, I created models with separate interaction terms that combine evangelicals and abortion attitudes and Catholics and abortion attitudes.

The results from the full model are displayed in the bottom panel of Figure 6.3, with the complete results in Table 6.2. The interaction terms are at the bottom: "I: Evang. & Abortion" & "I: Cath. & Abortion." The point estimates for these variables are clearly in the negative direction. Pro-life attitudes depress support for capital punishment for both evangelicals and Catholics. The confidence intervals are fairly wide, though, and this effect fails to reach statistical significance for evangelicals. Still, the effect is significant for Catholics. The model suggests at least some mass support for the Catholic consistent life ethic of opposing abortion and capital punishment – certainly for Catholics and perhaps even among evangelicals.

Because the linking of opposition to abortion and capital punishment is a relatively new, I split the models into two time periods, pre- and post-2000. The results are displayed graphically in Figure 6.4. Nearly all the variables

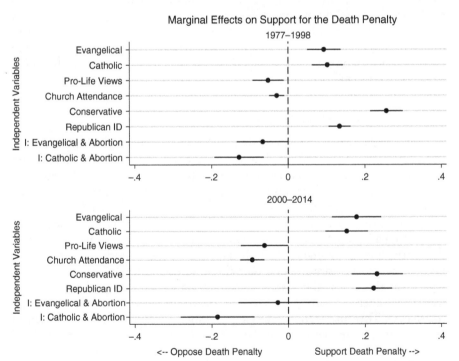

FIGURE 6.4. Marginal Effects of Support for Death Penalty in Two Time Periods. Logistic Regression Models with 95% Confidence Intervals. GSS, 1977–2014.

have a consistent relationship with capital punishment support over time, with the exception of the evangelical interaction. Surprisingly, prior to 2000, pro-life evangelicals were significantly more likely to have reduced support for the death penalty. From 2000 to 2014, the point estimate moves close to zero and is clearly insignificant. The Catholic interaction, however, remains. Anti-abortion attitudes depress Catholic support for the death penalty in all time periods, supporting the seamless garment approach promoted since 1980.

While abortion operated similarly for evangelicals and Catholics between 1977 and 1998, with pro-life views being related to reduced support for the death penalty, anti-abortion attitudes have no statistical effect on evangelicals' capital punishment views in the current period. Despite increasing evangelical calls for abolition, often in pro-life terms, support for the death penalty is high and unaffected by abortion. Unlike Catholics, who have had a consistent message of pairing death penalty abolition to abortion, evangelical leaders have used abortion arguments in two manners – supporting and opposing the death penalty. This conflict is evident in evangelical mass opinion, resulting in a null effect. Moreover, Southern Baptist clergy seem to have taken to the victim-oriented right-to-life approach. While there appears to have been an opportunity for the right-to-life message to move evangelicals toward death penalty abolition, this window of opportunity appears to have closed as conservatives have co-opted the pro-life language in support of capital punishment. These mixed messages may have helped pro-death penalty views to triumph within evangelicalism. Consistent, elite opposition, as with the Catholic Church, might be necessary to facilitate change.

Experimenting with Death Penalty Opinion

The mass and clergy findings regarding abortion and capital punishment, while important, only provide insight into the indirect relationship between abortion and capital punishment. To try and isolate the direct effects of the different frameworks evangelical leaders use to approach the death penalty, I developed a survey experiment, which was implemented in the Criminal Justice and Religion Survey (CJRS). My colleagues and I conducted the CJRS in November 2015 using a Survey Sampling International online panel to examine the effects that varying elite arguments in both support for and opposition to the death penalty. We surveyed a national sample of 1,400 adults, balanced by census region. In the CJRS, the respondents were randomly assigned to receive a treatment either supporting or opposing the death penalty (or a control of no treatment). Then individuals receiving treatments were randomly assigned to receive one of three versions of the corresponding prompt being made by a "local minister" at a "town hall meeting about faith and politics."[82]

In each scenario, the minister was asked whether he supported the death penalty. The minister then responded with one of six rationales, three supporting and three opposing the death penalty. The category of rationale was the same for those opposing and supporting: Right to Life, Justice, and Costs and Benefits.

The Right to Life approach focused on the competing pro-life justifications regarding capital punishment. The first mirrored the Catholic consistent life ethic, with the pastor saying:

I am pro-life, and whether that life is an unborn baby or a convicted murderer, we need to value the right to life. Therefore, I strongly oppose the death penalty.

The second mirrored the victim-centered approach:

I am pro-life, and I think that life is of such high value that the death penalty is the only proper punishment for people who murder innocent life. Therefore I strongly support the death penalty.

The Justice approach pitted the possibility of innocence versus retribution, drawing on the findings of Frank Baumgartner and his colleagues.[83] The minister opposing capital punishment said:

It is unjust to sentence people to death, because too often innocent people have been convicted of capital crimes. Therefore, I strongly oppose the death penalty.

The pastor supporting the death penalty declared:

Justice for the victim demands that murderers are put to death for taking innocent life. Therefore, I strongly support the death penalty.

Finally, the Costs and Benefits approach draws on a growing conservative concern with capital punishment, that its financial costs outweigh the benefits. This has been growing in the area of criminal justice reform, and it was one of the key arguments used when Nebraska outlawed the death penalty in 2015. In the survey prompt, the pastor opposing capital punishment said:

It costs the government more money to put a convicted criminal to death than it does to keep them in prison for life. As a country, we cannot afford to increase the costs of our criminal justice system. Therefore, I strongly oppose the death penalty.

The pastor supporting the death penalty countered with his own Costs and Benefits argument:

While it is certainly expensive to process criminals through death row, as a country we cannot afford the social costs of increased murder rates. Therefore, I strongly support the death penalty.

Following the prompts, respondents were asked two questions. First, those that received a treatment and not a control were asked to rate the *persuasiveness* of the pastor's argument about capital punishment on a 0–10 scale. Everyone, including those in the control group, was then asked for their opinion on capital punishment for persons convicted of murder. Options ranged from strongly favor to strongly oppose, with a neutral option. For those who were neutral or supported the death penalty for people convicted of murder, we asked a follow-up question: "Which punishment do you prefer for people convicted of murder?" The answer options were "the death penalty" or "life in prison with no chance of parole," along with "don't know."

Looking first at persuasiveness, across the entire sample, most of the death penalty justifications were rated at average or slightly above in persuasiveness. Arguments favoring capital punishment (5.56) were slightly more favorable than arguments opposing (5.22). This makes sense, as a slim majority still supports capital punishment.

Corresponding with the importance of the innocence frame, the Justice rationale for opposing the death penalty was rated as the most persuasive (5.82), though the Justice rationale for supporting the death penalty was nearly equal (5.75). The least persuasive argument was, by far, the Costs and Benefits approach to opposing the death penalty (4.73), despite some small government-favoring elites giving it credence. Regarding abortion, the total sample was more persuaded by the Right to Life argument in support of capital punishment (5.76) than the Right to Life argument against capital punishment (5.13). In fact, multivariate statistical models show that the Right to Life justification against the death penalty is the only frame that is not significantly more persuasive than the Costs and Benefits approach to opposing the death penalty.

Of primary interest is how evangelicals, particularly white evangelicals, respond to these varying arguments, especially the pro-life arguments. Figure 6.5 displays average persuasiveness for white evangelicals (right) and non-evangelicals (left) across all the issue frames, clustered by opposing and supporting the death penalty. For non-evangelicals, the biggest difference is that they are more persuaded by the Justice frame for opposing the death penalty than other arguments against capital punishment. This fits well with the narrative put forth by Baumgartner and his colleagues.[84] Non-evangelicals are equally persuaded by the Right to Life and Justice arguments for capital punishment, almost at the same levels that they rate the Justice frame in opposition.

Evangelicals are even more strongly persuaded by pro-death penalty arguments, which aligns with their solid majority support for capital punishment. That said, evangelicals too are quite persuaded by the Justice frame in opposition to the death penalty (6.16), as this matches any of the pro-death penalty frames. In fact, as compared to non-evangelicals, this justification is much more persuasive than the consistent life ethic (4.57) or the financial costs of executions (4.91). This cuts against conventional wisdom, especially for those on the evangelical left seeking to bring together anti-abortion, anti–death penalty, and pro–social welfare issues in a package of pro-life social justice issues. Perhaps it is innocence, not the "seamless garment," that would have the greatest effect for Christian abolitionists. This pattern also holds for Catholics, though not shown in Figure 6.5. The Justice frame opposing capital punishment

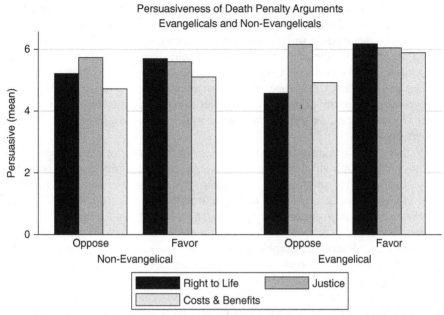

FIGURE 6.5. Average Persuasiveness of Death Penalty Justifications for Evangelicals and Non-Evangelicals. SSI, November 2015.

outperforms the pro-life rights frame (6.13 versus 5.26), though the Right to Life frame is more persuasive among Catholics than evangelicals. In general, there is little support for the consistent life ethic approach.

In favor of capital punishment, the three justifications are nearly equally persuasive for evangelicals, with the Right to Life frame being the most persuasive, though without a statistical difference. The main difference among Catholics, compared to Figure 6.5, is that they are less persuaded by the Costs and Benefits argument than are evangelicals. Despite most Catholic Church leaders opposing the death penalty, they are nearly equally persuaded by Rights and Justice pro–death penalty arguments as are evangelicals, whose leaders largely support capital punishment.

Multivariate statistical models, shown in Table 6.3, shed further light onto these findings. These linear regression models predict persuasiveness, with separate variables for each of the justifications, controls for party identification and church attendance (because they did not randomize adequately), and interactions between both evangelicals and Catholics and the various justifications. The Costs and Benefits justification for opposing the death penalty serves as the comparison category.

The interaction terms show that there are no significant differences for evangelicals in the persuasiveness of the arguments, compared to the Costs and Benefits argument against capital punishment. Rather, it appears that evangelicals are largely fixed in their view of the death penalty, though I will take this up next. In fact, the only clergy justification that approaches statistical significance is the Right to Life frame in opposition to the death penalty. But it has a negative coefficient, meaning that evangelicals are more likely to rate this argument as less persuasive than are non-evangelicals and non-Catholics. Catholics show more variance, but, surprisingly, they are more persuaded by the pro–death penalty arguments. Catholics rate the Right to Life argument for capital punishment, as well as the Justice argument, as more persuasive than others do.

If these elite arguments produce little differences in persuasiveness, it is unlikely that they will alter opinions, though the data allow us to investigate this. For the entire sample, 52% favored or strongly favored the death penalty, with 33% opposing and 26% taking a middle position. Of the 78% who favored capital punishment (or were in the middle), 63% chose the death penalty over life in prison without parole (37%) in a follow-up. Figure 6.6 displays these differences graphically for evangelicals and non-evangelicals. As expected, across all the treatments, evangelicals have higher levels of support for the death penalty than non-evangelicals.

Difference of means tests suggest that support for the death penalty does vary across treatments,[85] though this is reduced when taking into account the life-in-prison option.[86] Multivariate regression models, shown in Table 6.4, suggest the pro-death penalty Right to Life ($p = 0.10$), Justice ($p = 0.07$), and Costs and Benefits ($p = 0.03$) arguments increase support for the death penalty,

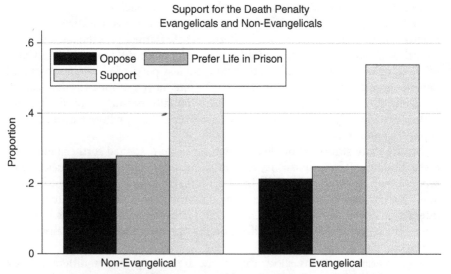

FIGURE 6.6. Support for the Death Penalty when Considering Life in Prison for Evangelicals and Non-Evangelicals. SSI, November 2015.

as compared to receiving no justification, for the entire sample.[87] If an individual received the Rights justification for the death penalty, the predicted probability that they would oppose the death penalty is 0.21, while the probability that they would support it more than doubles to 0.54. The increases are almost identical for the Justice and Costs and Benefits justifications to support capital punishment.

On the other hand, the opposition arguments have no effect on attitudes. There are also no significant interactive effects for evangelicals or Catholics. The elite arguments do not alter their opinions, whether I include the life in prison follow-up or not, at least not in this short survey experiment.

Discussion

These experimental tests of varying issue frames provide further insight into the relationship between religion and the death penalty in U.S. politics. Most importantly, both the general public and the religious subsets have stable death penalty attitudes. Though there is a two-decade trend of decreasing support for capital punishment, these attitudes are not easily altered by different arguments made by elites. In addition, as other prominent work has noted, the focus on the injustice of innocent persons being put to death is one of the most potent justifications for abolishing the death penalty. This argument is also seen as persuasive among the most punitive subsections of the public, evangelical Protestants.

The consistent life ethic approach – the criminal's right to life – first promulgated by Catholic leaders and now taken up by many evangelicals, does not have the same gravitas, however. It tests as one of the weakest justifications for both evangelicals and Catholics. That is not to say that abortion is unrelated to capital punishment, as the retributive approach that focuses on the sanctity of the victim's life – the victim's right to life – is viewed as very highly persuasive for evangelicals and Catholics and leads to Catholics being more supportive of capital punishment. This suggests that if religious elites, particularly evangelicals, continue to promulgate the right-to-life approach to supporting the death penalty, a cleavage between the general public and the religious public will persist.

CONCLUSION

Why have evangelicals diverged from their Catholic culture war partners in their support for capital punishment? It is not that evangelicals have failed to connect the death penalty to abortion, missing the consistent life ethic. Rather, evangelicals have effectively utilized right-to-life arguments to support conservative, law-and-order positions by emphasizing the victims' rights and the value of protecting life against murder. There is rights-claiming on both sides of the debate, as there are crosscutting pro-life messages within the domain of capital punishment, especially for evangelicals. The pro-life, pro–death penalty messages, in particular, seem to spur (or provide cover for) evangelical support for capital punishment and inhibit broad evangelical reforms, especially in recent decades.

Though the correlations are low over time, abortion attitudes work differently for evangelicals and Catholics, especially in the most recent period. Pro-life views depress Catholic support for the death penalty across all time periods, while they have little effect on evangelical attitudes, particularly in recent years. Testing specific elite frames, the pro-life attitudes in favor of capital punishment, which are often proffered by evangelical leaders, are seen as more persuasive and also increase general support for the death penalty, though this is not specific to Catholics or evangelicals. Moreover, the pro-life justifications for abolishing the death penalty are rated as non-persuasive. Religious abolitionists are better served by the innocence argument.

Thus, in the past evangelical elites responded to rank-and-file pressures by taking pro–death penalty positions and not wavering in the face of increasing societal preferences for abolition. Elites have bolstered their position by tapping into the pro-life movement and its rights-oriented perspective, especially in the past twenty years. This now reinforces these elite positions, as the rank-and-file respond favorably to abortion arguments.

Despite constituent public opinion being in their favor, evangelical elites appear to be increasingly reluctant to publicly favor capital punishment, which could alter the state of evangelical advocacy. So too could the increasing racial diversity within evangelicalism, which is leading some advocacy leaders, including Russell Moore of the SBC, to call for less punitive rhetoric and policies.[88] With the racial disparity in the application of capital punishment, it is not far-fetched to see capital punishment added to the list of evangelical reforms, along with prison reform and immigration reform.

That said, an increasingly vocal division remains with evangelicalism about the morality and prudence of capital punishment. The division is over the proper application of the abortion-related sanctity-of-life perspective: Should it be applied to the victim or to the offender?

To return to the opening, the evangelical division over capital punishment was evident in the aftermath of a federal jury sentencing Tamerlan Tsarnaev to death in May 2015. Opponents of capital punishment focused on the *offender's* – Tsarnaev's – right to life. Evangelical author and seminary professor, Scot McKnight, wrote from the perspective of the offender. "Christians can oppose the death penalty because they have hope and believe that God's grace can undo what has been done and remake the criminal into a person he or she was not previously."[89] Proponents, such as Albert Mohler, SBC leader and president of the Southern Baptist Theological Seminary, focused on the *victims'* rights to life and the demand for justice. In his "The Briefing" podcast, Mohler summarized, "Every single life is of infinite worth, because every single human being is made in God's image." But because of this, "some crimes simply demand the death penalty." For Mohler and his fellow evangelical supporters of the death penalty, their pro-life perspective demands such support. He described that supporting capital punishment is based not on vengeance, but on the sacredness of human life, not "retribution, but the necessity of justice."[90] On the whole, evangelicals still tend to agree with Mohler.

Though there is a vocal division, both abortion politics and rights politics continue to play an important role in evangelical perspectives on capital punishment. At the very least, since there are abortion-related, rights-based arguments on both sides of the issue, a sea change in public opinion (though perhaps not application) is unlikely, especially since abortion is a primary mode of representation for evangelical advocacy leaders. In the eyes of many, for those who are clearly guilty, the right to life demands the life of the murderer.

7

Where's the Right?

What Abortion Taught the Losers in the Gay Marriage Debate

At 10:00 in the morning on June 26, 2015, all eyes (and ears) awaited the decision from the nine black-robed jurists who would be ruling on perhaps the most consequential case in a generation. Television news stations interrupted programming to watch correspondents relay the ruling, and millions logged on to the website SCOTUSblog to be the first to know the outcome and read the opinion. The case was *Obergefell v. Hodges*, and the issue was same-sex marriage.

Justice Anthony Kennedy, the Ronald Reagan–appointed, centrist justice, delivered the opinion of the U.S. Supreme Court regarding constitutionality of state laws forbidding the license or recognition of same-sex marriages. In a 5–4 decision, the Court ruled that states could no longer deny marriage licenses or marriage recognition to same-sex couples. Justice Kennedy grounded his ruling in rights. The rationale is distilled in a long sentence on the twenty-second page of his opinion: "The right to marry is a fundamental right inherent in the liberty of the person, and under the Due Process and Equal Protection Clauses of the Fourteenth Amendment couples of the same-sex may not be deprived of that right and that liberty."[1] The Supreme Court identified the existence of the right of same-sex couples to marry, and it deemed this right fundamental, making its application universal and giving it a high level of constitutional protection.

The proponents for same-sex marriage had triumphed. While many had proffered equality arguments, based on the Fourteenth Amendment's Equal Protection Clause, same-sex marriage was won, both legally and politically, on the basis of rights. Kennedy, in particular, grounded his opinion in the liberty portion of the Fourteenth Amendment's Due Process Clause. The liberal proponents of the right to same-sex marriage had defeated conservatives, particularly evangelical and Catholic conservatives. In fact, in *Obergefell* and related cases, dozens of conservative religious groups filed briefs opposing the right to same-sex marriage. These included large national organizations such as the National Association of Evangelicals, the United States Conference of Catholic

Bishops, and the Church of Jesus Christ of Latter-Day Saints (Mormons), the Southern Baptist Convention and many other evangelical denominations, Christian advocacy groups such as the Family Research Council and the Christian Legal Society, and many evangelical seminaries, scholars, and leaders. But the left's argument for liberty had triumphed over the right's argument for morality, shared community values, and democratic politics, confirming the conventional wisdom of the past century of rights politics.

While a major conservative defeat, the politics of gay rights do not disprove the broader arc of conservative rights. Rather, they confirm the episodic process of rights learning and rights claiming. With the end of anti–gay marriage advocacy, the process of rights learning is in action. The politics of gay rights is the final blow to majoritarian Christian America. It has propelled evangelicals to consider themselves as a threatened minority, and it has impelled an increasing emphasis on rights claims, particularly the rights of religious freedom and free speech. Along the way, many leaders have prompted conservative Christians to learn from the pro-life movement in their response to the legality of same-sex marriage.

PROTECTING PUBLIC MORALITY AGAINST GAY RIGHTS

For decades, evangelical Christians were impassioned in their opposition to gay rights, lamenting the moral decay of society and prophesying the end of America if gay rights took hold. In a December 1994 interview with *Newsweek* magazine, Senator Jesse Helms (R-NC), a Southern Baptist, called gays "degenerates" and "weak, morally sick wretches." In 1988, Senator Majority Leader Trent Lott (R-MS) compared being gay to alcoholism, "sex addiction ... or kleptomania." When questioned about Lott's statements, House Majority Leader Richard Armey (R-TX) came to Lott's defense, saying, "The Bible is very clear on this. Now, both myself and Senator Lott believe very strongly in the Bible. I do not quarrel with the Bible on this subject."[2] Religious leaders were not much different in their approach. Dr. James Dobson of Focus on the Family, and founder of the Family Research Council, called same-sex attraction a "disorder" in his popular book parenting *Bringing Up Boys*.[3] Likewise, denominations, pastors, politicians, and advocacy groups resisted rights for gays and lesbians in many arenas. They stood in a majoritarian position, protecting the culture and public morality. This approach was ubiquitous, though a sketch of some of the history will suffice.

In 1976, the Southern Baptist Convention first addressed homosexuality in a resolution at their annual convention, urging churches "not to afford the practice of homosexuality any degree of approval through ordination, employment, or other designations of normal life-style."[4] The SBC reaffirmed this position in 1978. In a 1980 resolution, the rhetoric escalated, condemning "Gay Activists and liberal humanistic politicians" who pass ordinances under the "deceptive guise of human rights." It resolved "that our Convention deplore the proliferation of all homosexual practices, unnatural relations of any character, and sexual perversion whenever found in our society and reaffirm the traditional position of Southern Baptists that all such practices are sin and are condemned by the Word of God."[5] In 1985, the SBC officially opposed granting homosexuality the legal protection of minority group status "with attendant benefits or advantages,"[6] and in 1988 it "call[ed] upon all media to refuse advertising that promotes homosexuality or any other lifestyle that is destructive to the family."[7] Further, the 1988 convention linked homosexuality to "the erosion of moral sanity," blamed homosexual activity for the "introduction and spread of AIDS in the United States," and called it "not a normal lifestyle" and "an abomination in the eyes of God."[8]

In 1993, the SBC opposed gays in the military for being "incompatible with the requirements of military service" and "inconsistent to the Uniform Code of Military Justice," in addition to "endangering the life and health of military personnel."[9] The public affairs director of the National Association of Evangelicals, among others, joined them in their opposition, as did the Roman Catholic archbishop over the church's military archdiocese in Silver Spring, Maryland.[10] Further, the SBC chided "homosexual politics" for "masquerading today as 'civil rights,' in order to exploit the moral high ground of the civil rights movement."[11]

The general evangelical perspective from the mid-1970s to the 1990s was one of preserving community morality. It was a culturally dominant position, thwarting the rights claims of a small, unpopular minority. There were a few concerns about the rights of Christians being lost with the ascendance of gay rights, such as the rights of religious publishers to make decisions based on their beliefs,[12] though the overwhelming attention was on preserving the moral status of the community.

Rather than protecting rights, many evangelicals were actively opposed to LGBT activists procuring rights protections by gaining legal minority status and being protected from nondiscrimination measures. This was evident in the evangelical support for the passage of Amendment 2 to the Colorado Constitution in 1992, which forbid "the state of Colorado or any of its political subdivisions" from adopting policies granting LGBT people the ability "to claim any minority or protected status, quota preferences, or discrimination."[13] The group Colorado for Family Values organized the measure, heavily mobilizing voters in churches.[14] Evangelical organizations, such as the SBC, supported the amendment, with the Colorado Baptist General Convention unanimously endorsing it.[15] Even more, in 1993, the national denomination passed a resolution "oppos[ing] all effort to provide government endorsement, sanction, recognition, acceptance, or civil advantage on the basis of homosexuality."

When the Colorado Supreme Court struck down Amendment 2, which had passed with 53% of the vote, a leader of the SBC's advocacy group called the decision "supremely illogical on its face."[16] After the case reached the U.S. Supreme Court as *Romer v. Evans* in 1995, the SBC's Christian Life

Commission joined the Christian Legal Society, the National Association of Evangelicals, the Lutheran Church-Missouri Synod, Focus on the Family, and other evangelical organizations in supporting the constitutionality of the law. Interestingly, their common brief gave particular attention to religious liberty, arguing that adding sexual orientation to nondiscrimination requirements "imposes serious burdens upon religious exercise that exemptions do not sufficiently protect."[17] Their rights claim buttressed majoritarian politics.

The U.S. Supreme Court disagreed, siding with the gay rights activists in a 6–3 decision. The opinion, a precursor to *Obergefell*, was also written by Justice Kennedy. In a strongly worded dissent, Justice Scalia sounded the alarm for morality politics, as the Court turned "moral disapproval of homosexual conduct" into "animus."[18] In this dissent, as well as his dissent in *Lawrence v. Texas* (2003), Scalia suggested that the Court's rationale indicates that no moral prohibition of consensual sexuality will stand. These decisions began to orient some in the Christian Right toward rights arguments.[19] But at the same time, many conservative activists were entrenched, seeing an opportunity to capitalize on opposition to gay marriage.

The Immorality of Gay Marriage

Despite the warning from *Romer* and Justice Scalia, the Christian Right persisted in advocating the protection of morality, particularly in regard to gay marriage. In the mid-1990s, the issue of gay marriage arrived on the cultural scene, following the 1993 decision of the Hawaii Supreme Court to require a "compelling state interest" to deny same-sex marriages. The Hawaii Circuit Court proceeded in 1996 to rule that the state's ban on same-sex marriage was unconstitutional.[20] Evangelicals and their allies sought to curb any momentum toward the recognition of same-sex marriages and domestic partnerships. Following the Hawaii ruling, the Family Research Council called the decision a denial of "not only the wisdom of generations but the law of nature and nature's God."[21] In a 1996 resolution, the SBC proclaimed, "There is much scientific evidence showing that homosexual attractions are pathological, abnormal, and mostly if not entirely a matter of external influence, learned behavior, acquired taste and personal choice." After presenting a fervent biblical case opposing homosexuality and supporting traditional marriage, the resolution warned that "the United States of America will be placed at risk" if gay marriage is accepted. As such, the denomination "steadfastly oppose[d] the legalization of homosexual marriage."[22] That same year, the U.S. Congress complied, passing the Defense of Marriage Act (DOMA). DOMA was authored by Congressman Bob Barr (R-GA), who identified its need by declaring on the House floor, "The very foundations of our society are in danger of being burned. The flames of hedonism, the flames of narcissism, the flames of self-centered morality are licking at the very foundation of our society: the family unit."[23] Senator Robert Byrd

(D-WV) called giving same-sex relationships the status as heterosexual marriage "absurd," and Congressman Tom Coburn (R-OK) professed that his constituents believe "that homosexuality is immoral ... based on perversion ... based on lust."[24]

DOMA had two primary functions. Section 2 declared that no state would be required to recognize same-sex marriages from other states, and Section 3 defined that for all federal government entities the word "marriage" means "only a legal union between one man and one woman as husband and wife." Both houses of Congress passed the legislation by supermajorities, and President Bill Clinton signed it into law in September 1996.

In the political fights to thwart gay marriage, establishing a majoritarian morality position was again the emphasis of most evangelical activists. Gay rights activists were presented as an affront to American culture and American Christianity, and their rights were minimized. Majoritarian politics was the theme, though there was some concern about the future minority status of Christians if LGBT rights took hold. Within the SBC's 1996 resolution on same-sex marriage, it warned that the "recognition of homosexual marriages ... will certainly undermine, and may even restrain, the public communication, influence, and independence of individuals, groups, and institutions" who view gay marriage as immoral.[25] Other leaders expressed similar sentiments, though the primary emphasis of anti–gay marriage advocacy was the affirmative advocacy of morality, not the defensive advocacy of rights.

The last hurrah happened in 2004. After the Massachusetts Supreme Judicial Court ruled that the state's law against same-sex marriage violated its constitution and the Mayor of San Francisco began issuing same-sex marriage licenses, the issue ascended in cultural and political relevance. Political scientists David Campbell and J. Quin Monson identified a large spike in newspaper and broadcast media stories concerning gay marriage in the first half of 2004.[26] After this spike of attention, thirteen states put forth ballot measures that established marriage to be between one man and one woman, effectively banning gay marriage. This was a coordinated Republican strategy, with a focus on the general election.[27] All of these measures were successful, most passing by overwhelming numbers. Moreover, Campbell and Monson estimate that these ballot measures increased George W. Bush's electoral support among evangelicals, helping propel him to victory over John Kerry.[28] But the political tide was changing quickly, as gay marriage proponents grasped the increasingly potent "right to marriage" approach.

THE CHANGING TIDE OF RIGHTS

In 2008, Barack Obama opposed same-sex marriage as a presidential candidate, stating to audiences as diverse as mega-church pastor Rick Warren and MTV, "I believe that marriage is between a man and a woman. I am not in favor of gay marriage."[29] Yet, in 2011 the Obama administration declined to defend Section 3 of the DOMA, which required the federal government not to recognize same-sex marriages from other states, calling it unconstitutional.[30] In 2012, President Obama declared that his views had evolved in an interview with ABC News, "I've just concluded that for me personally it is important for me to go ahead and affirm that I think same-sex couples should be able to get married."[31]

Further, in 2008 California passed a state constitutional amendment – Proposition 8 – banning gay marriage through a ballot initiative effort. Proposition 8 declared that "only marriage between a man and a woman is valid or recognized in California," and it passed 52% to 48%.[32] Yet by 2010, the state of California decided not to defend Proposition 8, though it was democratically approved only two years prior.

Legal challenges to both DOMA and Proposition 8 arrived at the U.S. Supreme Court in 2013, under the case names *U.S. v. Windsor* and *Hollingsworth v. Perry*, respectively. The Obama administration formally opposed the laws restricting marriage in both cases, deeming them unconstitutional limitations on the rights of same-sex couples.[33] The Supreme Court declined to rule on the Proposition 8 case, declaring that one party lacked standing. In *Windsor*, the Court struck down Section 3 of DOMA, ruling that the federal government was required by the Constitution to recognize same-sex marriages as legitimate. Justice Kennedy again wrote the opinion, and with it the future outcome in *Obergefell* (2015), establishing a national right to same-sex marriage, was certainly all but determined.

While presidents, governors, and Supreme Court justices were evolving on gay marriage, public opinion, too, was changing quickly. Gallup found that the percent of Americans who supported gay marriages as being valid rose from 27% in 1996 when Congress passed DOMA to 60% just prior to the Supreme Court's *Obergefell* decision.[34] Pew reports a similar trend, showing that in 2011 for the first time more Americans supported same-sex marriage than opposed it.[35] Religious groups too increased their support, though evangelicals remained some of the most opposed to same-sex marriage. In Pew's religious landscape survey, evangelicals are among the least supportive of same-sex marriage, with only 28% favoring it in 2014. Catholics, by contrast, were twice as likely to favor same-sex marriage at 57%.[36]

Figure 7.1 uses data from the General Social Survey to plot evangelical and non-evangelical opposition to same-sex marriage over time (1988–2014), though the question was not asked between 1988 and 2004. The rate of change is much higher for non-evangelicals (dashed line), especially prior to 2006, as they became less opposed to same-sex marriage. From 2004 to 2014, total evangelical opposition (solid line) fell more than 20 points, while non-evangelical opposition fell more than 30 points. Though they are less opposed to the right to same-sex marriage, evangelicals remain one of the primary cultural holdouts.

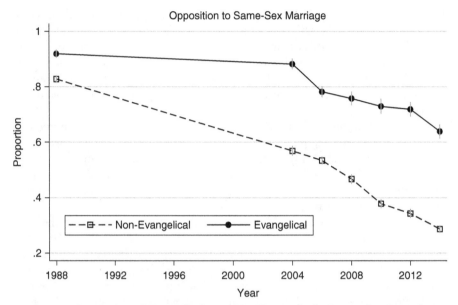

FIGURE 7.1. Proportion of Evangelicals and Non-Evangelicals Opposed to Same-Sex Marriage. GSS, 1988–2014.

The Collapse of Opposition to Same-Sex Marriage

Public opinion of the Christian Right's two primary moral issues – same-sex marriage and abortion – is behaving differently. Opposition to same-sex marriage is eroding, while pro-life attitudes are stable, and perhaps growing. Rights politics may be a cause. In a 2005 article, political scientist and religion scholar Ted Jelen suggested that conservatives' lack of a counter rights claim would be detrimental to their public support, especially in the face of a growing gay rights movement. Jelen describes the pro-life movement as the "clearest example" of a conservative religious position that emphasizes rights, also underscoring the effectiveness of the free exercise of religion as a fundamental human right.[37] Yet, he suggests that the communal language that seeks to rebuff same-sex marriage, such as "the sanctity of marriage," will "ultimately be unsuccessful," as it has no individualist grounding to compete against Lockean liberal arguments.[38] There is evidence of this in the data, even for evangelicals.

Beginning in 1974, the GSS asked respondents whether they approved or disapproved of same-sex relations. From 1974 to 2014, evangelicals have remained fairly steady in their high levels of disapproval of same-sex relations, only declining slightly even in the past decade. This is in the face of remarkable declines in disapproval of same-sex relations for non-evangelicals, with their rates of opposition cut in half from nearly 80% opposed to less than 40%. So

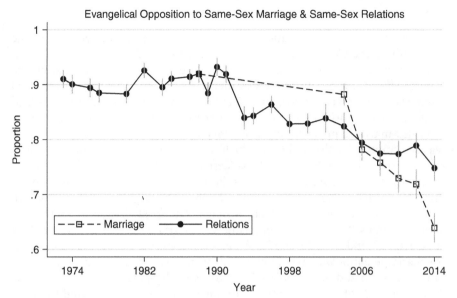

FIGURE 7.2. Proportion of Evangelical Opposition to Same-Sex Marriage and Same-Sex Relations. GSS, 1974–2014.

while evangelicals remain strongly supportive of traditional sexual morality, of late they have become more favorable toward same-sex marriage by a margin of about 15%. This gap is shown in Figure 7.2; the differentiation emerges after 2004 and has continued to grow. The vertical gray bars reflect standard errors, and when these do not overlap, we can consider the differences statistically significant. These show that evangelicals' perspective on same-sex relations versus same-sex marriage has flipped in the past few election cycles. In 2004, evangelicals were more likely to oppose same-sex marriage than same-sex relations, but since 2008, evangelicals are significantly more opposed to same-sex relations than same-sex marriage.

This gap between personal morality and support for legal rights suggests that in public policy evangelicals have been willing to cede ground to liberal rights-based arguments for gay marriage. Compare this to the steady opposition to abortion rights among evangelicals, as discussed in Chapter 2, and we can infer some support for Jelen's arguments. Moreover, my colleagues and I found that in 2011 there was no credible conservative counter rights claim to same-sex marriage as there was to issues such as abortion, education policy, and the death penalty.[39] All this considered, the absence of a counter rights claim has been detrimental to the traditional marriage coalition. A demand for public policy to reflect private morality has given way to an acceptance of individual rights to supersede personal morality, and this demand has structured the evangelicals' approach to politics.

SAME-SEX MARRIAGE: THE OTHER RIGHTS

The role of rights claims, and their absence, is further implicated by the aftermath of the Court's decision to mandate the legality and recognition of same-sex marriage nationwide. Even as the Supreme Court was hearing the *Obergefell* cases, a coalition of six evangelical organizations, three evangelical seminaries, and eleven Christian intellectuals – many of them evangelical – filed an *amicus curiae* brief indicating their concerns over how a ruling in favor of same-sex marriage might harm their right to free speech. The Liberty Institute was the counsel for the coalition, which included major players in evangelical politics, such as the Religious Broadcasters Association, the Billy Graham Evangelistic Association, Samaritan's Purse – the Christian charity led by Franklin Graham – and The Southern Baptist Theological Seminary, as well as its prominent president, Albert Mohler. The brief described conflicts in which religious "dissenters" from same-sex marriage have been "silenced by state actors," and then declared: "A decision from this Court imposing same-sex marriage nationwide would inevitably exacerbate these conflicts, and inexorably result in additional violations of free speech rights."[40]

The breadth of the conservative argument in this Christian Right *amicus* brief deserves attention. The religious coalition's position on free speech was so broad that it asked the Court to refrain from making a substantive legal ruling on a non–free speech issue in order to protect against the by-product of such a ruling – the potential for limiting free speech. As the brief put it, "This Court should affirm the decision below [upholding state bans on same-sex marriage] – in part to protect the First Amendment rights of those who disagree with same-sex marriage."[41] Ruling in favor of same-sex marriage would result in equality advocates using the decision "as a weapon to marginalize persons of faith."[42]

Even more, moments after the Supreme Court struck down state laws and established the fundamental right to same-sex marriage, religious advocates immediately shifted toward protecting their rights. Jordan Lorence, senior counsel of the Christian legal group Alliance Defending Freedom, spoke at a press conference outside the Supreme Court, stating, "We hope that this decision today will not be used as an excuse to ostracize, to demonize, or to punish people for holding views contrary to what five of the nine justices said today."[43] The Christian Right was quick to shift to rights politics.

While some conservatives, including presidential candidates Mike Huckabee and Rick Santorum, sought to challenge the ruling directly by blocking its implementation at the state level or calling for other federal institutions to reject the supremacy of the Supreme Court,[44] evangelicals, Catholics, and other political conservatives turned their attention to rights, particularly religious freedom and free speech rights. Several occurrences epitomize the post-*Obergefell* (and *Windsor*) approach to religion and gay rights. I focus on three: Kim Davis, Barronelle Stutzman, and the Indiana Religious Freedom Restoration Act.

The County Clerk

Kim Davis is a clerk in Rowan County, Kentucky, a government official who refused to issue marriage licenses to same-sex couples in the summer of 2015 following the Supreme Court's ruling in *Obergefell*. Citing her religious convictions of the evangelical Apostolic Church, Davis refused to personally issue the licenses. Additionally, because her name appeared on the official license, she prohibited any deputy clerks from issuing the licenses to gay couples. Davis's stance garnered national attention in the weeks following the Court's decision, and some prominent evangelicals, including presidential candidates Mike Huckabee of Arkansas and Ted Cruz of Texas, supported her. In September 2015, Davis was jailed after a federal judge found her in contempt of court for refusing to issue the licenses.[45] Liberty Counsel, the prominent Christian legal advocacy group focused on religious freedom, represented Davis, and when she was jailed, one of their lawyers proclaimed, "Today, for the first time in history, an American citizen has been incarcerated for having the belief of conscience that marriage is the union of one man and one woman." Senator Ted Cruz (R-TX) declared, "Today, judicial lawlessness crossed into judicial tyranny."[46] After her release, the Family Research Council announced that they would honor her at their Values Voter Summit for standing for her convictions and for religious liberty.[47]

While many evangelical Christians supported Davis, some conservatives took issue with her stance. Leaders of the SBC's Ethics and Religious Liberty Commission, for example, took a nuanced approach. They first chided the Supreme Court for putting state and local officials in these positions because the justices "impos[ed] their redefinition of marriage on the rest of the United States instead of allowing states to decide their own marriage policy." They then criticized the Kentucky governor for not seeking an accommodation for Davis. But on the merits, Russell Moore and the ERLC leadership could not fully support Davis's claim, as it was complicated by her status as a government employee. They wrote:

We must recognize the crucial difference between the religious liberty claims of private citizens and government officials.... . While government employees don't lose their constitutional protection *simply* because they work for the government, an individual whose office requires them to *uphold* or *execute* the law is a separate matter than the private citizen whose conscience is infringed upon as a *result* of the law.[48]

Despite the complicated case, Davis thrust the conflict of rights – religious liberty versus gay rights – onto the national stage.

The Small Business Owner

While the SBC leaders were hesitant to fully support Davis because of her government obligation, they did rally around the religious liberty claims of a private citizen, Barronelle Stutzman. Stutzman is the seventy-year-old owner of Arlene's Flowers, a small flower shop in Richland, Washington. In 2013, citing her religious beliefs, she refused to provide flowers for a same-sex wedding of a gay couple who were frequent customers of hers. The couple filed suit against Stutzman under Washington's antidiscrimination laws, and in early 2015 Stutzman lost, resulting in a $1,000 fine and more than $1 million in legal fees.[49] Stutzman is a Southern Baptist, and though less recognized than Davis, she too gained national attention, especially among conservatives. Her case represented the clash between religious freedom and gay rights, the state and individual liberty. In October 2014, Stutzman made an appearance at an ERLC conference on "The Gospel, Homosexuality and the Future of Marriage" in Nashville, Tennessee, stressing the importance of religious liberty.[50] The following summer, at the Southern Baptist Convention's 2015 annual meeting in Columbus, Ohio, she received a standing ovation when Russell Moore of the ERLC addressed her case as a fight for religious freedom. "Mrs. Stutzman knew that the truth is not up for sale and the Gospel doesn't bend to the highest bidder," Moore said.[51]

Stutzman's case epitomizes a variety of evangelical business owners and nonprofits who have run afoul of state and local nondiscrimination requirements because of their views on same-sex marriage. These cases include a baker from Colorado who declined to make a wedding cake for a same-sex couple, a photographer from New Mexico who refused to photograph a same-sex wedding, and an evangelical college in Massachusetts that faced accreditation pressures for its policies barring sexual relations for faculty or students outside of heterosexual marriage. In each, the religious individuals and institutions presented their First Amendment rights to religious freedom and free speech to protect their views on traditional morality. Success has been mixed. Gordon College in Massachusetts maintained its accreditation,[52] but the U.S. Supreme Court declined to hear Elane Photography's appeal of its nearly $7,000 fine for violating New Mexico's nondiscrimination ordinance,[53] as did the Colorado Supreme Court for Jack Phillips's refusal to bake a same-sex wedding cake.[54]

On February 16, 2017, the Washington Supreme Court upheld Stutzman's fine in her final state-based appeal. Christian Right religious freedom advocates were outraged, including ADF and the ERLC. ADF's senior counsel frustratingly responded, "Freedom of speech and religion aren't subject to the whim of a majority; they are constitutional guarantees." The ERLC's Moore argued that the ruling "shortchanges our nation's most fundamental freedom in favor of ideological conformity" and makes Stutzman "the target of a government that wants to steamroll her constitutional rights."[55] Both Stutzman and her conservative Christian allies are seeking a final hearing by the U.S. Supreme Court.

This growing conflict, and the fear among Christian conservatives, was foretold in the oral arguments of *Obergefell*, when Justice Samuel Alito asked Donald Verrilli, the Solicitor General for the Obama administration: "Well in the Bob Jones case [1983], the Court held that a college was not entitled to tax-exempt status if it opposed interracial marriage or interracial dating. So would the same apply to a university of college if it opposed same-sex marriage?" A flustered Verrilli responded: "You know, I don't think I can answer that question without knowing more specifics, but it's certainly going to be an issue. I don't deny that."[56] Almost immediately after the Supreme Court guaranteed the right to same-sex marriages in *Obergefell*, evangelical and Catholic advocacy groups and organizations began trying to secure their rights, shifting away from seeking to overturn the law. When the Washington Supreme Court ruled against Stutzman, ADF argued that the decision was about "crushing dissent," a position new to what at one time was the silent majority.[57] Cultural minority politics, centered on rights, was in full force.

The Legislative Remedy

For conservative Christians, a primary objective of rights politics has been procuring legislative responses to actual or hypothetical judicial decisions. In the wake of the Supreme Court's gay marriage rulings and state and local decisions to require religious businesses to provide services to same-sex couples, many states sought to enhance legislative protections for the religious freedom rights of individuals and nonprofits. Proponents titled these "Religious Freedom Restoration Acts," drawing on federal legislation that was passed by a Democratic Congress without opposition in 1993 and signed by President Bill Clinton. This legislation provided a robust protection for religious freedom, requiring the government to have a "compelling state interest" and use the "least restrictive means" to override an individual's right to religious freedom. The federal RFRA restored the requirements of prior Supreme Court cases before the right to free exercise was limited in 1990 by the Court's ruling in *Employment Division v. Smith*.[58] Because of *City of Boerne v. Flores* (1997), a Supreme Court ruling, the federal RFRA was limited in its scope, only applying to the federal government. In the wake of the *Boerne* decision, twenty-one states passed their own RFRAs.

Traditionally RFRAs protected religious minorities with little political clout, falling outside of the public spotlight and avoiding much of evangelicalism's purview. Following the 2010 Affordable Care Act and the ensuing requirement to provide contraceptives, the significance of the federal RFRA was realized. As discussed in Chapter 5, Hobby Lobby won its Supreme Court case because of the federal RFRA, and in turn several evangelical and Catholic institutions earned protection from government regulations. In the wake of a series of federal court rulings legalizing same-sex marriage, culminating with *Obergefell*, some states without RFRAs sought to enhance their religious freedom protections. These included Kansas, North Carolina, Arkansas, and, most prominently, Indiana.

In the spring of 2015, while awaiting the Court's *Obergefell* ruling, Indiana's proposed RFRA started to gain national attention. It was featured prominently in national newspapers, leading news broadcasts and filling social media feeds on the left and the right. Depending on one's position on the legislation, it was categorized as a license to discriminate or a protection of a vital freedom. At the end of March, Governor Mike Pence signed the law, but backlash ensued, with protests, public pressure, and businesses and sports institutions threatening to leave the state. On April 2, Pence signed legislative revisions to the law, seeking a compromise that softened the protections.[59]

Neither side was pleased. Some major media outlets began putting religious freedom in "scare quotes" in their headlines, signaling their disbelief in the claimed rights, while evangelicals, Catholics, and other supporters insisted on the importance of religious freedom for diverse viewpoints, even those that might be seen as discriminator. The battle over same-sex marriage had officially been recast: the right to equal treatment versus the right to religious freedom. But the larger significance has been largely ignored: the competitive frames portended the end of an era, as cultural majoritarian politics was in retreat, falling back to higher ground – religious liberty. Conservatives now were forced to argue a competing rights claim. It did not ensure victory, but it was an entre to debate in both politics and law.

LEARNING FROM THE PRO-LIFE MOVEMENT

In the wake of their cultural defeat regarding gay rights, conservative Christian activists have navigated toward the language of rights. This change in tactics was a natural reaction to a minority cultural position, and, in the process, Christian conservatives drew lessons from one of conservatisms' most profitable movements – the pro-life movement. As the Supreme Court was considering state-level restrictions on same-sex marriage, traditional marriage activists from both the Catholic and evangelical traditions began linking the pro-life movement with opposition to same-sex marriage. In a 2014 article in *Crisis Magazine*, a conservative, Catholic publication, Rachel Lu culled lessons from the pro-life movement for the defense of traditional marriage. She admitted that advocates for traditional marriage, unlike pro-life advocates, lacked "a core moral message around which to rally." To rectify this, she urged advocates to focus on the rights of children to have a mother and a father, indicating that this was successful in France.[60] That same year in *Baptist Press*, college professor Brian Cribb too drew lessons from the pro-life movement. He called evangelicals to accentuate the positives of biblical, heterosexual marriage, to argue "for" a position rather than "against" something, as the pro-life movement argued for life.[61] Evangelicals and Catholics were seeking more sophisticated, politically pragmatic arguments, as they had developed for the pro-life movement and other political positions.[62]

These lessons regarding the strategy of public arguments, as learned from the politics of abortion and applied to the same-sex marriage debate, continued to reverberate within conservative and religious circles. Writing to a broader conservative audience in *National Review*, Ryan Anderson, a Catholic and a leading activist opposing the legalization of same-sex marriage, credited the pro-life movement for its emphasis on the rights and dignity of the unborn. He then called conservatives to extend the pro-life movement to traditional marriage, because "decades of social-science research confirm that the best place on average for a child to grow up is with his married biological mom and dad."[63] This was echoed by evangelical commentator John Stonestreet of Breakpoint, part of Charles Colson's ministry. In an article titled "The Other Right," Stonestreet argued that "we believe that children not only have a right to *life*; they *also* have the right to a mom and a dad."[64]

Interestingly, the emphasis on "the other right" in the same-sex marriage debate seems to have gained traction in the United States after being stressed by Pope Francis, who has gained international attention for his softening of the Catholic Church's message toward those in the LGBT community. This rhetoric about the rights of children was central to the Vatican's conference on the "Complementarity of Man and Woman" in November 2014, with Pope Francis declaring in his keynote speech that "children have a right to grow up in a family with a father and a mother capable of creating a suitable environment for the child's development and emotional maturity."[65] Russell Moore of the ERLC, who was in attendance at the pope's invitation, responded immediately on social media, drawing the connection to the same-sex marriage debate. Moore wrote, "Pope Francis made clear that male/female complementary is essential to marriage and cannot be revised by contemporary ideologies."[66] Anderson and Stonestreet soon followed with their articles.

This line of argumentation is nascent, but the best-case scenario for conservatives would be what happened with the pro-life movement, where a compelling rights-based argument coalesced with scientific data to serve as a formidable counterweight to a social and political movement – abortion rights – that many thought was a foregone conclusion. Writing on the day of the Supreme Court's *Obergefell* decision, Russell Moore accentuated this link, titling his piece "We've Been Here Before: Lessons for the Marriage Debate from the Pro-Life Movement" and comparing *Obergefell* to *Roe*. Moore penned:

The pro-life movement's victories were only possible because its champions understood that legal consensus is never the final word. Imagine how much different the cause for life and dignity would look today if that first generation of pro-life advocates decided that being on the wrong side of history was just too high a price to pay. Thank God it was not for them, and God forbid it should be us. Let's follow their lead onward.[67]

Shortly after the Supreme Court decision, Ryan Anderson published his book, *Truth Overruled*, which seeks to craft a positive, public argument for traditional marriage and religious freedom. Anderson's book is endorsed by leading evangelicals such as Russell Moore, mega-church pastor Rick Warren, and author and public speaker Eric Metaxas. Throughout, he draws on the heritage of the pro-life movement. In the introduction, Anderson states, "Even those who disagree with the pro-life cause respect it and recognize that it has a legitimate place in the debate over public policy. And – this is crucial – it's because of that respect that pro-choice leaders generally respect the religious liberty and conscience rights of their pro-life fellow citizens."[68] Anderson emphasizes the need for improved public arguments, the importance of securing the rights to religious liberty and religious freedom, and the hope of a multi-generational strategy.

Many evangelical activists have hailed Anderson's book and adopted his emphasis on rights and his connection to the politics of abortion. In fact, the SBC invited Anderson to speak at an ERLC Conference on marriage and religious freedom in October 2014. (Recalling Chapter 4, it is no small feat for a Catholic to gain such prominence in Southern Baptist life.) Anderson's message to Southern Baptists drew on the lessons of the pro-life movement, emphasizing how pro-lifers gained tolerance from the wider society through their use of natural law and natural rights arguments. "Government ultimately should respect the rights of all citizens," Anderson said. "And a form of government that's respectful of free association and free contracts and free speech and free exercise of religion would protect citizens' rights to live according to their beliefs that marriage is a union of a man and a woman."[69] This connection to the First Amendment, the politics of abortion, and the politics of marriage appealed to his Southern Baptist partners, as they had been extending the pro-life movements to other domains. The mass public also seems to regard this approach better, as they are more favorable to rights-based religious liberty arguments that focus on pluralism than to rights-based arguments against same-sex marriage.[70]

CONCLUSION

The story of gay marriage advocacy confirms many of the lessons of the prior chapter. The Christian Right's most decisive culture war defeat – same-sex marriage – has instigated the process of rights politics, which has already been under way in other domains. Because of the legal and cultural victory for gay rights, evangelicals are more dependent on rights politics now than ever. In perhaps no other area are they a threatened minority, which is why there are increasing appeals on the right to rights and pluralism. Certainly evangelicals are not without political power, as seen by the success of state-level RFRAs and their potent legal teams, but they are in a defensive position in regard to sexual morality.

The lessons from the battle over gay rights fit well within the broader framework of the previous chapters, as this issue area displays active rights learning and rights claiming. The era of twentieth-century-style traditional cultural morality is ending, though that end is piecemeal and episodic, not total and linear, as parts of the Donald Trump campaign made manifest.

Evangelicals largely lost the battle over pornography laws several decades before they lost the battle over the definition of marriage. Out of the pornography defeat arose an advocacy strategy that utilized free speech to evangelicals' political and legal advantage. Over the past decade, evangelicals have lost the battle over the definition of marriage, and they have increasingly turned toward religious freedom. This will only increase. Sitting just below the surface is the politics of abortion, guiding and informing religious advocacy, at both the elite and rank-and-file levels.

Moreover, as we have seen in other areas of law and politics, some political liberals have embraced a new kind of community morality regarding equal treatment for sexual orientation, punishing dissent. In these situations, conservatives attack liberals for functioning as communitarians and demanding conformity, while liberals attack conservatives, saying that their embrace of human rights demands communitarian discrimination. At the very least, both now lay claim to rights. The mediating of these competing claims is likely to be the focus of religious politics for the foregoing future.

8

Conclusion

Rights, Reciprocity, and the Future of Conservative Religious Politics

On June 21, 2016, presumptive Republican presidential nominee Donald Trump held a meeting at Trump Tower with evangelical political leaders and activists. At the meeting, Trump announced his evangelical advisory board, which included prominent leaders of the Christian Right from the past three decades.[1] Many of the names appeared in earlier portions of this book, including Ralph Reed of the Faith and Freedom Coalition (formerly of the Family Research Council); Richard Land of Southern Evangelical Seminary (formerly of the Ethics & Religious Liberty Commission); James Dobson, founder of Focus on the Family; and Jerry Falwell, Jr. of Liberty University (son of Jerry Falwell, Sr.). After securing the Republican nomination, Trump gained the support of dozens of prominent Christian Right leaders. Some, such as Falwell,[2] offered their support willingly; others, such as Land, were more tepid, seeing Trump merely as a better choice than the Democratic nominee Hillary Clinton.[3]

Not all of evangelicalism was supportive of Trump, however. In fact, the latter wave of evangelical leaders was quite critical of his candidacy for his lack of moral character (both personal and in business), his rhetoric toward minorities and immigrants, and his lack of support for the pro-life movement. Many conservative evangelical activists were active in the "Never Trump" movement, including Russell Moore of the ERLC and conservative blogger Erick Erickson.[4] So when Trump met with evangelical leaders on June 21, he was seeking to rally support from an important part of his base, some of which had been tepid or even vocally opposed to him. At the meeting, a young evangelical activist, Eric Teetsel, made an uninvited appearance. Teetsel was the former executive director of the Manhattan Declaration, which focused on religious advocacy against abortion and gay marriage and for religious liberty. In late 2015, the Marco Rubio (R-FL) presidential campaign hired Teetsel as its Director of Faith Outreach.

On this June morning, Teetsel was in New York City advocating for a conservative alternative to Trump to join the presidential race, but this particular morning he decided to make a statement to his fellow evangelicals. He stopped by a local drug store, bought some poster board, and made a homemade protest sign, which read in bold red letters: "Torture is not pro-life; Racism is not pro-life; Misogyny is not pro-life; Murdering the children of terrorists is not pro-life."[5] Teetsel was protesting Trump's actions and statements that seemed to go against the tenets of evangelical Christianity. Yahoo News ran a story on Teetsel's protest with a picture of his homemade sign, and it soon echoed across social media. Russell Moore declared on Twitter, "Eric Teetsel is right about what it means to be pro-life."[6]

Teetsel's message is instructive for contemporary evangelical activism. First, abortion is the touchstone of evangelical politics. Evangelical leaders tie their political advocacy in other areas to abortion in order to both represent their constituents and to serve as a prophetic witness, seeking to change their views. In the process, evangelicals have learned the value of rights. Prior chapters have shown how conservative rights claims were proffered in the areas of free speech and religious liberty, seeking to protect the place of conservative Christians in the public square. Christians were also mobilized against health care reform initiatives and both for and against the legalization of capital punishment using religious rights claims. In all these cases, the politics of abortion has been a frequent message used by elites to connect lesser political issues to the most salient position – pro-life – or teach constituents about the need to take a different position. Over the past forty years, the politics of abortion activated *rights learning* and *rights claiming* among both evangelical elites and the rank-and-file.

On his homemade protest sign, Teetsel used abortion to display *rights learning* and *rights claiming*, though so too did many evangelical Trump supporters, focusing not on specific economic or immigration policies, but on Trump's opportunity to appoint at least one Supreme Court justice who could overturn *Roe v. Wade* and his promises to protect religious liberty for evangelicals. But in addition to *rights learning* and *rights claiming*, Teetsel was arguing for something greater, something beyond evangelicals themselves – *rights extending*.

AN OPPORTUNITY FOR RIGHTS EXTENDING

The preceding chapters have largely stopped after investigating evangelical *rights learning* and *rights claiming*, begging a question: What are the broader implications of conservative rights politics? One option is that an emphasis on rights could balkanize and polarize, degrading democratic discourse as factions cling to uncompromising positions. Legal scholar Mary Ann Glendon developed this thesis twenty-five years ago in her influential book *Rights Talk*,[7] and she has been joined by others.[8] Political Scientist Geoffrey Layman too raised this concern in the conclusion of his influential book, speaking specifically about abortion. Layman lamented that not only have the two political parties "taken highly polarized cultural stands, but they have treated the issues superficially, using the emotional language of fundamental rights – the 'fundamental right to life' of the unborn or the 'fundamental constitutional liberty' of every woman to make her own reproductive decisions – rather than providing reasoned explanations of their positions."[9] A large concern with rights politics is that the fabric of communal and political life will be lost through rights-induced polarization.

While polarization is certainly a concern, at the same time, evangelical rights politics have the potential to teach them about others' rights. Attention to rights might be part of the political process. As Ted Jelen put it in 2005, rights-based rhetoric may be the most broadly accessible form of discourse.[10] Furthermore, once individuals learn about rights and understand their value in a pluralistic system, they may become likely to support the rights of those with whom they disagree. In fact, my coauthors and I have previously found evidence supporting this, as conservative political candidates who employ rights-based justifications for their positions are seen by the public as more moderate, not more polarized, than candidates who employ moral justifications.[11]

As such, the politics of abortion have the potential to activate *rights extending* among American evangelicals. If this is true, political liberals and pluralists should celebrate this outcome of conservative Christian politics. Even though large segments of the public would disagree with conservative positions on abortion, marriage, and perhaps religious liberty, we should all commend the process if it taught religious elites and a substantial portion of the public to support the rights of opponents.[12]

Returning to the Teetsel example, his homemade sign was trying to extend the argument of human dignity vouchsafed by the right to life to the human dignity of Muslims, women, and enemy combatants. Certainly this is not a panacea, as his sign and his message did not cause evangelicals *en masse* to reject Trump or remove their names from his advisory board, and most of them voted for a candidate who espoused intolerant views. But if the average evangelical respects the rights of opponents more now than before and engages in greater political tolerance, then we should welcome the progress (though not perfection) made by conservative rights politics. In what follows, I briefly discuss data regarding the evolution of evangelical support for rights and political tolerance.

RESPECT FOR RIGHTS AND POLITICAL TOLERANCE

For the past six decades, many social scientists have analyzed individuals' respect for citizens' rights. Within the academic literature, this has come to be called *political tolerance* – when individuals acknowledge the equal rights of their political opponents. The study of political tolerance began with the work of sociologist Samuel Stouffer in 1955,[13] and it has persisted among several streams of sociological and political science research.[14] Over the course of this research, religion has stood out as a primary inhibitor of political tolerance.[15] Religiously traditional people, including the more dogmatic, authoritarian, and threatened, are on average more intolerant than others,[16] though there is some recent counterevidence that religious beliefs and practices can enhance tolerance.[17]

Chapter 3 provides some insight into evangelical political tolerance regarding free speech. Recall one of the primary measures of support for free speech was taken from a battery of questions from the General Social Survey about political minority groups – atheists, racists, communists, militarists, and homosexuals. These GSS questions are frequently employed as a measure of political tolerance, deemed the "fixed-group" approach. Those with a higher support for the political rights of these groups have greater tolerance, and vice versa.[18] Chapter 3 measured support for free speech with an aggregate index of whether individuals would allow members of a minority group to speak in public. Figure 3.1 showed that evangelicals have consistently trailed others in their support for free speech since 1976. That said, evangelical support for free speech has increased over the period, and it has increased at a greater rate than among non-evangelicals. In fact, evangelical tolerance for free speech was at its highest level ever in 2014, up almost 20% since 2008. Moreover, since 1998, evangelicals who score higher on the pro-life scale are more tolerant of free speech for political minorities than are evangelicals who score lower on the pro-life scale, accounting for a variety of other political and demographic variables.[19]

Similarly, the same data set asks a battery of questions about affording rights to homosexuals. Questions include whether a homosexual should be allowed to make a speech in the community, whether a homosexual should be allowed to teach in a college or university, and whether books on homosexuality should be allowed in the library. As with free speech, I combined these into an index of political tolerance for homosexuals. The standardized index ranges from 0 to 1, with higher values representing more tolerance. Figure 8.1 displays the results for evangelicals and non-evangelicals from 1973 to 2014, and the results look similar to those regarding free speech. Evangelicals consistently (and significantly) trail non-evangelicals in their tolerance for gays and lesbians, but their tolerance levels have increased quite dramatically. Evangelical tolerance for homosexuals has doubled since the early 1970s and grown 30% since the early 1990s.

Multivariate models provide some evidence that opposition to gay rights is not in lockstep with its culture war partner – abortion. The models, listed in full in Table 8.1 in Appendix B, indicate that more pro-life abortion attitudes, as well as being an evangelical, in general are related to decreased tolerance for gays and lesbians. Yet, the models also suggest that there is a contingent effect; anti-abortion attitudes may actually increase tolerance for gays and lesbians among conservative Christians of late. Prior to 2000, pro-life attitudes

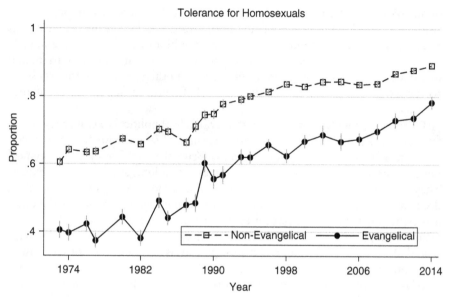

FIGURE 8.1. Evangelical and Non-Evangelical Tolerance for Homosexuals over Time. GSS, 1973–2014.

promoted more intolerance among evangelicals, but since 2000, pro-life attitudes help increase evangelical tolerance, though at insignificant levels.[20] For Catholics, pro-life attitudes consistently and significantly increase their likelihood of extending tolerance to gays and lesbians in both time periods. The politics of abortion may be teaching Christians the value of extending rights.

In a recent academic article, my colleagues, Paul Djupe and Ted Jelen, and I have examined rights extending in a more direct way.[21] We conducted a survey framing experiment that tested the effect of conservative-based rights claims on political tolerance. In the survey, participants had to read a short statement given by a political candidate or a clergy member regarding the owner of a photography business that refused to offer her service for a same-sex wedding based on her religious beliefs. The issue draws on the religious liberty versus gay rights controversies that are discussed in Chapter 7, and it almost exactly recounts the case *Elane Photography v. Willock* (2014). When the advocate (clergy or candidate) offered his position on the issue in the news snippet, he was randomly assigned to state his position with a different justification: morality, free speech, and religious liberty. This allowed us to isolate the effects of the different kind of justifications (morality, secular rights, and religious rights) against each other and a control condition (no justification).

To assess political tolerance, we employed a "least-liked group" approach pioneered by social scientists John L. Sullivan, James E. Piereson, and George E. Marcus in 1982.[22] Participants were given six groups across the ideological spectrum – immigrants, Tea Party members, Muslims, homosexuals, Christian fundamentalists, and atheists – and then asked to identify which one they liked the least or disagreed with the most. The least-liked approach produces a similar measure of political tolerance to the GSS fixed-group approach, with some caveats in recent years.[23] In our survey, evangelicals were most likely to choose atheists as their least-liked group, with Muslims second. Once respondents selected their least-liked group, they were asked a series of questions about whether they were willing to extend rights to this group including their ability to rally, run for office, make a speech, teach, keep a book in the library, and be free from a phone tap.

The justifications by a political candidate did not affect respondents' tolerance levels, but the clergy, however, did alter tolerance levels. The results are displayed graphically in Figure 8.2. When clergy employed a rights justification – free speech and religious liberty – the survey takers responded with more tolerant attitudes toward their least-liked group. This was especially true of evangelicals. The free speech frame enhanced tolerance, though outside of significance, but the religious liberty frame improved tolerance more than double the free speech frame, solidly within significance.

The implication here should not be missed by the discussion of statistical significance. When a religious elite presented evangelicals with a cue that

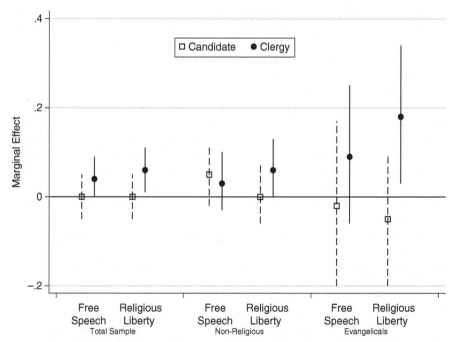

FIGURE 8.2. Marginal Effects of Conservative Rights Frames on Political Tolerance for Evangelicals and the Non-Religious with 90% Confidence Intervals. MTurk, 2015.

supported their political position on a politically charged issue, evangelicals reacted with increased tolerance for outsiders. Instead of triggering a defensive posture (and lower tolerance), the in-group's claiming of rights produced an extending effect, broadening democratic inclusion for ideological enemies.

This finding suggests that the evangelical emphases on religious liberty and abortion in their support for Trump, championed by many such as popular evangelical author Eric Metaxas,[24] could prime evangelicals to be willing to protect fundamental political rights of others. This will be borne out over time, though the glaring, early exception seems to be evangelicals' opinions of immigrants and refugees, following Trump's calls for a border wall with Mexico and for the halting of admission of Islamic immigrants and refugees following the 2015 terrorist attacks in Paris and San Bernardino, California. That said, in late 2015, my colleagues and I used survey data to argue that anti-Muslim bias is more a function of Republican identity than evangelicalism.[25] Untangling this is difficult, because evangelicalism and Republicanism are intertwined, but a brief example provides some insight into the process of rights extending.

SBC Mosque Controversy

In the summer and fall of 2010, a controversy arose over a proposal for a Muslim group to build an Islamic cultural center and mosque in lower Manhattan, only two blocks from the site of the September 11, 2001 attacks on the World Trade Center. This event elicited strong reactions from the American public, with nearly 60% disapproving of the building of this Islamic center, according to an August 26, 2010 Religious News Service poll.[26] Many religious leaders made public pronouncements and took policy positions regarding the appropriateness of the center. Because this was a controversy of the role of minority religions in American society and First Amendment rights, at least in part, the views of religious leaders frequently came to the fore. The Southern Baptist Convention's ERLC objected to the building of the Muslim center near Ground Zero. President Richard Land declared, "I defend the right for Muslims to have places of worship in lower Manhattan, but not at Ground Zero. . . . The right to religious freedom doesn't include the right to have a religious worship place wherever you want."[27] Land argued for limiting the rights of religious non-allies.

In opposing the Islamic cultural center near Ground Zero, Land's position was likely consistent with the views of many of his conservative Christian constituents, who probably opposed the building of this Muslim center in Manhattan's financial district. Land's position, however, was controversial in religious liberty circles. Baptists have been leaders in the area of religious liberty, as discussed in Chapter 4. Because of this reputation, supporting limitations on the rights of religious groups to establish facilities was seen as a misapplication of the Baptist heritage of defending religious freedom. In this case, *rights claiming* did not lead to *rights extending*.

In September 2010, however, Land joined the Anti-Defamation League's newly created Interfaith Coalition on Mosques. His participation showed his solidarity with the religious freedom rights of Muslims, despite resisting the Ground Zero Islamic cultural center. In being involved, Land was lending his name in support of "those involved in legal efforts to defend American Muslims who are having their legal rights under the First Amendment denied or curtailed by zoning commission and city councils."[28] Rights extending was gaining momentum.

Land's membership in the Interfaith Coalition on Mosques sparked significant controversy among Southern Baptists. In October 2010, the ERLC responded to constituents by posting an article entitled "Setting the Record Straight" on its website. The article discussed Land's view on the Ground Zero mosque and cultural center, his involvement in the Interfaith Coalition, his views on radical Islam, and his perspective on partnering with outside organizations. It explained that he sought to defend religious freedom, oppose radical Islam, and be sensitive to Americans' feelings about Ground Zero.[29] This was not enough to quell the controversy, and in January 2011, Land withdrew from the Interfaith Coalition. He wrote, "While many Southern Baptists share my deep commitment to religious freedom and the right of Muslims to have places of worship, they also feel that a Southern Baptist denominational leader filing suit to allow individual mosques to be built is 'a bridge too far.'"[30] Land later commented to the *Associated Press* that Southern Baptists felt that Interfaith Coalition was engaged in advocacy rather than merely defense of religious liberty, which crossed the line for an SBC agency leader. He said, "I don't agree with that perception, but it's widespread and I have to respect it."[31] While Chapter 4 shows how evangelicals came to embrace religious liberty over and above church-state separation in order to protect the role of faith in the public square, in 2011 the largest evangelical denomination was reluctant to extend these religious freedom rights to an opponent.

Flash forward only five years, and the stakes of religious liberty for evangelical Christians have grown. As Chapters 5 and 7 detail, the passage of the Affordable Care Act and the legalization of same-sex marriage have wrought legal controversies pitting religious conscience against government regulation. Their hegemony is under threat. In turn, evangelicals have become staunch supporters of religious liberty, backing Christian bakers, florists, and photographers, advocating for religious craft stores and Amish cabinetmakers, and supporting religious colleges and Catholic nuns. The SBC was a leader in these fights for religious freedom for evangelicals and their allies.

In 2014, Southern Baptists and other evangelical groups advocated for the extending of broad religious liberty rights to a typical opponent – a Muslim prisoner. In *Holt v. Hobbs*, Abdul Muhammad sued the Arkansas Department of Corrections, arguing that a rule prohibiting him from growing a beard in order to practice his religious beliefs violated his right to religious freedom. The International Mission Board of the Southern Baptist Convention, as well as other evangelical organizations, filed an *amicus* brief, urging the Supreme

Court to protect Muhammad's right to religious freedom. In January 2015, a unanimous Court sided with the prisoner. Russell Moore of the ERLC praised the decision. "Religious liberty isn't a prize earned by those with the most political clout," said Moore. "Christians and others should be glad, especially in a time when the most basic liberties are routinely dismissed in many corners of our national debate."[32] Rights claiming had promoted rights extending.

The next year, Moore and the SBC would go further. A community of Muslims in New Jersey had been repeatedly denied the ability to build a mosque, despite complying with zoning requirements. A diverse group of twenty religious and civil rights groups, including Moore's ERLC, filed a brief with the federal district court in New Jersey supporting the religious freedom rights of this community of Muslims.[33] Two weeks later, the ERLC organized an interfaith conversation on religious liberty, where Moore expanded on the need to extend religious freedom rights to others. "We need to identify and see where others are receiving pressure and persecution and marginalization, and stand up for one another. When a city council in the Bible Belt attempts to bar a mosque, evangelicals need to stand against such government action."[34]

The next month, the ERLC's support for the New Jersey mosque ignited controversy at the SBC's annual convention in St. Louis, Missouri. A messenger from Arkansas motioned that "all Southern Baptist officials or offices who support the rights of Muslims to build Islamic mosques in the United States be immediately removed from their position within the Southern Baptist Convention." A later motion asked the ERLC to remove its name from the *amicus* brief. Both motions were ruled out of order, exceeding the authority of messengers, but Moore later responded. He asserted, "What it means to be a Baptist is to support soul freedom for everybody," receiving applause from the SBC audience. "Brothers and sisters, when you have a government that says 'we can decide whether or not a house of worship can be constructed based upon the theological beliefs of that house of worship,' then there are going to be Southern Baptist churches in San Francisco and New York and throughout the country that are not going to be able to build."[35] The link between rights claiming and rights extending was clear.

With this defense, the SBC overwhelmingly supported the ERLC's position supporting the mosque. Five years prior, the denomination's advocacy arm had capitulated when pressured regarding its support for religious liberty for Muslims, but in 2016 it stood firm in its extension of rights to a very controversial group. As religious freedom became increasingly important to evangelicals and they have become increasingly identified with minority politics, they have begun to realize the need to defend it broadly, both for themselves and for others. Yet, this move toward rights extending is not perfect. While Moore's SBC entity (the ERLC) stood firm on defending the religious freedom rights of Muslims, the SBC's international missions agency withdrew their support for the *amicus* brief in early 2017 after intense protest from some within the denomination.[36]

This pattern of two steps forward and one step back is typical. Both *rights learning* and *rights extending* are processes that play out in episodes and are best viewed longitudinally. Despite events that suggest otherwise, the overarching evidence from both elites and public opinion data suggests that evangelicals are learning to value their rights *and* their opponents' rights, and the prompting of conservative rights arguments can reinforce this. If abortion has transformed the culture wars to be about rights, it has also helped enhance the rights of all.

THE BIG PICTURE

The evidence from the preceding chapters suggests a simple truth: evangelical politics are changing, while at the same time staying the same. Abortion has been the central, enduring theme of evangelical politics since the 1970s. Certainly a variety of other issues have and continue to matter in electoral politics and public opinion polls, but the politics of abortion endure in their front-and-center place within evangelical politics. The obvious battles over the legality of abortion remain, especially considering the variety of state-level restrictions on abortion that have been passed in the last decade, their defeat in the recent *Whole Women's Health v. Hellerstedt* (2016), and the ensuing legal challenges that will be prompted by a potentially changing Supreme Court. But importantly, the politics of abortion seem to be on the move, making their home in other issues. As evangelical elites have become more established players in conservative politics and as issues have become more complex, the easy issue of abortion has been used as a political shortcut. Elites justify their advocacy expansion and teach their constituents about new issues by referencing the politics of abortion. Because of this, scholars of religion and politics should consider abortion the primary means of representation in conservative Christian politics. Due to the stability of abortion attitudes, especially for the younger generation, this can be expected to persist.

While abortion remains central to the political agenda of evangelicals, they have also turned toward rights. The politics of rights have now become ubiquitous in conservative and evangelical politics, as rights discourse has found its way into a host of issues. The pro-life movement too has been present in this shift, as it was the gateway to this new realm of politics. The politics of abortion taught evangelicals about the value of rights politics, and specific pro-life issues, such as the right to protest, initiated a need to grasp rights politics, both for themselves and for their opponents.

This turn toward rights has been accentuated by continued cultural decline among American evangelicals. Rights matter as the culture changes and mainstream groups loose ground. No longer are evangelicals the silent majority or the active cultural force. In fact, many see themselves as the persecuted minority, being trampled by the secular left. Religious demographer Robert Jones, CEO of the Public Religion Research Institute, has recently documented this change.[37] This minority status is perhaps partly why Trump gained the support of many, seeking to turn back the cultural tide as Jones has discussed.[38]

On the rights front, minority groups are often the most protective of their political rights, because the majority threatens them. In taking an active role in rights politics, especially free speech and religious liberty, evangelical elites, despite the temporary success of the Trump campaign, are signaling a shift from Christian America to post-Christian America. Having the dominant cultural voice may no longer be an option, and evangelicals are not pollyannaish on this. Instead, evangelicals are seeking to ensure that they have a voice in politics and culture. Prominent evangelicals are realizing this and stating it publicly. Russell Moore, leader of the SBC's advocacy arm, admitted in 2014, "The new reality is an increasingly post-Christian America, an increasingly secularizing America."[39] In this kind of America, evangelicals are learning the value of rights.

While evangelicals are learning the value of rights politics, there are potential downsides for both activists and the broader polity. While social movements have achieved a variety of successes through rights politics, it may come with a cost to the movement. Rights movements are more professionalized, and professionalization can decrease the momentum of the grassroots.[40] Others have identified the "myth of rights," where legal victories can lull activists into a false sense of security.[41] Frequently politicizing such fundamental rights as religious freedom may also produce backlash effects, degrading broad legal and political support and making the fights all the more difficult and polarized. Universal rights talk may also deprive the American public of the diverse streams of political culture that have been central to our national identity, especially the political traditions of ordered liberty, morality, and the common good that have been shaped by Christianity.[42]

Moreover, rights talk is not going to be an instant cure for the concerns of conservatives and liberals. It is not a magic potion that will allow evangelicals to obtain everything they want from politics, or suddenly make conservative evangelicals talk and vote like liberal Democrats. Drawing on the categories of American culture outlined by Robert Bellah and his colleagues a generation ago, evangelical political discourse surely will continue to be mixed, combining a liberal, individualist commitment to rights with republican sensibilities, though perhaps less biblical versions of political culture than in eras past. Evangelicals will continue to be unlikely to be expressive individualists, opposing sexual license and abortion rights, but they are likely to be increasingly tolerant of cultural pluralism, particularly if the favor is returned.[43]

Though evangelicals are unlikely to speak, act, and vote like their counterparts do, liberals should celebrate the increased emphasis on rights within evangelical politics. As evangelicals have come to consider, create, and claim their own rights, they have also learned to value other people's rights to a much greater degree. Combine this with previous work that suggests that evangelicals have increasingly engaged in deliberative forms of a democracy, a hallmark of contemporary liberalism, and there is much to commend.[44] This should spur American politics and culture toward a "confident pluralism," to use the phrase of legal scholar John Inazu.[45] Integrated, not isolated, pluralism is the way forward, where citizens work out respect for each other's rights in social and political institutions. Social scientists Robert Putnam and David Campbell provide some hope for this, as they find that in the past, religion has navigated the combination of religious diversity and religious devotion in American society through integrated social networks.[46] These integrated networks, along with respect for rights, are the way forward.

It is easy to lose sight of the big picture as our immediate cultural and political battles our fought, but this useful irony is worth attention, especially for those who value political liberalism. Over the past four decades, the central issue in American the culture wars – abortion – has helped teach evangelicals, the forbearers of morality and communitarianism, the value of individual rights. Though perhaps a bit unorthodox, much of evangelicalism has now been converted. As such, the politics of abortion might be responsible for our future détente in the culture wars of yesteryear. At the very least, it will change the nature of our politics.

Epilogue

On June 27, 2016 the U.S. Supreme Court struck a blow to conservative Christians when it declared in *Whole Women's Health v. Hellerstedt* that Texas's restrictions on abortion were unconstitutional. The 5–3 decision jeopardized a host of gains that the pro-life movement had made over the past decade. While *Roe v. Wade* remained in place, pro-life activists had instituted state-level restrictions to limit access to abortion in several locales. These were the greatest practical successes of the pro-life movement in two decades, but the *Hellerstedt* decision raised doubts about the sustainability of this strategy. Even more, if certain restrictions on the right to an abortion could not survive a legal challenge, what hope was there to overturn *Roe*?

The *Hellerstedt* decision was only the latest in a series of defeats for conservative Christians. In the summer of 2016, evangelicals and their Catholic allies seemed to be in retreat, as American politics and culture were rapidly changing. A year earlier, the Supreme Court legalized gay marriage across the nation. Rather than sparking a backlash, the public, even the evangelical public, seemed to accept the result. In the first half of 2016, the battle shifted from marriage altars to public restrooms, with the federal government and others supporting the right of transgender individuals to use bathrooms matching their gender identity. Only ten years prior, many states had passed constitutional amendments limiting marriage to be between one man and one woman; now transgender rights were prevailing. The pace of cultural and political change was swift, and it coalesced with demographic shifts. The Pew Research Center, for example, reported that the number of religiously unaffiliated Americans increased by almost 50% from 2007 to 2014 (from 16% to 23%), while the percentage of Christians declined from 78% to 71%. Christianity and Christian moral politics were on the decline.

Many evangelical activists were aware of this changing cultural and political tide. While they pushed for local majoritarian changes, like the Texas abortion restrictions, they were at the same time pursuing a minority rights strategy, especially in national politics, procuring greater legal protections. In their retreat, conservative Christians sought to secure their rights to dissent, supporting religious freedom and free speech rights for religious organizations and individuals that disagreed with same-sex marriage and the expansion of LGBT rights. But even this push toward rights was tenuous, as politicians, the press, and the public opposed many efforts to codify more religious freedom protections, dubbing them a license to discriminate.

The religious freedom rights of organizations had been bolstered in 2014 with the Supreme Court's 5–4 decision in *Burwell v. Hobby Lobby*. The death of the conservative Supreme Court stalwart, Justice Antonin Scalia in February 2016, however, put this decision (and the status of broad religious freedom protections) in jeopardy. President Barack Obama nominated Merrick Garland to replace Scalia. Though a moderate liberal, Garland was likely to be closer in his views of religious freedom to Obama appointee Justice Elena Kagan, a dissenter in the Hobby Lobby case, than Scalia.

By the end of June, Senate Majority Leader Mitch McConnell (R-KY) had been able to secure a delay in considering Garland as Scalia's Supreme Court replacement until after the November election. Yet, even the eight justices that remained ruled against the Texas abortion restrictions in *Hellerstedt*. The election was unlikely to alter this decision. Moreover, the prospects of the election appeared bleak for conservatives. Donald Trump had defeated the favored candidates of evangelical elites, Ted Cruz and Marco Rubio, for the Republican nomination. Though Trump had some evangelical backing among elites and more among the rank-and-file, many were skeptical of him. The national polling averages had him trailing Democratic candidate Hillary Clinton in the upcoming election by about 5 points. A loss would certainly cement evangelicals' minority status, as Clinton would further ingrain progressive Obama-era policies, while likely altering the make-up of the Supreme Court for decades to come.

Given this context, the push toward minority politics was palpable among leading conservative Christian activists. They talked frequently about their rights, about protecting difference, dissent, and pluralism. As this book discusses, this "rights turn" in conservative Christian politics was not novel. It had been developing, both among elites and the rank-and-file, for twenty years. But in 2015 and 2016, a rights-based emphasis seemed to be gaining significant momentum, with the presidential election, the Supreme Court, and the culture all moving against Christian majoritarianism in America. It is no coincidence that during this period conservative author Rod Dreher even called for evangelicals and other traditional Christians to engage in the "Benedict Option," where they embrace their minority status and retreat to local Christian communities.

Only 144 days after *Hellerstedt*, the narrative changed, or so it seemed. On November 8, 2016, Donald Trump was elected the 45th President of the United

States, with upwards of 75% of white evangelicals voting for him. After the election, Republicans controlled the presidency, Congress, and most state governments. Republicans would surely be able to put a young conservative on the Supreme Court to replace Scalia, and Obama-era executive orders, like those mandating the protection of gender identity, would end. Perhaps Christian rights politics would be put on hold for a new wave of moral majority politics.

Rather than a repudiation of the conservative Christian shift toward rights politics, the election of Donald Trump presents a more complicated, realistic picture. This is to be expected as one analyzes the leading edge of evangelical political change. Evangelicals still have enough political power to win elections, especially in certain states, but the demographic trends are unfavorable. This highlights a tension within evangelicalism. Should the emphasis be on a return to the cultural dominance of a Christian America or the securing of Christian pluralism? In an election between Clinton and Trump, both the majoritarian-oriented and rights-oriented evangelicals saw benefits in the election of Trump.

The evolution of evangelical politics toward rights that I discuss in this book cannot be curtailed by a single election. The rights shift is episodic, often structured by threats and opportunities, but the trajectory remains. Despite the election of Trump and the majoritarian policies that might follow, the trend in evangelical politics is toward rights and pluralism. Evangelicals of all stripes increasingly understand this, either explicitly or implicitly. The trend, however, does not guarantee that it will be employed in every case, and there remains a tension among evangelicals, many who do not want to forgo the perceived near-term benefits of the moral majority for the future protections of a pluralistic minority.

The tension among evangelicals has been evident in a recent controversy around Russell Moore, the leader of the Southern Baptist Convention's advocacy organization. As the book recounts, Moore has been a leader in the evangelical shift toward rights over the past decade. Following the election of Trump, however, Moore came under intense scrutiny from some prominent members of the denomination. Moore was an outspoken critic of Trump throughout the Republican primary and general election campaign, and he has also advocated for broad religious freedom rights for Muslims, arguing that supporting religious freedom for all is both morally right and will better protect Christians. Increasingly, prominent Southern Baptists have opposed Moore's advocacy, and in early 2017 several large churches threatened to withdraw their financial support for the organization. In March, opposition to Moore reached a crescendo, when it appeared he might be asked to resign.

Moore has survived, remaining head of the Southern Baptist organization at the time of this writing. Many younger Southern Baptists and evangelicals who agreed with Moore's rights-based advocacy, even rights for all, supported him. Perhaps more important, Moore has been a fervent pro-life advocate throughout his tenure, and abortion advocacy has persisted at the top of his organization's priority list. Despite some serious differences, Moore's steady commitment to evangelicalisms' first priority – anti-abortion politics – may have provided him enough latitude to navigate a pluralistic, rights-based advocacy within conservative Christianity.

The tensions evident in the Trump election and the Moore controversy illuminate that the change in evangelical politics detailed in this book, while real, is also "in process." The book's themes are both the evangelical shift toward rights politics and the role of abortion in facilitating that shift. Abortion politics initiated evangelicals into minority politics. It helped teach them about the importance of rights politics, both in rhetoric and in legal advocacy, it helped expand their advocacy in new directions, and it helped evangelicals come to promote the expansion of rights to others. Changes *have happened* in evangelical politics, and changes *are happening*. Conservative Christian politics are not the same today as they were in 1984, though the Trump and Moore experiences suggest that many of those impulses remain, sometimes below the surface and sometimes bubbling to the surface.

Over the past year, conservative Christian politics have been in flux. It is possible that in the short term, evangelical politics will move away from rights politics, especially while they hold institutional political power. Their cultural power, however, appears to be declining, and the rising generation of advocacy leaders are pursuing a pluralistic strategy. While we may see discreet counterexamples, the arc of evangelical advocacy is bending toward minority, rights-based politics, as the book describes. This should be a salve to the scars of our culture wars.

Appendix A

Variables and Coding

GENERAL SOCIAL SURVEY (1977–2014)

Dependent Variables

FREE SPEECH SCALE: Additive Index of the questions about whether disfavored groups should be able to "make a speech in your (city/town/community)," ranging from 0–5:

Atheists – "somebody who is against all churches and religion;" 0 = no; 1 = yes.

Communists – "a man who admits he is a communist;" 0 = no; 1 = yes.

Militarists – "a person who advocates doing away with elections and letting the military run the country;" 0 = no; 1 = yes.

Homosexuals – "a man who admits that he is a homosexual;" 0 = no; 1 = yes.

Racists – "a person who believes that Blacks are genetically inferior;" 0 = no; 1 = yes.

PORNOGRAPHY LAW: "Which of these statements comes closest to your feelings about pornography laws?" 1 = always illegal; 2 = illegal under 18; 3 = always legal.

SCHOOL PRAYER RULING: "The United States Supreme Court has ruled that no state or local government may require the reading of the Lord's Prayer or Bible verses in public schools. What are your views on this – do you approve or disapprove of the court ruling?" 0 = approve; 1 = disapprove

HEALTH CARE: "In general, some people think that it is the responsibility of the government in Washington to see to it that people have help in paying for doctors and hospital bills. Others think that these matters are not the responsibility of the federal government and that people should take care of these things themselves." Ranges from 1 ("Government should help") to 5 ("People should help themselves")

CAPITAL PUNISHMENT: "Do you favor of oppose the death penalty for persons convicted of murder?" 0 = oppose; 1= favor

SAME-SEX MARRIAGE: "Homosexual couples should have the right to marry one another." 0 = support; 1 = oppose

HOMOSEXUAL RELATIONS: "What about sexual relations between two adults of the same-sex;" 0 = not wrong; 1 = wrong

HOMOSEXUAL TOLERANCE SCALE: Additive Index of the questions about whether "a man who admits that he is a homosexual" should be able to

> Allowed to make a speech in the community; 0 = no; 1= yes
>
> Have a book in the library in favor of homosexuality; 0 = no; 1= yes
>
> Allowed to teach in a college or university; 0 = no; 1= yes

Independent Variables

ABORTION SCALE: Additive index ranging from 0–7 of the questions about "whether or not you think it should be possible for a pregnant woman to obtain a legal abortion:"

> "The woman wants it for any reason;" 0 = yes; 1 = no.
>
> "The woman's own health is seriously endangered by the pregnancy;" 0 = yes; 1 = no.
>
> "The family has a very low income and cannot afford any more children;" 0 = yes; 1 = no.
>
> "She became pregnant as a result of rape;" 0 = yes; 1 = no.
>
> "She is married and does not want any more children;" 0 = yes; 1 = no.
>
> "There is a strong chance of serious defect in the baby;" 0 = yes; 1 = no.
>
> "She is not married and does not want to marry the man;" 0 = yes; 1 = no.

PARTY-ID: 0) strong Democrat; 1) weak Democrat 2) Independent leaning Democrat 3) Independent 4) Independent leaning Republican 5) weak Republican 6) strong Republican.

IDEOLOGY: 0) extremely liberal; 1) liberal; 2) slightly liberal; 3) moderate; 4) slightly conservative; 5) conservative; 6) extremely conservative.

GOV'T DO MORE: Should the government in Washington do more or less? Ranges from 1 ("should do more") to 5 ("government does too much")

PRESIDENT'S PARTY: 0 = Democrat; 1 = Republican

GOV. CONFIDENCE: Additive index of confidence in executive, legislative, and judicial branches of the federal government. 1 = hardly any; 2 = only some; 3 = great deal, for each. Index ranges from 3–9.

TRUST IN PEOPLE: Can people be trusted? 1 = yes; 0 = no

RELIGIOUS TRADITION: Used Steensland, et al.'s "Measure of American Religion" syntax, as updated by Stetzer and Burge's "Reltrad Coding Problems and a New Repository" to compute religious tradition (RELTRAD). Unaffiliated is the reference category.
 EVANGELICAL PROTESTANT
 BLACK PROTESTANT
 MAINLINE PROTESTANT
 JEWISH
 OTHER FAITH
 UNAFFILIATED

ATTENDANCE: How often do you attend religious services? 0 = never; 1 = once a year or less; 2 = once a month or less; 3 = two-three times per month; 4 = weekly or nearly weekly; 5 = more than once a week

I: EVANG. AND ABORTION VIEWS: Interaction between Evangelical Religious Tradition and Abortion Scale (evangelical x abortion scale).

I: CATHOLIC AND ABORTION VIEWS: Interaction between Catholic Religious Tradition and Abortion Scale (catholic x abortion scale).

EDUCATION: Degree: 0 = Less than high school; 1 = High school; 2 = Junior College; 3 = Bachelor's degree; 4 = Graduate degree.

MALE: Sex of respondent. 1 = Male; 0 = Female.

WHITE: 1 = White; 0 = Non-white.

CHILDREN: Does respondent have any children? 0 = No; 1 = Yes.

AGE: Age of respondent in years.

HEALTH: Would you say your own health, in general, is excellent (2), good (1), or poor (0)?

YEAR: Survey Year.

SOUTHERN BAPTIST CLERGY SURVEYS (1980–2008)

Dependent Variables

SCHOOL PRAYER AMENDMENT: "We need a constitutional amendment to permit prayer as a regular exercise in schools." 0) strongly disagree; 1) disagree; 2) not sure; 3) agree; 4) strongly agree

TUITION TAX CREDITS: "Do you favor tuition assistance for Christian schools" / "The government should provide vouchers to help pay for their children to attend private or religious schools." 0) strongly disagree; 1) disagree; 2) not sure; 3) agree; 4) strongly agree

BAPTIST JOINT COMMITTEE: How good a job is the Baptist Joint Committee (BJC) DOING: 0) poor; 1) fair; 2) good; 3) excellent

CHRISTIAN LIFE COMMISSION: How good a job is the Christian Life Commission (CLC) doing: 0) poor; 1) fair; 2) good; 3) excellent

HEALTH CARE: "We need government-sponsored national health insurance so that everyone can get adequate medical care." 1 = strongly agree; 2 = agree; 3 = not sure; 4 = disagree; 5 = strongly disagree

DEATH PENALTY: "I oppose capital punishment" 1 = strongly agree; 2 = agree; 3 = not sure; 4 = disagree; 5 = strongly disagree

Abortion Variable

ANTI-ABORTION AMENDMENT: "We need a constitutional amendment prohibiting all abortions unless to save a mother's life, or in the case of rape or incest." 0) strongly disagree; 1) disagree; 2) not sure; 3) agree; 4) strongly agree

Political Variables

IDEOLOGY: 0) extremely liberal; 1) liberal; 2) slightly liberal; 3) moderate; 4) slightly conservative; 5) conservative; 6) extremely conservative

PARTY-ID: 0) strong Democrat; 1) weak Democrat 2) Independent leaning Democrat 3) Independent 4) Independent leaning Republican 5) weak Republican 6) strong Republican

PRESIDENT'S PARTY: 0 = Democrat; 1 = Republican

GOV. SOLVE SOCIAL PROBS.: "The federal government should do more to solve social problems such as unemployment, poverty, and poor housing." 1 = strongly agree; 2 = agree; 3 = not sure; 4 = disagree; 5 = strongly disagree

Religious Variables

RELIGIOUS BELIEFS: a first order factor analysis five questions coded from 0) strongly disagree; 1) disagree; 2) not sure; 3) agree; 4) strongly agree. The religious beliefs questions are: 1) Adam and Eve were real historical figures; 2) the Bible is inerrant in all matters; 3) Jesus was born of a virgin; 4) the Devil really exists; and 5) women should not be ordained as clergy

Personal Factors and Controls

SEMINARY EDUCATION: 0) none; 1) Bible college; 2) some seminary; 3) seminary graduate; 4) post-graduate work

NON-SEMINARY EDUCATION: 0) grade school; 1) high school; 2) some college; 3) college graduate; 4) post-graduate work

CHURCH SIZE: 0) 1–99; 2) 100–199; 2) 200–299; 3) 300–499; 4) 500–999; 5) over 999

AGE: 0) under 30; 1) 30–39; 2) 40–49; 3) 50–59; 4) over 50

YEAR: survey year

AMERICAN NATIONAL ELECTION STUDY (2000)

Dependent Variable

CAMPAIGN FINANCE REFORM: "Recently, there has been a lot of talk about campaign finance reform. Some people believe that we should protect government from excessive influence from campaign contributors. Others think that protecting freedom of individuals to financially support political candidates and parties is more important. Which is closer to the way you think..." 0 = "Protecting the freedom of individuals;" 1 = "Protect the government from excessive influence."

Independent Variables

ABORTION: "Please tell me which one of the opinions best agrees with your view:" 1 = "By law, abortion should never be permitted;" 2 = The law should permit abortion only in case of rape, incest, or when the woman's life is in danger;" 3 = "The law should permit abortion for reasons other than rape, incest, or danger to the woman's life, but only after the need for the abortion has been clearly established;" 4 = "By law, a woman should always be able to obtain an abortion as a matter of personal choice."

ABORTION IMPORTANCE: "How important is [abortion] to your personally?" 1 = Not at all important; 2) Not too important; 3) Somewhat important; 4) Very important; 5) Extremely important

PARTY-ID: 0 = Strong Democrat; 1 = Weak Democrat 2 = Independent leaning Democrat 3 = Independent 4 = Independent leaning Republican 5 = Weak Republican 6 = Strong Republican.

RELIGIOUS TRADITION: Followed a modified version of Steensland et al., "Measure of American Religion" and Layman, *The Great Divide*. Unaffiliated is the reference category.

EVANGELICAL: The following religious identifications are classified as evangelical: **Other Denomination:** "Evangelical United Brethren;" "Christian or Just Christian" and Attendance is greater than "never;" "Church (or Churches) of Christ" and not United Church of Christ; "Church of God;" "Assembly of God;" "Holiness;" "Pentecostal;" "Non-Denominational – Protestant" and Attendance is greater than "never." **Baptist:** "Baptist Convention;" "American Baptist Association" and Non-Black; "Independent Baptist;" "Other" and Non-Black; "Don't know" and Non-Black. **Lutheran:** "Missouri Synod." **Methodist:** "Other" and Non-Black; "Don't know" and Non-Black. **Reformed:** "Christian Reformed Church." **Brethren:** "Church of the Brethren;" "Plymouth Brethren."

BLACK PROTESTANT
MAINLINE PROTESTANT
CATHOLIC

OTHER FAITH
JEWISH
UNAFFILIATED
WHITE: 0 = Non-White; 1 = White.
HISPANIC: 0 = Non-Hispanic; 1 = Hispanic.
AGE: Age of respondent in years.
FEMALE: Sex of respondent. 1 = Male; 2 = Female.
EDUCATION: 0 = Less than high school; 1 = High school; 2 = Junior
   College; 3 = Bachelor's degree; 4 = Advanced degree.
ABORTION-EVANGELICAL INTERACTION: Evangelical Religious
   Tradition x Abortion Attitude.
ABORTION-CATHOLIC INTERACTION: Catholic Religious Tradition x
   Abortion Attitude.

SURVEY SAMPLING INTERNATIONAL SURVEYS

Experimental Frames

Free Speech

Right to Life
   During the 2014 election season, a local minister participated in a town
      hall meeting about faith and politics. The minister was asked
      whether he supported the extension of free speech privileges, even
      to those with whom he may disagree. The minister responded by
      saying: "Decisions about free speech should be guided by our under-
      standing of rights. I am pro-life, and I want to ensure that my free
      speech right to protest abortion is protected. We must protect the
      rights of disfavored groups, because we may become disfavored.
      Therefore, I strongly support expansive free speech."
Anti-Abortion
   During the 2014 election season, a local minister participated in a town
      hall meeting about faith and politics. The minister was asked
      whether he supported the extension of free speech privileges, even
      to those with whom he may disagree. The minister responded by
      saying: "Decisions about free speech should be guided by the politics
      of abortion. I oppose abortion, and I do not want others to deny my
      ability to express these views. Therefore, I strongly support expan-
      sive free speech."
Control
   During the 2014 election season, a local minister participated in a town
      hall meeting about faith and politics. The minister was asked
      whether he supported the extension of free speech privileges, even
      to those with whom he may disagree. The minister responded by
      saying: "Yes, I support expansive free speech."

Health Care

Right to Life

During the 2014 election season, a local minister participated in a town hall meeting about faith and politics. The minister was asked whether he supported the creation of a national health insurance program. The minister responded by saying: "Decisions about health care should be guided by our understanding of rights. I am pro-life, and every national health care proposal for the past twenty-five years opposes the right to life of the unborn by expanding and funding the abortion industry. Therefore, I strongly oppose creating a national health insurance program."

Anti-Abortion

During the 2014 election season, a local minister participated in a town hall meeting about faith and politics. The minister was asked whether he supported the creation of a national health insurance program. The minister responded by saying: "Decisions about health care should be guided by our understanding of abortion. I oppose abortion, and every national health care proposal for the past 25 years has expanded and funded the abortion industry. Therefore, I strongly oppose creating a national health insurance program."

Control

During the 2014 election season, a local minister participated in a town hall meeting about faith and politics. The minister was asked whether he supported the creation of a national health insurance program. The minister responded by saying: "No, I oppose creating a national health insurance program."

Death Penalty

Oppose

Right to Life

Last week, a local minister participated in a town hall meeting about faith and politics. The minister was asked whether he supported the death penalty. The minister responded by saying: "Decisions about capital punishment should be guided by our understanding of rights. I am pro-life, and whether that life is an unborn baby or a convicted murderer, we need to value the right to life. Therefore, I strongly oppose the death penalty."

Justice

Last week, a local minister participated in a town hall meeting about faith and politics. The minister was asked whether he supported the death penalty. The minister responded by saying: "Decisions about capital punishment should be guided by our understanding of justice. It is unjust to sentence people to death, because too often innocent people have been convicted of capital crimes. Therefore, I strongly oppose the death penalty."

Costs and Benefits

Last week, a local minister participated in a town hall meeting about faith and politics. The minister was asked whether he supported the death penalty. The minister responded by saying: "Decisions about capital punishment should be guided by our understanding of costs and benefits. It costs the government more money to put a convicted criminal to death than it does to keep them in prison for life. As a country, we cannot afford to increase the costs of our criminal justice system. Therefore, I strongly oppose the death penalty."

Support

Right to Life

Last week a local minister participated in a town hall meeting about faith and politics. The minister was asked whether he supported the death penalty. The minister responded by saying: "Decisions about capital punishment should be guided by our understanding of rights. I am pro-life, and I think that life is of such high value that the death penalty is the only proper punishment for people who murder innocent life. Therefore, I strongly support the death penalty."

Justice

Last week, a local minister participated in a town hall meeting about faith and politics. The minister was asked whether he supported the death penalty. The minister responded by saying: "Decisions about capital punishment should be guided by our understanding of justice. Justice for the victim demands that murders are put to death for taking innocent life. Therefore, I strongly support the death penalty."

Costs and Benefits

Last week, a local minister participated in a town hall meeting about faith and politics. The minister was asked whether he supported the death penalty. The minister responded by saying: "Decisions about capital punishment should be guided by our understanding of costs and benefits. While it is certainly expensive to process criminals through death row, as a country we cannot afford the social costs of increased murder rates. Therefore, I strongly support the death penalty."

Control: No prompt

Dependent Variables

PERSUASIVE: "Do you find the minister's comments (on topic) persuasive?" Scale from o (not credible) to 10 (extremely persuasive)

FREE SPEECH: "Do you think there are circumstances in which the First Amendment's free speech protections should be limited, or do you think there should be no limits?" Scale from o (often need limits) to 10 (no limits)

HEALTH CARE: "Which of the options below comes closest to your view?" 1 = "the federal government should directly provide health insurance to all legal residents;" 2 = "the federal government should require individuals to obtain health insurance, and should offer subsidies to reduce the cost, but should not directly provide health insurance;" 3 = "the federal government should provide funding to the states to assist people in getting health insurance coverage, but it should not provide health insurance to individuals;" 4 = "the federal government should not be involved in providing individuals health insurance coverage;" 5 = Don't know / no opinion;

Recoding for simplicity: o = favor national health care proposals (options 1 and 2 in main question); 1 = oppose national health care proposals (options 3 and 4 in main question)

DEATH PENALTY: Variable is constructed from two questions: 1) "Do you strongly favor, favor, oppose, or strongly oppose the death penalty for persons convicted of murder?" 2) If you support the death penalty, "Which punishment do you prefer for people convicted of murder:" the death penalty; life in prison with no chance of parole; or don't know.

Final Coding: Oppose = o; Life in prison = 1; Support = 2

Independent Variables

RELIGIOUS TRADITION: Coded affiliation with religious denominations, following Steensland, et al.'s "The Measure of American Religion" syntax for GSS. Computed religious tradition (RELTRAD) categories, with unaffiliated is the reference category.
EVANGELICAL PROTESTANT
BLACK PROTESTANT
MAINLINE PROTESTANT
JEWISH
OTHER FAITH
UNAFFILIATED

ABORTION ATTITUDES: o = always be able to obtain; 1 = only if need is clear; 2 = only for rape, incest, etc.; 3 = never permitted

PARTY-ID: 1) strong Democrat; 2) weak Democrat 3) Independent leaning Democrat 4) Independent 5) Independent leaning Republican 6) weak Republican 7) strong Republican.

POLITICAL IDEOLOGY: 1) extremely liberal; 2) liberal; 3) slightly liberal; 4) moderate; 5) slightly conservative; 6) conservative; 7) extremely conservative.

ATTENDANCE: How often do you attend religious services? 1 = never; 2 = a few times a year; 3 = once or twice a month; 4 = almost every week; 5 = once a week; 6 = more often than once a week

EDUCATION: Degree: 0 = Less than high school; 1 = High school; 2 = Junior College; 3 = Bachelor's degree; 4 = Graduate degree.

MALE: Sex of respondent. 1 = Male; 0 = Female.

WHITE: 1 = White; 0 = Non-white.

AGE: Age of respondent in years.

Appendix B

Statistical Tables

TABLE 3.1. *GSS: Linear Regression Models of Free Speech Attitudes and Pornography Laws*

IVs	FREE SPEECH SCALE				PORNOGRAPHY LAWS	
	All Years (Rob. SEs)	1977–1989 (Rob. SEs)	1990–1997 (Rob. SEs)	1998–2014 (Rob. SEs)	1977–1997 (Rob. SEs)	1998–2014 (Rob. SEs)
Evangelical	−0.56**	−0.64**	−0.57**	−0.52**	0.86	0.72*
	(0.06)	(0.09)	(0.13)	(0.10)	(0.10)	(0.10)
Black	−0.38**	−0.61**	−0.31†	−0.37**	1.28†	1.64**
Protestant	(0.07)	(0.11)	(0.18)	(0.12)	(0.18)	(0.29)
Catholic	−0.17**	−0.18**	−0.20†	−0.23**	1.01	1.12
	(0.04)	(0.07)	(0.11)	(0.06)	(0.09)	(0.11)
Mainline Prot.	−0.28**	−0.37**	−0.34**	−0.18*	0.81*	0.73**
	(0.04)	(0.07)	(0.11)	(0.07)	(0.08)	(0.08)
Other Faith	−0.16**	−0.16	−0.17	−0.20*	0.66**	0.77†
	(0.06)	(0.10)	(0.14)	(0.10)	(0.09)	(0.12)
Jewish	−0.27**	−0.23†	−0.36†	−0.35**	1.66*	1.69*
	(0.09)	(0.13)	(0.20)	(0.14)	(0.35)	(0.43)
Evang. and	0.01	−0.04†	0.01	0.04†	0.90**	0.98
Abor.	(0.01)	(0.02)	(0.03)	(0.02)	(0.02)	(0.03)
Interaction						
Abortion	−0.11**	−0.10**	−0.10**	−0.12**	0.86**	0.83**
(Favor-	(0.01)	(0.01)	(0.02)	(0.01)	(0.01)	(0.02)
Oppose)						
Party-ID	0.04**	0.02†	0.04*	0.04**	1.01	1.00
(Dem.-	(0.01)	(0.01)	(0.02)	(0.01)	(0.01)	(0.02)
Repub.)						

(continued)

TABLE 3.1. *(continued)*

IVs	FREE SPEECH SCALE				PORNOGRAPHY LAWS	
	All Years (Rob. SEs)	1977–1989 (Rob. SEs)	1990–1997 (Rob. SEs)	1998–2014 (Rob. SEs)	1977–1997 (Rob. SEs)	1998–2014 (Rob. SEs)
Ideology (Lib.-Conserv.)	−0.05** (0.01)	−0.06** (0.02)	−0.07** (0.03)	−0.04* (0.02)	0.89** (0.02)	0.89** (0.02)
Gov. Confidence (Low-High)	0.01 (0.01)	0.02 (0.01)	−0.01 (0.02)	−0.01 (0.01)	0.99 (0.02)	0.98 (0.02)
Attendance (Never-Always)	−0.07** (0.01)	−0.10** (0.02)	−0.05* (0.03)	−0.05** (0.02)	0.80** (0.01)	0.85** (0.02)
Education	0.37** (0.01)	0.42** (0.02)	0.37** (0.03)	0.31** (0.02)	1.11** (0.03)	1.12** (0.03)
Age	−0.17** (0.01)	−0.21** (0.02)	−0.16** (0.03)	−0.10** (0.02)	0.72** (0.01)	0.73** (0.02)
Children	0.01 (0.03)	0.02 (0.05)	0.02 (0.07)	−0.04 (0.05)	0.90** (0.05)	0.75** (0.06)
Male	0.13** (0.03)	0.03 (0.04)	0.27** (0.06)	0.17** (0.04)	2.05** (0.10)	2.12** (0.14)
White	0.25** (0.05)	0.12 (0.08)	0.20† (0.12)	0.33** (0.06)	0.81* (0.08)	1.02 (0.01)
Year	0.01** (0.001)	0.02** (0.01)	0.001 (0.02)	0.004 (0.004)	1.01 (0.004)	1.02** (0.01)
Constant	−21.51 (2.40)	−42.77 (10.12)	2.95 (30.25)	−3.62 (7.76)	–	–
Cut 1	–	–	–	–	10.17 (8.08)	41.85 (11.89)
Cut 2	–	–	–	–	14.25 (8.08)	46.63 (11.90)
N	13947	6486	2501	4960	8534	5100
R^2	0.20	0.22	0.17	0.17	0.27	0.26

Notes: The statistical significance notations are: † = $p \leq 0.10$; * = $p \leq 0.05$; ** = $p \leq 0.01$. Robust standard errors are in parentheses. Adjusted Count R^2 used for the Pornography Laws models.

TABLE 3.2. *ANES 2000: Logistic Regression Models of Opposition to Campaign Finance Reform, Odds Ratios*

IVs	Campaign Finance – Oppose (SEs)	Campaign Finance – Don't Know (SEs)
Evangelical	1.34	1.26
	(0.42)	(0.29)
Black Protestant	1.78	2.25*
	(0.87)	(0.72)
Catholic	1.26	1.10
	(0.38)	(0.24)
Mainline Prot.	1.02	1.03
	(0.32)	(0.24)
Other Faith	1.04	1.37
	(0.40)	(0.36)
Jewish	1.58	1.35
	(0.83)	(0.61)
Abortion	1.12	0.98
(Favor-Oppose)	(0.09)	(0.06)
Abortion Importance	–	0.87*
(Not-Very)		(0.05)
Party-ID	1.15**	0.99
(Dem.-Repub.)	(0.05)	(0.03)
Gov. Thermometer	1.01†	1.01*
(Low-High)	(0.01)	(0.003)
Attendance	1.02	0.89†
(Never-Always)	(0.08)	(0.06)
Education	0.88†	0.51**
	(0.07)	(0.03)
Age	1.00	0.97**
	(0.01)	(0.004)
Children	0.93	1.04
	(0.18)	(0.16)
Male	1.19	0.48**
	(0.19)	(0.06)
White	1.13	0.87
	(0.31)	(0.17)
Constant	0.14	11.87
	(0.07)	(5.22)
N	926	1426
Adj. Count R²	0.00	0.17

Notes: The statistical significance notations are: † = p ≤ 0.10; * = p ≤ 0.05; ** = p ≤ 0.01. Standard errors are in parentheses.

TABLE 3.3. *SSI Evangelical: Linear Regression Models of How Anti-Abortion Frames Affect Support for Free Speech*

IVs	Persuasive (SEs)	Support for Free Speech (SEs)
Right To Life Frame	0.87**	−0.80
	(0.25)	(0.71)
Anti-Abortion Frame	0.24	0.45
	(0.25)	(0.71)
Abortion Attitudes (pro-anti)	0.49**	0.08
	(0.09)	(0.19)
Party-ID (Dem.-Repub.)	−	−0.08
		(0.11)
Education	−0.05	−0.01
	(0.11)	(0.31)
White	0.51*	−0.06
	(0.25)	(0.31)
Right To Life and Abortion Views Interaction	−	−0.36
		(0.27)
Anti-Abortion and Abortion Views Interaction	−	0.17
		(0.27)
Right To Life and Party-ID Interaction	−	0.29*
		(0.15)
Anti-Abortion and Party-ID Interaction	−	−0.10
		(0.15)
Constant	5.13	0.10
	(0.36)	(0.04)
N	562	559
Adj. R^2	0.07	0.002

Notes: The statistical significance notations are: † = $p \leq 0.10$; * = $p \leq 0.05$; ** = $p \leq 0.01$. Standard errors are in parentheses. The Control Frame is the comparison category for the frames.

TABLE 3.4. *SSI Evangelical: ANOVA Randomization Checks of Treatments*

IVs	FREE SPEECH		HEALTH CARE	
	Mean	P-Value	Mean	P-Value
Female		0.50		0.83
Right To Life	0.64		0.68	
Anti-Abortion	0.70		0.71	
Control	0.69		0.71	
Party-ID		0.95		0.12
Right To Life	4.43		4.62	
Anti-Abortion	4.49		4.65	
Control	4.43		4.27	
Age		0.98		0.14
Right To Life	45.65		45.65	
Anti-Abortion	42.21		42.21	
Control	43.28		43.28	
White		0.64		0.04*
Right To Life	0.77		0.84	
Anti-Abortion	0.79		0.79	
Control	0.75		0.74	
Education		0.33		0.23
Right To Life	2.32		2.33	
Anti-Abortion	2.17		2.32	
Control	2.24		2.18	
Parent		0.49		0.13
Right To Life	0.66		0.70	
Anti-Abortion	0.63		0.61	
Control	0.69		0.65	
Abortion Attitudes		0.34		0.23
Right To Life	1.65		1.60	
Anti-Abortion	1.73		1.80	
Control	1.82		1.72	

Notes: The statistical significance notations are: † = $p \leq 0.10$; * = $p \leq 0.05$; ** = $p \leq 0.01$.

TABLE 4.1. *SBC Clergy: Ordered Logistic Regression Models of Church-State Views, Odds Ratios*

IVs	POSITIVE VIEW OF THE BAPTIST JOINT COMMITTEE	FAVOR SCHOOL PRAYER AMENDMENT	FAVOR TUITION TAX CREDITS
	Odds Ratios (Rob. SEs)	Odds Ratios (Rob. SEs)	Odds Ratios (Rob. SEs)
Abortion Amendment (Oppose-Favor)	0.81** (0.04)	2.04** (0.09)	1.36** (0.05)
Ideology (Lib.-Conserv.)	0.71** (0.04)	1.38** (0.07)	1.35** (0.06)
Party-ID (Dem.-Repub.)	0.92** (0.03)	1.03 (0.02)	1.17** (0.03)
Religious Beliefs	0.63** (0.05)	1.54** (0.09)	1.22** (0.07)
Seminary Education	0.94 (0.04)	0.87** (0.03)	0.97 (0.03)
Education	0.90* (0.05)	0.93* (0.02)	0.95 (0.04)
Church Size	0.97 (0.03)	0.94** (0.02)	0.94** (0.02)
Age	1.13** (0.05)	1.05 (0.03)	0.89** (0.03)
Year	1.00 (0.01)	0.98** (0.01)	1.03** (0.01)
Cut Point 1	−3.14 (22.25)	−37.83 (10.23)	65.92 (9.99)
Cut Point 2	−1.71 (22.25)	−35.67 (10.22)	67.61 (9.99)
Cut Point 3	0.41 (22.26)	−34.95 (10.22)	68.28 (10.00)
Cut Point 4	–	−33.38 (10.22)	70.06 (10.00)
N	1718	2866	2867
Adj. Count R²	0.21	0.22	0.11

Notes: The statistical significance notations are: † = p ≤ 0.10; * = p ≤ 0.05; ** = p ≤ 0.01. Robust standard errors are in parentheses.

TABLE 4.2. *GSS: Logistic Regression Models of Opposition to Supreme Court's School Prayer Ruling, Odds Ratios*

IVs	All Years (Rob. SEs)
Evangelical	2.98**
	(0.26)
Black Protestant	3.29**
	(0.35)
Catholic	1.84**
	(0.12)
Mainline Prot.	1.90**
	(0.13)
Other Faith	0.98
	(0.10)
Jewish	0.45**
	(0.08)
Evang. and Abor. Interaction	0.98
	(0.02)
Abortion (Favor-Oppose)	1.11**
	(0.02)
Party-ID (Dem.-Repub.)	1.03**
	(0.01)
Ideology (Lib.-Conserv.)	1.16**
	(0.02)
Attendance (Never-Always)	1.10**
	(0.02)
Education	0.74**
	(0.01)
Age	1.17**
	(0.02)
Children	1.20**
	(0.05)
Male	0.90**
	(0.04)
White	0.71**
	(0.05)
Year	1.00
	(0.002)
Constant	0.001
	(0.004)
N	13149
Adj. Count R^2	0.26

Notes: The statistical significance notations are: † = $p \leq 0.10$; * = $p \leq 0.05$; ** = $p \leq 0.01$. Robust standard errors are in parentheses.

TABLE 5.1. *SBC Clergy: Ordered Logistic Regression Models of Health Care Attitudes, Odds Ratios*

IVs	All Years (Rob. SEs)	1988–1992 (Rob. SEs)	1996–2008 (Rob. SEs)
Abortion Amend. (Oppose-Favor)	1.09*	1.05	1.12†
	(0.05)	(0.07)	(0.07)
Party-ID	1.30**	1.31**	1.29**
(Dem.-Repub.)	(0.04)	(0.05)	(0.05)
Gov. Solve Social Probs.	2.03**	1.92**	2.14**
(Favor-Oppose)	(0.09)	(0.13)	(0.13)
President's Party	1.15	–	1.40
(Dem.-Repub.)	(0.10)		(0.34)
Religious Beliefs	1.10†	1.07	1.18*
	(0.06)	(0.09)	(0.09)
Seminary Education	1.05†	1.06	1.05
	(0.04)	(0.06)	(0.06)
Education	1.07†	1.07	1.06
	(0.05)	(0.05)	(0.07)
Church Size	1.08**	1.03	1.11**
	(0.03)	(0.04)	(0.04)
Age	0.96	0.98	0.93
	(0.04)	(0.05)	(0.05)
Survey Year	1.08**	1.03	1.06*
	(0.01)	(0.03)	(0.03)
Cut Point 1	149.52	64.30	114.76
	(13.70)	(66.10)	(57.01)
Cut Point 2	151.39	66.23	116.53
	(13.71)	(66.11)	(57.02)
Cut Point 3	152.51	67.32	117.69
	(13.72)	(66.11)	(57.02)
Cut Point 4	154.05	68.79	119.29
	(13.72)	(66.11)	(57.02)
N	2111	967	1144
Adj. Count R^2	0.22	0.13	0.18

Notes: The statistical significance notations are: † = $p \leq 0.10$; * = $p \leq 0.05$; ** = $p \leq 0.01$. Robust standard errors are in parentheses.

TABLE 5.2. *GSS: Ordered Logistic Regression Models of Health Care Attitudes, Odds Ratios*

IVs	All Years (Rob. SEs)	1975–1992 (Rob. SEs)	1993–2014 (Rob. SEs)
Evangelical	1.28**	1.42**	1.23**
	(0.09)	(0.17)	(0.10)
Black Protestant	1.01	1.03	1.00
	(0.10)	(0.17)	(0.12)
Catholic	1.11†	1.11	1.11
	(0.07)	(0.13)	(0.08)
Mainline Prot.	1.17*	1.25*	1.18*
	(0.08)	(0.14)	(0.09)
Other Faith	1.14	1.49*	1.03
	(0.11)	(0.25)	(0.12)
Jewish	0.89	1.03	0.83
	(0.12)	(0.27)	(0.13)
Abortion	1.02**	1.00	1.03**
(Favor-Oppose)	(0.01)	(0.02)	(0.01)
Party-ID	1.18**	1.11**	1.22**
(Dem.-Repub.)	(0.01)	(0.02)	(0.02)
Gov't Do More	1.82**	1.68**	1.89**
(Favor-Oppose)	(0.04)	(0.06)	(0.05)
President's Party	0.89**	–	0.82**
(Dem.-Repub.)	(0.04)		(0.04)
Gov. Confidence	0.98†	0.94**	0.99
(Low-High)	(0.01)	(0.02)	(0.02)
Attendance	1.04**	1.06**	1.02
(Never-Always)	(0.02)	(0.03)	(0.02)
Personal Health	0.87**	0.92†	0.85**
(Excellent-Poor)	(0.02)	(0.04)	(0.03)
Education	1.00	0.97	1.02
	(0.02)	(0.03)	(0.02)
Age	1.04**	1.03	1.04*
	(0.02)	(0.03)	(0.02)
Children	1.10*	1.10	1.10†
	(0.05)	(0.08)	(0.06)
Male	1.07†	0.93	1.14**
	(0.04)	(0.06)	(0.05)
White	1.10	1.21†	1.06
	(0.07)	(0.14)	(0.08)
Year	1.00	0.94**	1.01†
	(0.002)	(0.01)	(0.003)
Cut Point 1	−4.65	−133.58	14.18
	(4.42)	(27.92)	(6.77)
Cut Point 2	−3.59	−132.54	15.27
	(4.42)	(27.92)	(6.77)

(*continued*)

TABLE 5.2. (*continued*)

IVs	All Years (Rob. SEs)	1975–1992 (Rob. SEs)	1993–2014 (Rob. SEs)
Cut Point 3	−1.77 (4.42)	−130.70 (27.92)	17.10 (6.77)
Cut Point 4	−0.69 (4.42)	−129.59 (27.92)	18.17 (6.77)
N	10455	3583	6872
Adj. Count R²	0.12	0.11	0.14

Notes: The statistical significance notations are: † = p ≤ 0.10; * = p ≤ 0.05; ** = p ≤ 0.01. Robust standard errors are in parentheses. Unaffiliated is the comparison category for religious affiliation.

TABLE 5.3. *SSI Evangelical: Linear Regression Models of Perceived Persuasiveness of Anti-Health Care Frames and Their Effects on Opposition to Health Care*

IVs	PERSUASIVENESS (Standardized Coefficients)		OPPOSITION TO HEALTH CARE (Odds Ratios)	
	Standard Model (SEs)	Interactive Model (SEs)	Standard Model (SEs)	Interactive Model (SEs)
Right To Life Frame	1.49** (0.30)	−0.39 (0.51)	0.88 (0.22)	0.25* (0.16)
Anti-Abortion Frame	1.04** (0.30)	−1.02† (0.55)	1.37 (0.35)	0.70 (0.36)
Abortion Attitudes (pro-anti)	2.54** (0.34)	0.38** (0.54)	1.13 (0.11)	1.14 (0.11)
Party-ID (Dem.-Repub.)	1.58** (0.40)	1.62** (0.39)	1.49** (0.08)	1.49** (0.08)
White	0.01 (0.34)	0.01 (0.33)	1.97* (0.53)	0.98 (0.41)
Age	1.65** (0.54)	1.63** (0.53)	1.01* (0.01)	1.01† (0.01)
Parent	−0.30 (0.27)	−0.28 (0.26)	1.58* (0.35)	1.68* (0.38)
Right To Life and Abortion Views Interaction	–	3.28** (0.75)	–	4.56* (3.18)
Anti-Abortion and Abortion Views Interaction	–	2.70** (0.47)	–	2.44⁰·¹³ (1.44)
Constant	1.47 (0.42)	2.70 (0.47)	0.06 (0.02)	0.10 (0.04)
N	513	513	514	514
Adj. R²	0.21	0.25	0.33	0.32

Notes: The statistical significance notations are: † = p ≤ 0.10; * = p ≤ 0.05; ** = p ≤ 0.01. Standard errors are in parentheses. The Control Frame is the comparison category for the frames.

TABLE 6.1. *SBC Clergy: Ordered Logistic Regression Models of Support for the Death Penalty, Odds Ratios*

IVs	All Years (Rob. SEs)	1988–1996 (Rob. SEs)	2000–2008 (Rob. SEs)
Abortion Amend. (Oppose-Favor)	1.11*	1.08	1.17*
	(0.05)	(0.07)	(0.08)
Party-ID	1.07*	1.12**	1.00
(Dem.-Repub.)	(0.03)	(0.04)	(0.05)
Ideology	1.67**	1.65**	1.73**
(Lib.-Conserv.)	(0.10)	(0.14)	(0.16)
Religious Beliefs	1.94**	1.86**	2.05**
	(0.06)	(0.18)	(0.24)
Seminary Education	0.99	0.92	1.08
	(0.04)	(0.05)	(0.07)
Education	1.04	0.99	1.10
	(0.05)	(0.06)	(0.08)
Church Size	1.00	0.98	1.01
	(0.03)	(0.03)	(0.04)
Age	0.97**	0.95	0.98
	(0.01)	(0.05)	(0.08)
Survey Year	0.97**	1.00	1.02
	(0.01)	(0.02)	(0.03)
Cut Point 1	−60.65	−7.98	47.03
	(14.37)	(36.43)	(46.50)
Cut Point 2	−59.63	−6.90	47.97
	(14.37)	(36.42)	(46.51)
Cut Point 3	−59.02	−6.39	48.74
	(14.36)	(36.42)	(46.51)
Cut Point 4	−56.85	−4.15	50.85
	(14.36)	(36.42)	(46.51)
N	2107	1269	838
Adj. Count R^2	0.18	0.19	0.18

Notes: The statistical significance notations are: † = $p \leq 0.10$; * = $p \leq 0.05$; ** = $p \leq 0.01$. Robust standard errors are in parentheses.

TABLE 6.2. *GSS: Logistic Regression Models of Support for the Death Penalty, Odds Ratios*

IVs	REGULAR MODEL All Years (Rob. SEs)	INTERACTION MODELS All Years (Rob. SEs)	1977–1998 (Rob. SEs)	2000–2014 (Rob. SEs)
Evangelical	1.90**	1.98**	1.74**	2.56**
	(0.15)	(0.20)	(0.23)	(0.45)
Black Protestant	1.17	1.10	1.01	1.29
	(0.12)	(0.12)	(0.14)	(0.24)
Catholic	1.48**	2.00**	1.83**	2.23**
	(0.11)	(0.19)	(0.23)	(0.34)
Mainline Prot.	1.64**	1.58**	1.44**	1.88**
	(0.12)	(0.12)	(0.14)	(0.24)
Other Faith	1.29*	1.23*	1.17	1.27
	(0.14)	(0.13)	(0.16)	(0.21)
Jewish	1.72**	1.75**	2.02**	1.50†
	(0.27)	(0.27)	(0.44)	(0.36)
I: Evang. and Abortion Views	–	0.96†	0.95†	0.98
		(0.02)	(0.03)	(0.04)
I: Catholic and Abortion Views	–	0.89**	0.90**	0.87**
		(0.02)	(0.03)	(0.03)
Abortion (Favor-Oppose)	0.91**	0.95**	0.96**	0.96*
	(0.01)	(0.01)	(0.02)	(0.03)
Party-ID (Dem.-Repub.)	1.17**	1.17**	1.14**	1.22**
	(0.01)	(0.01)	(0.02)	(0.03)
Ideology (Lib.-Conserv.)	1.27**	1.27**	1.29**	1.23**
	(0.02)	(0.02)	(0.04)	(0.04)
Gov. Confidence (Low-High)	1.01	1.01	1.02	0.98
	(0.01)	(0.01)	(0.02)	(0.02)
Trust in People (High-Low)	1.25**	1.24**	1.23**	1.25**
	(0.06)	(0.06)	(0.07)	(0.10)
Attendance (Never-Always)	0.91**	0.91**	0.94**	0.84**
	(0.15)	(0.02)	(0.02)	(0.02)
Education	0.89**	0.90**	0.91**	0.88**
	(0.02)	(0.02)	(0.02)	(0.03)
Age	0.97†	0.97†	0.99	0.95†
	(0.02)	(0.02)	(0.02)	(0.03)
Children	1.20**	1.19**	1.22**	1.16†
	(0.06)	(0.06)	(0.08)	(0.10)
Male	1.52**	1.51**	1.51**	1.55**
	(0.06)	(0.06)	(0.08)	(0.11)
White	2.26**	2.28**	2.40**	2.19**
	(0.15)	(0.15)	(0.22)	(0.22)

IVs	REGULAR MODEL	INTERACTION MODELS		
	All Years (Rob. SEs)	All Years (Rob. SEs)	1977–1998 (Rob. SEs)	2000–2014 (Rob. SEs)
Year	0.99**	0.99**	1.02**	1.00
	(0.002)	(0.001)	(0.004)	(0.01)
Constant	1.14e7	1.59e7	1.86e-15	507.33
	(4.58e7)	(6.41e5)	(1.58e-14)	(7914.19)
N	13074	13074	8849	4225
Adj. Count R²	0.06	0.06	0.02	0.15

Notes: The statistical significance notations are: † = p ≤ 0.10; * = p ≤ 0.05; ** = p ≤ 0.01. Robust standard errors are in parentheses.

TABLE 6.3. *SSI Full: Regression Models of How Various Frames Affect Support for Capital Punishment*

IVs	PERSUASIVE		SUPPORT FOR CAPITAL PUNISHMENT	
	Regular Model	*Interactive Model*	*Regular Model*	*Interactive Model*
	OLS Coefficient (SEs)	OLS Coefficient (SEs)	Odds Ratio (SEs)	Odds Ratio (SEs)
Right To Life (Opp.) Frame	0.40	0.35	1.07†	0.96
	(0.29)	(0.37)	(0.20)	(0.23)
Right To Life (Fav.) Frame	0.95**	0.60	1.37	1.27
	(0.29)	(0.39)	(0.26)	(0.33)
Justice (Opp.) Frame	1.13**	0.78*	1.05	1.16
	(0.29)	(0.38)	(0.20)	(0.29)
Justice (Fav.) Frame	0.95**	0.52	1.42†	1.29
	(0.29)	(0.38)	(0.27)	(0.33)
Costs and Benefits (Opp.) Frame	–	–	1.01	1.01
			(0.20)	(0.26)
Costs and Benefits (Fav.) Frame	0.54†	0.26	1.53*	1.45
	(0.29)	(0.38)	(0.30)	(0.37)
Evangelical	–	−0.23	–	1.18
		(0.56)		(0.41)
Catholic	–	−0.74	–	1.27
		(0.49)		(0.45)
Party-ID (Dem.-Repub.)	−0.04	−0.04	0.85**	0.86**
	(0.04)	(0.04)	(0.02)	(0.02)

(*continued*)

TABLE 6.3. (*continued*)

IVs	PERSUASIVE		SUPPORT FOR CAPITAL PUNISHMENT	
	Regular Model	Interactive Model	Regular Model	Interactive Model
	OLS Coefficient (SEs)	OLS Coefficient (SEs)	Odds Ratio (SEs)	Odds Ratio (SEs)
Attendance	0.29**	0.28	0.89**	0.88**
(Low-High)	(0.05)	(0.06)	(0.03)	(0.03)
I: Rights (Opp.) and	–	–0.88	–	1.55
Evangelical		(0.84)		(0.86)
I: Rights (Fav.) and	–	0.41	–	1.11
Evangelical		(0.74)		(0.53)
I: Justice (Opp.) and	–	0.48	–	0.90
Evangelical		(0.76)		(0.45)
I: Justice (Fav.) and	–	0.57	–	1.28
Evangelical		(0.77)		(0.65)
I: Costs and Ben. (Opp.)	–	–	–	1.36
and Evang.				(0.71)
I: Costs and Ben. (Fav.) and	–	0.65	–	1.60
Evangelical		(0.83)		(0.90)
I: Rights (Opp.) and	–	0.53	–	1.16
Catholic		(0.69)		(0.56)
I: Rights (Fav.) and Catholic	–	1.25†	–	1.01
		(0.71)		(0.51)
I: Justice (Opp.) and	–	0.96	–	0.67
Catholic		(0.70)		(0.32)
I: Justice (Fav.) and	–	1.11	–	1.01
Catholic		(0.69)		(0.49)
I: Costs and Ben. (Opp.)	–	–	–	0.81
and Catholic				(0.39)
I: Costs and Ben. (Fav.) and	–	0.68	–	0.86
Catholic		(0.68)		(0.41)
Constant / Cut 1	4.13	4.41	–1.99	–1.89
	(0.32)	(0.37)	(0.21)	(0.23)
Cut 2	–	–	–0.76	–0.66
			(0.20)	(0.23)
N	1235	1221	1326	1312
Adj. R² /Adj. Count	0.04	0.04	–0.01	–0.003

Notes: The statistical significance notations are: † = p ≤ 0.10; * = p ≤ 0.05; ** = p ≤ 0.01. Standard errors are in parentheses. The Control Frame is the comparison category for the frames.

TABLE 6.4. *SSI Full: ANOVA Randomization Checks of Treatments*

IVs	Mean (Favor)	Mean (Oppose)	Mean (Control)	P-Value
Female				0.50
Right to Life	0.48	0.52	0.50	
Justice	0.51	0.51		
Costs and Benefits	0.48	0.49		
Control				
Party-ID				0.14
Right to Life	4.16	4.48	4.38	
Justice	4.15	4.52		
Costs and Benefits	4.37	4.56		
Control				
Age				0.72
Right to Life		45.65		
Justice		42.21		
Costs and Benefits		43.28		
Control				
White				0.80
Right to Life	0.84	0.79	0.81	
Justice	0.82	0.83		
Costs and Benefits	0.83	0.82		
Control				
Education				0.76
Right to Life	3.94	3.81	3.71	
Justice	3.87	3.93		
Costs and Benefits	3.87	3.75		
Control				
Parent				0.59
Right to Life	1.33	1.28	1.38	
Justice	1.32	1.26		
Costs and Benefits	1.31	1.31		
Control				
Abortion Attitudes				0.80
Right to Life	2.01	1.94	2.14	
Justice	1.99	1.96		
Costs and Benefits	1.92	2.07		
Control				
Church Attendance				0.11
Right to Life	2.86	2.50	2.60	
Justice	2.67	2.48		
Costs and Benefits	2.52	2.65		
Control				

Notes: The statistical significance notations are: $\dagger$ = p $\leq$ 0.10; * = p $\leq$ 0.05; ** = p $\leq$ 0.01.

TABLE 8.1. *GSS: Ordered Logistic Regression Models of Tolerance of Homosexuals, Odds Ratios*

IVs	1977–1999 (Rob. SEs)	2000–2014 (Rob. SEs)
Evangelical	0.45**	0.52**
	(0.04)	(0.06)
Black Protestant	0.74**	0.74**
	(0.07)	(0.09)
Catholic	0.75**	0.84
	(0.06)	(0.10)
Mainline Prot.	0.70**	0.96
	(0.05)	(0.09)
Other Faith	0.75	0.85
	(0.07)	(0.11)
Jewish	1.60**	1.11
	(0.29)	(0.27)
Evang. and Abor. Interaction	0.96*	1.04
	(0.02)	(0.03)
Cath. and Abor. Interaction	1.09**	1.09**
	(0.02)	(0.03)
Abortion (Favor-Oppose)	0.84**	0.82**
	(0.01)	(0.01)
Party-ID (Dem.-Repub.)	0.99	1.01
	(0.01)	(0.02)
Ideology (Lib.-Conserv.)	0.88**	0.87**
	(0.01)	(0.02)
Attendance (Never-Always)	0.88**	0.91**
	(0.01)	(0.02)
Education	1.71**	1.60**
	(0.03)	(0.04)
Age	0.78**	0.79**
	(0.01)	(0.02)
Children	0.90**	0.85**
	(0.04)	(0.05)
Male	0.79**	0.75**
	(0.03)	(0.04)
White	1.35**	1.56**
	(0.09)	(0.11)
Year	1.05**	1.04**
	(0.003)	(0.01)
Cut Point 1	93.37	91.66
	(5.33)	(10.79)
Cut Point 2	94.05	92.35
	(5.33)	(10.79)
Cut Point 3	94.97	93.33
	(5.33)	(10.80)
N	15799	8922
Adj. Count R^2	0.11	0.01

Notes: The statistical significance notations are: † = $p \leq 0.10$; * = $p \leq 0.05$; ** = $p \leq 0.01$. Robust standard errors are in parentheses. Unaffiliated is the comparison category for religious affiliation.

Notes

CHAPTER 1

1. See e.g., John Rawls, *Political Liberalism*, expanded ed. (New York: Columbia University Press, 2005). Ronald Dworkin, *Taking Rights Seriously* (Cambridge, MA: Harvard University Press, 1978).
2. See e.g., Stephen L. Carter, *The Culture of Disbelief* (New York: Anchor, 1991). Robert P. George, *Making Men Moral: Civil Liberties and Public Morals* (New York: Oxford University Press, 1995).
3. Robert N. Bellah et al., *Habits of the Heart: Individualism and Commitment in American Life* (Berkeley: University of California Press, 1985), 27–35.
4. Wayne Batchis, *The Right's First Amendment: The Politics of Free Speech and the Return of Conservative Libertarianism* (Stanford, CA: Stanford University Press, 2016).
5. Mary Ann Glendon, *Rights Talk: The Impoverishment of Political Discourse* (New York: Free Press, 1991), 14.
6. Louis Hartz, *The Liberal Tradition in America: An Interpretation of Political Thought* (New York: Harcourt, Brace, and World, 1955).
7. See e.g., John P. Diggins, *The Lost Soul of American Politics: Virtue, Self-Interest, and the Foundations of Liberalism* (Chicago: University of Chicago Press, 1984). Russell L. Hanson, *The Democratic Imagination in America: Conversations with Our Past* (Princeton, NJ: Princeton University Press, 1985). Barry Alan Shain, *The Myth of American Individualism: The Protestant Origins of American Political Thought* (Princeton, NJ: Princeton University Press, 1994). Rogers M. Smith, "Beyond Tocqueville, Myrdal, and Hartz: The Multiple Traditions in America," *American Political Science Review* 87, no. 3 (1993). Michael P. Zuckert, *The Natural Rights Republic: Studies in the Foundation of the American Political Tradition* (South Bend, IN: University of Notre Dame Press, 1996).
8. See e.g., William McLoughlin, *Soul Liberty: The Baptists' Struggle in New England, 1630–1833* (Hanover, NH: University Press of New England, 1991). Rhys H. Williams, "Visions of the Good Society and the Religious Roots of American Political

Culture," *Sociology of Religion* 60, no. 1 (1999). John Witte, Jr., *The Reformation of Rights: Law, Religion, and Human Rights in Early Modern Calvinism* (New York: Cambridge University Press, 2007).

9. Richard L. Pacelle, Jr., *The Transformation of the Supreme Court's Agenda: From the New Deal to the Reagan Administration* (Boulder, CO: Westview Press, 1991).

10. See e.g., Charles R. Epp, *The Rights Revolution: Lawyers, Activists, and Supreme Courts in Comparative Perspective* (Chicago: University of Chicago Press, 1998). Jonathan Goldberg-Hiller, *The Limits to Union: Same-Sex Marriage and the Politics of Civil Rights* (Ann Arbor: University of Michigan Press, 2004). Michael W. McCann, *Rights at Work: Pay Equity Reform and the Politics of Legal Mobilization* (Chicago: University of Chicago Press, 1994). Mark V. Tushnet, *NAACP's Legal Strategy against Segregated Education, 1925–1950* (Chapel Hill: University of North Carolina Press, 2005).

11. James Davison Hunter, *Culture Wars: The Struggle to Define America* (New York: Basic Books, 1991).

12. Steven M. Teles, *The Rise of the Conservative Legal Movement: The Battle for Control of the Law* (Princeton, NJ: Princeton University Press, 2008).

13. Glendon, *Rights Talk*.

14. Ted G. Jelen, "Political Esperanto: Rhetorical Resources and Limitations of the Christian Right in the United States," *Sociology of Religion* 66, no. 3 (2005).

15. Batchis, *The Right's First Amendment*.

16. Matthew C. Moen, "From Revolution to Evolution: The Changing Nature of the Christian Right," *Sociology of Religion* 55, no. 3 (1994). Jelen, "Political Esperanto."

17. Jon A. Shields, *The Democratic Virtues of the Christian Right* (Princeton, NJ: Princeton University Press, 2009).

18. Steven P. Brown, *Trumping Religion: The New Christian Right, the Free Speech Clause, and the Courts* (Tuscaloosa: University of Alabama Press, 2002); Hans J. Hacker, *The Culture of Conservative Christian Litigation* (Lanham, MD: Rowman & Littlefield, 2005). Teles, *The Rise of the Conservative Legal Movement*. Joshua C. Wilson, *The Street Politics of Abortion: Speech, Violence, and America's Culture Wars* (Stanford, CA: Stanford University Press, 2013). Batchis, *The Right's First Amendment*.

19. Batchis's *The Right's First Amendment* is an exception here, as he identifies the reemergence of libertarian stream of American conservatism as the primary cause of the right's shift in free speech advocacy.

20. Barry Hankins, *Uneasy in Babylon: Southern Baptist Conservatives and American Culture* (Tuscaloosa: University of Alabama Press, 2002). William McLoughlin, *New England Dissent 1960–1833: The Baptists and the Separation of Church and State* (Cambridge, MA: Harvard University Press, 1971).

21. Philip Hamburger, *Separation of Church and State* (Cambridge, MA: Harvard University Press, 2002). Andrew R. Lewis, "Abortion Politics and the Decline of the Separation of Church and State: The Southern Baptist Case," *Politics & Religion* 7, no. 3 (2014).

22. Daniel K. Williams, *Defenders of the Unborn: The Pro-Life Movement before Roe v. Wade* (New York: Oxford University Press, 2016).

23. See Hamburger, *Separation of Church and State*.

24. Williams, *Defenders of the Unborn.*
25. Lewis, "Abortion Politics and the Decline of the Separation of Church and State." Carin Robinson, "Cross-Cutting Messages and Political Tolerance: An Experiment Using Evangelical Protestants," *Political Behavior* 32, no. 4 (2010).
26. For elites and pro-life rights, see: Moen, "From Revolution to Evolution." For the mass public and pro-life rights, see: Ted G. Jelen, "Changes in the Attitudinal Correlates of Opposition to Abortion," *Journal for the Scientific Study of Religion* 27, no. 2 (1988).
27. Robert Booth Fowler et al., *Politics and Religion in America: Faith, Culture, and Strategic Choices*, 3rd ed. (Boulder, CO: Westview Press, 2004).
28. Scott Ainsworth and Itai Sened, "The Role of Lobbyists: Entrepreneurs with Two Audiences," *American Journal of Political Science* 37, no. 3 (1993). Ken Kollman, *Outside Lobbying: Public Opinion and Interest Group Strategies* (Princeton, NJ: Princeton University Press, 1998). Terry M. Moe, *The Organization of Interests: Incentives and the Internal Dynamics of Political Interest Groups* (Chicago: University of Chicago Press, 1980). "Toward a Broader View of Interest Groups," *Journal of Politics* 43, no. 2 (1981). James Q. Wilson, *Political Organizations* (New York: Basic Books, 1973).
29. Theda Skocpol, *Diminished Democracy: From Membership to Management in American Civil Life* (Norman: University of Oklahoma Press, 2003). "APSA Presidential Address: Voice and Inequality: The Transformation of American Civic Democracy," *Perspectives on Politics* 2, no. 1 (2004). Robert D. Putnam, *Bowling Alone: The Collapse and Revival of American Community* (New York: Simon & Schuster, 2000). James L. Guth et al., "Onward Christian Soldiers: Religious Activist Groups in American Politics," in *Interest Group Politics*, ed. Alan J. Cigler and Burdett A. Loomis (Washington, DC: CQ Press, 1995).
30. Dennis Chong and James N. Druckman, "Framing Theory," *Annual Review of Political Science* 10 (2007). John R. Zaller, *The Nature and Origins of Mass Opinion* (New York: Cambridge University Press, 2002).
31. Ted G. Jelen and Clyde Wilcox, "Causes and Consequences of Public Attitudes toward Abortion: A Review and Research Agenda," *Political Research Quarterly* 56, no. 4 (2003). "U.S. Public Becoming Less Religious," *Pew Research Center* (2015), www.pewforum.org/2015/11/03/u-s-public-becoming-less-religious/.
32. Elizabeth Adell Cook, Ted G. Jelen, and Clyde Wilcox, *Between Two Absolutes: Public Opinion and the Politics of Abortion* (Boulder, CO: Westview, 1992).
33. John H. Evans, "Have Americans' Attitudes Become More Polarized? An Update," *Social Science Quarterly* 84, no. 1 (2003).
34. John P. Hoffman and Sherrie Mills Johnson, "Attitudes toward Abortion among Religious Traditionalists in the United States: Change or Continuity?," *Sociology of Religion* 66, no. 2 (2005).
35. Robert D. Putnam and David E. Campbell, *American Grace: How Religion Divides and Unites Us* (New York: Simon & Schuster, 2010), 393.
36. Mitchell Killian and Clyde Wilcox, "Do Abortion Attitudes Lead to Party Switching?," *Political Research Quarterly* 61, no. 4 (2008). See also: Greg D. Adams, "Abortion: Evidence of Issue Evolution," *American Journal of Political Science* 41, no. 3 (1997).
37. Donald P. Haider-Markel and Mark R. Joslyn, "Gun Policy, Opinion, Tragedy and Blame Attribution: The Conditional Influence of Issue Frames," ibid., 63, no. 2 (2001). Thomas E. Nelson, Rosalee A. Clawson, and Zoe M. Oxley, "Media

Framing of a Civil Liberties Conflict and Its Effect on Tolerance," *American Political Science Review* 91, no. 3 (1997).

38. Jelen, "Political Esperanto."
39. Paul A. Djupe et al., "Rights Talk: The Opinion Dynamics of Rights Framing," *Social Science Quarterly* 95, no. 3 (2014).
40. For the rise of the religiously unaffiliated or "nones," see: Putnam and Campbell, *American Grace*. Though there is some debate among social scientists about the appropriate measurement of the "nones" and the cause of their increase, religious prominence is certainly on the decline in America. See also: "U.S. Public Becoming Less Religious," *Pew Research Center*.
41. Alan I. Abramowitz, "It's Abortion, Stupid: Policy Voting in the 1992 Presidential Election," *Journal of Politics* 57, no. 1 (1995). Adams, "Abortion." Killian and Wilcox, "Do Abortion Attitutudes Lead to Party Switching?"
42. David C. Leege et al., *The Politics of Cultural Differences: Social Change and Voter Mobilization Strategies in the Post-New Deal Period* (Princeton, NJ: Princeton University Press, 2002). For an historical account that emphasizes race, see: Randall Balmer, "The Real Origins of the Religious Right. They'll Tell You It Was Abortion. Sorry, the Historical Record's Clear: It Was Segregation," *Politico*, May 27, 2014.
43. For a political science account, see: Ryan L. Claassen, *Godless Democrats and Pious Republicans? Party Activists, Party Capture and the "God Gap"* (New York: Cambridge University Press, 2015). For an historical account, see: Darren Dochuk, *From Bible Belt to Sun Belt: Plain-Folk Religion, Grassroots Politics, and the Rise of Evangelical Conservatism* (New York: W.W. Norton, 2011).
44. For the evolution of cultural politics and party mobilization, see: Leege et al., *The Politics of Cultural Differences*. For the evolution of rights-based pro-life opinion within evangelicalism, see: Jelen, "Changes in the Attitudinal Correlates of Opposition to Abortion."
45. Chapter 2 will provide more detail about the history of National Right to Life Committee and its relationship between Catholics and evangelicals.
46. For the Southern Baptists, see: "Religious Liberty Bill before Congress Highlights Difference among Baptists," *SBC Today*, July 26, 1991; Brian Bolduc, "The Church and the RFRA," *National Review*, February 17, 2012.
47. Tony Cook, "Gov. Mike Pence Signs 'Religious Freedom' Bill in Private," *Indiana Star*, April 2, 2015.
48. See Glendon, *Rights Talk*.
49. For deliberation, see: Amy Guttman and Dennis Thompson, *Democracy and Disagreement* (Cambridge: Belknap Press, 1996). Shields, *The Democratic Virtues of the Christian Right*. For tolerance, see: Paul A. Djupe, Andrew R. Lewis, and Ted G. Jelen, "Rights, Reflection, and Reciprocity: Implications of the Same-Sex Marriage Debate for Tolerance and the Political Process," *Politics & Religion* 9, no. 3 (2016).
50. Alexis de Tocqueville, *Democracy in America*, trans. Delba Wintrop (Chicago: University of Chicago Press, 2002).
51. Guttman and Thompson, *Democracy and Disagreement*.
52. Shields, *The Democratic Virtues of the Christian Right*.
53. For a legal and political theory perspective, see: John D. Inazu, *Confident Pluralism: Surviving and Thriving through Deep Difference* (Chicago: University of Chicago Press, 2016).

54. George Marsden, "The Evangelical Denomination," in *Introduction: Evangelicalism and Modern America*, ed. George Marsden (Grand Rapids, MI: William B. Erdmans, 1984). "Contemporary American Evangelicalism," in *Southern Baptists & American Evangelicals: The Conversation Continues*, ed. David S Dockery (Nashville, TN: Broadman & Holman, 1993). In modern America, evangelical Protestants typically participate in the National Association of Evangelicals, while mainline Protestants, an even more diverse group of Protestants that includes many progressive, liberal, and neo-orthodox Protestants, participate in the National Council of Churches. For additional resources on the definition of evangelical, see: David W. Bebbington, *Evangelicalism in Modern Britain: A History from the 1730s to the 1980s* (London: Unwin Hyman, 1989). Also see: National Association of Evangelicals, "What Is an Evangelical?," (2009), www.nae.net/church-and-faith-partners/what-is-an-evangelical.

55. For the debate among Southern Baptists about whether they are evangelicals, see: David S. Dockery, ed., *Southern Baptists & American Evangelicals: The Conversation Continues* (Nashville: Broadman & Holman, 1993). James Leo Garrett, Jr., E. Glenn Hinson, and James E. Tull, *Are Southern Baptists "Evangelicals"?* (Macon, GA: Mercer University Press, 1983). Hankins, *Uneasy in Babylon*. In general, the SBC moderates who led the denomination until the 1980s were less accepting of the evangelical label, while many SBC conservatives who have led the SBC since the 1980s have embraced the term. Religion and politics scholars, however, consistently choose to classify Southern Baptists as evangelicals. Though some Southern Baptists may eschew the label, their affiliation aligns with evangelicalism theologically, historically, and politically. See: Corwin E. Smidt, Lyman A. Kellstedt, and James L. Guth, "The Role of Religion in American Politics: Explanatory Theories and Associated Analytical and Measurement Issues," in *Oxford Handbook on Religion and American Politics*, ed. Corwin E. Smidt, Lyman A. Kellstedt, and James L. Guth (New York: Oxford University Press, 2009).

56. For an overview, see: Putnam and Campbell, *American Grace*. Smidt, Kellstedt, and Guth, "The Role of Religion in American Politics." Corwin E. Smidt, *American Evangelicals Today* (Lanham, MD: Rowman & Littlefield, 2013).

57. For an alternative approach, see: Bob Smientana, "What Is an Evangelical? Four Questions Offer New Definition," *Christianity Today*, November 19, 2015.

58. Brian Steensland et al., "The Measure of American Religion: Toward Improving the State of the Art," *Social Forces* 79, no. 1 (2000). When using the General Social Survey, I use Stetzer and Burge's update of coding Steensland et al.'s religious tradition coding: Ed Stetzer and Ryan P. Burge, "Reltrad Coding Problems and a New Repository," *Politics & Religion* 9, no. 1 (2016).

59. Thomas Kidd, "Polls Show Evangelicals Support Trump. But the Term 'Evangelical' Has Become Meaningless," *The Washington Post*, July 22, 2016; Russell Moore, "Russell Moore: Why This Election Makes Me Hate the Word 'Evangelical'," ibid., February 29 .

60. Smidt, Kellstedt, and Guth, "The Role of Religion in American Politics."

61. Claassen, *Godless Democrats and Pious Republicans?* Lyman A. Kellstedt et al., "A Gentle Stream or a 'River Glorious'? The Religious Left in the 2004 Election," in *A Matter of Faith: Religion in the 2004 Presidential Election*, ed. David E. Campbell (Washington, DC: Brookings Institution Press, 2007).

62. Williams, *Defenders of the Unborn*, xi–xiv. See also: *God's Own Party: The Making of the Christian Right* (New York: Oxford University Press, 2010).
63. See e.g., Ronald J. Sider, *Completely Pro-Life: Building a Consistent Stance* (Downers Grove, IL: InterVarsity Press, 1987).
64. *The Associated Press Stylebook*, 39th ed. (New York: Basic Books, 2004), emphasis in the original.
65. These clergy data are a part of the Cooperative Clergy Study Project.

CHAPTER 2

1. Jimmy Carter, "White House Conference on Families Statement Announcing Conference," in *The American Presidency Project* (1978).
2. J. Brooks Flippen, *Jimmy Carter, the Politics of Family, and the Rise of the Religious Right* (Athens: University of Georgia Press, 2011). Leo P. Ribuffo, "Family Policy Past as Prologue: Jimmy Carter, the White House Conference on Families, and the Mobilization of the New Christian Right," *Review of Policy Research* 23, no. 2 (2006).
3. Victoria Irwin, "Factions Seek Control of Family Conference," *Christian Science Monitor,* February 13, 1980.
4. "Family Conference Officials Downplay Abortion Issue," *The Argus-Press*, June 18, 1980. Ribuffo.
5. Williams, *Defenders of the Unborn*.
6. Christina Wolbrecht, *The Politics of Women's Rights: Parties, Positions, and Change* (Princeton, NJ: Princeton University Press, 2000).
7. Claassen, *Godless Democrats and Pious Republicans?*
8. The elections of 1992 and 1996 appear to be the exceptions, as only about 50% of evangelicals voted for Republicans. Moreover, Claassen's percentages perhaps underestimate white evangelical support for Republican candidates, compared to other methods that define evangelicals as Protestants who self-identify as "born-again" Christians rather than members of an evangelical congregation. Ibid., 93.
9. Gregory A. Smith and Jessica Martinez, *How the Faithful Voted: A Preliminary 2016 Analysis* (Washington, DC: Pew Research Center, 2016).
10. Geoffrey Layman, *The Great Divide: Religious and Cultural Conflict in American Party Politics* (New York: Columbia University Press, 2001).
11. Claassen, *Godless Democrats and Pious Republicans?*
12. Leege et al., *The Politics of Cultural Differences.*
13. Claassen, *Godless Democrats and Pious Republicans?*, 107. See also: Leege et al., *The Politics of Cultural Differences.*
14. Adams, "Abortion." Killian and Wilcox, "Do Abortion Attitudes Lead to Party Switching?." Ted G. Jelen, "Culture Wars and the Party System: Religion and Realignment," in *Culture Wars in American Politics: Critical Reviews of a Popular Thesis*, ed. Rhys H. Williams (Hawthorne, NY: Aldine de Gruyter, 1997).
15. Edward G. Carmines and James A. Stimson, *Issue Evolution: Race and the Transformation of American Politics* (Princeton, NJ: Princeton University Press, 1989). Leege et al., *The Politics of Cultural Differences.*
16. Layman, *The Great Divide.* That said, Leege et al. and Layman differ about the specific time period where cultural politics matter for partisan change, with Leege et al. suggesting a later date.

17. Evans, "Have Americans' Attitudes Become More Polarized?"
18. Williams, *Defenders of the Unborn*, 111.
19. Ibid.
20. Ibid., 114. See: "A Protestant Affirmation on the Control of Human Reproduction," *Christianity Today*, November 1968. Robert D. Visscher, "Therapeutic Abortion: Blessing or Murder," ibid., September 27.
21. Williams, *Defenders of the Unborn*.
22. *Resolution on Abortion* (St Louis: Southern Baptist Convention, 1971).
23. *Abortion* (National Association of Evangelicals, 1971).
24. Technically *Roe* allowed regulations regarding abortion in the second trimester as well as the third, but second-trimester regulations could only be to safeguard the health of the mother, not the survival of the fetus.
25. W. Barry Garrett, "High Court Holds Abortion to Be 'a Right of Privacy'," *Baptist Press*, January 31, 1973.
26. Robert O'Brien, "Abortion Court Decision Interpreted by Attorney," ibid., January 29.
27. For a discussion of Wood's positions, see Chapter 4, as well as: Pam Parry, *On Guard for Religious Liberty: Six Decades of the Baptist Joint Committee* (Macon, GA: Smith & Helwys, 1996).
28. Williams, *Defenders of the Unborn*, 118.
29. *Abortion* (National Association of Evangelicals, 1973).
30. *Resolution on Abortion* (St Louis: Southern Baptist Convention, 1980).
31. See e.g., Nancy Tatom Ammerman, *Baptist Battles: Social Change and Religious Conflict in the Southern Baptist Convention*, 2nd ed. (New Brunswick, NJ: Rutgers University Press, 1995). Hankins, *Uneasy in Babylon*. Arthur Emery Farnsley II, *Southern Baptist Politics: Authority and Power in the Restructuring of an American Denomination* (University Park: Penn State University Press, 1994).
32. For a review of the SBC's organizational change and its split with the BJC, see: Andrew R. Lewis, "The Southern Baptist Church-State 'Culture War': The Internal Politics of Denominational Advocacy" (Ph.D. Dissertation, American University, 2011). See also: Hankins, *Uneasy in Babylon*. Ammerman, *Baptist Battles*.
33. For a review, see: Jelen and Wilcox, "Causes and Consequences of Public Attitudes toward Abortion."
34. Ibid.
35. Cook, Jelen, and Wilcox, *"Between Two Absolutes.*
36. Clyde Wilcox and Barbara Norrander, "Of Moods and Morals: The Dynamics of Opinion on Abortion and Gay Rights," in *Understanding Public Opinion*, ed. Barbara Norrander and Clyde Wilcox (Washington, DC: CQ Press, 2002). George F. Bishop, Robert W. Oldendick, and Alfred J. Tuchfarber, "The Importance of Replicating a Failure to Replicate: Order Effects on Abortion Items," *Public Opinion Quarterly* 49, no. 1 (1985).
37. This Pro-Life Index is quite reliable with an Eigenvalue of 3.84 and a Cronbach's Alpha of 0.89.
38. Elizabeth Adell Cook, Ted G. Jelen, and Clyde Wilcox, "Measuring Abortion Attitudes: Methodological and Substantive Lessons from the CBS/New York Times Surveys," *Family Planning Perspectives* 25, no. 3 (1993).
39. Paul DiMaggio, John Evans, and Bethany Bryson, "Have American's Social Attitudes Become More Polarized?," *American Journal of Sociology* 102, no. 3 (1996). Evans, "Have Americans' Attitudes Become More Polarized?"

40. Cook, Jelen, and Wilcox, *Between Two Absolutes.*
41. Wilcox and Norrander, "Of Moods and Morals."
42. Carmines and Stimson. "The Two Faces of Issue Voting," *American Political Science Review* 74, no. 1 (1980).
43. Layman, *The Great Divide.*
44. Adams, "Abortion."
45. Abramowitz, "It's Abortion, Stupid," 176.
46. Elizabeth Adell Cook, Ted G. Jelen, and Clyde Wilcox, "Issue Voting in U.S. Senate Elections: The Abortion Issue in 1990," *Congress & the Presidency* 21, no. 1 (1994). "Issue Voting in Gubernatorial Elections: Abortion and Post-*Webster* Politics," *Journal of Politics* 56, no. 1 (1994).
47. Thomas M. Carsey and Geoffrey C. Layman, "Changing Sides or Changing Minds? Party Conversion, Issue Conversion, and Partisan Change on the Abortion Issue," *American Journal of Political Science* 50, no. 2 (2006).
48. Adams, "Abortion." Killian and Wilcox, "Do Abortion Attitutudes Lead to Party Switching?"
49. Carsey and Layman, "Changing Sides or Changing Minds?"
50. Killian and Wilcox, "Do Abortion Attitutudes Lead to Party Switching?."
51. Several scholars have shown party identity to be a deeply rooted, difficult to alter social identity on par with one's religion or ethnicity. Donald Green, Bradley Palmquist, and Eric Schickler, *Partisan Hearts and Minds: Political Parties and the Social Identities of Voters* (New Haven, CT: Yale University Press, 2002).
52. These are technically called *amici curiae* briefs, and groups or individuals who want to indicate their view on a case, advocate a particular legal position, or indicate how their constituents will be affected file them.
53. See, Putnam and Campbell, *American Grace,* 390. See also, Kristin Luker, *Abortion and the Politics of Motherhood* (Berkeley: University of California Press, 1984).
54. See e.g., Shields, *The Democratic Virtues of the Christian Right.*
55. See e.g., Skocpol, "APSA Presidential Address: Voice and Inequality: The Transformation of American Civic Democracy."; Guth et al., "Onward Christian Soldiers."
56. See e.g., Linda Gordon, *The Moral Property of Women: A History of Birth Control Politics in America,* 4th ed. (Urbana: University of Illinois Press, 2002). Luker, *Abortion and the Politics of Motherhood.* Robert O. Self, *All in the Family: The Realignment of American Democracy since the 1960s* (New York: Hill and Wang, 2012). Rickie Solinger, *Reproductive Politics: What Everyone Needs to Know* (New York: Oxford University Press, 2013).
57. Cook, Jelen, and Wilcox, *Between Two Absolutes.* Ted G. Jelen, David F. Damore, and Thomas Lamatsch, "Gender, Employment Status, and Abortion: A Longitudinal Analysis," *Sex Roles* 47, no. 7/8 (2002).
58. Williams, *Defenders of the Unborn.* See also: Mary Ziegler, *After Roe: The Lost History of the Abortion Debate* (Cambridge, MA: Harvard University Press, 2015).
59. Williams, *Defenders of the Unborn,* 3.
60. Ibid., 88–100.
61. "United States Declaration of Independence" (1776).
62. United Nations, "The Universal Declaration of Human Rights" (1948).
63. "Fifth Amendment of the United States Constitution."
64. Williams, *Defenders of the Unborn,* 97.

65. For a religious and political history of Schaeffer, see: Barry Hankins, *Francis Schaeffer and the Shaping of Evangelical America* (Grand Rapids, MI: Wm. B. Eerdmans, 2008).

66. For Schaeffer's impact on Land, see: Hankins, *Uneasy in Babylon*, 23.

67. Williams writes, "Francis Schaeffer, a popular evangelical writer who may have done more than any other person to mobilize evangelicals on behalf of the pro-life cause, framed the abortion issue as part of a broader narrative on national moral decline." Williams, *Defenders of the Unborn*, 237.

68. See also Hankins, *Francis Schaeffer and the Shaping of Evangelical America*.

69. Ibid., 180–91.

70. Williams, *Defenders of the Unborn*.

71. See Jerry Falwell, *Strength for the Journey: An Autobiography* (New York: Simon & Schuster, 1987).

72. Williams, *Defenders of the Unborn*, 237.

73. Jerry Falwell, *How You Can Help Clean up America* (Lynchburg, VA: Liberty Publishing Company, 1978).

74. Witte, *The Reformation of Rights*.

75. Ibid., xi.

76. McLoughlin, *Soul Liberty: The Baptists' Struggle in New England, 1630–1833*.

77. *Human Rights* (National Association of Evangelicals, 1956).

78. *Declaration of Human Rights* (Atlanta, GA: Southern Baptist Convention, 1978).

79. Williams, *Defenders of the Unborn*, 9.

80. See e.g., Matthew C. Moen, *The Transformation of the Christian Right* (Tuscaloosa: University of Alabama Press, 1992). Laura Grindstaff, "Abortion and the Popular Press: Mapping Media Discourse from *Roe* to *Webster*," in *Abortion Politics in the United States and Canada: Studies in Public Opinion*, ed. Ted G. Jelen and Marthe A. Chandler (Westport, CT: Praeger, 1994).

81. Moen, "From Revolution to Evolution."

82. Ted G. Jelen, "Respect for Life, Sexual Morality, and Opposition to Abortion," *Review of Religious Research* 25, no. 3 (1984).

83. "Changes in the Attitudinal Correlates of Opposition to Abortion."

84. See e.g., Mark J. Rozell and Clyde Wilcox, *Second Coming: The Christian Right in Virginia Politics* (Baltimore: Johns Hopkins University Press, 1996). Layman, *The Great Divide*. Justin Watson, *The Christian Coalition: Dreams of Restoration, Demands for Recognition* (New York: St. Martin's Griffin, 1999).

85. Ralph Reed, *Active Faith: How Christians Are Changing the Soul of American Politics* (New York: Free Press, 1996).

86. Moen, "From Revolution to Evolution."

87. Shields, *The Democratic Virtues of the Christian Right*.

88. *Resolution on Abortion* (Southern Baptist Convention, 1980).

89. *Resolution on the Partial-Birth Abortion Ban* (New Orleans, LA: Southern Baptist Convention, 1996).

90. *On the Sanctity of Human Life* (Columbus, OH: Southern Baptist Convention, 2015).

91. Dallas A. Blanchard, *The Anti-Abortion Movement and the Rise of the Religious Right: From Polite to Fiery Protest* (New York: MacMillan, 1994).

92. Liam Stack, "A Brief History of Deadly Attacks on Abortion Providers," *The New York Times*, November 29, 2015.

93. Wilson, *The Street Politics of Abortion.*

94. See: Hacker, *The Culture of Conservative Christian Litigation.*
   Ann Southworth, *Lawyers of the Right: Professionalizing the Conservative Coalition* (Chicago: University of Chicago Press, 2008). Dennis R. Hoover and Kevin R. den Dulk, "Christian Conservatives Go to Court: Religion and Legal Mobilization in the United States and Canada," *International Political Science Review* 25, no. 1 (2004).

95. Wilson, *The Street Politics of Abortion,* 164. Kevin den Dulk, "In Legal Culture, but Not of It: The Role of Cause Lawyers in Evangelical Legal Mobilization," in *Cause Lawyers and Social Movements,* ed. Austin Sarat and Stuart Scheingold (Stanford, CA: Stanford University Press, 2006).

96. Teles, *The Rise of Conservative Legal Movement.* Amanda Hollis-Brusky, *Ideas with Consequences: The Federalist Society and the Conservative Counterrevolution* (New York: Oxford University Press, 2015). Southworth, *Lawyers of the Right.*

97. Hollis-Brusky, *Ideas with Consequences.*

98. Jelen, "Political Esperanto," 309–10.

99. Williams, *Defenders of the Unborn,* 267.

100. Hacker, *The Culture of Conservative Christian Litigation.*

101. Wilson, *The Street Politics of Abortion,* 161–62.

102. Ibid., 163.

103. Southworth, *Lawyers of the Right.* Hollis-Brusky, *Ideas with Consequences.*

104. Leege et al., *The Politics of Cultural Differences.*

105. Wilson, *The Street Politics of Abortion,* 162.

106. See e.g., Leege et al., *The Politics of Cultural Differences.* Abramowitz, "It's Abortion, Stupid." Killian and Wilcox, "Do Abortion Attitudes Lead to Party Switching?." Claassen, *Godless Democrats and Pious Republicans?* Layman, *The Great Divide.*

107. See e.g., Moen, *The Transformation of the Christian Right.* Hacker, *The Culture of Conservative Christian Litigation.* Wilson, *The Street Politics of Abortion.*

CHAPTER 3

1. Ross Douthat, "The Blasphemy We Need," *The New York Times,* January 7, 2015.

2. Family Research Council, "In Atlanta, Family Research Council's Tony Perkins Stands with Fired Chief, Challenges Mayor Reed's Intimidating Message," news release, January 13, 2015, www.frc.org/newsroom/in-atlanta-family-research-coun cils-tony-perkins-stands-with-fired-fire-chief-challenges-mayor-reeds-intimidating-message. Perkins used the example of the *Charlie Hebdo* attacks to chastise liberal restrictions on religious people's free expression of their faith, including the Atlanta fire chief who was fired because of his view on gay rights.

3. Nick Eicher, "Why 'Je Suis Charlie' Should Give Christians Pause," *World Magazine,* January 19, 2015.

4. Franklin Graham, "Franklin Graham: Are There Limits to Religious Mockery," *Decision Magazine,* March 2, 2015.

5. Joe Carter, "Us, Them, and Good Men: Choosing Sides on Offensive Speech," *Canon and Culture,* February 20, 2015.

6. John L. Allen, "After Charlie Hebdo, Pope Says Free Speech Has Limits," *Crux*, January 15, 2015.

7. Examples include: Tracinski Robert, "The Message of Charlie Hebdo: Europe, Welcome to the ISIS Era," *The Federalist*, January 7, 2015. Kim R. Holmes, "Charlie Hebdo, Intolerance, and the Problem of Double Standards," (2015), www.heritage.org/research/commentary/2015/2/charlie-hebdo-intolerance-and-the-problem-of-double-standards. Sean Davis, "Men without Chests: How C. S. Lewis Predicted Charlie Hebdo Censorship," *The Federalist*, January 8, 2015.

8. Falwell's legal battle was covered in *Christianity Today* and *Baptist Press*, though neither offered an editorial position. See e.g., "Falwell Wins $200,000 for Emotional Distress in a Suit against Hustler Magazine," *Christianity Today*, January 18, 1985. "Falwell Loses Hustler Suit," *Christianity Today*, April 8, 1988. Kathy Palen, "High Court to Review Falwell-Flynt Case," *Baptist Press*, April 3, 1987. Stan Hastey, "No Damages for Falwell, Supreme Court Rules," ibid., February 25, 1988.

9. Douglas O. Linder, "The Falwell v. Flynt Trial," http://law2.umkc.edu/faculty/projects/ftrials/falwell/trialaccount.html; Rodney Smolla, *Jerry Falwell v. Larry Flynt: The First Amendment on Trial* (1988).

10. *Hustler Magazine v. Falwell*, 485 U.S. 46 (1988).

11. Ibid.

12. "Falwell Loses Hustler Suit," 48.

13. Batchis, *The Right's First Amendment*.

14. In evaluating political conservatives, Batchis, by contrast, gives credit to the increasing ideological commitment to libertarianism on the right.

15. In this chapter, I am setting aside the role of free speech arguments in granting religious groups equal access to public facilities. This line of cases begins in *Widmar v. Vincent* (1981), and evangelicals, including the Southern Baptists, were heavily involved in this issue. See: Brown, *Trumping Religion*. I will revisit this a bit in Chapter 4, which addresses the evolution of church-state law and politics.

16. See Bellah et al., *Habits of the Heart*.

17. *Resolution Concerning Obscenity in Literature* (Houston, TX: Southern Baptist Convention, 1953).

18. Theo Sommerkamp, "Campaign against Indecency Mapped," *Baptist Press*, August 14, 1957.

19. *Alcohol Advertising* (National Association of Evangelicals, 1958). *Obscene Literature* (National Association of Evangelicals, 1958).

20. *Resolution on Pornographic Literature* (Louisville, KY: Southern Baptist Convention, 1959).

21. Fred Kaplan, "The Day Obscenity Became Art," *The New York Times*, July 20, 2009.

22. A. C. Miller, "The Christian Citizen in Community Action," *Baptist Press*, May 22, 1959.

23. Ibid.

24. *Obscenity* (National Association of Evangelicals, 1965).

25. Ibid.

26. *Resolution on Pornographic Materials* (Houston, TX: Southern Baptist Convention, 1968).

27. *Pornography and the Courts* (National Association of Evangelicals, 1969).
28. "Baptist Leader Asks Public Funds to Fight Pornography," *Baptist Press*, May 13, 1970.
29. Ibid.
30. See Bellah et al., *Habits of the Heart*.
31. *Resolution on Pornography* (Atlanta, GA: Southern Baptist Convention, 1986)
32. *Obscenity* (National Association of Evangelicals). *Pornography and the Courts* (National Association of Evangelicals).
33. The BJC is an umbrella group based in Washington, DC that advocated for the SBC and other Baptist groups on religious liberty and other public affairs issues. After conservatives gained control of the SBC in the 1980s, the denomination ended its partnership with the BJC. See: Lewis, "The Southern Baptist Church-State 'Culture War'." "Abortion Politics and the Decline of the Separation of Church and State."
34. David E. Anderson, "Churches Seek Renewed Social Activist Role," *Nashua Telegraph*, March 2, 1974.
35. W. Barry Garrett, "Baptist Body Declares Its Position on Equal Rights," *Baptist Press*, March 7, 1974.
36. "Public Financing Passes Senate; House Outlook Dim," ibid., April 15.
37. David B. Magleby and Candice J. Nelson, *The Money Chase: Congressional Campaign Finance Reform* (Washington, DC: Brookings Institution Press, 2010), 153.
38. "SBC Leaders Agree with Resignation; Register Sadness," *Baptist Press*, August 9, 1974.
39. Hollis-Brusky, *Ideas with Consequences*. Hollis-Brusky suggests that one of the primary reasons there was no conservative momentum against campaign finance laws was that conservative legal advocacy networks did not yet exist. The Federalist Society would not develop for nearly another decade.
40. See: ibid. Batchis, *The Right's First Amendment*.
41. "House Votes 385 to 16 to Ban Flag Mutilation," *Baptist Press*, June 22, 1967.
42. Beth Hayworth, "Graham Calls for Spiritual Renewal to Honor America," ibid., July 7, 1970.
43. "Court Upholds Student Use of Flag for Peace," ibid., June 26, 1974.
44. Williams, *Defenders of the Unborn*.
45. Brown, *Trumping Religion*.
46. "Roundup for Monday A.M.," *Baptist Press*, June 10, 1984.
47. For more on Schaeffer's renouncing of evangelicalism and conservative politics, see: Frank Schaeffer, *Crazy for God: How I Grew up as One of the Elect, Helped Found the Religious Right, and Lived to Take All (or Almost All) of It Back* (Boston, MA: Da Capo Press, 2008). Mark Oppenheimer, "Son of Evangelical Royalty Turns His Back, and Tells the Tale," *The New York Times*, August 19, 2011.
48. For more on conservative religious legal advocacy organizations, see: Hacker, *The Culture of Conservative Christian Litigation*. For the development of religious advocacy organizations to support free speech in abortion protest cases, see: Wilson, *The Street Politics of Abortion*.
49. The controversial groups are atheists, racists, communists, militarists, and homosexuals. There is not a distinguishable conservative/liberal split in tolerating the speech of some groups over others. Liberals and conservatives both approve more

of homosexual and atheist speech than racist, communist, and militarist speech, though liberals approve of this speech at greater levels than conservatives do. Thus, the scale, which has an alpha of 0.83 and a first-order factor analysis that produces an Eigenvalue of 2.36, is appropriate.

50. For a review, see: James L. Gibson, "Measuring Political Tolerance and General Support for Pro-Civil Liberties Policies: Notes, Evidence, and Cautions," *Public Opinion Quarterly* 77, no S1 (2013).

51. Wilson, *The Street Politics of Abortion*.

52. Operation Rescue is an anti-abortion organization founded by Randall Terry in 1986 to engage in civil disobedience to seek to draw attention to the abortion issue and curtail abortions. Strategies included sit-ins, protests, blockades of abortion clinics, and sidewalk counseling in front of clinics. Under the Operation Rescue umbrella are many fairly autonomous state and local chapters.

53. Tom Strode, "Supreme Court Hears Operation Rescue Case," *Baptist Press*, November 19, 1991.

54. "Congress Approves Outlawing Abortion Clinic Blockades," *Baptist Press*, November 19, 1993.

55. Gwen Ifill, "Clinton Signs Bill Banning Blockades and Violent Acts at Abortion Clinics," *The New York Times*, May 27, 1994.

56. *Resolution on the Freedom of Choice Act, Hyde Amendment* (Houston, TX: Southern Baptist Convention, 1993).

57. Tom Strode, "Supreme Court's Term Confirms Commitment to Abortion Rights," *Baptist Press*, July 7, 2000.

58. Christian Legal Society, "Brief of the National Hispanic Christian Leadership Conference, International Society for Krishna Consciousness, Untied States Conference of Catholic Bishops, American Bible Society, Christian Medical Association, Ethics & Religious Liberty Commission of the Southern Baptist Convention, Institutional Religious Freedom Alliance, Intervarsity Christian Fellowship/USA, Lutheran Church-Missouri Synod, National Association of Evangelicals, and Christian Legal Society, Amicus Curiae.," in *Eleanor McCullen, et al. v. Martha Coakley, et al.* (Washington, DC, 2014).

59. For more on the development of free speech litigation and legal organizations through abortion protest cases, see: Wilson, *The Street Politics of Abortion*.

60. Staff, "Court Hears Case on Students' Rights," *Baptist Press*, March 20, 2007.

61. Ibid. Though *Baptist Press* cited evangelical involvement in this case approvingly, the Southern Baptists did not participate as *amicus curiae*. In an interview with the author in 2010, Richard Land said that the ERLC supported free speech but could not file in support of pro-drug language. Richard D. Land, "Interview with the Author." August 9 and 13, 2010, Nashville, TN.

62. Liberty Counsel, "U.S. Supreme Court Rules in Favor of Free Speech in Funeral Protest Case," news release, March 2, 2011, www.lc.org/index.cfm?PID=14100& PRID=1040.

63. Ibid.

64. Richard Land, "When Freedoms Are Curtailed: Verbal Terrorism," *Baptist Press*, November 6, 2007.

65. Hannah Cummings, "High Court Weighs Speech Limits in Westboro Case," ibid., October 7, 2010.

66. One exception is the Texas Mexican Baptist Convention, which passed a resolution supporting respect for the flag in June 1989. See Orville Scott, "Texas Baptist Convention Challenged to 'Arise, Build'," ibid., June 29, 1989.
67. The case is *Sable Communications of California v. FCC* (1989).
68. Staff, "Appeals Court Nominee Tells Panel Devotion to Law Is Issue," *Baptist Press*, September 19, 2002.
69. Christian Coalition of America, "Christian Coalition Expresses Disappointment with Senators That Opposed the Flag Amendment," news release, June 28, 2006.
70. Kelly Boggs, "First-Person: Limits to the First Amendment," *Baptist Press*, September 17, 2010.
71. The unaffiliated or secular are the comparison category.
72. Hollis-Brusky, *Ideas with Consequences*.
73. Batchis, *The Right's First Amendment*.
74. Charlotte Allen, "The Right to Life Lobby vs. McCain," *The Weekly Standard*, April 30, 2007.
75. See: Tom Strode, "Campaign-Finance Bill Violates Free-Speech Rights, Critics Say," *Baptist Press*, April 3, 2001. See also: *U.S. Senate Passes McCain-Feingold Bill to Restrict Free Speech*, 59–41 (National Right to Life Committee, April 30, 2001).
76. *On Protecting Free Speech in Campaign Finance Legislation* (New Orleans, LA: Southern Baptist Convention, 2001).
77. Tom Strode, "ACLJ Seeking to Overturn Campaign Finance Reform Law," *Baptist Press* April 5, 2002.
78. For the Federalist Society's talking points, see: Hollis-Brusky, *Ideas with Consequences*.
79. Strode, ACLJ Seeking to Overturn Campaign Finance Reform Law.
80. Tom Strode, "ERLC, Others Decry Ruling on Campaign Reform Law," *Baptist Press*, December 11, 2003.
81. "High Court Hears Pro-Life Issue Ads Case," ibid., April 26, 2007.
82. "Supreme Court Protects Issue Ads," *Baptist Press*, June 26, 2007.
83. Richard Land, "First-Person: Is Kagan the Right Choice for the Court?," ibid., June 29, 2010.
84. *National Right to Life Board of Directors' Resolution Honoring James Bopp* (National Right to Life, 2013).
85. Tom Strode, "Court Backs Pro-Life Ads as Free Speech," *Baptist Press*, June 16, 2014.
86. Ibid.
87. See: John Sides, "Why Campaign Finance Reform is Hard," The Monkey Cage, August 2, 2012, http://themonkeycage.org/2012/08/why-campaign-finance-reform-is-hard/.
88. Tom Strode, "NEA's Frohmayer Resigns; Critics Credit Buchanan," *Baptist Press*, February 24, 1992.
89. "Hight Court Hears Arguments over NEA Decency Standard," *Baptist Press*, April 1, 1998.
90. See Appendix A for the prompts and question wording.
91. The full models are in Table 3.4 in Appendix B, and the results of the randomization are in Table 3.5 in Appendix B.

92. See e.g., Samuel Smith, "FRC's Tony Perkins, 50 Conservative Activists Reportedly Plan to Endorse Ted Cruz," *Christian Post*, December 16, 2015.
93. Geoffrey Layman, "Where Is Trump's Evangelical Base? Not in Church," *The Washington Post*, March 29, 2016.
94. Emily Cadei, "2016: The End of the Culture Wars as We Know Them," *Newsweek*, May 11, 2016.
95. Tobin Grant, "Did White Evangelical Support for Trump Drop Due to Lower Turnout?," *Religion News Service*, November 14, 2016; Smith and Martinez, "How the Faithful Voted."

CHAPTER 4

1. See David Roach, "Baptists 'Not Threatened' by Pope's U.S. Visit," *Baptist Press*, September 21, 2015.
2. Tina Susman, "Philadelphia Plans Intense Security for Pope Francis Visit–Some Say Too Intense," *Los Angeles Times*, September 1, 2015.
3. Julia Terruso, "City's Share of $17 Million Papal-Visit Costs: $8 Million," *Philadelphia Inquirer*, December 4, 2015.
4. George Sheridan, "Southern Baptists, Pope Interact During U.S. Visit," *Baptist Press*, October 22, 1979. Stan Hastey, "Judge Orders Reimbursement for Cost of Papal Platform," ibid., November 16.
5. M. Kelly Tillery, "You Can Fight City Hall: The Case of the Pope's Platform," *The Philadelphia Lawyer*, Winter 2010.
6. "Cities Hosting Pope Francis Must Take Pains to Protect Church-State Separation, Says Americans United," news release, August 31, 2015, www.au.org/media /press-releases/cities-hosting-pope-francis-must-take-pains-to-protect-church-state-separation.
7. Terruso, "City's Share of $17 Million Papal-Visit Costs."
8. Hamburger, *Separation of Church and State*.
9. Roach, "Baptists 'Not Threatened' by Pope's U.S. Visit."
10. Ibid.
11. Tom Strode, "Pope's Speech Troubling, Southern Baptists Say," ibid., September 25.
12. Ibid.
13. Ibid.
14. Ira C. Lupu, "Reconstructing the Establishment Clause: The Case against Discretionary Accommodation of Religion," *University of Pennsylvania Law Review* 140 (1991): 557.
15. See e.g., *Widmar v. Vincent* (1981), *Rosenberg v. University of Virginia* (1995), and *Good News Club v. Milford Central School* (2001).
16. See e.g., Brown. Ted G. Jelen and Clyde Wilcox, *Public Attitudes toward Church and State* (Armonk, NY: M. E. Sharpe, 1995). Also, for the electoral impact of public opinion on the Establishment Clause, see: Jeremiah J. Castle, "The Electoral Impact of Public Opinion on Religious Establishment," *Journal for the Scientific Study of Religion* 54, no. 4 (2015).
17. For a review, see: Donald L. Drakeman, *Church, State, and Original Intent* (New York: Cambridge University Press, 2010).

18. Jelen and Wilcox, *Public Attitudes toward Church and State*. Ted G. Jelen, *To Serve God and Mammon: Church-State Relations in American Politics* (Boulder, CO: Westview Press, 2000).
19. Hacker, *The Culture of Conservative Christian Litigation*.
20. Farnsley II, *Southern Baptist Politics*. Hankins, *Uneasy in Babylon*. Lewis, "The Southern Baptist Church-State 'Culture War'." Charles McDaniel, "Guest Editorial: The Decline of the Separation Principle in the Baptist Tradition of Religious Liberty," *Journal of Church and State* 50 (2008).
21. Hunter, *Culture Wars*. Layman, *The Great Divide*.
22. See: Jelen and Wilcox, "Causes and Consequences of Public Attitudes toward Abortion."
23. Thomas C. Berg, "Anti-Catholicism and Modern Church-State Relations," *Loyola University of Chicago Law Journal* 33, no. 1 (2001).
24. Hankins, *Uneasy in Babylon*, 189.
25. McLoughlin, *New England Dissent 1960–1833. Soul Liberty*.
26. For a political analysis of this split, see: Lewis, "The Southern Baptist Church-State 'Culture War'."
27. "Brief of Amici Curiae General Conference of Seventh-Day Adventists and the Joint Conference Committee," in *Everson v. Board of Education of the Township of Ewing* (Washington, DC: Joint Conference Committee, 1947). Hamburger, 458.
28. Daryl R. Fair, "The *Everson* Case in the Context of New Jersey Politics," in *Everson Revisited: Religion, Education, and Law at the Crossroads*, ed. Jo Renee Formicola and Humbert Morken (Lanham, MD: Rowman & Littlefield, 1997).
29. "Government Aid to Church Schools," (Nashville: Sunday School Board of the Southern Baptist Convention, 1947). Hamburger, *Separation of Church and State*, 464.
30. Stanley LeRoy Hastey, "A History of the Baptist Joint Committee on Public Affairs, 1946–1971" (Ph.D. Dissertation, Southern Baptist Theological Seminary, 1973), 73. Along with these public criticisms, Philip Hamburger identifies several letters from Southern Baptist ministers, found within the private papers of Justice Hugo Black (the author of the *Everson* decision), that were critical of the Supreme Court's decision and frequently declared anti-Catholic sentiment.
31. McCall also urged the BJC to withdraw the BJC's *amicus* brief. Parry, *On Guard for Religious Liberty*, 17.
32. *Resolution on Concerning Use of Tax Funds and Tax-Supported Schools by Religious Organizations* (Houston, TX: Southern Baptist Convention, 1953).
33. Stan Hastey, "The History and Contributions of the Baptist Joint Committee on Public Affairs," *Baptist History and Heritage* 20, no. 3 (1985). Parry, *On Guard for Religious Liberty*.
34. Hamburger, *Separation of Church and State*.
35. The three Supreme Court cases addressing these issues are: *Engle v. Vitale* (1962), *Abington Township School District v. Schempp* (1963), and *Murray v. Curlett* (1963).
36. Hastey, "The History and Contributions of the Baptist Joint Committee on Public Affairs." Parry, *On Guard for Religious Liberty*.
37. *Resolution on Voluntary Prayer* (St. Louis, MO: Southern Baptist Convention, 1971).
38. See: Ammerman, *Baptist Battles*. Hankins, *Uneasy in Babylon*. Oran P. Smith, *The Rise of Baptist Republicanism* (New York: New York University Press, 1997). I have chosen to use the terms "moderates" and "conservatives" when discussing

the two sides within the Southern Baptist conflict, following the lead of historian Barry Hankins in his book *Uneasy in Babylon*. While there are problems with assigning political labels to this religious controversy, I prefer these labels as they accurately represent the political and religious elements of the division without using words that can be taken pejoratively.

39. Richard D. Land, "Restoring Our Religious Freedom While Preserving Our Baptist Heritage," Ethics & Religious Liberty Commission, 1997, http://erlc.com/article/restoring-our-religious-freedom-while-preserving-our-baptist-heritage/.

40. Michael W. McConnell, "Accommodation of Religion: An Update and a Response to the Critics," *George Washington Law Review* 60 (1992).

41. Land, "Interview with the Author."

42. "Restoring Our Religious Freedom While Preserving Our Baptist Heritage." "Interview with the Author."

43. "Interview with the Author."

44. These findings for the SBC clergy are consistent with General Social Survey responses of rank-and-file Southern Baptists. Throughout the 1980s and 1990s, Southern Baptists were more likely than all others to oppose the Supreme Court's school prayer rulings and favor increased prayer in school. See Lewis, "The Southern Baptist Church-State 'Culture War': The Internal Politics of Denominational Advocacy."

45. Land, "Interview with the Author."

46. Hankins, *Uneasy in Babylon*. Hunter, *Culture Wars*.

47. Parry, *On Guard for Religious Liberty*.

48. American Ethical Union et al., "Brief for Amici Curiae American Ethical Union: American Humanist Association; Board of Church and Society, United Methodist Church; Catholics for a Free Choice, Church of the Brethren; Department of Church Women of the Division of Homeland Ministries, Christian Church (Disciples of Christ); National Federation of Temple Sisterhoods; National Women's Conference of the American Ethical Union; Unitarian Universalist Association; Unitarian Universalist Federation; Union of American Hebrew Congregations; Young Women's Christian Association," in *Patricia A. Harris v. Cora McRae, et al.* (Brooklyn, NY, 1979), 18.

49. Parry, *On Guard for Religious Liberty*.

50. American Jewish Congress et al., "Brief of American Jewish Congress, Board of Church and Society of the United Methodist Church, National Women's Conference of the American Ethical Union, New York State Council of Churches, Union of American Hebrew Congregations and Unitarian Universalist Women's Federation, Amici Curiae," in *John H. Poelker v. Jane Doe* (New York, 1976), 4.

51. "Baptists among Signers of Abortion Rights Statement," *Baptist Public Affairs*, October 26, 1979.

52. *McRae v. Califano* 1980

53. Stan Hastey, "Wood Hails Ruling Upholding Federal Abortion Funding," *Baptist Press*, January 17, 1980, 3.

54. American Ethical Union et al., "Brief for Amici Curiae," 3.

55. National Council of Churches of Christ in the U.S.A., "Brief of Amicus Curiae on Behalf of the National Council of Churches of Christ in the U.S.A.," in *Patricia Harris, et al. v. Cora McRae* (San Francisco, 1980). United Presbyterian Church in the U.S.A., "The United Presbyterian Church in the U.S.A. For Leave to File Brief

Amicus Curiae out of Time and Brief Amicus Curiae," in *Patricia Harris, et al. v. Cora McRae, et al.* (San Francisco, 1980).

56. United States Catholic Conference, "Brief of the United States Catholic Conference, Amicus Curiae," in *Patricia R. Harris v. Cora McRae, et al.* (Washington, DC, 1980). The United States Catholic Conference combined with the National Conference of Catholic Bishops in 2001, forming the United States Conference of Catholic Bishops.

57. *Harris, Secretary of Health and Human Services v. McRae et al.*, 448 U.S. 297 (1980), 21.

58. Paige Patterson, "Interview with the Author," August 8, 2010, Philadelphia, PA.

59. "Majority Report of SBC Executive Committee on Baptist Joint Committee," *Baptist Today*, June 10, 1990. Emphasis in the original.

60. "Baptists Will Examine Evangelism, Freedom," *Baptist Public Affairs*, September 8, 1981.

61. See e.g., Skeet Workman, "Letter to Rev. Gary Young," August 27, 1986.

62. Baptist Joint Committee on Public Affairs et al., "Brief of the Baptist Joint Committee on Public Affairs, the American Jewish Committee, and Americans United for the Separation of Church and State as Amici Curiae in Support of Appellees," in *Otis R. Bowen v. Chan Kendrick, et al.* (Washington, DC, 1988), 6.

63. Louis Moore, "CLC Files Briefs in Supreme Court," *Baptist Press*, February 27, 1989.

64. Lutheran Church-Missouri Synod et al., "Brief of the Lutheran Church- Missouri Synod, the Christian Life Commission of the Southern Baptist Convention and the National Association of Evangelicals as Amici Curiae in Support of Appellants," in *William L. Webster, et al. v. Reproductive Heath Services, et al.* (St. Louis, 1989), 11–12.

65. Ibid., 11.

66. In 1993, the RFRA legislation passed the U.S. Congress overwhelmingly, though it has become more controversial of late as many evangelical and Catholic individuals and groups are using its strong religious freedom protections to object to laws requiring the coverage of contraceptive care and the provision of certain services for same-sex marriages. These controversies will be covered more in Chapters 5 and 7.

67. "Religious Liberty Bill before Congress Highlights Difference among Baptists," 1.

68. Ibid.

69. Tom Strode, "CLC Endorses RFRA; BJC Mum on Abortion," *Light*, October–December 1991, 15.

70. Incidentally, in two decades this legislation would become central to contemporary evangelical legal advocacy.

71. The correlations range from 0.37 in 1984 to 0.40 in 1992.

72. James Dunn, "Interview with the Author," August 4 and September 6, 2010, Philadelphia, PA.

73. Land, "Interview with the Author."

74. Hamburger, *Separation of Church and State*, 376.

75. George W. Truett, Baptists and Religious Liberty, (Nashville: The Sunday School Board of the Southern Baptist Convention, 2011 [1920]), www.bjconline.org/index.php?option=com_content&task=view&id=51&Itemid=73.

76. American Jewish Congress et al., "Brief of American Jewish Congress," 8.

77. See e.g., Paul D. Simmons, "Religious Liberty and the Abortion Debate," *Journal of Church and State* 32, no. 3 (1990).
78. Hankins, *Uneasy in Babylon*, 171.
79. United States Catholic Conference et al., "Brief Amicus Curiae of the United States Catholic Conference, the Christian Life Commission, Southern Baptist Convention, and the National Association of Evangelicals in Support of Respondents and Cross-Petitioners," in *Planned Parenthood of Southeastern Pennsylvania, et al. v. Robert P. Casey, et al.* (Washington, DC, 1992), 6.
80. Various, "Evangelicals and Catholics Together: The Christian Mission in the Third Millennium," *First Things*, May 1994.
81. Martin King, "Land and Lewis Remove Names from Controversial Document," *Baptist Press*, April 7, 1995, 1.
82. The results are similar using the American National Election Study.
83. The favorability gap between evangelicals and those who are neither evangelical nor Catholic, however, has increased, as these non-Catholics and non-evangelicals rate Catholics more poorly.
84. *Resolution on Religious Liberty and No Establishment of Religion* (Philadelphia, PA: Southern Baptist Convention, 1972).
85. James Dunn, "Public Money for Public Purposes," *Baptist Public Affairs*, June 29, 1981.
86. "Interview with the Author."
87. Land, "Interview with the Author."
88. Correlation results are: 0.31 in 1984; 0.30 in1988; 0.53 in 1992; and 0.38 in 1996.
89. *Resolution on Parental Choice in Education* (Atlanta, GA: Southern Baptist Convention, 1991).
90. *Resolution on Parental Choice on Education* (New Orleans, LA: Southern Baptist Convention, 1996).
91. Land, "Interview with the Author."
92. Ethics and Religious Liberty Commission of the Southern Baptist Convention et al., "Brief of the Ethics and Religious Liberty Commission of the Southern Baptist Convention, the National Association of Evangelicals, and the Convocation of Anglicans in North America as Amici Curiae in Support of Petitioners," in *Arizona Christian School Tuition Organization v. Kathleen M. Winn, et al.* (Nashville, TN: 2010).
93. Land, "Interview with the Author."
94. Hankins, *Uneasy in Babylon*.
95. Land quoted in ibid., 23.
96. Land, "Interview with the Author."
97. American Ethical Union et al., "Brief for Amici Curiae," 7–10.
98. Baptist Joint Committee on Public Affairs et al., "Brief of the Baptist Joint Committee."
99. Americans United for the Separation of Church and State, "Brief of Americans United for the Separation of Church and State as Amicus Curiae in Support of Appellees," in *William L. Webster, et al. v. Reproductive Health Services, et al.* (Washington, DC, 1989).
100. Tom Strode, "BJCPA Asks Supreme Court to Maintain Religion Test," *SBC Today*, September 20, 1991, 5.

101. Michael Whitehead, "CLC to Court: Squeeze out *Lemon*: Restore True Liberty to First Amendment, Commission Requests," *Salt* 4, no. 1 (1994).
102. Land, "Interview with the Author."
103. "Brief of Amicus Curiae of the Southern Baptist Convention Ethics & Religious Liberty Commission in Support of Petitioner," in *Town of Greece v. Galloway* (2014), 1, 19.
104. "Brief of Amici Curiae Dr. Daniel L. Akin; Dr. Darrell L. Bock; Dr. D.A. Carson; Dr. C. Stephen Evans; Dr. Wayne Grudem; Dr. James M. Hamilton; Dr. H. Wayne House; Dr. Peter A. Lillback; Dr. R. Albert Mohler, Jr.; and J. Michael Thigpen in Support of the Petitioner and Reversal.," in *Town of Greece v. Galloway* (2014), 1.
105. "Brief of Baptist Joint Committee for Religious Liberty, General Synod of the United Church of Christ, and Rev. Gradye Parsons, Stated Clerk of the General Assembly of the Presbyterian Church (U.S.A.) as Amici Curiae in Support of Respondents," in *Town of Greece v. Galloway*," (2014), 5, 8.
106. For evangelical free speech and religious freedom advocacy, see: Brown. For rights talk among American evangelicals, see: Djupe et al., "Rights Talk."
107. CBS, "Southern Baptist Leader Calls for Fresh Approach in 'Increasingly Post-Christian America'," *CBS News*, April 18, 2014, www.cbsnews.com/news/new-southern-baptist-leader-russell-moore-calls-for-a-change-in-tone/.
108. Tom Strode, "ERLC Brief Opposes Hostility against Religion," *Baptist Press*, April 26, 2016.
109. Hunter, *Culture Wars*.
110. "Brief of the Southern Baptist Theological Seminary, the Ethics & Religious Liberty Commission, the International Mission Board, and Dr. R. Albert Mohler, Jr. as *Amici Curiae* in Support of Petitioners," in *Zubik v. Burwell*" (2016).
111. "Brief of the Baptist Joint Committee as Amicus Curiae in Support of Respondents" in *Zubik v. Burwell* (2016), 6.

CHAPTER 5

1. All passages from the Bible are quoted from the New International Version translation.
2. Certainly some evangelicals, particularly racial minorities, have always supported increased government health care, but this chapter focuses on conservative, white evangelicalism.
3. There is almost no mention of health care in most of the recent histories of the Christian Right, including: Williams, *God's Own Party*. Matthew Avery Sutton, *American Apocalypse: A History of Modern Evangelicalism* (Cambridge, MA: Belknap Press of Harvard University Press, 2014). Dochuk, *From Bible Belt to Sun Belt*.
4. For an overview public opinion work, see: Juliane Corman and David Levin, "The Polls–Trends: Support for Government Provision of Health Care and the Patient Protection and Affordable Care Act," *Public Opinion Quarterly* 80, no. 1 (2016). For public opinion and interest group analysis of early health care advocacy, see: Lawrence R. Jacobs, *The Health of Nations: Public Opinion and the Making of American and British Health Policy* (Ithaca, NY: Cornell University Press, 1993).

5. Lawrence Jacobs and Suzanne Mettler, "Why Public Opinion Changes: The Implications for Health and Health Policy," *Journal of Health Policy, Politics, and Law* 36, no. 6 (2011). David L. Eckles and Brian F. Schaffner, "Loss Aversion and the Framing of the Health Care Reform Debate," *The Forum* 8, no. 1 (2010).

6. Williams, *God's Own Party*.

7. Sutton, *American Apocalypse*.

8. "Protestants Score Truman Health Plan," *The New York Times*, March 5, 1950, 15.

9. United Nations, "The Universal Declaration of Human Rights."

10. For prophecy language, see: Sutton, *American Apocalypse*.

11. "Church Tax Privileges to Remain, Corman Says," *Baptist Press*, October 8, 1975.

12. "Testimony Endorses National Health Care," *Baptist Press*, November 14, 1975.

13. See e.g., James Lee Young, "Baptist Call for Attitude Change by Church on Aging," ibid., October 25, 1974.

14. "Declaration of Human Rights," (Southern Baptist Convention).

15. "House Votes to Bar Abortion Aid for Victims of Rape and Incest," *The New York Times*, August 3, 1977.

16. Adam Clymer, "Abortion Aid Barred by Bell in Rape Case: He Rules That Current Law Makes No Exceptions for Victims," ibid., August 2, 1, 13.

17. The exceptions for the prohibition on Medicaid funding were often part of the political strategy employed by supporters and opponents. For example, in 1977 pro-abortion supporters forced House Republicans to take a vote to remove all exceptions, including when the mother's life was at stake. See: Martin Tolchin, "House Bars Medicaid Abortions and Funds for Enforcing Quotas," ibid., June 18, 49.

18. "House Votes to Bar Abortion Aid for Victims of Rape and Incest," ibid., August 3, 11.

19. "They Said Legal Abortions Would Stop and Illegal Ones Would Multiply," *Christianity Today*, October 23, 1981, 57.

20. John Maust, "The Abortion Issue: Exercising Religion Freely on Both Sides," ibid., September 5, 1980, 24.

21. *McRae v. Califano* 491 F.Supp. 630 (1980).

22. Hastey, "Wood Hails Ruling Upholding Federal Abortion Funding," 3.

23. American Ethical Union et al., "Brief of Amici Curaie," 3.

24. National Council of Churches of Christ in the U.S.A., "Brief of Amicus Curiae." United Presbyterian Church in the U.S.A., "The United Presbyterian Church in the U.S.A. For Leave to File."

25. United States Catholic Conference, "Brief of the United States Catholic Conference."

26. *Harris v. McRae et al.*, 21.

27. *Resolution on Abortion* (Southern Baptist Convention, 1980).

28. "Thursday Afternoon Resolutions," *Baptist Press*, June 8, 1980.

29. "Abortion Factions Skirmish over Koop Appointment," *Christianity Today*, May 8, 1981, 46.

30. Beth Spring, "New Problems in Congress for Antiabortionists," ibid., February 4, 1983, 60.

31. "Mark Hatfield Taps into the Real Power on Capitol Hill," ibid., October 22, 1982, 18.

32. Tom Minnery and Kenneth S. Kantzer, "It's Too Soon to Quit," ibid., December 17, 10–11.
33. *Resolution on Hunger and Poverty* (St. Louis, MO: Southern Baptist Convention, 1987).
34. Ibid.
35. See Vicente Navarro, *The Politics of Health Policy: The U.S. Reforms, 1980–1994* (Cambridge, MA: Blackwell, 1994).
36. William J. Clinton, "Remarks on Signing Memorandums in Medical Research and Reproductive Helath and an Exchange with Reporters," The American Presidency Project, 1993.
37. Tom Strode, "Clinton Rescinds Abortion Policies; Pro-Lifers Won't Retreat, Land Says," *Baptist Press*, January 25, 1993.
38. Kim A. Lawton, "Clinton Abortion Actions Usher in a New Era," *Christianity Today*, March 8, 1993, 52.
39. Robin Toner, "Clinton Would End Ban on Aid to Poor Seeking Abortions," *The New York Times*, March 30, 1993.
40. Ibid.
41. Chip Alford, "Messengers Oppose Clinton's Views, Urge Him to Biblical Morality," *Baptist Press*, June 23, 1993.
42. *Resolution on the Freedom of Choice Act, Hyde Amendment* (Houston, TX: Southern Baptist Convention, 1993).
43. *On President William Jefferson Clinton* (Houston, TX: Southern Baptist Convention, 1993).
44. Religious News Service, "Southern Baptists Decry Clinton Ideas," *Chicago Tribune*, June 18, 1993, 8.
45. Jack Chambers, "Baptists Pray for Prodigal President," *Wall Street Journal*, June 15, 1993, C18.
46. "SBC Messengers Likely to Consider Resolution on Clinton's Views," *Baptist Press*, June 13, 1993.
47. Timothy C. Morgan, "Clinton Draws Ire of SBC," July 19, 1993, 54.
48. William J. Eaton and Paul Richter, "First Lady's Health Plan Talk Hailed," *Los Angeles Times*, September 21, 1993, 1.
49. Gwen Ifill, "New Health Plan, Old Abortion Fight," *The New York Times*, October 4, 1993, A14.
50. William Kristol, "Defeating President Clinton's Health Care Proposal," Project for a Republican Future, 1993.
51. David Schiedermayer, "Healing the Health-Care System," *Christianity Today*, October 25, 1993, 16.
52. Ifill, "New Health Plan," A14.
53. John W. Kennedy, "Rx for America," *Christianity Today*, April 25, 1994, 38.
54. Robin Toner, "Hillary Clinton Opens Campaign to Answer Critics of Health Plan," *The New York Times*, February 16, 1994, A11.
55. Merrill Matthews Jr., "Don't Punish the Healthy," *Christianity Today*, April 25, 1994, 10.
56. *Resolution on Health Care Reform* (Orlando, FL: Southern Baptist Convention, 1994).
57. See e.g., Kristol, "Defeating President Clinton's Health Care Proposal."

58. Kennedy, "Rx for America," 38.
59. Adam Clymer, "Hillary Clinton Says Administration Was Misunderstood on Health Care," *The New York Times*, October 3, 1994, A12.
60. Tom Strode, "Full Abortion Rights Promoted in CBF-Funded Agency's Journal," *Baptist Press*, February 2, 1998.
61. Russell D. Moore, "Land, Other Ethicists, Evaluate Medical Dilemmas at Conference," ibid., March 9.
62. See also: R. Albert Mohler, Jr., "A Threat to the Disabled & Everyone," ibid., August 10, 2007; Jerry Pierce, "Oxford Bioethicist: Life's Value Evident Even to Unbelievers," ibid., June 9, 2005.
63. Tom Strode, "Health Care Is a 'National Dilemma': 'Vigorous' Debate Ahead, Land Says," ibid., May 13, 2003.
64. "White House Finalizes Health Coverage for Unborn Children Despite Criticism," *Baptist Press*, October 1, 2002.
65. Madison Trammel, "Health Care, Everyone?" *Christianity Today*, July 2006, 18.
66. "The Health Care Crunch," ibid., February 5, 2008, 20–21.
67. Charles Colson and Catherine Larson, "We Need Health-Care Reform," ibid., August 2009, 64.
68. Ethics & Religious Liberty Commission, "Fifteen Principles for Needed Health Care Reform," Nashville, TN: Ethics & Religious Liberty Commission, 2009. See also: Staff, "ERLC Lays out 15 Principles Needed for Health Care Reform," *Baptist Press*, November 11, 2009.
69. Ethics & Religious Liberty Commission, "Fifteen Principles for Needed Health Care Reform." See also: Staff, "ERLC Lays out 15 Principles Needed for Health Care Reform."
70. Tom Strode, "Despite Endorsement by Some, Sebelius 'Unfit' for HHS Role, Pro-Life Leaders Say," ibid., March 6.
71. Richard D. Land, "Giant Steps to Gov. Health Care?," ibid., February 4 .
72. Staff, "Head-Counting Begins as Obama Prepares Address," ibid., September 8.
73. "Land-Endorsement Statement Urges New Start," *Baptist Press*, September 14, 2009.
74. Ken Connor, "First-Person: Health Care & Moral Schizophrenia," ibid., November 17.
75. "Family Research Council Urges Pro-Life Senators to 'Denounce' Abortion Funding," *Catholic News Agency*, November 19, 2009.
76. M.Z. Hemingway, "Stunned by Stupak," *Christianity Today*, January 2010, 13.
77. Sarah Kliff, "Stupak's Last Stand," *Newsweek*, March 21, 2010.
78. Staff, "Pro-Lifers Nearly Unanimous in Dismay," *Baptist Press*, March 22, 2010.
79. Family Research Council Action, "FRC Action Statement on Congressman Bart Stupak's Retirement" (2010).
80. Kliff, "Stupak's Last Stand."
81. Tom Strode, "Obama Recess Appointment 'Dangerous' for the Elderly, SBC Ethicist Land Says," *Baptist Press*, July 8, 2010.
82. The SBC, for example, passed a resolution against morning after pills in 1991. *Resolution on Sanctity of Human Life* (Atlanta, GA: Southern Baptist Convention, 1991).
83. "Obama Admin. Reaffirms: Health Care Plans Must Cover Abortion-Causing Drugs," *Baptist Press*, January 20, 2012.
84. Ethics & Religious Liberty Commission, "Letter to HHS: Comment on Failed Religious 'Accommodation'," April 8, 2013.

85. National Association of Evangelicals, "HHS Proposed Rule Jeopardizes Religious Freedom," February 1, 2013, www.nae.net/hhs-proposed-rule-jeopardizes-religious-freedom/.

86. Tom Strode, "Letter to Obama: It's Not Just Catholics Who Oppose HHS over 'Contraception Mandate'," *Baptist Press*, January 6, 2012.

87. Steven Ertelt, "154 Members of Congress Object to Pro-Abortion Obama Mandate," *Life News*, February 7, 2012.

88. Amy Sullivan, "Articles of Faith: Why Republicans Don't Want to Debate Birth Control," *Time*, August 12, 2011.

89. Strode, "Obama Admin. Reaffirms."

90. David Jackson, "Catholic Institutions Sue Obama over Birth Control Mandate," *USA Today*, May 21, 2012.

91. Eric Marrapodi, "Wheaton College Sues Administration over Contraception Mandate," *CNN*, July 18, 2012.

92. Roy Hayhurst, "Hawkins Reminds Messengers of Baptist Pledge," *Baptist Press*, June 21, 2012.

93. The Becket Fund for Religious Liberty, "HHS Mandate Information Central," www.becketfund.org/hhsinformationcentral.

94. In the clergy data, the ideology and abortion measures are correlated quite highly at 0.50. To try and isolate the independent effect of abortion, I measure ideology with the question: whether the government should do more to solve social problems. This item is less correlated with abortion (0.20).

95. Odds ratio (OR) = 1.12; p = 0.06.

96. OR = 1.30; p = 0.03.

97. The health care variable is available beginning in 1975, but 1983 is the first year where both the health care and the abortion scale measures are available.

98. See Hollis-Brusky, *Ideas with Consequences*.

99. American Center for Law and Justice, "Health Care Legislation & Litigation" (2012).

100. Family Research Council, "Family Research Council Says Supreme Court Health Care Ruling Jeopardizes Future of Liberty," June 28, 2012, www.frcblog.com/2012/06/scotus-health-care-ruling-jeopardizes-future-of-liberty/.

101. American Center for Law and Justice, "ACLJ: Supreme Court Urged to Reject IRS Regulations Authorizing Illegal Obamacare Subsidies" (2015), https://aclj.org/obamacare/aclj-supreme-court-urged-to-reject-irs-regulations-authorizing-illegal-obamacare-subsidies. The much less prominent Texas Black Americans for Life and the Life Education Resource Network also filed briefs.

102. Family Research Council, "Family Research Council: Supreme Court Subjects Obamacare to Linguistic Gymnastics," June 25, 2015, www.frc.org/newsroom/family-research-council-supreme-court-subjects-obamacare-to-linguistic-gymnastics.

103. Because of their secular ties, partisanship and ideology may have more sway on their activities than other religious groups.

104. National Association of Evangelicals, "NAE Files Supreme Court Brief for Hobby Lobby, Conestoga," January 28, 2014, www.nae.net/nae-files-supreme-court-brief-for-hobby-lobby-conestoga/.

105. *Hippocratic Oath* (Baltimore, MD: Johns Hopkins University Press, 2015), http://guides.library.jhu.edu/c.php?g=202502&p=1335752.

CHAPTER 6

1. Russell Berman, "How Nebraska Abolished the Death Penalty," *The Atlantic*, May 27, 2015. Julie Bosman, "Nebraska Bans Death Penalty, Defying a Veto," *The New York Times*, May 27, 2015.
2. See Frank Baumgartner, Emily Williams, and Kaneesha Johnson, "Americans Are Turning against the Death Penalty. Are Politicians Far Behind?," *The Washington Post, The Monkey Cage*, December 7, 2015.
3. Frank R. Baumgartner, Suzanna L. De Boef, and Amber E. Boydstun, *The Decline of the Death Penalty and the Discovery of Innocence* (New York: Cambridge University Press, 2008).
4. Jon Cohen, "Most Want Death Penalty for Dzhokhar Tsarnaev If He Is Convicted of Boston Bombing," *The Washington Post*, May 1, 2013.
5. Jennifer Agiesta, "Poll: 53% Say Boston Bomber Should Face Death Penalty," *CNN*, April 21, 2015.
6. Evan Allen, "Few Favor Death for Dzhokhar Tsarnaev, Poll Finds," *Boston Globe*, April 26, 2015.
7. Agiesta, "Poll."
8. Ron Sider, Professor at Eastern Seminary and founder of Evangelicals for Social Action, is a prime example. See: Tim Stafford, "Ron Sider's Unsettling Crusade," *Christianity Today*, March 1, 2000.
9. Chester L. Britt, "Race, Religion and Support for the Death Penalty: A Research Note.," *Justice Quarterly* 15 (1998). James D. Unnever, Francis T. Cullen, and John P. Bartkowski, "Images of God and Public Support for Capital Punishment: Does a Close Relationship with a Loving God Matter?," *Criminology* 44, no. 4 (2006). Robert L. Young, "Religious Orientation, Race, and Support for the Death Penalty," *Journal of the Scientific Study of Religion* 31, no. 1 (1992).
10. Christopher D. Bader et al., "Divine Justice: The Relationship between Images of God and Attitudes toward Capital Punishment," *Criminal Justice Review* 35, no. 1 (2010). James D. Unnever and Francis T. Cullen, "Reassessing the Racial Divide in Support for Capital Punishment: The Continuing Significance of Race," *Journal of Research in Crime and Delinquency* 44, no. 1 (2007).
11. Harold G. Grasmick, Robert J. Burski Jr., and Brenda Sims, "Religious Beliefs and Public Support for the Death Penalty for Juveniles and Adults," *Journal of Crime and Justice* 16, no. 2 (1993). Britt, "Race, Religion, and Support for the Death Penalty." James D. Unnever, Francis T. Cullen, and Bonnie S. Fisher, "Empathy and Public Support for Capital Punishment," *Journal of Crime and Justice* 28, no. 1 (2005). Young, "Religious Orientation, Race, and Support for the Death Penalty."
12. Kevin H. Wozniak and Andrew R. Lewis, "Reexamining the Effect of Christian Denominational Affiliation on Death Penalty Support," *Journal of Criminal Justice* 38, no. 5 (2010).
13. Harold G. Grasmick et al., "Religion, Punitive Justice, and Support for the Death Penalty," *Justice Quarterly* 10, no. 2 (1993). See also: Harold G. Grasmick et al., "Protestant Fundamentalism and the Retributive Doctrine of Punishment," *Criminology* 30, no. 1 (1992).
14. One exception is Carin Robinson's doctoral dissertation. She evaluates the effectiveness of different religious frames for and against capital punishment, evaluating both the arguments and the source of the elite cue. Though she talks about the

different approaches, Robinson does not directly examine pro-life arguments for and against capital punishment, however. Carin Robinson, "Doctrine, Discussion and Disagreement: Evangelical Protestant Interaction with Catholics in American Politics" (Ph.D. Dissertation, Georgetown University, 2008).

15. Jonathan Merritt, "In a Groundbreaking Vote, Latino Evangelicals Call for End to Death Penalty," *The Washington Post*, March 30, 2015.

16. "Poll: Younger Christians Less Supportive of the Death Penalty," *The Washington Post*, January 18, 2014.

17. Shane Claiborne, "If It Weren't for Jesus, I Might Be Pro-Death Too," (Red Letter Christians, 2014). *Executing Grace: How the Death Penalty Killed Jesus and Why It's Killing Us* (New York: HarperOne, 2016).

18. Angela Wang, "The Death Penalty Today: Is It Just?," (Prison Fellowship, September 19, 2012).

19. There was a documented diversity of opinion about capital punishment among the leaders of Prison Fellowship. So while they were critical of the current application of capital punishment in America, they refrained from calling for its abolition. See: Randy Frame, "A Matter of Life and Death," *Christianity Today*, August 14, 1995.

20. Sarah Eekhoff Zylstra, "Evangelicals Now Officially Divided on Death Penalty," ibid., October 19, 2015.

21. Joanna Piacenza, "Support for Death Penalty by Religious Affiliation," (Public Religion Research Institute, April 9, 2015).

22. Avery Cardinal Dulles, "Catholicism & Capital Punishment," *First Things*, April 2001.

23. See Joseph Cardinal Bernardin, "A Consistent Ethic of Life: An American-Catholic Dialogue," Gannon Lecture, Fordham University, 1983. "A Consistent Ethic of Life: Continuing the Dialogue" (1984).

24. United States Conference of Catholic Bishops, "The Church's Anti-Death Penalty Position," www.usccb.org/issues-and-action/human-life-and-dignity/death-penalty-capital-punishment/catholic-campaign-to-end-the-use-of-the-death-penalty.cfm.

25. *On Capital Punishment* (Orlando, FL: Southern Baptist Convention, 2000).

26. Philip Pullela, "Pope Calls for Worldwide Abolition of Death Penalty," *Reuters*, February 21, 2016.

27. Sarah Pulliam Bailey and Karen Tumulty, "How a Southern Baptist Leader Became Surprising Voice on Confederate Flag," *The Washington Post*, June 24, 2015.

28. Russell Moore, "Is the Pope Right About the Death Penalty?" *Russellmoore.com* (2016), www.russellmoore.com/2016/02/21/is-the-pope-right-about-the-death-penalty/.

29. Kimberly J. Cook, *Divided Passions: Public Opinions on Abortion and the Death Penalty* (Lebanon, NH: Northeastern University Press, 1998).

30. Moore, "Is the Pope Right about the Death Penalty?."

31. Methodist Church, "Doctrines and Disciplines of the Methodist Church," (1956). See also: Tom McAnally, "Death Penalty Continues Despite Church's 50-Year Opposition," *United Methodist News Service*, October 10, 2006.

32. United Presbyterian Church in the USA, "Minutes of the 171st General Assembly" (1959), 384. See also: Presbyterian Mission Agency, "Capital Punishment" (2016).

33. *Abolition of the Death Penalty* (National Council of Churches, 1968).

34. Ibid.

35. "North Carolina Issue on Trustees Delayed," *Baptist Press*, November 17, 1962. "Wake Forest Trustee Plan Fails to Carry," *Baptist Press*, November 17, 1963.
36. "Virginia Baptists OK Strong Resolutions," *Baptist Press*, November 13, 1965.
37. "Recommendations of the Christian Life Commission," *Baptist Press*, May 21, 1964.
38. "Strong Race Statement Loses to Softer One," *Baptist Press*, May 23, 1964. See also: Jerry Sutton, *A Matter of Conviction: A History of Southern Baptist Engagement with the Culture* (Nashville, TN: Ethics and Religious Liberty Commission of the SBC, 2008).
39. "Arkansas Editor Commends Death Sentence Commutation," *Baptist Press*, January 4, 1971.
40. Ibid.
41. See: ProCon.org, "31 States with the Death Penalty and 19 States with Death Penalty Bans," ProCon. In 1967, the Arkansas governor declared a moratorium on executions, later commuting the sentences of all fifteen death row inmates in 1970. In 1972, Pennsylvania's state supreme court ruled that capital punishment violated the state constitution.
42. Ramsey Clark, "To Abolish the Death Penalty," Statement Before the Senate Judiciary Committee (1968). See also: Corinna Barrett Lain, "Furman Fundamentals," *Washington Law Review* 82, no. 1 (2007): 30.
43. "Court Hears Arguments against Death Penalty," *Baptist Press*, January 18, 1972.
44. Ibid.
45. Quoted in Bob Woodward and Scott Armstrong, *The Brethren* (New York: Simon & Schuster, 1979), 219. See also: Lee Epstein and Thomas G. Walker, *Constitutional Law for a Changing America: Rights, Liberties, and Justice*, 8th ed. (Thousand Oaks, CA: CQ Press), 576.
46. David Gooch, "Conference Speakers Disagree on Law and Order," July 17, 1973.
47. Epstein and Walker, *Constitutional Law for a Changing America*, 583.
48. *Gregg v. Georgia*, 428 U.S. 153 (1976).
49. Stan L. Hastey, "High Court Upholds Capital Punishment," July 2, 1976.
50. Sutton describes, "Surprisingly, nothing was mentioned concerning capital punishment." Sutton, *A Matter of Conviction*, 222.
51. Jim Newton, "Colson Opposes Capital Punishment," *Baptist Press*, June 13, 1979.
52. Marshall Shelley, "The Death Penalty: Two Sides of a Growing Issue," *Christianity Today*, March 2, 1984, 16.
53. Lutheran Church-Missouri Synod, "Convention Resolution 2–38" (1967). "Report on Capital Punishment" (1976).
54. "Report on Capital Punishment."
55. *Capital Punishment* (National Association of Evangelicals, 1972). *Capital Punishment* (National Association of Evangelicals, 1973).
56. "*Capital Punishment*" (National Association of Evangelicals, 1972)
57. See also: *Abortion* (National Association of Evangelicals, 1971); *Abortion* (National Association of Evangelicals, 1973).
58. See: Stafford, "Ron Sider's Unsettling Crusade." Glen H. Stassen and David P. Gushee, *Kingdom Ethics: Following Jesus in Contemporary Context* (Downers Grove, IL: Intervarsity Press, 2003).
59. Shelley, "The Death Penalty," 17.
60. Ibid.

61. Norma Jameson, "Smaw Offers His Life for Death Row Men," *Baptist Press*, July 28, 1981.
62. See: Ammerman, *Baptist Battles*. Hankins, *Uneasy in Babylon*. Lewis, "The Southern Baptist Church-State 'Culture War'."
63. "Baker Keeps Post with 15-15 Vote," *Baptist Press*, September 18, 1987; Sutton, *A Matter of Conviction*.
64. Dan Martin, "CLC Search Committee Selects Richard Land," *Baptist Press*, September 7, 1988.
65. "CLC Directors Elect Land on 23–2 Ballot," *Baptist Press*, September 15, 1988.
66. Marv Knox, "Southern Baptist Agency Drops Surgeon General's AIDS Report," September 16, 1988.
67. Frame, "A Matter of Life and Death," 50.
68. Ibid.
69. *On Capital Punishment* (Southern Baptist Convention)
70. "Conservatives Rethink Death Penalty," *Christianity Today*, April 6, 1998, 19.
71. "Text of Texas Gov. Bush's Statement on Karla Faye Tucker," *CNN*, February 3, 1998.
72. "The Lesson of Karla Faye Tucker," *Christianity Today*, April 6, 1998, 16.
73. Steve Achord, "Pastor: Baptists Should Learn from Karla Faye Tucker's Life," *Baptist Press*, February 5, 1998.
74. Sarah Eekhoff Zylstra, "Capital Doubts," *Christianity Today*, February 19, 2008, 20.
75. Marvin Olasky, "Dead Seriousness," *World Magazine*, October 19, 2013. See also: David Neff, "Executing Justice?," *Christianity Today*, March 2014. Marvin Olasky, "Against Death Penalty Extremism," *World Magazine*, October 11, 2013.
76. "Theologian's Pen Pal Faces Execution Again," *Christianity Today*, July 2015, 17.
77. Holly Yan, Catherine E. Shoichet, and Moni Basu, "Georgia Inmate Kelly Gissendaner Executed after Failed Appeals," *CNN*, September 30, 2015.
78. David P. Gushee, Richard Land, and Glen Stassen, "How Biblical Is It to Be Pro-Life and Support the Death Penalty?," *Christianity Today*, February 2012, 42–43.
79. R. Albert Jr. Mohler, "Why Christians Should Support the Death Penalty," *CNN Belief Blog*, May 1, 2014.
80. Sarah Pulliam Bailey, "Bobby Jindal's Vision," *Christianity Today*, March 2011, 51.
81. Wozniak and Lewis, "Reexamining the Effect of Christian Denominational Affiliation on Death Penalty Support."
82. See Appendix A for the complete wording of these treatments.
83. Baumgartner, De Boef, and Boydstun, *The Decline of the Death Penalty and the Discovery of Innocence*.
84. Ibid.
85. $p = 0.003$
86. $p = 0.09$
87. The p-values are: Right to Life ($p = 0.10$), Justice ($p = 0.07$), and Costs and Benefits ($p = 0.03$).
88. Russell Moore, "A White Church No More," *The New York Times*, May 6, 2016.
89. Scot McKnight, "The Death Penalty: American Law vs. Christianity" (Jesus Creed, Patheos), May 18, 2015, www.patheos.com/blogs/jesuscreed/2015/05/18/the-death-penalty-american-law-vs-christianity/.
90. R. Albert Mohler, Jr. "The Briefing" (albertmohler.com), May 18, 2015.

CHAPTER 7

1. *Obergefell v. Hodges,* 576 U.S. __ (2015), 22.
2. David Lightman, "Rhetoric on Gays Rekindles Republican Debate," *Hartford Courant,* June 30, 1998.
3. James Dobson, *Bringing up Boys* (Wheaton, IL: Tyndale House, 2001).
4. *Resolution on Homosexuality* (Norfolk, VA: Southern Baptist Convention, 1976).
5. *Resolution on Homosexuality* (St. Louis, MO: Southern Baptist Convention, 1980).
6. *Resolution on Homosexuality* (Dallas, TX: Southern Baptist Convention, 1985).
7. *Resolution on Persecution of Christians* (San Antonio, TX: Southern Baptist Convention, 1988).
8. *Resolution on Homosexuality* (San Antonio, TX: Southern Baptist Convention, 1988).
9. *Resolution on Homosexuality, Military Service and Civil Rights* (Houston, TX: Southern Baptist Convention, 1993).
10. "Religious Leaders Divided over Gays in Military," *Los Angeles Times,* April 3, 1993.
11. *Resolution on Homosexuality, Military Service and Civil Rights* (Southern Baptist Convention).
12. *Resolution on Persecution of Christians* (Southern Baptist Convention).
13. "Amendment 2," in *Colorado Constitution* (1992).
14. Dirk Johnson, "Colorado Homosexuals Feel Betrayed," *The New York Times,* November 8, 1992.
15. Tom Strode, "Colorado Court Rejection of Amendment 2 Criticized," *Baptist Press,* October 14, 1994.
16. Ibid.
17. "CLC Joins Brief Opposing Ruling for Homosexual Rights," *Baptist Press,* July 28, 1995.
18. *Romer v. Evans,* 517 U.S. 620 (1996). Scalia Dissenting.
19. In *Lawrence v. Texas* (2003), the Supreme Court ruled 6–3 that state laws criminalizing homosexual activity violated individual liberty under the Fourteenth Amendment's Due Process Clause. In his dissent, Justice Scalia opined, "State laws against bigamy, same-sex marriage, adult incest, prostitution, and obscenity are likewise sustainable only in light of *Bowers'* [a Supreme Court Case from 1986] validation of laws based on moral choices. Every single one of these laws is called into question by today's decision." *Lawrence v. Texas,* 539 U.S. 558 (2003). Scalia Dissenting
20. Carey Goldberg, "Hawaii Judge Ends Gay-Marriage Ban," *The New York Times,* December 4, 1996.
21. Ibid.
22. *Resolution on Homosexual Marriage* (New Orleans, LA: Southern Baptist Convention, 1996).
23. Ariane De Vogue, "Congress Evolves on DOMA, Same-Sex Marriage," December 6, 2012. In 2008, after converting to the Libertarian Party, Barr apologized for his role in DOMA. Also see: Bob Barr, "No Defending the Defense of Marriage Act," *Los Angeles Times,* January 5, 2009.
24. De Vogue, "Congress Evolves on DOMA."
25. *Resolution on Homosexual Marriage* (Southern Baptist Convention).

26. David E. Campbell and J. Quin Monson, "The Case of Bush's Reelection: Did Gay Marriage Do It?," in *A Matter of Faith: Religion in the 2004 Presidential Election*, ed. David E. Campbell (Washington, DC: Brookings, 2007).
27. See: Putnam and Campbell, *American Grace*.
28. Campbell and Monson, "The Case of Bush's Reelection."
29. This quote comes from his interview with MTV in November 2008. In April 2008, Obama told Rick Warren, "I believe that marriage is the union between a man and a woman." Mackenzie Weinger, "Evolve: Obama Gay Marriage Quotes," *Politico*, May 9, 2012.
30. Charlie Savage and Sheryl Gay Stolberg, "In Shift, U.S. Says Marriage Act Blocks Gay Rights," *The New York Times*, February 23, 2011.
31. Weinger, "Evolve."
32. Tamara Audi, Justin Scheck, and Christopher Lawton, "California Votes for Prop 8," *The Wall Street Journal*, November 5, 2008.
33. Christi Parsons and David G. Savage, "Obama Administration Urges Supreme Court to Strike Down Prop 8," *Los Angeles Times*, February 28, 2013. Josh Gerstein, "Brief Fuels Gay Marriage Speculation," *Politico*, February 22, 2013.
34. Gallup, "Marriage," 2016, www.gallup.com/poll/117328/marriage.aspx.
35. Pew Research Center, "Gay Marriage," www.pewresearch.org/data-trend/domestic-issues/attitudes-on-gay-marriage/.
36. "Views About Same-Sex Marriage," www.pewforum.org/religious-landscape-study/views-about-same-sex-marriage/.
37. Jelen, "Political Esperanto," 310.
38. Ibid., 319–20.
39. Djupe et al., "Rights Talk"
40. "Brief Amici Curiae Religious Organizations, Public Speakers, and Scholars Concerned About Free Speech in Support of Respondents," in *Obergefell v. Hodges* (2015), 10.
41. Ibid., 32.
42. Ibid., 31.
43. "NBC Nightly News," June 26, 2015. See also: Pete Williams and Halimah Abdullah, "Landmark: Supreme Court Rules Same-Sex Marriage Legal Nationwide," NBC Nightly News, June 26, 2015.
44. In an op-ed in *USA Today* after the Supreme Court decision, Huckabee declared, "As president, I will never bow down to the false gods of judicial supremacy." "Mike Huckabee: Fight Gay Marriage Judicial Tyranny," *USA Today*, June 26, 2015. Similarly, Rick Santorum said, "The stakes are too high and the issue too important to simply cede the will of the people to five unaccountable justices." Carrie Dunn and Rafferty Andrew, "2016 Candidates React to Supreme Court's Gay Marriage Ruling," *NBC News*, June 26, 2015. Further, several conservative legal and political scholars, led by Robert P. George of Princeton University, signed a statement urging resistance to *Obergefell*. See: "Statement Calling for Consitutional Resistance to *Obergefell v. Hodges*," American Principles Project, 2015.
45. Ed Payne and Jason Hanna, "After Kim Davis Is Jailed, Clerk's Office Issues Marriage License to Gay Couple," *CNN*, September 4, 2015.
46. Alan Blinder and Tamar Lewin, "Clerk in Kentucky Chooses Jail over Deal on Same-Sex Marriage," *The New York Times*, September 3, 2015.

47. "Kentucky County Clerk Kim Davis to Be Honored at Values Voter Summit," September 14, 2015, www.frc.org/newsroom/kentucky-county-clerk-kim-davis-to-be-honored-at-values-voter-summit.

48. Russell Moore and Andrew T. Walker, "Need We Jail Each Other over Marriage Licenses?," September 4, 2015, http://erlc.com/resource-library/articles/need-we-jail-each-other-over-marriage-licenses. Emphasis in the original.

49. Nicholas K. Geranios, "Gay-Wedding Bias Case Big Surprise to Florist," *Seattle Times*, April 11, 2015.

50. Tom Strode, "Marriage Crisis Predated Gay Marriage, Conf. Speakers Say," *Baptist Press*, October 28, 2014.

51. Art Toalston and Erin Roach, "ERLC to Open Mideast Office, Honors Embattled Florist," ibid., June 18, 2015.

52. "Joint Statement by Gordon College and the Commission on Institutions of Higher Education, NEASC," NEASC, 2015.

53. Robert Barnes, "Supreme Court Declines Case of Photographer Who Denied Service to Gay Couple," *The Washington Post*, April 7, 2014.

54. Donna Bryson, "Colorado Court: Ruling Stands That Baker Can't Cite Religion," *Associated Press*, April 25, 2016.

55. Diana Chandler, "Florist Aims for Supreme Court for Religious Liberty," *Baptist Press*, February 16, 2017.

56. Sarah Pulliam Bailey, "Could Religious Institutions Lose Tax-Exempt Status over Supreme Court's Gay Marriage Case?," *Washington Post*, April 28, 2015.

57. Chandler, "Florist Aims for Supreme Court for Religious Liberty."

58. The test was established in *Sherbert v. Verner* (1963) and *Wisconsin v. Yoder* (1972), but it was limited by *Oregon v. Smith* (1990).

59. Tony Cook and Tom LoBianco, "Indiana Governor Signs Amended 'Religious Freedom' Law," *USA Today*, April 2, 2015.

60. Rachel Lu, "Pro-Life Lessons for the Defense of Marriage," *Crisis Magazine*, January 29, 2014.

61. Bryan Cribb, "First Person: Same-Sex Marriage & the Pro-Life Example," *Baptist Press*, September 29, 2014.

62. See e.g., Moen, *The Transformation of the Christian Right*. Wilson, *The Street Politics of Abortion*.

63. Ryan T. Anderson and Sarah Torre, "The Right to Life and a Culture of Marriage," *National Review*, December 10, 2014.

64. John Stonestreet, "The Other Right," *Breakpoint*, December 22, 2014.

65. Michelle Boorstein, "Pope Says Children Have a Right to Grow up in a Family with a Father and a Mother," *The Washington Post*, November 17, 2014.

66. Ibid.

67. Russell Moore, "We've Been Here Before: Lessons for the Marriage Debate from the Pro-Life Movement," *Russellmoore.com*, June 26, 2015, www.russellmoore.com/2015/06/26/weve-been-here-before-lessons-for-the-marriage-debate-from-the-pro-life-movement/.

68. Ryan T. Anderson, *Truth Overruled: The Future of Marriage and Religious Freedom* (Washington, DC: Regnery, 2015), 2.

69. Tom Strode, "Bolster Family, ERLC Speakers Urge," *Baptist Press*, October 30, 2014.

70. See: Djupe et al., "Rights Talk." Djupe, Lewis, and Jelen, "Rights, Reflections, and Reciprocity.

CHAPTER 8

1. Kate Shellnutt and Sarah Eekhoff Zylstra, "Who's Who of Trump's Tremendous Faith Advisors," *Christianity Today*, June 22, 2016.
2. Robert Costa and Jenna Johnson, "Evangelical Leader Jerry Falwell Jr. Endorses Trump," *The Washington Post*, January 26, 2016.
3. Chad Groening, "Putting a 'Lesser Evil' in the White House," *One News Now*, June 10, 2016.
4. Moore, "A White Church No More." Erik Erickson, "I Will Not Vote for Donald Trump. Ever," The Resurgent, July 11, 2016, http://theresurgent.com/i-will-not-vote-for-donald-trump-ever/. See also, Elizabeth Dias, "Donald Trump's Feud with Evangelical Leader Reveals Fault Lines," *Time*, May 9, 2016.
5. John Ward, "Former Rubio Adviser Holds Homemade Anti-Trump Sign Outside Evangelical Meeting," *Yahoo! News*, June 21, 2016. Emphasis in the original.
6. Russell Moore, Twitter post, June 21, 2016, 1:49 p.m., https://twitter.com/drmoore/status/745312725132152834.
7. Glendon, *Rights Talk*.
8. Bellah et al., *Habits of the Heart*. Michael J. Sandel, *Democracy's Discontent: America in Search of a Public Philosophy* (Cambridge, MA: Harvard University Press, 1998).
9. Layman, *The Great Divide*, 328–29.
10. Jelen, "Political Esperanto."
11. Djupe et al., "Rights Talk."
12. This joins prior analyses that find that conservative rights politics enhance the professionalization, sophistication, and democratic discourse of religious organizations. See e.g., Wilson, *The Street Politics of Abortion*. Shields, *The Democratic Virtues of the Christian Right*. Moen, *The Transformation of the Christian Right*.
13. Samuel C. Stouffer, *Communism, Conformity, and Civil Liberties* (New York: Doubleday, 1955).
14. For a review, see: Gibson, "Measuring Political Tolerance and General Support for Pro-Civil Liberties Policies."
15. For a review, see: Paul A. Djupe, ed. *Religion and Political Tolerance in America: Advances in the State of the Art* (Philadelphia: Temple University Press, 2015). Putnam and Campbell, *American Grace*.
16. Ted G. Jelen and Clyde WIlcox, "Denominational Preference and the Dimensions of Political Tolerance," *Sociological Analysis* 51, no. 1 (1990). Stephen T. Mockabee, "A Question of Authority: Religion and Cultural Conflict in the 2004 Election," *Political Behavior* 29, no. 2 (2007). Sam Reimer and Jerry Z. Park, "Tolerant (in)Civility: A Longitudinal Analysis of White Conservative Protestants' Willingness to Grant Civil Liberties," *Journal for the Scientific Study of Religion* 40, no. 4 (2001).
17. Marie A. Eisenstein, *Religion and the Politics of Tolerance* (Waco, TX: Baylor University Press, 2008).

18. See e.g., James L. Gibson, "Alternative Measures of Political Tolerance: Must Tolerance Be 'Least-Liked'?," *American Journal of Political Science* 36, no. 2 (1992). "Measuring Political Tolerance and General Support for Pro-Civil Liberties Policies."

19. See Figure 3.3.

20. $p = 0.16$

21. See: Djupe, Lewis, and Jelen, "Rights, Reflection, and Reciprocity."

22. John L. Sullivan, James E. Piereson, and George E. Marcus, *Political Tolerance and American Democracy* (Chicago: University of Chicago Press, 1982).

23. In a recent review, James Gibson finds that the different measures "share a common source in larger political values, but they also include strong doses of idiosyncratic (and systematic) variance as well." Gibson, "Measuring Political Tolerance and General Support for Pro-Civil Liberties Policies," 61. For example, Gibson suggests that the inclusion of "Communists" in recent fixed-group batteries decreases the compatibility of the fixed-group and least-liked group approach, because Americans' perspective on communists is quite different today. As such, in order to get a full picture of political tolerance, it may be best to analyze both the fixed-group and least-liked approaches, as I do here. See Gibson, "Measuring Political Tolerance and General Support for Pro-Civil Liberties Policies;" "Alternative Measures of Political Tolerance: Must Tolerance Be 'Least-Liked'?"

24. Eric Metaxas, "Should Christians Vote for Trump?," *Wall Street Journal*, October 12, 2016.

25. Andrew R. Lewis, Paul A. Djupe, and Jacob R. Neiheisel, "Republicanism Trumps Religion When It Comes to Anti-Muslim Sentiment," *FiveThirtyEight*, December 10, 2015.

26. Nicole Neroulias, "RNS: Poll: Majority Opposes Mosque near Ground Zero, Sees Site as 'Sacred Ground'," *Religion News Service*, August 26, 2010.

27. Elizabeth Wood, "Ground Zero Mosque Too Close for Comfort, SBC's Land Says," *Baptist Press*, August 13, 2010.

28. Ethics & Religious Liberty Commission, "Setting the Record Straight," *ERLC.com*, March 10, 2010, http://erlc.com/article/setting-the-record-straight/.

29. Ibid.

30. Hastings Dwayne, "Land Withdraws Form Interfaith Coalition," *Baptist Press*, January 21, 2011.

31. Associated Press, "Southern Baptist Leader Leaves Mosque Coalition," *Associated Press*, January 25, 2011.

32. Tom Strode, "Court Upholds Inmate's Religious Liberty," *Baptist Press*, January 20, 2015.

33. The Becket Fund for Religious Liberty, "Christians, Jews, Sikhs, Hindus Defend New Jersey Mosque" (2016), www.becketfund.org/amicus-brief-defends-new-jersey-islamic-society/.

34. Tom Strode, "All Need Religious Liberty, Baptist, Others Contend," *Baptist Press*, May 25, 2016.

35. Michael Gryboski, "Russell Moore Takes on Critics at SBC for Supporting Religious Freedom for Muslims to Build Mosques," *Christian Post*, June 16, 2016.

36. Sarah Eekhoff Zylstra, "Southern Baptists Back Away from Backing Mosques," *Christianity Today*, February 8, 2017.

37. Robert P. Jones, *The End of White Christian America* (New York: Simon & Schuster, 2016).
38. "The Rage of White, Christian America," *The New York Times*, November 10, 2016.
39. CBS, "Southern Baptist Leader Calls for Fresh Approach in 'Increasingly Post-Christian America'."
40. See e.g., Wilson, *The Street Politics of Abortion*.
41. Stuart A. Scheingold, *The Politics of Rights: Lawyers, Public Policy, and Political Change*, 2nd ed. (Ann Arbor: University of Michigan Press, 2004).
42. For more, see Glendon, *Rights* Talk, 12–17.
43. Bellah et al., *Habits of the Heart*.
44. Shields, *The Democratic Virtues of the Christian Right*.
45. Inazu, *Confident Pluralism*.
46. Putnam and Campbell, *American Grace*.

References

"Abolition of the Death Penalty." National Council of Churches, 1968.

"Abortion." National Association of Evangelicals, 1971.

"Abortion." National Association of Evangelicals, 1973.

"Abortion Factions Skirmish over Koop Appointment." *Christianity Today*, May 8, 1981, 46.

Abramowitz, Alan I. "It's Abortion, Stupid: Policy Voting in the 1992 Presidential Election." *Journal of Politics* 57, no. 1 (1995): 176–86.

Achord, Steve. "Pastor: Baptists Should Learn from Karla Faye Tucker's Life." *Baptist Press*, February 5, 1998.

Adams, Greg D. "Abortion: Evidence of Issue Evolution." *American Journal of Political Science* 41, no. 3 (1997): 718–37.

Agiesta, Jennifer. "Poll: 53% Say Boston Bomber Should Face Death Penalty." *CNN*, April 21, 2015.

Ainsworth, Scott, and Itai Sened. "The Role of Lobbyists: Entrepreneurs with Two Audiences." *American Journal of Political Science* 37, no. 3 (1993): 834–66.

"Alcohol Advertising." National Association of Evangelicals, 1958.

Alford, Chip. "Messengers Oppose Clinton's Views, Urge Him to Biblical Morality." *Baptist Press*, June 23, 1993.

Allen, Charlotte. "The Right to Life Lobby vs. McCain." *The Weekly Standard*, April 30, 2007.

Allen, Evan. "Few Favor Death for Dzhokhar Tsarnaev, Poll Finds." *Boston Globe*, April 26, 2015.

Allen, John L. "After Charlie Hebdo, Pope Says Free Speech Has Limits." *Crux*, January 15, 2015.

"Amendment 2." In *Colorado Constitution*, 1992.

American Center for Law and Justice. "ACLJ: Supreme Court Urged to Reject IRS Regulations Authorizing Illegal Obamacare Subsidies." 2015. https://aclj.org/obamacare/aclj-supreme-court-urged-to-reject-irs-regulations-authorizing-illegal-obamacare-subsidies.

"Health Care Legislation & Litigation." 2012.

American Jewish Congress et al. "Brief of American Jewish Congress, Board of Church and Society of the United Methodist Church, National Women's Conference of the American Ethical Union, New York State Council of Churches, Union of American Hebrew Congregations and Unitarian Universalist Women's Federation, Amici Curiae." In *John H. Poelker v. Jane Doe*. New York, 1976.

Americans United for the Separation of Church and State. "Brief of Americans United for the Separation of Church and State as Amicus Curiae in Support of Appellees." In *William L. Webster, et al. v. Reproductive Health Services, et al*. Washington, DC, 1989.

Ammerman, Nancy Tatom. *Baptist Battles: Social Change and Religious Conflict in the Southern Baptist Convention*. 2nd ed. New Brunswick, NJ: Rutgers University Press, 1995.

American Ethical Union et al. "Brief for Amici Curiae American Ethical Union; American Humanist Association; Board of Church and Society, United Methodist Church; Catholics for a Free Choice, Church of the Brethren; Department of Church Women of the Division of Homeland Ministries, Christian Church (Disciples of Christ); National Federation of Temple Sisterhoods; National Women's Conference of the American Ethical Union; Unitarian Universalist Association; Unitarian Universalist Federation; Union of American Hebrew Congregations; Young Women's Christian Association." In *Patricia A. Harris v. Cora McRae, et al*. Brooklyn, NY, 1979.

Anderson, David E. "Churches Seek Renewed Social Activist Role." *Nashua Telegraph*, March 2, 1974.

Anderson, Ryan T. *Truth Overruled: The Future of Marriage and Religious Freedom*. Washington, DC: Regnery, 2015.

Anderson, Ryan T., and Sarah Torre. "The Right to Life and a Culture of Marriage." *National Review*, December 10, 2014.

"Arkansas Editor Commends Death Sentence Commutation." *Baptist Press*, January 4, 1971.

Associated Press. "Southern Baptist Leader Leaves Mosque Coalition." *Associated Press*, January 25, 2011.

The Associated Press Stylebook. 39th ed. New York: Basic Books, 2004.

Audi, Tamara, Justin Scheck, and Christopher Lawton. "California Votes for Prop 8." *The Wall Street Journal*, November 5, 2008.

Bader, Christopher D., Scott A. Desmond, F. Carson Mencken, and Byron R. Johnson. "Divine Justice: The Relationship between Images of God and Attitudes toward Capital Punishment." *Criminal Justice Review* 35, no. 1 (2010): 90–106.

"Baker Keeps Post with 15–15 Vote." *Baptist Press*, September 18, 1987.

Balmer, Randall. "The Real Origins of the Religious Right. They'll Tell You It Was Abortion. Sorry, the Historical Record's Clear: It Was Segregation." *Politico*, May 27, 2014.

Baptist Joint Committee on Public Affairs, et al. "Brief of the Baptist Joint Committee on Public Affairs, the American Jewish Committee, and Americans United for the Separation of Church and State as *Amici Curiae* in Support of Appellees." In *Otis R. Bowen v. Chan Kendrick, et al*. Washington, DC, 1988.

"Baptist Leader Asks Public Funds to Fight Pornography." *Baptist Press*, May 13, 1970.

"Baptists among Signers of Abortion Rights Statement." *Baptist Public Affairs*, October 26, 1979.

"Baptists Will Examine Evangelism, Freedom." *Baptist Public Affiars*, September 8, 1981.

Barnes, Robert. "Supreme Court Declines Case of Photographer Who Denied Service to Gay Couple." *The Washington Post*, April 7, 2014.

Barr, Bob. "No Defending the Defense of Marriage Act." *Los Angeles Times*, January 5, 2009.

Batchis, Wayne. *The Right's First Amendment: The Politics of Free Speech and the Return of Conservative Libertarianism*. Stanford, CA: Stanford University Press, 2016.

Baumgartner, Frank R., Suzanna L. De Boef, and Amber E. Boydstun. *The Decline of the Death Penalty and the Discovery of Innocence*. New York: Cambridge University Press, 2008.

Baumgartner, Frank, Emily Williams, and Kaneesha Johnson. "Americans Are Turning against the Death Penalty. Are Politicians Far Behind?" *The Washington Post*, December 7, 2015.

Bebbington, David W. *Evangelicalism in Modern Britain: A History from the 1730s to the 1980s*. London: Unwin Hyman, 1989.

Becket Fund for Religious Liberty. "Christians, Jews, Sikhs, Hindus Defend New Jersey Mosque." May 11, 2016. www.becketfund.org/amicus-brief-defends-new-jersey-islamic-society/.

"HHS Mandate Information Central." www.becketfund.org/hhsinformationcentral.

Bellah, Robert N., Steve M. Tipton, William M. Sullivan, Richard Madsen, and Ann Swidler. *Habits of the Heart: Individualism and Commitment in American Life*. Berkeley: University of California Press, 1985.

Berg, Thomas C. "Anti-Catholicism and Modern Church-State Relations." *Loyola University Chicago Law Journal* 33, no. 1 (2001): 121–72.

Berman, Russell. "How Nebraska Abolished the Death Penalty." *The Atlantic*, May 27, 2015.

Bishop, George F., Robert W. Oldendick, and Alfred J. Tuchfarber. "The Importance of Replicating a Failure to Replicate: Order Effects on Abortion Items." *Public Opinion Quarterly* 49, no. 1 (1985): 105–14.

Blanchard, Dallas A. *The Anti-Abortion Movement and the Rise of the Religious Right: From Polite to Fiery Protest*. New York: MacMillan, 1994.

Blinder, Alan, and Tamar Lewin. "Clerk in Kentucky Chooses Jail over Deal on Same-Sex Marriage." *The New York Times*, September 3, 2015.

Boggs, Kelly. "First-Person: Limits to the First Amendment." *Baptist Press*, September 17, 2010.

Bolduc, Brian. "The Church and the RFRA." *National Review*, February 17, 2012.

Boorstein, Michelle. "Pope Says Children Have a Right to Grow up in a Family with a Father and a Mother." *The Washington Post*, November 17, 2014.

Bosman, Julie. "Nebraska Bans Death Penalty, Defying a Veto." *The New York Times*, May 27, 2015.

"Brief Amici Curiae Religious Organizations, Public Speakers, and Scholars Concerned about Free Speech in Support of Respondents." In *Obergefell v. Hodges*. Washington, DC, 2015.

"Brief of Amici Curiae Dr. Daniel L. Akin; Dr. Darrell L. Bock; Dr. D.A. Carson; Dr. C. Stephen Evans; Dr. Wayne Grudem; Dr. James M. Hamilton; Dr. H. Wayne House; Dr. Peter A. Lillback; Dr. R. Albert Mohler, Jr.; and J. Michael Thigpen in Support of the Petitioner and Reversal." In *Town of Greece v. Galloway*. Washington, DC, 2014.

"Brief of Amici Curiae General Conference of Seventh-Day Adventists and the Joint Conference Committee." In *Everson v. Board of Education of the Township of Ewing*. Washington, DC: Joint Conference Committee, 1947.

"Brief of Amicus Curiae of the Southern Baptist Convention Ethics & Religious Liberty Commission in Support of Petitioner." In *Town of Greece v. Galloway*. Washington, DC, 2014.

"Brief of Baptist Joint Committee for Religious Liberty, General Synod of the United Church of Christ, and Rev. Gradye Parsons, Stated Clerk of the General Assembly of the Presbyterian Church (U.S.A.) as Amici Curiae in Support of Respondents." In *Town of Greece v. Galloway*. Washington, DC, 2014.

"Brief of the Baptist Joint Committee as Amicus Curiae in Support of Respondents." In *Zubik v. Burwell*. Washington, DC, 2016.

"Brief of the Southern Baptist Theological Seminary, the Ethics & Religious Liberty Commission, the International Mission Board, and Dr. R. Albert Mohler, Jr. as Amici Curiae in Support of Petitioners." In *Zubik v. Burwell*. Washington, DC, 2016.

Britt, Chester L. "Race, Religion and Support for the Death Penalty: A Research Note." *Justice Quarterly* 15 (1998): 175–91.

Brown, Steven P. *Trumping Religion: The New Christian Right, the Free Speech Clause, and the Courts*. Tuscaloosa: University of Alabama Press, 2002.

Bryson, Donna. "Colorado Court: Ruling Stands That Baker Can't Cite Religion." *Associated Press*, April 25, 2016.

Cadei, Emily. "2016: The End of the Culture Wars as We Know Them." *Newsweek*, May 11, 2016.

Campbell, David E., and J. Quin Monson. "The Case of Bush's Reelection: Did Gay Marriage Do It?" In *A Matter of Faith: Religion in the 2004 Presidential Election*, edited by David E. Campbell. Washington, DC: Brookings, 2007.

"Capital Punishment." National Association of Evangelicals, 1972.

"Capital Punishment." National Association of Evangelicals, 1973.

Carmines, Edward G., and James A. Stimson. *Issue Evolution: Race and the Transformation of American Politics*. Princeton, NJ: Princeton University Press, 1989.

"The Two Faces of Issue Voting." *American Political Science Review* 74, no. 1 (1980): 78–91.

Carsey, Thomas M., and Geoffrey C. Layman. "Changing Sides or Changing Minds? Party Conversion, Issue Conversion, and Partisan Change on the Abortion Issue." *American Journal of Political Science* 50, no. 2 (2006): 464–77.

Carter, Jimmy. "White House Conference on Families Statement Announcing Conference." *The American Presidency Project*, 1978.

Carter, Joe. "Us, Them, and Good Men: Choosing Sides on Offensive Speech." *Canon and Culture*, February 20, 2015.

Carter, Stephen L. *The Culture of Disbelief*. New York: Anchor, 1991.

Castle, Jeremiah J. "The Electoral Impact of Public Opinion on Religious Establishment." *Journal for the Scientific Study of Religion* 54, no. 4 (2015): 814–32.

CBS. "Southern Baptist Leader Calls for Fresh Approach in 'Increasingly Post-Christian America'." *CBS News*, April 18, 2014. www.cbsnews.com/news/new-southern-baptist-leader-russell-moore-calls-for-a-change-in-tone/

Chambers, Jack. "Baptists Pray for Prodigal President." *Wall Street Journal*, June 15, 1993, C18.

Chandler, Diana. "Florist Aims for Supreme Court for Religious Liberty." *Baptist Press*, February 16, 2017.

Chong, Dennis, and James N. Druckman. "Framing Theory." *Annual Review of Political Science* 10 (2007): 103–26.

Christian Coalition of America. "Christian Coalition Expresses Disappointment with Senators That Opposed the Flag Amendment." news release, June 28, 2006.

Christian Legal Society. "Brief of the National Hispanic Christian Leadership Conference, International Society for Krishna Consciousness, Untied States Conference of Catholic Bishops, American Bible Society, Christian Medical Association, Ethics & Religious Liberty Commission of the Southern Baptist Convention, Institutional Religious Freedom Alliance, Intervarsity Christian Fellowship/USA, Lutheran Church-Missouri Synod, National Association of Evangelicals, and Christian Legal Society, Amicus Curiae." In *Eleanor McCullen, et al. v. Martha Coakley, et al.* Washington, DC, 2014.

"Church Tax Privileges to Remain, Corman Says." *Baptist Press*, October 8, 1975.

"Cities Hosting Pope Francis Must Take Pains to Protect Church-State Separation, Says Americans United." news release., August 31,, 2015, www.au.org/media/press-releases/cities-hosting-pope-francis-must-take-pains-to-protect-church-state-separation.

Claassen, Ryan L. *Godless Democrats and Pious Republicans? Party Activists, Party Capture and the "God Gap."* New York: Cambridge University Press, 2015.

Claiborne, Shane. *Executing Grace: How the Death Penalty Killed Jesus and Why It's Killing Us*. New York: HarperOne, 2016.

"If It Weren't for Jesus, I Might Be Pro-Death Too." Red Letter Christians, 2014.

Clark, Ramsey. "To Abolish the Death Penalty." Statement Before the Senate Judiciary Committee. July 2, 1968.

Clinton, William J. "Remarks on Signing Memorandums in Medical Research and Reproductive Health and an Exchange with Reporters." The American Presidency Project, 1993.

Clymer, Adam. "Abortion Aid Barred by Bell in Rape Case: He Rules That Current Law Makes No Exceptions for Victims." *The New York Times*, August 2, 1977, 1, 13.

"Hillary Clinton Says Administration Was Misunderstood on Health Care." *The New York Times*, October 3, 1994, A12.

Cohen, Jon. "Most Want Death Penalty for Dzhokhar Tsarnaev If He Is Convicted of Boston Bombing." *The Washington Post*, May 1, 2013.

Colson, Charles, and Catherine Larson. "We Need Health-Care Reform." *Christianity Today*, August 2009, 64.

Connor, Ken. "First-Person: Health Care & Moral Schizophrenia." *Baptist Press*, November 17, 2009.

"Conservatives Rethink Death Penalty." *Christianity Today*, April 6, 1998, 19.

Cook, Elizabeth Adell, Ted G. Jelen, and Clyde Wilcox. *Between Two Absolutes: Public Opinion and the Politics of Abortion*. Boulder, CO: Westview, 1992.

"Issue Voting in Gubernatorial Elections: Abortion and Post-*Webster* Politics." *Journal of Politics* 56, no. 1 (1994): 187–99.

"Issue Voting in U.S. Senate Elections: The Abortion Issue in 1990." *Congress & the Presidency* 21, no. 1 (1994): 99–112.

"Measuring Abortion Attitudes: Methodological and Substantive Lessons from the CBS/New York Times Surveys." *Family Planning Perspectives* 25, no. 3 (1993): 118–21.

Cook, Kimberly J. *Divided Passions: Public Opinions on Abortion and the Death Penalty.* Lebanon, NH: Northeastern University Press, 1998.

Cook, Tony. "Gov. Mike Pence Signs 'Religious Freedom' Bill in Private." *Indiana Star,* April 2, 2015.

Cook, Tony, and Tom LoBianco. "Indiana Governor Signs Amended 'Religious Freedom' Law." *USA Today,* April 2, 2015.

Corman, Juliane, and David Levin. "The Polls–Trends: Support for Government Provision of Health Care and the Patient Protection and Affordable Care Act." *Public Opinion Quarterly* 80, no. 1 (2016): 114–79.

Costa, Robert, and Jenna Johnson. "Evangelical Leader Jerry Falwell Jr. Endorses Trump." *The Washington Post,* January 26, 2016.

"Court Hears Arguments against Death Penalty." *Baptist Press,* January 18, 1972.

"Court Upholds Student Use of Flag for Peace." *Baptist Press,* June 26, 1974.

Cribb, Bryan. "First Person: Same-Sex Marriage & the Pro-Life Example." *Baptist Press,* September 29, 2014.

Cummings, Hannah. "High Court Weighs Speech Limits in Westboro Case." *Baptist Press,* October 7, 2010.

Davis, Sean. "Men without Chests: How C. S. Lewis Predicted Charlie Hebdo Censorship." *The Federalist,* January 8, 2015.

De Vogue, Ariane. "Congress Evolves on DOMA, Same-Sex Marriage." December 6, 2012.

"Declaration of Human Rights." Atlanta, GA: Southern Baptist Convention, 1978.

den Dulk, Kevin. "In Legal Culture, but Not of It: The Role of Cause Lawyers in Evangelical Legal Mobilization." In *Cause Lawyers and Social Movements,* edited by Austin Sarat and Stuart Scheingold. Stanford, CA: Stanford University Press, 2006.

Dias, Elizabeth. "Donald Trump's Feud with Evangelical Leader Reveals Fault Lines." *Time,* May 9, 2016.

Diggins, John P. *The Lost Soul of American Politics: Virtue, Self -Interest, and the Foundations of Liberalism.* Chicago: University of Chicago Press, 1984.

DiMaggio, Paul, John Evans, and Bethany Bryson. "Have Americans' Social Attitudes Become More Polarized?" *American Journal of Sociology* 102, no. 3 (1996): 690–755.

Djupe, Paul A., ed. *Religion and Political Tolerance in America: Advances in the State of the Art.* Philadelphia: Temple University Press, 2015.

Djupe, Paul A., Andrew R. Lewis, and Ted G. Jelen. "Rights, Reflection, and Reciprocity: Implications of the Same-Sex Marriage Debate for Tolerance and the Political Process." *Politics & Religion* 9, no. 3 (2016): 630–48.

Djupe, Paul A., Andrew R. Lewis, Ted G. Jelen, and Charles D. Dahan. "Rights Talk: The Opinion Dynamics of Rights Framing." *Social Science Quarterly* 95, no. 3 (2014): 652–68.

Dobson, James. *Bringing up Boys.* Wheaton, IL: Tyndale House, 2001.

Dochuk, Darren. *From Bible Belt to Sun Belt: Plain-Folk Religion, Grassroots Politics, and the Rise of Evangelical Conservatism.* New York: W.W. Norton, 2011.

Dockery, David S., ed. *Southern Baptists & American Evangelicals: The Conversation Continues.* Nashville: Broadman & Holman, 1993.

Douthat, Ross. "The Blasphemy We Need." *The New York Times,* January 7, 2015.

Drakeman, Donald L. *Church, State, and Original Intent*. New York: Cambridge University Press, 2010.

Dulles, Avery Cardinal. "Catholicism & Capital Punishment." *First Things*, April 2001, 30–35.

Dunn, Carrie, and Rafferty Andrew. "2016 Candidates React to Supreme Court's Gay Marriage Ruling." *NBC News*, June 26, 2015.

Dunn, James. "Interview with the Author." (August 4 & September 6, 2010). Philadelphia, PA

"Public Money for Public Purposes." *Baptist Public Affairs*, June 29, 1981.

Dwayne, Hastings. "Land Withdraws Form Interfaith Coalition." *Baptist Press*, January 21, 2011.

Dworkin, Ronald. *Taking Rights Seriously*. Cambridge, MA: Harvard University Press, 1978.

Eaton, William J., and Paul Richter. "First Lady's Health Plan Talk Hailed." *Los Angeles Times*, September 21, 1993, 1.

Eckles, David L., and Brian F. Schaffner. "Loss Aversion and the Framing of the Health Care Reform Debate." *The Forum* 8, no. 1 (2010): Article 7.

Eicher, Nick. "Why 'Je Suis Charlie' Should Give Christians Pause." *World Magazine*, January 19, 2015.

Eisenstein, Marie A. *Religion and the Politics of Tolerance*. Waco, TX: Baylor University Press, 2008.

Epp, Charles R. *The Rights Revolution: Lawyers, Activists, and Supreme Courts in Comparative Perspective*. Chicago: University of Chicago Press, 1998.

Epstein, Lee, and Thomas G. Walker. *Constitutional Law for a Changing America: Rights, Liberties, and Justice*. 8th ed. Thousand Oaks, CA: CQ Press.

Erickson, Erick. "I Will Not Vote for Donald Trump. Ever." *The Resurgent*, July 11, 2016, http://theresurgent.com/i-will-not-vote-for-donald-trump-ever/.

Ertelt, Steven. "154 Members of Congress Object to Pro-Abortion Obama Mandate." *Life News*, February 7, 2012.

Ethics & Religious Liberty Commission. "Letter to HHS: Comment on Failed Religious 'Accommodation'." April 8, 2013.

"Setting the Record Straight." *ERLC.com*. March 10, 2010. http://erlc.com/article/setting-the-record-straight/.

"Fifteen Principles for Needed Health Care Reform." Nashville, TN: Ethics & Religious Liberty Commission, 2009.

Ethics and Religious Liberty Commission of the Southern Baptist Convention et al. "Brief of the Ethics and Religious Liberty Commission of the Southern Baptist Convention, the National Association of Evangelicals, and the Convocation of Anglicans in North America as Amici Curiae in Support of Petitioners." In *Arizona Christian School Tuition Organization v. Kathleen M. Winn, et al*. Nashville, 2010.

Evans, John H. "Have Americans' Attitudes Become More Polarized? An Update." *Social Science Quarterly* 84, no. 1 (2003): 71–90.

Fair, Daryl R. "The Everson Case in the Context of New Jersey Politics." Chap. 1–22 In *Everson Revisited: Religion, Education, and Law at the Crossroads*, edited by Jo Renee Formicola and Humbert Morken. Lanham, MD: Rowman & Littlefield, 1997.

Falwell, Jerry. *How You Can Help Clean up America*. Lynchburg, VA: Liberty Publishing Company, 1978.

Strength for the Journey: An Autobiography. New York: Simon & Schuster, 1987.
"Falwell Loses Hustler Suit." *Christianity Today*, April 8, 1988, 48.
"Falwell Wins $200,000 for Emotional Distress in a Suit against Hustler Magazine." *Chrisianity Today*, January 18, 1985, 47.
"Family Conference Officials Downplay Abortion Issue." *The Argus-Press*, June 18, 1980.
Family Research Council. "Family Research Council Says Supreme Court Health Care Ruling Jeopardizes Future of Liberty." June 28, 2012.
"In Atlanta, Family Research Council's Tony Perkins Stands with Fired Chief, Challenges Mayor Reed's Intimidating Message." news release, January 13, 2015, www.frc.org/newsroom/in-atlanta-family-research-councils-tony-perkins-stands-with-fired-fire-chief-challenges-mayor-reeds-intimidating-message.
"Family Research Council: Supreme Court Subjects Obamacare to Linguistic Gymnastics." June 25, 2015. www.frc.org/newsroom/family-research-council-supreme-court-subjects-obamacare-to-linguistic-gymnastics.
Family Research Council Action. "FRC Action Statement on Congressman Bart Stupak's Retirement." 2010.
"Family Research Council Urges Pro-Life Senators to 'Denounce' Abortion Funding." *Catholic News Agency*, November 19, 2009.
Farnsley II, Arthur Emery *Southern Baptist Politics: Authority and Power in the Restructuring of an American Denomination*. University Park, PA: Penn State University Press, 1994.
"Fifth Amendment of the United States Constitution."
Flippen, J. Brooks. *Jimmy Carter, the Politics of Family, and the Rise of the Religious Right*. Athens: University of Georgia Press, 2011.
Fowler, Robert Booth, Allen D. Hertzke, Laura R. Olson, and Kevin R. den Dulk. *Politics and Religion in America: Faith, Culture, and Strategic Choices*. 3rd ed. Boulder, CO: Westview Press, 2004.
Frame, Randy. "A Matter of Life and Death." *Christianity Today*, August 14, 1995, 50.
Gallup. "Marriage." 2016, www.gallup.com/poll/117328/marriage.aspx.
Garrett, James Leo, Jr., E. Glenn Hinson, and James E. Tull. *Are Southern Baptists "Evangelicals"?* Macon, GA: Mercer University Press, 1983.
Garrett, W. Barry. "Baptist Body Declares Its Position on Equal Rights." *Baptist Press*, March 7, 1974.
"High Court Holds Abortion to Be 'a Right of Privacy'." *Baptist Press*, January 31, 1973.
George, Robert P. *Making Men Moral: Civil Liberties and Public Morals*. New York: Oxford University Press, 1995.
Geranios, Nicholas K. "Gay-Wedding Bias Case Big Surprise to Florist." *Seattle Times*, April 11, 2015.
Gerstein, Josh. "Brief Fuels Gay Marriage Speculation." *Politico*, February 22, 2013.
Gibson, James L. "Alternative Measures of Political Tolerance: Must Tolerance Be 'Least-Liked'?" *American Journal of Political Science* 36, no. 2 (1992): 560–77.
"Measuring Political Tolerance and General Support for Pro-Civil Liberties Policies: Notes, Evidence, and Cautions." *Public Opinion Quarterly* 77, no. S1 (2013): 45–68.
Glendon, Mary Ann. *Rights Talk: The Impoverishment of Political Discourse*. New York, NY: Free Press, 1991.

Goldberg, Carey. "Hawaii Judge Ends Gay-Marriage Ban." *The New York Times*, December 4, 1996.

Goldberg-Hiller, Jonathan. *The Limits to Union: Same-Sex Marriage and the Politics of Civil Rights*. Ann Arbor: University of Michigan Press, 2004.

Gooch, David. "Conference Speakers Disagree on Law and Order." July 17, 1973.

Gordon, Linda. *The Moral Property of Women: A History of Birth Control Politics in America*. 4th ed. Urbana: University of Illinois Press, 2002.

"Government Aid to Church Schools." Nashville: Sunday School Board of the Southern Baptist Convention, 1947.

Graham, Franklin. "Franklin Graham: Are There Limits to Religious Mockery." *Decision Magazine*, March 2, 2015.

Grant, Tobin. "Did White Evangelical Support for Trump Drop Due to Lower Turnout?" *Religion News Service*, November 14, 2016.

Grasmick, Harold G., Robert J. Burski Jr., and Brenda Sims. "Religious Beliefs and Public Support for the Death Penalty for Juveniles and Adults." *Journal of Crime and Justice* 16, no. 2 (1993): 59–86.

Grasmick, Harold G., John K. Cochran, Robert J. Bursik Jr., and M' Lou Kimpel. "Religion, Punitive Justice, and Support for the Death Penalty." *Justice Quarterly* 10, no. 2 (1993): 289–314.

Grasmick, Harold G., Elizabeth Davenport, Mitchell B. Chamlin, and Robert J. Bursik Jr. "Protestant Fundamentalism and the Retributive Doctrine of Punishment." *Criminology* 30, no. 1 (1992): 21–45.

Green, Donald, Bradley Palmquist, and Eric Schickler. *Partisan Hearts and Minds: Political Parties and the Social Identities of Voters*. New Haven, CT: Yale University Press, 2002.

Gregg v. Georgia, 428 U.S. 153 (1976).

Grindstaff, Laura. "Abortion and the Popular Press: Mapping Media Discourse from *Roe* to *Webster*." In *Abortion Politics in the United States and Canada: Studies in Public Opinion*, edited by Ted G. Jelen and Marthe A. Chandler, 57–88. Westport, CT: Praeger, 1994.

Groening, Chad. "Putting a 'Lesser Evil' in the White House." *One News Now*, June 10, 2016.

Gryboski, Michael. "Russell Moore Takes on Critics at SBC for Supporting Religious Freedom for Muslims to Build Mosques." *Christian Post*, June 16, 2016.

Gushee, David P., Richard Land, and Glen Stassen. "How Biblical Is It to Be Pro-Life and Support the Death Penalty?" *Christianity Today*, February 2012, 42–43.

Guth, James L., John C. Green, Lyman A. Kellstedt, and Corwin E. Smidt. "Onward Christian Soldiers: Religious Activist Groups in American Politics." In *Interest Group Politics*, edited by Alan J. Cigler and Burdett A. Loomis, 55–76. Washington, DC: CQ Press, 1995.

Guttman, Amy, and Dennis Thompson. *Democracy and Disagreement*. Cambridge: Belknap Press, 1996.

Hacker, Hans J. *The Culture of Conservative Christian Litigation*. Lanham, MD: Rowman & Littlefield, 2005.

Haider-Markel, Donald P., and Mark R. Joslyn. "Gun Policy, Opinion, Tragedy and Blame Attribution: The Conditional Influence of Issue Frames." *American Journal of Political Science* 63, no. 2 (2001): 520–43.

Hamburger, Philip. *Separation of Church and State*. Cambridge, MA: Harvard University Press, 2002.

Hankins, Barry. *Francis Schaeffer and the Shaping of Evangelical America*. Grand Rapids, MI: Wm. B. Eerdmans, 2008.

 Uneasy in Babylon: Southern Baptist Conservatives and American Culture. Tuscaloosa: University of Alabama Press, 2002.

Hanson, Russell L. *The Democratic Imagination in America: Conversations with Our Past*. Princeton, NJ: Princeton University Press, 1985.

Harris, Secretary of Health and Human Services v. McRae et al., 448 U.S. 297 (1980).

Hartz, Louis. *The Liberal Tradition in America: An Interpretation of Political Thought*. New York: Harcourt, Brace, and World, 1955.

Hastey, Stan. "No Damages for Falwell, Supreme Court Rules." *Baptist Press*, February 25, 1988.

 "The History and Contributions of the Baptist Joint Committee on Public Affairs." *Baptist History and Heritage* 20, no. 3 (1985): 35–43.

 "Wood Hails Ruling Upholding Federal Abortion Funding." *Baptist Press*, January 17, 1980, 2–3.

 "Judge Orders Reimbursement for Cost of Papal Platform." *Baptist Press*, November 16, 1979.

Hastey, Stan L. "High Court Upholds Capital Punishment." July 2, 1976.

Hastey, Stanley LeRoy. "A History of the Baptist Joint Committee on Public Affairs, 1946–1971." Ph.D. Dissertation, Southern Baptist Theological Seminary, 1973.

Hayhurst, Roy. "Hawkins Reminds Messengers of Baptist Pledge." *Baptist Press*, June 21, 2012.

Hayworth, Beth. "Graham Calls for Spiritual Renewal to Honor America." *Baptist Press*, July 7, 1970.

"The Health Care Crunch." *Christianity Today*, February 5, 2008.

Hemingway, M.Z. "Stunned by Stupak." *Christianity Today*, January 2010, 13.

Hippocratic Oath. Johns Hopkins, 2015, http://guides.library.jhu.edu/c.php?g=202502 &p=1335752.

Hoffman, John P., and Sherrie Mills Johnson. "Attitudes toward Abortion among Religious Traditionalists in the United States: Change or Continuity?" *Sociology of Religion* 66, no. 2 (2005): 161–82.

Hollis-Brusky, Amanda. *Ideas with Consequences: The Federalist Society and the Conservative Counterrevolution*. New York: Oxford University Press, 2015.

Holmes, Kim R. "Charlie Hebdo, Intolerance, and the Problem of Double Standards." February 5, 2015). www.heritage.org/research/commentary/2015/2/charlie-hebdo-intolerance-and-the-problem-of-double-standards.

Hoover, Dennis R., and Kevin R. den Dulk. "Christian Conservatives Go to Court: Religion and Legal Mobilization in the United States and Canada." *International Political Science Review* 25, no. 1 (2004): 9–34.

"House Votes 385 to 16 to Ban Flag Mutilation." *Baptist Press*, June 22, 1967.

"House Votes to Bar Abortion Aid for Victims of Rape and Incest." *The New York Times*, August 3, 1977, 11.

"Human Rights." National Association of Evangelicals, 1956.

Hunter, James Davison. *Culture Wars: The Struggle to Define America*. New York: Basic Books, 1991.

Hustler Magazine v. Falwell, 485 U.S. 46 (1988).

Ifill, Gwen. "Clinton Signs Bill Banning Blockades and Violent Acts at Abortion Clinics." *The New York Times*, May 27, 1994.

"New Health Plan, Old Abortion Fight." *The New York Times*, October 4, 1993, A14.

Inazu, John D. *Confident Pluralism: Surviving and Thriving through Deep Difference.* Chicago: University of Chicago Press, 2016.

Irwin, Victoria. "Factions Seek Control of Family Conference." *Christian Science Monitor*, February 13, 1980.

Jackson, David. "Catholic Institutions Sue Obama over Birth Control Mandate." *USA Today*, May 21, 2012.

Jacobs, Lawrence, and Suzanne Mettler. "Why Public Opinion Changes: The Implications for Health and Health Policy." *Journal of Health Policy, Politics, and Law* 36, no. 6 (2011): 917–33.

Jacobs, Lawrence R. *The Health of Nations: Public Opinion and the Making of American and British Health Policy.* Ithaca, NY: Cornell University Press, 1993.

Jameson, Norma. "Smaw Offers His Life for Death Row Men." *Baptist Press*, July 28, 1981.

Jelen, Ted G. "Culture Wars and the Party System: Religion and Realignment." In *Culture Wars in American Politics: Critical Reviews of a Popular Thesis*, edited by Rhys H. Williams, 145–58. Hawthorne, NY: Aldine de Gruyter, 1997.

"Changes in the Attitudinal Correlates of Opposition to Abortion." *Journal for the Scientific Study of Religion* 27, no. 2 (1988): 211–28.

"Political Esperanto: Rhetorical Resources and Limitations of the Christian Right in the United States." *Sociology of Religion* 66, no. 3 (2005): 303–21.

"Respect for Life, Sexual Morality, and Opposition to Abortion." *Review of Religious Research* 25, no. 3 (1984): 220–31.

To Serve God and Mammon: Church-State Relations in American Politics. Boulder, CO: Westview Press, 2000.

Jelen, Ted G., David F. Damore, and Thomas Lamatsch. "Gender, Employment Status, and Abortion: A Longitudinal Analysis." *Sex Roles* 47, no. 7/8 (2002): 321–30.

Jelen, Ted G., and Clyde Wilcox. "Causes and Consequences of Public Attitudes toward Abortion: A Review and Research Agenda." *Political Research Quarterly* 56, no. 4 (2003): 489–500.

Public Attitudes toward Church and State. Armonk, NY: M. E. Sharpe, 1995.

Jelen, Ted G., and Clyde Wilcox. "Denominational Preference and the Dimensions of Political Tolerance." *Sociological Analysis* 51, no. 1 (1990): 69–81.

Johnson, Dirk. "Colorado Homosexuals Feel Betrayed." *The New York Times*, November 8, 1992.

"Joint Statement by Gordon College and the Commission on Institutions of Higher Education, NEASC." NEASC, 2015.

Jones, Robert P. *The End of White Christian America.* New York: Simon & Schuster, 2016.

"The Rage of White, Christian America." *The New York Times*, November 10, 2016.

Joseph Cardinal Bernardin. "A Consistent Ethic of Life: An American-Catholic Dialogue." Gannon Lecture, Fordham University, 1983.

"A Consistent Ethic of Life: Continuing the Dialogue." 1984.

Kaplan, Fred. "The Day Obscenity Became Art." *The New York Times*, July 20, 2009.

Kellstedt, Lyman A., Corwin E. Smidt, John C. Green, and James L. Guth. "A Gentle Stream or a 'River Glorious'? The Religious Left in the 2004 Election." In *A Matter of Faith: Religion in the 2004 Presidential Election*, edited by David E. Campbell, 232–58; 13. Washington, DC: Brookings Institution Press, 2007.

Kennedy, John W. "Rx for America." *Christianity Today*, April 25, 1994, 38.

"Kentucky County Clerk Kim Davis to Be Honored at Values Voter Summit." September 14, 2015. www.frc.org/newsroom/kentucky-county-clerk-kim-davis-to-be-honored-at-values-voter-summit.

Kidd, Thomas. "Polls Show Evangelicals Support Trump. But the Term 'Evangelical' Has Become Meaningless." *The Washington Post*, July 22, 2016.

Killian, Mitchell, and Clyde Wilcox. "Do Abortion Attitudes Lead to Party Switching?" *Political Research Quarterly* 61, no. 4 (2008): 561–73.

King, Martin. "Land and Lewis Remove Names from Controversial Document." *Baptist Press*, April 7, 1995.

Kliff, Sarah. "Stupak's Last Stand." *Newsweek*, March 21, 2010.

Knox, Marv. "Southern Baptist Agency Drops Surgeon General's AIDS Report." September 16, 1988.

Kollman, Ken. *Outside Lobbying: Public Opinion and Interest Group Strategies*. Princeton, NJ: Princeton University Press, 1998.

Kristol, William. "Defeating President Clinton's Health Care Proposal." Project for a Republican Future, 1993.

Lain, Corinna Barrett. "Furman Fundamentals." *Washington Law Review* 82, no. 1 (2007): 30.

Land, Richard. "First-Person: Is Kagan the Right Choice for the Court?" *Baptist Press*, June 29, 2010.

"When Freedoms Are Curtailed: Verbal Terrorism." *Baptist Press*, November 6, 2007.

Land, Richard D. "Giant Steps to Gov. Health Care?" *Baptist Press*, February 4, 2009.

"Interview with the Author." (August 9 & 13, 2010). Nashville, TN.

"Restoring Our Religious Freedom While Preserving Our Baptist Heritage." Ethics & Religious Liberty Commission, 1997, http://erlc.com/article/restoring-our-religious-freedom-while-preserving-our-baptist-heritage/.

Lawrence v. Texas, 539 U.S. 558 (2003).

Lawton, Kim A. "Clinton Abortion Actions Usher in a New Era." *Christianity Today*, March 8, 1993, 52.

Layman, Geoffrey. *The Great Divide: Religious and Cultural Conflict in American Party Politics*. New York: Columbia University Press, 2001.

"Where Is Trump's Evangelical Base? Not in Church." *The Washington Post*, March 29, 2016.

Leege, David C., Kenneth D. Wald, Brian S. Krueger, and Paul D. Mueller. *The Politics of Cultural Differences: Social Change and Voter Mobilization Strategies in the Post-New Deal Period*. Princeton, NJ: Princeton University Press, 2002.

"The Lesson of Karla Faye Tucker." *Christianity Today*, April 6, 1998, 16.

Lewis, Andrew R. "Abortion Politics and the Decline of the Separation of Church and State: The Southern Baptist Case." *Politics & Religion* 7, no. 3 (2014): 521–49.

"The Southern Baptist Church-State 'Culture War': The Internal Politics of Denominational Advocacy." Ph.D. Dissertation, American University, 2011.

Lewis, Andrew R., Paul A. Djupe, and Jacob R. Neiheisel. "Republicanism Trumps Religion When It Comes to Anti-Muslim Sentiment." *FiveThirtyEight*, December 10, 2015.

Liberty Counsel. "U.S. Supreme Court Rules in Favor of Free Speech in Funeral Protest Case." news release, March 2, 2011, www.lc.org/index.cfm?PID=14100&PRID=1040.

Lightman, David. "Rhetoric on Gays Rekindles Republican Debate." *Hartford Courant*, June 30, 1998.

Linder, Douglas O. "The Falwell v. Flynt Trial." http://law2.umkc.edu/faculty/projects/ftrials/falwell/trialaccount.html.

Lu, Rachel. "Pro-Life Lessons for the Defense of Marriage." *Crisis Magazine*, January 29, 2014.

Luker, Kristin. *Abortion and the Politics of Motherhood*. Berkeley: University of California Press, 1984.

Lupu, Ira C. "Reconstructing the Establishment Clause: The Case against Discretionary Accommodation of Religion." *University of Pennsylvania Law Review* 140 (1991): 555–612.

Lutheran Church-Missouri Synod. "Convention Resolution 2–38." 1967.

"Report on Capital Punishment." 1976.

Lutheran Church-Missouri Synod et al. "Brief of the Lutheran Church – Missouri Synod, the Christian Life Commission of the Southern Baptist Convention and the National Association of Evangelicals as Amici Curiae in Support of Appellants." In *William L. Webster, et al. v. Reproductive Heath Services, et al.* St. Louis, 1989.

Magleby, David B., and Candice J. Nelson. *The Money Chase: Congressional Campaign Finance Reform*. Washington, DC: Brookings Institution Press, 2010.

"Majority Report of SBC Executive Committee on Baptist Joint Committee." *Baptist Today*, June 10, 1990.

"Mark Hatfield Taps into the Real Power on Capitol Hill." *Christianity Today*, October 22, 1982, 18.

Marrapodi, Eric. "Wheaton College Sues Administration over Contraception Mandate." *CNN*, July 18, 2012.

Marsden, George. "Contemporary American Evangelicalism." In *Southern Baptists & American Evangelicals: The Conversation Continues*, edited by David S. Dockery, 27–39. Nashville: Broadman & Holman, 1993.

"The Evangelical Denomination." In *Introduction: Evangelicalism and Modern America*, edited by George Marsden, vii-xix. Grand Rapids, MI: William B. Erdmans, 1984.

Martin, Dan. "CLC Directors Elect Land on 23–2 Ballot." *Baptist Press*, September 15, 1988.

"CLC Search Committee Selects Richard Land." *Baptist Press*, September 7, 1988.

Matthews Merrill, Jr. "Don't Punish the Healthy." *Christianity Today*, April 25, 1994, 10.

Maust, John. "The Abortion Issue: Exercising Religion Freely on Both Sides." *Christianity Today*, September 5, 1980, 24.

McAnally, Tom. "Death Penalty Continues Despite Church's 50-Year Opposition." *United Methodist News Service*, October 10, 2006.

McCann, Michael W. *Rights at Work: Pay Equity Reform and the Politics of Legal Mobilization*. Chicago: University of Chicago Press, 1994.

McConnell, Michael W. "Accommodation of Religion: An Update and a Response to the Critics." *George Washington Law Review* 60 (1992): 685–742.

McDaniel, Charles. "Guest Editorial: The Decline of the Separation Principle in the Baptist Tradition of Religious Liberty." *Journal of Church and State* 50 (2008): 413–30.

McKnight, Scot. "The Death Penalty: American Law vs. Christianity." Jesus Creed, Patheos, May 18, 2015. www.patheos.com/blogs/jesuscreed/2015/05/18/the-death-penalty-american-law-vs-christianity/.

McLoughlin, William. *New England Dissent 1960–1833: The Baptists and the Separation of Church and State.* Cambridge, MA: Harvard University Press, 1971.

Soul Liberty: The Baptists' Struggle in New England, 1630–1833. Hanover, NH: University Press of New England, 1991.

McRae v. Califano, 491 F.Supp. 630 (1980).

Merritt, Jonathan. "In a Groundbreaking Vote, Latino Evangelicals Call for End to Death Penalty." *The Washington Post*, March 30, 2015.

"Poll: Younger Christians Less Supportive of the Death Penalty." *The Washington Post*, January 18, 2014.

Metaxas, Eric. "Should Christians Vote for Trump?" *Wall Street Journal*, October 12, 2016.

Methodist Church. "Doctrines and Disciplines of the Methodist Church." 1956.

"Mike Huckabee: Fight Gay Marriage Judicial Tyranny." *USA Today*, June 26, 2015.

Miller, A. C. "The Christian Citizen in Community Action." *Baptist Press*, May 22, 1959.

Minnery, Tom, and Kenneth S. Kantzer. "It's Too Soon to Quit." *Christianity Today*, December 17, 1982, 10–11.

Mockabee, Stephen T. "A Question of Authority: Religion and Cultural Conflict in the 2004 Election." *Political Behavior* 29, no. 2 (2007): 221–48.

Moe, Terry M. *The Organization of Interests: Incentives and the Internal Dynamics of Political Interest Groups.* Chicago: University of Chicago Press, 1980.

"Toward a Broader View of Interest Groups." *Journal of Politics* 43, no. 2 (1981): 531–43.

Moen, Matthew C. "From Revolution to Evolution: The Changing Nature of the Christian Right." *Sociology of Religion* 55, no. 3 (1994): 345–57.

The Transformation of the Christian Right. Tuscaloosa: University of Alabama, 1992.

Mohler, R. Albert Jr. "The Briefing." albertmohler.com, May 18, 2015.

"A Threat to the Disabled & Everyone." *Baptist Press*, August 10, 2007.

"Why Christians Should Support the Death Penalty." *CNN Belief Blog*, May 1, 2014.

Moore, Louis. "CLC Files Briefs in Supreme Court." *Baptist Press*, February 27, 1989.

Moore, Russell. "Is the Pope Right about the Death Penalty?" *Russellmoore.com* February 21, 2016. www.russellmoore.com/2016/02/21/is-the-pope-right-about-the-death-penalty/.

"Russell Moore: Why This Election Makes Me Hate the Word 'Evangelical'." *The Washington Post*, February 29, 2016.

"Twitter Post." (June 21, 2016, 1:49 p.m.) https://twitter.com/drmoore/status/745312725132152834.

"We've Been Here Before: Lessons for the Marriage Debate from the Pro-Life Movement." *Russellmoore.com*, June 26, 2015. www.russellmoore.com/2015/06/26/weve-been-here-before-lessons-for-the-marriage-debate-from-the-pro-life-movement/.

"A White Church No More." *The New York Times*, May 6, 2016.

Moore, Russell D. "Land, Other Ethicists, Evaluate Medical Dilemmas at Conference." *Baptist Press*, March 9, 1998.

Moore, Russell, and Andrew T. Walker. "Need We Jail Each Other over Marriage Licenses?" September 4, 2015. http://erlc.com/resource-library/articles/need-we-jail-each-other-over-marriage-licenses.

Morgan, Timothy C. "Clinton Draws Ire of SBC." July 19, 1993, 54.

National Association of Evangelicals. "HHS Proposed Rule Jeopardizes Religious Freedom." February 1, 2013. www.nae.net/hhs-proposed-rule-jeopardizes-reli gious-freedom/

"NAE Files Supreme Court Brief for Hobby Lobby, Conestoga." January 28, 2014. www.nae.net/nae-files-supreme-court-brief-for-hobby-lobby-conestoga/

"What Is an Evangelical?" March 7, 2009. www.nae.net/church-and-faith-partners/ what-is-an-evangelical.

National Council of Churches of Chirst in the U.S.A. "Brief of Amicus Curiae on Behalf of the National Council of Churches of Christ in the U.S.A." In *Patricia Harris, et al. v. Cora McRae*. San Francisco, 1980.

"National Right to Life Board of Directors' Resolution Honoring James Bopp." National Right to Life, 2013.

Navarro, Vicente. *The Politics of Health Policy: The U.S. Reforms, 1980–1994*. Cambridge, MA: Blackwell, 1994.

"NBC Nightly News." June 26, 2015.

Neff, David. "Executing Justice?" *Christianity Today*, March 2014.

Nelson, Thomas E., Rosalee A. Clawson, and Zoe M. Oxley. "Media Framing of a Civil Liberties Conflict and Its Effect on Tolerance." *American Political Science Review* 91, no. 3 (1997): 567–83.

Neroulias, Nicole. "RNS: Poll: Majority Opposes Mosque near Ground Zero, Sees Site as 'Sacred Ground'." *Religion News Service*, August 26, 2010.

Newton, Jim. "Colson Opposes Capital Punishment." *Baptist Press*, June 13, 1979.

"North Carolina Issue on Trustees Delayed." *Baptist Press*, November 17, 1962.

O'Brien, Robert. "Abortion Court Decision Interpreted by Attorney." *Baptist Press*, January 29, 1973.

Obergefell v. Hodges, 576 U.S. __ (2015).

"Obscene Literature." National Association of Evangelicals, 1958.

"Obscenity." National Association of Evangelicals, 1965.

Olasky, Marvin. "Against Death Penalty Extremism." *World Magazine*, October 11, 2013.

"Dead Seriousness." *World Magazine*, October 19, 2013.

"On Capital Punishment." Orlando, FL: Southern Baptist Convention, 2000.

"On President William Jefferson Clinton." Houston, TX: Southern Baptist Convention, 1993.

"On Protecting Free Speech in Campaign Finance Legislation." New Orleans, LA: Southern Baptist Convention, 2001.

"On the Sanctity of Human Life." Columbus, OH: Southern Baptist Convention, 2015.

Oppenheimer, Mark. "Son of Evangelical Royalty Turns His Back, and Tells the Tale." *The New York Times*, August 19, 2011.

Pacelle, Richard L. Jr. *The Transformation of the Supreme Court's Agenda: From the New Deal to the Reagan Administration*. Boulder, CO: Westview Press, 1991.

Palen, Kathy. "High Court to Review Falwell-Flynt Case." *Baptist Press*, April 3, 1987.

Parry, Pam. *On Guard for Religious Liberty: Six Decades of the Baptist Joint Committee*. Macon, GA: Smith & Helwys, 1996.

Parsons, Christi, and David G. Savage. "Obama Administration Urges Supreme Court to Strike Down Prop 8." *Los Angeles Times*, February 28, 2013.

Patterson, Paige. Interview with the Author. (August 18, 2010). Philadelphia, PA.

Payne, Ed, and Jason Hanna. "After Kim Davis Is Jailed, Clerk's Office Issues Marriage License to Gay Couple." *CNN*, September 4, 2015.

Pew Research Center. "Gay Marriage." www.pewresearch.org/data-trend/domestic-issues/attitudes-on-gay-marriage/.

"Views about Same-Sex Marriage." www.pewforum.org/religious-landscape-study/views-about-same-sex-marriage/.

Piacenza, Joanna. "Support for Death Penalty by Religious Affiliation." Public Religion Research Institute, April 9, 2015.

Pierce, Jerry. "Oxford Bioethicist: Life's Value Evident Even to Unbelievers." *Baptist Press*, June 9, 2005.

"Pornography and the Courts." National Association of Evangelicals, 1969.

Presbyterian Mission Agency. "Capital Punishment." 2016.

ProCon.org. "31 States with the Death Penalty and 19 States with Death Penalty Bans." ProCon.

"A Protestant Affirmation on the Control of Human Reproduction." *Christianity Today*, November 1968, 18–19.

"Protestants Score Truman Health Plan." *The New York Times*, March 5, 1950, 15.

"Public Financing Passes Senate; House Outlook Dim." *Baptist Press*, April 15 1974.

Pullela, Philip. "Pope Calls for Worldwide Abolition of Death Penalty." *Reuters*, February 21, 2016.

Pulliam Bailey, Sarah. "Bobby Jindal's Vision." *Christianity Today*, March 2011, 51.

"Could Religious Institutions Lose Tax-Exempt Status over Supreme Court's Gay Marriage Case?" *The Washington Post*, April 28, 2015.

Pulliam Bailey, Sarah, and Karen Tumulty. "How a Southern Baptist Leader Became Surprising Voice on Confederate Flag." *The Washington Post*, June 24, 2015.

Putnam, Robert D. *Bowling Alone: The Collapse and Revival of American Community*. New York: Simon & Schuster, 2000.

Putnam, Robert D., and David E. Campbell. *American Grace: How Religion Divides and Unites Us*. New York: Simon & Schuster, 2010.

Rawls, John. *Political Liberalism*. expanded ed. New York: Columbia University Press, 2005.

"Recommendations of the Christian Life Commission." *Baptist Press*, May 21, 1964.

Reed, Ralph. *Active Faith: How Christians Are Changing the Soul of American Politics*. New York: Free Press, 1996.

Reimer, Sam, and Jerry Z. Park. "Tolerant (in)Civility: A Longitudinal Analysis of White Conservative Protestants' Willingness to Grant Civil Liberties." *Journal for the Scientific Study of Religion* 40, no. 4 (2001): 735–45.

"Religious Leaders Divided over Gays in Military." *Los Angeles Times*, April 3, 1993.

"Religious Liberty Bill before Congress Highlights Difference among Baptists." *SBC Today*, July 26, 1991.

Religious News Service. "Southern Baptists Decry Clinton Ideas." *Chicago Tribune*, June 18, 1993, 8.

"Resolution Concerning Obscenity in Literature." Houston, TX: Southern Baptist Convention, 1953.

"Resolution on Abortion." St Louis, MO: Southern Baptist Convention, 1980.

"Resolution on Abortion." St Louis, MO: Southern Baptist Convention, 1971.

"Resolution on Concerning Use of Tax Funds and Tax-Supported Schools by Religious Organizations." Houston, TX: Southern Baptist Convention, 1953.

"Resolution on Health Care Reform." Orlando, FL: Southern Baptist Convention, 1994.

"Resolution on Homosexual Marriage." New Orleans, LA: Southern Baptist Convention, 1996.

"Resolution on Homosexuality." San Antonio, TX: Southern Baptist Convention, 1988.

"Resolution on Homosexuality." Dallas, TX: Southern Baptist Convention, 1985.

"Resolution on Homosexuality." St. Louis, MO: Southern Baptist Convention, 1980.

"Resolution on Homosexuality." Norfolk, VA: Southern Baptist Convention, 1976.

"Resolution on Homosexuality, Military Service and Civil Rights." Houston, TX: Southern Baptist Convention, 1993.

"Resolution on Hunger and Poverty." St. Louis, MO: Southern Baptist Convention, 1987.

"Resolution on Parental Choice in Education." Atlanta, GA: Southern Baptist Convention, 1991.

"Resolution on Parental Choice on Education." New Orleans, LA: Southern Baptist Convention, 1996.

"Resolution on Persecution of Christians." San Antonio, TX: Southern Baptist Convention, 1988.

"Resolution on Pornagraphic Materials." Hoston, TX: Southern Baptist Convention, 1968.

"Resolution on Pornographic Literature." Louisville, KY: Southern Baptist Convention, 1959.

"Resolution on Pornography." Atlanta, GA: Southern Baptist Convention, 1986.

"Resolution on Religious Liberty and No Establishment of Religion." Philadelphia, PA: Southern Baptist Convention, 1972.

"Resolution on Sanctity of Human Life." Atlanta, GA: Southern Baptist Convention, 1991.

"Resolution on the Freedom of Choice Act, Hyde Amendment." Houston, TX: Southern Baptist Convention, 1993.

"Resolution on the Partial-Birth Abortion Ban." New Orleans, LA: Southern Baptist Convention, 1996.

"Resolution on Voluntary Prayer." St. Louis, MO: Southern Baptist Convention, 1971.

Ribuffo, Leo P. "Family Policy Past as Prologue: Jimmy Carter, the White House Conference on Families, and the Mobilization of the New Christian Right." *Review of Policy Research* 23, no. 2 (2006): 311–38.

Roach, David. "Baptists 'Not Threatened' by Pope's U.S. Visit." *Baptist Press*, September 21, 2015.

Robert, Tracinski. "The Message of Charie Hebdo: Europe, Welcome to the ISIS Era." *The Federalist*, January 7, 2015.

Robinson, Carin. "Cross-Cutting Messages and Political Tolerance: An Experiment Using Evangelical Protestants." *Political Behavior* 32, no. 4 (2010): 495–515.

"Doctrine, Discussion and Disagreement: Evangelical Protestant Interaction with Catholics in American Politics." Ph.D. Dissertation, Georgetown University, 2008.

Romer v. Evans, 517 U.S. 620 (1996).

"Roundup for Monday A.M." *Baptist Press*, June 10, 1984.

Rozell, Mark J., and Clyde Wilcox. *Second Coming: The Christian Right in Virginia Politics*. Baltimore: Johns Hopkins University Press, 1996.

Sandel, Michael J. *Democracy's Discontent: America in Search of a Public Philosophy*. Cambridge, MA: Harvard University Press, 1998.

Savage, Charlie, and Sheryl Gay Stolberg. "In Shift, U.S. Says Marriage Act Blocks Gay Rights." *The New York Times*, February 23, 2011.

"SBC Leaders Agree with Resignation; Register Sadness." *Baptist Press*, August 9, 1974, 4.

"SBC Messengers Likely to Consider Resolution on Clinton's Views." *Baptist Press*, June 13, 1993.

Schaeffer, Frank. *Crazy for God: How I Grew up as One of the Elect, Helped Found the Religious Right, and Lived to Take All (or Almost All) of It Back*. Boston: Da Capo Press, 2008.

Scheingold, Stuart A. *The Politics of Rights: Lawyers, Public Policy, and Political Change*. 2nd ed. Ann Arbor: University of Michigan Press, 2004.

Schiedermayer, David. "Healing the Health-Care System." *Christianity Today*, October 25, 1993, 16.

Scott, Orville. "Texas Baptist Convention Challenged to 'Arise, Build'." *Baptist Press*, June 29, 1989.

Self, Robert O. *All in the Family: The Realignment of American Democracy since the 1960s*. New York: Hill and Wang, 2012.

Shain, Barry Alan. *The Myth of American Individualism: The Protestant Origins of American Political Thought*. Princeton, NJ: Princeton University Press, 1994.

Shelley, Marshall. "The Death Penalty: Two Sides of a Growing Issue." *Christianity Today*, March 2, 1984, 17.

Shellnutt, Kate, and Sarah Eekhoff Zylstra. "Who's Who of Trump's Tremendous Faith Advisors." *Christianity Today*, June 22, 2016.

Sheridan, George. "Southern Baptists, Pope Interact During U.S. Visit." *Baptist Press*, October 22, 1979.

Shields, Jon A. *The Democratic Virtues of the Christian Right*. Princeton, NJ: Princeton University Press, 2009.

Sider, Ronald J. *Completely Pro-Life: Building a Consistent Stance*. Downers Grove, IL: InterVarsity Press, 1987.

Sides, John. "Why Campaign Finance Reform Is Hard." The Monkey Cage, 2012. http://themonkeycage.org/2012/08/why-campaign-finance-reform-is-hard/.

Simmons, Paul D. "Religious Liberty and the Abortion Debate." *Journal of Church and State* 32, no. 3 (1990): 567–84.

Skocpol, Theda. "APSA Presidential Address: Voice and Inequality: The Transformation of American Civic Democracy." *Perspectives on Politics* 2, no. 1 (2004): 3–20.

Diminished Democracy: From Membership to Management in American Civil Life. Norman: University of Oklahoma, 2003.

Smidt, Corwin E. *American Evangelicals Today*. Lanham, MD: Rowman & Littlefield, 2013.

Smidt, Corwin E., Lyman A. Kellstedt, and James L. Guth. "The Role of Religion in American Politics: Explanatory Theories and Associated Analytical and Measurement Issues." In *Oxford Handbook on Religion and American Politics*, edited by Corwin E. Smidt, Lyman A. Kellstedt and James L. Guth, 3–42. New York: Oxford University Press, 2009.

Smientana, Bob. "What Is an Evangelical? Four Questions Offer New Definition." *Christianity Today*, November 19, 2015.

Smith, Gregory A., and Jessica Martinez. "How the Faithful Voted: A Preliminary 2016 Analysis." Pew Research Center, 2016.

Smith, Oran P. *The Rise of Baptist Republicanism*. New York, NY: New York University Press, 1997.

Smith, Rogers M. "Beyond Tocqueville, Myrdal, and Hartz: The Multiple Traditions in America." *American Political Science Review* 87, no. 3 (1993): 549–66.

Smith, Samuel. "FRC's Tony Perkins, 50 Conservative Activists Reportedly Plan to Endorse Ted Cruz." *Christian Post*, December 16, 2015.

Smolla, Rodney. *Jerry Falwell v. Larry Flynt: The First Amendment on Trial*. 1988.

Solinger, Rickie. *Reproductive Politics: What Everyone Needs to Know*. New York: Oxford University Press, 2013.

Sommerkamp, Theo. "Campaign against Indecency Mapped." *Baptist Press*, August 14, 1957.

Southworth, Ann. *Lawyers of the Right: Professionalizing the Conservative Coalition*. Chicago: University of Chicago Press, 2008.

Spring, Beth. "New Problems in Congress for Antiabortionists." *Christianity Today*, February 4, 1983, 60.

Stack, Liam. "A Brief History of Deadly Attacks on Abortion Providers." *The New York Times*, November 29, 2015.

Staff. "Appeals Court Nominee Tells Panel Devotion to Law Is Issue." *Baptist Press*, September 19, 2002.

"Court Hears Case on Students' Rights." *Baptist Press*, March 20, 2007.

"ERLC Lays out 15 Principles Needed for Health Care Reform." *Baptist Press*, November 11, 2009.

"Head-Counting Begins as Obama Prepares Address." *Baptist Press*, September 8, 2009.

"Land-Endorsement Statement Urges New Start." *Baptist Press*, September 14, 2009.

"Pro-Lifers Nearly Unanimous in Dismay." *Baptist Press*, March 22, 2010.

Stafford, Tim. "Ron Sider's Unsettling Crusade." *Christianity Today*, March 1, 2000.

Stassen, Glen H., and David P. Gushee. *Kingdom Ethics: Following Jesus in Contemporary Context*. Downers Grove, IL: Intervarsity Press, 2003.

"Statement Calling for Consitutional Resistance to *Obergefell v. Hodges*." American Principles Project, 2015.

Steensland, Brian, Jerry Z. Park, Mark D. Regnerus, Lynn D. Robinson, W. Bradford Wilcox, and Robert D. Woodberry. "The Measure of American Religion: Toward Improving the State of the Art." *Social Forces* 79, no. 1 (2000): 291–318.

Stetzer, Ed, and Ryan P. Burge. "Reltrad Coding Problems and a New Repository." *Politics & Religion* 9, no. 1 (2016): 187–90.

Stonestreet, John. "The Other Right." *Breakpoint*, December 22, 2014.

Stouffer, Samuel C. *Communism, Conformity, and Civil Liberties*. New York: Doubleday, 1955.

Strode, Tom. "ACLJ Seeking to Overturn Campaign Finance Reform Law." *Baptist Press*, April 5, 2002.

"All Need Religious Liberty, Baptist, Others Contend." *Baptist Press*, May 25, 2016.

"BJCPA Asks Supreme Court to Maintain Religion Test." *SBC Today*, September 20, 1991.

"Bolster Family, ERLC Speakers Urge." *Baptist Press*, October 30, 2014.

"Campaign-Finance Bill Violates Free-Speech Rights, Critics Say." *Baptist Press*, April 3, 2001.

"CLC Endorses RFRA; BJC Mum on Abortion." *Light*, October-December 1991.

"CLC Joins Brief Opposing Ruling for Homosexual Rights." *Baptist Press*, July 28, 1995.

"Clinton Rescinds Abortion Policies; Pro-Lifers Won't Retreat, Land Says." *Baptist Press*, January 25, 1993.

"Colorado Court Rejection of Amendment 2 Criticized." *Baptist Press*, October 14, 1994.

"Congress Approves Outlawing Abortion Clinic Blockades." *Baptist Press*, November 19, 1993.

"Court Backs Pro-Life Ads as Free Speech." *Baptist Press*, June 16, 2014.

"Court Upholds Inmate's Religious Liberty." *Baptist Press*, January 20, 2015.

"Despite Endorsement by Some, Sebelius 'Unfit' for HHS Role, Pro-Life Leaders Say." *Baptist Press*, March 6, 2009.

"ERLC Brief Opposes Hostility against Religion." *Baptist Press*, April 26, 2016.

"ERLC, Others Decry Ruling on Campaign Reform Law." *Baptist Press*, December 11, 2003.

"Full Abortion Rights Promoted in CBF-Funded Agency's Journal." *Baptist Press*, February 2, 1998.

"Health Care Is a 'National Dilemma': 'Vigorous' Debate Ahead, Land Says." *Baptist Press*, May 13, 2003.

"High Court Hears Pro-Life Issue Ads Case." *Baptist Press*, April 26, 2007.

"Hight Court Hears Arguments over NEA Decency Standard." *Baptist Press*, April 1, 1998.

"Letter to Obama: It's Not Just Catholics Who Oppose HHS over 'Contraception Mandate'." *Baptist Press*, January 6, 2012.

"Marriage Crisis Predated Gay Marriage, Conf. Speakers Say." *Baptist Press*, October 28, 2014.

"NEA's Frohmayer Resigns; Critics Credit Buchanan." *Baptist Press*, February 24, 1992.

"Obama Admin. Reaffirms: Health Care Plans Must Cover Abortion-Causing Drugs." *Baptist Press*, January 20, 2012.

"Obama Recess Appointment 'Dangerous' for the Elderly, SBC Ethicist Land Says." *Baptist Press*, July 8, 2010.

"Pope's Speech Troubling, Southern Baptists Say." *Baptist Press*, September 25, 2015.

"Supreme Court Hears Operation Rescue Case." *Baptist Press*, November 19, 1991.

"Supreme Court Protects Issue Ads." *Baptist Press*, June 26, 2007.

"Supreme Court's Term Confirms Commitment to Abortion Rights." *Baptist Press*, July 7, 2000.

"White House Finalizes Health Coverage for Unborn Children Despite Criticism." *Baptist Press*, October 1, 2002.

"Strong Race Statement Loses to Softer One." *Baptist Press*, May 23, 1964.

Sullivan, Amy. "Articles of Faith: Why Republicans Don't Want to Debate Birth Control." *Time*, August 12, 2011.

Sullivan, John L., James E. Piereson, and George E. Marcus. *Political Tolerance and American Democracy*. Chicago: University of Chicago Press, 1982.

Susman, Tina. "Philadelphia Plans Intense Security for Pope Francis Visit – Some Say Too Intense." *Los Angeles Times*, September 1, 2015.

Sutton, Jerry. *A Matter of Conviction: A History of Southern Baptist Engagement with the Culture*. Nashville: Ethics and Religious Liberty Commission of the SBC, 2008.

Sutton, Matthew Avery. *American Apocalypse: A History of Modern Evangelicalism*. Cambridge, MA: Belknap Press of Harvard University Press, 2014.

Teles, Steven M. *The Rise of the Conservative Legal Movement: The Battle for Control of the Law*. Princeton, NJ: Princeton University Press, 2008.

Terruso, Julia. "City's Share of $17 Million Papal-Visit Costs: $8 Million." *Philadelphia Inquirer*, December 4, 2015.

"Testimony Endorses National Health Care." *Baptist Press*, November 14, 1975.

"Text of Texas Gov. Bush's Statement on Karla Faye Tucker." *CNN*, February 3, 1998.

"Theologian's Pen Pal Faces Execution Again." *Christianity Today*, July 2015, 17.

"They Said Legal Abortions Would Stop and Illegal Ones Would Multiply." *Christianity Today*, October 23, 1981, 57.

"Thursday Afternoon Resolutions." *Baptist Press*, June 8, 1980.

Tillery, M. Kelly. "You Can Fight City Hall: The Case of the Pope's Platform." *The Philadelphia Lawyer*, Winter 2010, 20.

Toalston, Art, and Erin Roach. "ERLC to Open Mideast Office, Honors Embattled Florist." *Baptist Press*, June 18, 2015.

Tocqueville, Alexis de. *Democracy in America*. Translated by Delba Wintrop. Chicago: University of Chicago Press, 2002.

Tolchin, Martin. "House Bars Medicaid Abortions and Funds for Enforcing Quotas." *The New York Times*, June 18, 1977, 49.

Toner, Robin. "Clinton Would End Ban on Aid to Poor Seeking Abortions." *The New York Times*, March 30, 1993.

"Hillary Clinton Opens Campaign to Answer Critics of Health Plan." *The New York Times*, February 16, 1994, A11.

Trammel, Madison. "Health Care, Everyone?" *Christianity Today*, July 2006, 18.

Truett, George W. *Baptists and Religious Liberty*. Nashville: The Sunday School Board of the Southern Baptist Convention, 2011 [1920]. www.bjconline.org/index.php?option=com_content&task=view&id=51&Itemid=73.

Tushnet, Mark V. *NAACP's Legal Strategy against Segregated Education,1925–1950*. Chapel Hill: University of North Carolina Press, 2005.

"U.S. Public Becoming Less Religious." *Pew Research Center*, November 3, 2015. www.pewforum.org/2015/11/03/u-s-public-becoming-less-religious/.

"U.S. Senate Passes McCain-Feingold Bill to Restrict Free Speech, 59–41." National Right to Life Committee, April 30, 2001.

United Nations. "The Universal Declaration of Human Rights." 1948.

United Presbyterian Church in the USA. "Minutes of the 171st General Assembly."
    1959.
"The United Presbyterian Church in the U.S.A. For Leave to File Brief Amicus Curiae
    out of Time and Brief Amicus Curiae." In *Patricia Harris, et al. v. Cora McRae,
    et al.* San Francisco, 1980.
United States Catholic Conference. "Brief of the United States Catholic Conference,
    Amicus Curiae." In *Patricia R. Harris v. Cora McRae, et al.* Washington, DC,
    1980.
United States Catholic Conference et al. "Brief Amicus Curiae of the United States
    Catholic Conference, the Christian Life Commission, Southern Baptist Convention,
    and the National Association of Evangelicals in Support of Respondents and Cross-
    Petitioners." In *Planned Parenthood of Southeastern Pennsylvania, et al. v. Robert
    P. Casey, et al.* Washington, DC, 1992.
United States Conference of Catholic Bishops. "The Church's Anti-Death Penalty
    Position." http://www.usccb.org/issues-and-action/human-life-and-dignity/death-pen
    alty-capital-punishment/catholic-campaign-to-end-the-use-of-the-death-penalty.cfm.
"United States Declaration of Independence." 1776.
Unnever, James D., and Francis T. Cullen. "Reassessing the Racial Divide in Support for
    Capital Punishment: The Continuing Significance of Race." *Journal of Research in
    Crime and Delinquency* 44, no. 1 (2007): 124–58.
Unnever, James D., Francis T. Cullen, and John P. Bartkowski. "Images of God and
    Public Support for Capital Punishment: Does a Close Relationship with a Loving
    God Matter?" *Criminology* 44, no. 4 (2006): 835–66.
Unnever, James D., Francis T. Cullen, and Bonnie S. Fisher. "Empathy and Public Support
    for Capital Punishment." *Journal of Crime and Justice* 28, no. 1 (2005): 1–34.
Various. "Evangelicals and Catholics Together: The Christian Mission in the Third
    Millennium." *First Things*, May 1994.
"Virginia Baptists OK Strong Resolutions." *Baptist Press*, November 13, 1965.
Visscher, Robert D. "Therapeutic Abortion: Blessing or Murder." *Christianity Today*,
    September 27, 1968, 6–8.
"Wake Forest Trustee Plan Fails to Carry." *Baptist Press*, November 17, 1963.
Wang, Angela. "The Death Penalty Today: Is It Just?": Prison Fellowship, September 19,
    2012.
Ward, John. "Former Rubio Adviser Holds Homemade Anti-Trump Sign Outside
    Evangelical Meeting." *Yahoo! News*, June 21, 2016.
Watson, Justin. *The Christian Coalition: Dreams of Restoration, Demands for Recog-
    nition.* New York: St. Martin's Griffin, 1999.
Weinger, Mackenzie. "Evolve: Obama Gay Marriage Quotes." *Politico*, May 9, 2012.
Whitehead, Michael. "CLC to Court: Squeeze out *Lemon*: Restore True Liberty to First
    Amendment, Commission Requests." *Salt* 4, no. 1 (1994): 1, 4.
Wilcox, Clyde, and Barbara Norrander. "Of Moods and Morals: The Dynamics of
    Opinion on Abortion and Gay Rights." In *Understanding Public Opinion*, edited
    by Barbara Norrander and Clyde Wilcox, 121–47. Washington, DC: CQ Press,
    2002.
Williams, Daniel K. *Defenders of the Unborn: The Pro-Life Movement before Roe v.
    Wade.* New York: Oxford University Press, 2016.

God's Own Party: The Making of the Christian Right. New York: Oxford University Press, 2010.

Williams, Pete, and Halimah Abdullah. "Landmark: Supreme Court Rules Same-Sex Marriage Legal Nationwide." NBC Nightly News, 2015.

Williams, Rhys H. "Visions of the Good Society and the Religious Roots of American Political Culture." *Sociology of Religion* 60, no. 1 (1999): 1–34.

Wilson, James Q. *Political Organizations.* New York: Basic Books, 1973.

Wilson, Joshua C. *The Street Politics of Abortion: Speech, Violence, and America's Culture Wars.* Stanford, CA: Stanford University Press, 2013.

Witte, John Jr. *The Reformation of Rights: Law, Religion, and Human Rights in Early Modern Calvinism.* New York: Cambridge University Press, 2007.

Wolbrecht, Christina. *The Politics of Women's Rights: Parties, Positions, and Change.* Princeton, NJ: Princeton University Press, 2000.

Wood, Elizabeth. "Ground Zero Mosque Too Close for Comfort, SBC's Land Says." *Baptist Press,* August 13, 2010.

Woodward, Bob, and Scott Armstrong. *The Brethren.* New York: Simon & Schuster, 1979.

Workman, Skeet. "Letter to Rev. Gary Young." August 27, 1986.

Wozniak, Kevin H., and Andrew R. Lewis. "Reexamining the Effect of Christian Denominational Affiliation on Death Penalty Support." *Journal of Criminal Justice* 38, no. 5 (2010): 1082–89.

Yan, Holly, Catherine E. Shoichet, and Moni Basu. "Georgia Inmate Kelly Gissendaner Executed after Failed Appeals." CNN, September 30, 2015.

Young, James Lee. "Baptist Call for Attitude Change by Church on Aging." *Baptist Press,* October 25, 1974, 4–6.

Young, Robert L. "Religious Orientation, Race, and Support for the Death Penalty." *Journal of the Scientific Study of Religion* 31, no. 1 (1992): 76–87.

Zaller, John R. *The Nature and Origins of Mass Opinion.* New York: Cambridge University Press, 2002.

Ziegler, Mary. *After Roe: The Lost History of the Abortion Debate.* Cambridge, MA: Harvard University Press, 2015.

Zuckert, Michael P. *The Natural Rights Republic: Studies in the Foundation of the American Political Tradition.* South Bend, IN: University of Notre Dame Press, 1996.

Zylstra, Sarah Eekhoff. "Capital Doubts." *Christianity Today,* February 19, 2008.

"Evangelicals Now Officially Divided on Death Penalty." *Christianity Today,* October 19, 2015.

"Southern Baptists Back Away from Backing Mosques." *Christianity Today,* February 8, 2017.

Index